Satire:

An Anthology

Ashley Brown
John L. Kimmey

UNIVERSITY OF SOUTH CAROLINA

THOMAS Y. CROWELL
HARPER & ROW, PUBLISHERS
New York Hagerstown San Francisco London

Sponsoring Editor: Phillip W. Leininger
Project Editor: Rhonda Roth
Production Supervisor: Kewal K. Sharma
Compositor: Cherry Hill Composition
Printer: The Maple Press Co.
Binder: The Maple Press Co.

Satire: An Anthology

Library of Congress Cataloging in Publication Data
Main entry under title:

Satire : an anthology.
  Bibliography: p.
  Includes index.
  1. Satire. I. Brown, Ashley, Date-   II. Kim-
mey, John Lansing, Date-
PN6231.S2S34 1977   808.87   77-24925
ISBN 0-690-01524-0

Grateful acknowledgment is made for use of the following material:

W. H. Auden, "The Unknown Citizen," copyright 1940 and renewed 1968 by W. H. Auden. Reprinted from *Collected Shorter Poems 1927–1957* by W. H. Auden, by permission of Random House, Inc. and Faber & Faber Ltd.

Wililam H. Barber, "Voltaire's Use of Irony," from W. H. Barber, *Voltaire: Candide*, Studies in French Literature, no. 5 (1960), pp. 35–40. Reprinted by permission of Edward Arnold (Publishers) Ltd.

Donald Barthelme, "City Life," reprinted with the permission of Farrar, Straus & Giroux, Inc. from *City Life* by Donald Barthelme; copyright © 1969, 1970 by Donald Barthelme.

Ashley Brown, "A Note on American Satire," excerpted from "Allen Tate as Satirist" by Ashley Brown. Copyright © 1968 by *Shenandoah:* The Washington and Lee University Review, with the permission of the Editor.

Geoffrey Chaucer, "The Nun's Priest's Tale," from *The Canterbury Tales*, translated by Nevill Coghill for Penguin Classics. Copyright © 1951, 1958, 1960 by Nevill Coghill. Reprinted by permission of Penguin Books, Ltd.

E. E. Cummings, "I Sing of Olaf," copyright 1931, 1959 by E. E. Cummings. Reprinted from his volume *Complete Poems 1913–1962* by permission of Harcourt Brace Jovanovich, Inc.

T. S. Eliot, "Mr. Apollinax," from *Collected Poems 1909–1962* by T. S. Eliot, copyright 1936 by Harcourt Brace Jovanovich, Inc.; copyright © 1963, 1964 by T. S. Eliot. Reprinted by permission of Harcourt Brace Jovanovich and Faber & Faber Ltd.

Robert C. Elliott, "Satire and Magic: History. 1. Greece," from Robert C. Elliott, *The Power of Satire: Magic, Ritual, Art* (copyright © 1960 by Princeton Paperback, 1966), pp. 3–15. Reprinted by permission of Princeton University Press.

Erasmus, "Charon," from Erasmus, *Ten Colloquies*, translated by Craig R. Thompson, copyright © 1957 by the Liberal Arts Press, Inc. Reprinted by permission of the publisher, the Bobbs-Merrill Company, Inc.

Northrop Frye, "The Nature of Satire," reprinted from *University of Toronto Quarterly* 14 (October 1944) by permission of the author and University of Toronto Press.

Anthony Hecht, "The Dover Bitch: A Criticism of Life," from *The Hard Hours* by Anthony Hecht. Copyright © 1960 by Anthony E. Hecht. Originally appeared in *Transatlantic Review*. Reprinted by permission of Atheneum Publishers.

Stanley Edgar Hyman, "The Rape of the Lock," first published in *The Hudson Review* 12, no. 3 (Autumn 1960). Reprinted by permission of Mrs. Stanley Edgar Hyman.

Juvenal, "Satire III," from *The Satires of Juvenal*, translated by Rolfe Humphries. Copyright © 1958 by Indiana University Press. Reprinted by permission of the publisher.

Alvin Kernan, "Juvenal, 'Prince of Satyrists,'" from *The Cankered Muse*. Copyright © 1959. Reprinted by permission of Yale University Press.

Lucian, "Hermes and Charon," reprinted by permission of the publisher and the Loeb Classical Library from Lucian, *The Dialogues of the Dead*, translated by M. D. MacLeod (Cambridge, Mass.: Harvard University Press), © 1961 by the President and Fellows of Harvard College.

H. L. Mencken, "Hell and Its Outskirts," © 1948, 1976 by The New Yorker Magazine, Inc. Reprinted by permission.

Ishmael Reed, "The Gangster's Death," copyright © 1972 by Ishmael Reed. Reprinted by permission of the author.

Karl Shapiro, "The Humanities Building," copyright © 1974 by Karl Shapiro. Reprinted from *Adult Bookstore* by Karl Shapiro, by permission of Random House, Inc. Originally appeared in *The New Yorker*.

John Speirs, "The Nun's Priest's Tale," reprinted by permission of Faber & Faber Ltd. from *Chaucer the Maker* by John Speirs.

Wallace Stevens, "A High-Toned Old Christian Woman," copyright 1923 and renewed 1951 by Wallace Stevens. Reprinted from *The Collected Poems of Wallace Stevens*, by permission of Alfred A. Knopf, Inc.

Allen Tate, "A Note on Elizabethan Satire," reprinted from *Essays of Four Decades*, © 1959 by Allen Tate, by permission of The Swallow Press Inc., Chicago.

Jean-Claude van Itallie, *Almost Like Being*, reprinted by permission of International Creative Management. Copyright © 1965, 1966, 1967 by Jean-Claude van Itallie (Revised.) © Copyright, 1966, by Jean-Claude van Itallie (as unpublished dramatic compositions). CAUTION: Professionals and amateurs are hereby warned that the plays in this volume are subject to a royalty. They are fully protected under the copyright laws of the United States of America, and of all countries covered by the International Copyright Union (including the Dominion of Canada and the rest of the British Commonwealth), and of all countries covered by the Pan-American Copyright Convention and the Universal Copyright Convention, and of all countries with which the United States has reciprocal copyright relations. All rights, including professional, amateur, motion picture, recitation, lecturing, public reading, radio broadcasting, television, and the rights of translation into foreign languages are strictly reserved. Particular emphasis is laid on the question of readings, permission for which must be secured from the author's agent in writing. All inquiries (except for amateur rights) should be addressed to Bridget Aschenberg, International Creative Management, 40 W. 57th St., New York, New York 10019. The amateur acting rights of the plays in this volume are controlled exclusively by the Dramatists Play Service, Inc., 440 Park Avenue South, New York, N.Y. 10016. No amateur performance of *War, The Hunter and the Bird, Almost Like Being, I'm Really Here* or *Where Is de Queen?* may be given without obtaining in advance the written permission of the Dramatists Play Service, Inc., and paying the requisite fee. "When I Fall in Love" by Victor Young and Edward Heyman. © Copyright, 1952, by Northern Music Corporation and Victor Young Publications, Inc. Used by Permission. All Rights Reserved. "Almost Like Being" was first published in the *Tulane Drama Review* 9, No. 4 (Summer 1965).

Gore Vidal, "Book Report," copyright © 1956 by Gore Vidal. Reprinted from *Homage to Daniel Shays: Collected Essays 1952–1972* by Gore Vidal, by permission of Random House, Inc.

Richard Wilbur, Introduction to Moliere's *The Misanthrope*, translated by Richard Wilbur, copyright © 1954, 1955 by Richard Wilbur. Reprinted by permission of Harcourt Brace Jovanovich, Inc.

Contents

Criticism

Preface

This book has three purposes. The first is to acquaint the student with the history of satire from the Greeks to the moderns. We include not only some of the major authors and important works but also an outline of the development of this literary mode. The second purpose is to define key terms such as Menippean satire, mock-epic, and high and low burlesque, and to discuss their significance. Headnotes provide biographical data and brief critical commentary. The third purpose is to offer essays that discuss the evolution as well as the nature of satire and that provide analyses of a few of the outstanding selections. A bibliography lists well-known satires and useful books and articles.

Naturally, it is impossible in a volume of this kind to do more than present a limited number of writers. Our choice has been guided first by the desire to cover the mode adequately in all its variety without losing sight of its main trends. In the section on tradition we stress those satirists who reveal the continuity of the genre and whose contribution has been influential. We begin with a representative group of contemporary authors so that students can familiarize themselves with current satiric themes and techniques before confronting the literary works of more distant times. The critical essays are chosen on the basis of their comprehensiveness and the ease and incisiveness with which they discuss the selections included. They should prove valuable for students writing papers.

The uses of this book are several. It can fit into introduction to literature or genre courses, English or comparative literature surveys. What is more, its flexibility and variety enhance the appeal for students on different levels and with different literary interests. An instructor can proceed through the anthology chronologically or thematically, by form or by style. Certainly there are few genres so rewarding to study in terms of literary devices and none that expose the weaknesses of humanity and society with such conviction and cunning.

Ashley Brown
John L. Kimmey

Satire

Introduction

Satire, one of the oldest literary modes, has not always been admired in the way that tragedy and comedy have been. People who are happy with the world as it is find satirists destructive and malicious. And indeed some of the greatest satirists were not the most agreeable of persons. But the editors of this anthology consider the mode an important and exhilarating way of dealing with human experience, and no student of literature should overlook its variety and power. Over the centuries satire has appealed on occasion to writers as different as Chaucer and Shakespeare. In our century we can easily see it in the work of James Joyce and T. S. Eliot, writers who fit into other literary modes more conveniently. Today the satiric impulse is certainly widespread, as shown by the popularity of novelists like Gore Vidal and Philip Roth, journalists like Art Buchwald and Hunter Thompson, and entertainers like Mort Sahl and the late Lenny Bruce.

Satire typically works through subtlety and suggestion rather than through bluntness and plain statement. It avoids the direct approach of propaganda and sermon in favor of the indirect method of art. Choosing a subject such as politics or pedantry, satirists set out to attack with moral fervor. But instead of slashing and decrying, they express themselves in a complex and often witty way. The object is ridicule, not simple invective. In short, satire begins with denunciation and ends with an appeal to the critical understanding of the reader.

The early history and evolution of satire are fairly clear. The first satirist we know about, Archilochus (seventh century B.C.), was a Greek poet who followed Homer. Robert C. Elliott, in *The Power of Satire*, from which we have drawn a chapter for this anthology, gives us a brilliant account of the lost world of the poet, and the student should turn to his essay for enlightenment. Werner Jaeger, a famous Hellenist of the last generation, said that the poetry of Archilochus was "born of the need of the free individual to see and solve the problem of human life outside the mystic content of epic poetry, which had hitherto been the only sphere in which it could be posed or answered." This remark suggests something about satirists generally. They frequently follow "heroic" writers like Homer and Virgil, or Spenser and Milton, or Scott and Fenimore Cooper, and direct some of their most characteristic thrusts at the pretensions of heroism. (Mark Twain's essay, "Literary Offenses of Fenimore Cooper," is a case in point.) Werner Jaeger's remark also suggests that from the beginning, the "critical understanding" was involved in satire.

In the ancient world the term "satire" appeared at a relatively late stage. It is derived from the Latin *satura*, meaning a "mixture" or "medley" as derived from *satura lanx*, a bowl of first fruits. (Note that the Greeks did not have the word.) Satire has kept this "mixed" quality much of the time: verse and prose, sublime and vulgar styles, the effect of an improvisation. It is worth remarking here that writers and critics in the Middle Ages and the Renaissance mistakenly thought that *satire* was derived from the Greek *satyr*, and thus they acted on the assumption that it should be "rough" and even obscene in its effects.

Although the Romans established the forms of satire that we have inherited, the characteristic tone is evident earlier in the plays of Aristophanes (circa 448–380 B.C.), an Athenian Greek who found much to denounce in the public life of his city-state. Some of his plays, such as the *Lysistrata* (an attack on the folly of war) and *The Clouds* (an attack on the Socratic school of philosophy), are still performed, and a modern audience does not object to the indecencies that offended our grandparents.

But classical satire did not develop in the form of drama. Following Aristophanes, the Greek cynic Menippus (circa 340–270 B.C.) lent his name to one of the major forms perfected by the Romans, Menippean satire, a prose narrative which usually contains some verse and which often descends to the popular and coarse in its attack on folly. Two famous examples from Latin literature are the *Satyricon*, attributed to Petronius Arbiter; and *The Golden Ass*, written in the second century A.D. by Lucius Apuleius. Both have been translated into English recently, and the *Satyricon* is widely read today. Petronius (who died in A.D. 65) presents an extraordinary picture of the dissolute Rome of Nero. His narrative is typical of the loose plotting and improvisation of the form, and here and there we have entire scenes that anticipate the technique of the modern novel. Encolpius, the roguish anti-hero, has his modern descendants, for instance Thomas Mann's Felix Krull. Menippean satire, then, is a term that we can later apply in an extended sense to narratives such as *Don Quixote* and *Candide*, with their plots based on accumulations of adventures. In an influential book, *The Anatomy of Criticism*, Northrop Frye refers to it as a species of prose fiction that presents "people as mouthpieces of the ideas they represent" in contrast to the novel proper, such as *Madame Bovary*, with its great emphasis on characterization. He also observes that shorter forms of Menippean satire, developed in the Roman world, became the models that were followed many centuries later in the Renaissance.

An important figure in satirical history is Lucian, a late Greek writer, represented in this anthology by a dialogue, "Hermes and Charon." After studying the philosophy of the Stoics in his youth, he renounced it and turned to a new literary form, the satirical dialogue, for which he is chiefly famous. These short Menippean works show his questioning spirit and hatred of sham; they are applied in particular to the myths of the old religion and to philosophy. "Hermes and Charon" is one of the *Dialogues of the Dead* which are set in the lower world. Heroes such as Hercules, Alexander, and Achilles are rowed across the river by the ferryman Charon, who frequently appears as a commentator. In this familiar setting the vanities of the heroes are exposed at death; the irony is often quite grim. But, as Professor Frye points out, the dramatic interest of these dialogues is in a conflict of ideas rather than of characters. Lucian's common sense philosophical attitude was not attractive to the Christian Middle Ages, and in any case Greek ceased to be the language of the educated class. But with its revival by the Renaissance Humanists, who were of course men of the Church wishing to reform theology, Lucian's dialogues provided a sophisticated method of criticism. Erasmus and Thomas More imitated them directly, and they influenced Rabelais, Shakespeare (in the "tragical satire," *Timon of Athens*), Ben Jonson (in *Volpone*), Voltaire, Swift, and Peacock.

The other type of satire that the Romans perfected is formal verse satire. The ancestor in this case was the Greek Bion (circa 325 B.C.), a contemporary of Menippus. As Cynics, both held that virtue was the goal of life, but their doctrine eventually came to a kind of insolent self-righteousness. (Although their works were lost, their successors credit them with being pioneers in the satirical art.) The "rough" improvisation associated with the wandering preacher Bion—a form of diatribe—was to become the guise of much Roman verse satire. But as satire became more formal, more indirect in method, the diatribe diminished in importance. The Roman poets Horace, Persius, and Juvenal were chiefly responsible for this development, and their practice affected most classical satires in English poetry. Horace, who lived during the "golden age" of Augustus Caesar, and who was evidently a happy man, censured follies and vices with what John Dryden called a "fine raillery." Poets such as Marvell and Pope admired and imitated the special tone of Horace's work, and his influence on English poetry has been extensive. In this anthology we include both his satire on city life (popularly called "The Town Mouse and the Country Mouse") and Juvenal's *Satire III*, an attack on the vices and dangers of the city by one who was doubtless led to his disillusionment by sad experience. Juvenal, who lived more than a century after Horace, saw the Empire in its decline. For his fictional situation he has himself addressed by Umbricius, a bitter citizen who is about to desert Rome for Naples, and thus he "distances" himself from his wrong feelings. Verse satire at this stage reached a level of formal achievement seldom equaled, and Juvenal, like Horace, has been frequently imitated since the sixteenth century. (The student who wishes to follow up *Satire III* may read Dr. Johnson's "London" (1738), which is modeled on it, but recast in the style of the English Augustan Age.) The Juvenalian tone of denunciation is something we often find, and Shakespeare, in *Timon of Athens*, manages to sustain it for much of a full-length play.

If the Christian Middle Ages were not sympathetic to classical satire in verse or prose, what happened to the impulse to denounce? The typical medieval form of satire was the "complaint," which might as well be called a direct attack on vice; that is, the moralist's voice, sometimes strident, always earnest, creates the momentum and the mood. Sometimes this comes out in an allegorical work such as *Piers Plowman*, the famous visionary poem written by one of Chaucer's contemporaries, where there is an almost systematic cataloguing of vices. Although it is the work of a learned man, such satire is not of a "civilized" order—there is no indirection, no urbanity. A racier kind of satire operated in popular culture, much of it subliterary in the way of the oral tradition. Chaucer, whose poetic range was wide, did not hesitate to use for his purpose the fabliau (the coarse tale of ordinary life) or the beast fable (a story in which animals act like human beings). In his hands the ancient folk story of Chanticleer and the Fox is elevated to high art in "The Nun's Priest's Tale." This joyous poem, a mock-epic in which a trivial situation is treated in an absurdly elaborate style, is the work of a great comic writer, and its depiction of pride is anything but grim.

Although satire, sometimes identified with comedy, can be very funny, it is basically concerned with exposing some flaw or excess. Indeed no humor is necessary (as in Dr. Johnson's "London"). But the ways of exposing flaws and excesses are many, and the satirist can adopt various attitudes, including the playful and witty as well as the vitriolic. Juvenal is wise in putting his denunciation of Rome into the speech of a poor decent citizen who can endure no more of the corruption; the poet thus avoids the self-pity which is so unattractive. The satirist differs from the comic artist in not quite accepting the world as it is. An example is Byron's *Don Juan.* Although this long comic poem contains satirical passages, such as the mock dedication that we include in this anthology, Byron does not carry out a sustained indictment of society, and, in fact, he gives the impression of delighting in its incongruities. (However, his "Vision of Judgment," contemporary with *Don Juan* and written in the same stanzaic form, is unquestionably a strongly felt satire on the political situation in the England of 1821.) Returning to Juvenal once more, we might observe his *fiction,* his make-believe situation, as a way of mounting his attack. This is important, and the true satirists always observe it, no matter what the state of their feelings.

It is impossible in this brief introduction to do more than suggest the various forms that satire took from the Renaissance onward. But we can mention four. If Erasmus reestablished the satiric dialogue as a terse way of criticizing ideas, Rabelais (circa 1494–1553) in *Gargantua and Pantagruel* developed what might be called the encyclopedic narrative, in which the excesses of learning are exposed by being "blown up" out of proportion. (Rabelais, like Erasmus, was opposed to the scholastic philosophers of the Church.) This kind of narrative itself is large and digressive; it ridicules through exaggeration. Its influence can be easily traced in Swift's *Battle of the Books* and *Gulliver's Travels* (Book III), in Pope's *Dunciad* and Sterne's *Tristram Shandy* in the eighteenth century; in *Bouvard and Pécuchet* (1881), Flaubert's great gibe at the clichés of his time; and in certain parts of Joyce's *Ulysses* (1922).

The year after Rabelais' death an unknown writer in Spain published *The Life of Lazarillo de Tormes,* a short narrative that is considered the first picaresque novel. The word *pícaro* has an uncertain etymology, but it refers to an irresponsible rogue or drifter, another kind of anti-hero. The picaresque novel is not necessarily a satire, but its satirical potentialities are considerable. Lazarillo, the young drifter, looks at the social institutions of Spain such as the Church and the aristocracy from the underside, and the implied criticism cuts deep. Some scholars think the unknown author was a follower of Erasmus; in any case his book and those of Erasmus were put on the Index in Spain in 1559. But by that time the damage had been done; the novel was soon translated into French and English. And the picaresque novel became one of the major forms of narrative art in Europe and America: Henry Fielding's *Tom Jones*, Fernández de Lizardi's *The Itching Parrot* (written in Mexico in 1816), Nikolai Gogol's *Dead Souls* (1842), and Saul Bellow's *The Adventures of Augie March* are all descended from *Lazarillo*.

During the next century another literary form in which satire could operate reached a high level of development in France with Molière. This is the comedy of manners, the witty play dealing with the morals and manners of high society. The characters are types, such as clever young men, intellectual ladies, jealous husbands, and fops. (Molière's theatrical conventions grew out of commedia dell' arte, a popular acting tradition based on stock characters and intrigues.) But he lived during a great period in French culture with an intellectual and social élite at its center. Francis Fergusson has observed that the direction he gave comedy was "away from the folk tradition of farce, and toward rationality, literature, and the realistic imitation of contemporary character; in short, toward modern drama as we know it." Plays such as *The Misanthrope*, *Tartuffe*, *The Miser*, and the lighter *Highbrow Ladies* are not only satirical comedies set in the Paris of Louis XIV, they are commentaries on permanent vagaries of human nature. Molière has no equal but many followers in the theaters of Europe: Congreve and Wycherly in England, Goldoni in Italy, and Marivaux and Beaumarchais in France.

Contemporary with Molière was the poet-critic Nicolas Boileau (1636–1711), the perfect type of neoclassical writer who observed the strictest rules in his art. He was the author of *The Lectern*, a mock-epic that brought a new urbanity to formal verse satire. This poem, hardly 1000 lines long, concerns a trivial dispute between two ecclesiastics in Paris. Its salient feature is the elevation of style, for which the *Aeneid* is the principal model. The neoclassical age still cherished the idea of epic as the most important literary form; lacking that, the mock-epic, with its blending of epic dignity and the corrosive venom of satire, was the most satisfactory substitute. Boileau's works were soon translated into English by various poets, including the Earl of Rochester and Samuel Butler, and they were much admired by Dryden, the leading poet of the Restoration. *The Lectern* made possible Dryden's own work in mock-epic, notably *Mac Flecknoe* (1682), and somewhat later Pope's *Rape of the Lock* and *Dunciad* carried forward this genre, which for many readers represents the highest achievement in English verse satire. Mock-epic is a species of *high burlesque*, where the trivial subject is treated in a style proper to epic or poetic tragedy. The opposite tendency, *low burlesque*, is represented by Samuel Butler's *Hudibras* (1662). Here the dignified subject is treated in a low style. Butler, a royalist in a period of political turmoil, intensely disliked the Puritan clergy and rulers of Cromwell's generation, and his Puritan knight, Hudibras, is made ridiculous by style as much as anything else; the heroic world is cut down to size:

> The sun had long since in the lap
> Of Thetis taken out his nap,
> And, like a lobster boiled, the morn
> From black to red began to turn;
> When Hudibras, whom thoughts and aching
> 'Twixt sleeping kept all night and waking,
> Began to rub his drowsy eyes,
> And from his couch prepared to rise. . .

Though satire tends to be anti-heroic, the satirist is not frivolous (even when his manner is an assumed frivolity). He is usually a moralist and unlikely to accept big ideas and ideals without question. Aristophanes had good reason to write the *Lysistrata*, and Shakespeare treated the same antiwar theme more comprehensively in *Troilus and Cressida*, the finest dramatic satire in English. *The Rape of the Lock* was written in the aftermath of Milton's *Paradise Lost*, the most impressive epic or "heroic" poem in our literature. The climactic part of the epic has Eve succumbing to temptation and eating the forbidden fruit; hence the Fall of Man. Much of the epic "machinery" (the angels and their activities) is there to make the event in the Garden of Eden seem vast in importance. Pope, an admirer of Milton, wittily uses certain phases of Milton's poem for satirical purposes. His climactic incident is the loss of a foolish society girl's lock of hair. By surrounding this trivial incident with a considerable array of "machinery" (in this case a small army of flimsy sylphs), Pope makes the supernatural devices of Milton's poem seem ridiculous—at least in the social setting of eighteenth-century London. We can say, then, that this is a first-rate example of *literary* satire, in which a certain kind of grand style is turned against itself. A good satirist is almost invariably a good rhetorician; that is, one who knows how to manipulate styles to witty advantage.

In speaking earlier of Archilochus, we mentioned the "critical understanding" to which satire should appeal. The reader often must be able to see the discrepancy between style and subject. Of all the English satirists, Swift perhaps makes the most demands on the reader's judgment. In the famous last book of *Gulliver's Travels* we are presented with two alternatives: the repulsive Yahoos (the representation of men) and the beautiful Houyhnhnms, the "reasonable" horses who gain so much by the comparison. The reader should discern that the kind of "reason" that we get in these horses is limited and unworthy of the truly enlightened.

Swift's real moral standard is never directly stated: readers must locate it for themselves, given the alternatives. Similarly, in "A Modest Proposal" the tone of the essay is so "reasonable," and modern readers may consider overpopulation such a danger, that they could get well into the satire before they realized that they were in effect approving a mass murder. What Swift wants to do is to shock the public into awareness.

Looking back to the neoclassical satirists, we can point out certain formal qualities that made possible their successes, especially in verse. For instance, most satirists in French and English for almost two centuries (from 1600 to 1800) wrote in couplets. The heroic couplet (a pair of rhymed iambic pentameter lines, usually end-stopped) has an epigrammatic quality that makes it suitable for satire: it delivers a concentration of effect that no other verse form can. Pope, in a pair of couplets in *The Rape of the Lock*, thus epitomizes an entire society, from the judge in his courtroom to the society girl applying her makeup at her dressing table:

> The hungry judges soon the sentence sign,
> And wretches hang that jurymen may dine;
> The merchant from th' exchange returns in peace,
> And the long labors of the toilet cease.

This kind of precise elegance often is associated with the comedy of manners (which of course can be written in prose), but the satirist can turn the couplet to other purposes. Thus Blake, who inherited the eighteenth-century instinct for epigram, wrote:

> Pity would be no more
> If we did not make somebody Poor . . . .

There are, however, other forms that the poet-satirist can use, and indeed the proliferation of forms that began with the Romantic movement offered many possibilities. Burns, for instance, in "Holy Willie's Prayer," uses the conventional form of a prayer, which is absolutely right for this exposure of Calvinist hypocrisy. Wallace Stevens, an American poet of our century, satirizes the Protestantism of his youth, but his method is more complex; he writes a poem based on elaborate symbols. These are just two examples of how satirists have developed the genre since Pope.

Although the impulse to satirize is a powerful force in our culture today, a number of critics believe that the mode is difficult to practice. Among them is the late W. H. Auden, preeminently a comic poet, who made this pertinent observation:

> Satire flourishes in a homogeneous society where satirist and audience share the same view as to how normal people can be expected to behave,

and in times of relative stability and contentment, for satire cannot deal
with serious evil and suffering. In an age like our own, it cannot flourish
except in intimate circles as an expression of private feuds: in public life
the evils and sufferings are so serious that satire seems trivial and the
only possible kind of attack is prophetic denunciation.

It is true that our era is not a time of "relative stability" and that the
satiric impulse is rarely sustained And Auden is probably right in maintaining that the satirist and the audience no longer agree on standards.
For instance, a writer like Vladimir Nabokov in *Lolita* is apt to be misunderstood by many of his readers, a fact that makes his attack on the
social and sexual mores of our society all the more savage. Nevertheless,
the satirist today has had some successes in dealing with major topics.

Those writers who have enjoyed the greatest successes are frequently
the very ones who have adapted traditional forms to contemporary materials. George Orwell's *Animal Farm* is the beast fable brought up to date.
Harsher and sparer than "The Nun's Priest's Tale," this satire on communism retains the essence of Chaucer's gibe at humankind by reducing
human beings to the level of barnyard animals and thus mocking their
bustling self-importance. Evelyn Waugh's early novels, such as *Vile
Bodies* and *A Handful of Dust*, are in part comedies of manners concerned
with the antics of upper-class English society. Though the characters are less inhibited than those of Molière, their wit and their intrigues are similar in many respects. And though Waugh does not estab-
lish absolute standards against which to judge the world he ridicules, he
does value, as one critic notes, "order in social and personal life." Joseph
Heller's *Catch-22* is still another work whose form remains conventional
despite the unconventional attitudes and ideas expressed. It is a Menippean satire on air force bureaucracy with an anti-hero, Yossarian, a
combination of naive Candide and conniving rogue. Professor Frye's description of such satire fits the novel:

> The Menippean satire deals less with people as such than with mental
> attitudes. Pedants, bigots, cranks, parvenus, virtuosi, enthusiasts, rapa-
> cious and incompetent professional men of all kinds, are handled in
> terms of their occupational approach to life as distinct from their social
> behavior.

A current writer who has had both popular and critical success in
recent years and who sees himself as a satirist in the tradition of Petronius, Juvenal, Apuleius, and Peacock is Gore Vidal. He is one of the few
living satirists to comment at length on the state of the mode today. His
essay "Satire in the 1950's" argues vigorously for a revival of a moribund
art. Unlike Auden he considers the present, despite its lack of a homo-

geneous society and stability, a good time for satire since it is "most useful" and "most used" during a period of "serious confusion" and "dramatic change." To prove his point Vidal cites examples of its achievement when the Roman Republic was declining: "Cicero satirized radicals, Catullus satirized the mysteriously amiable Caesar, and Horace ticked off a number of highly placed bores." The trouble is that in America, the new Roman Republic, we tolerate too much and question and laugh at our most cherished beliefs too little. Some of the topics, he insists, that should be attacked are "Christianity, Psychiatry, Marxism, Romantic Love, Xenophobia, Science." And the best vehicle for launching such an attack is the novel, which Vidal himself has employed so effectively to bring truth "to a solemn canting world."

Vidal's "Book Report" as well as Anthony Hecht's "Dover Bitch," both included in this anthology, are good examples of satire using the traditional device of parody to mock an overserious world. Parody is the deriding of a literary work by imitating its form and style in a degrading and humorous manner. It is related to mock-epic. But Vidal and Hecht are doing more than caricaturing a specific kind of criticism and a specific kind of poem. They are making critical judgments, one about the solemn way a certain type of reader views historical fiction and the foolishness of that fiction itself, and the other about the pomposity with which oversensitive people pontificate on the sad state of the world. Donne's parody of Marlowe's "The Passionate Shepherd to His Love" contains the same double-barreled mockery of an outmoded style and attitude.

Three other authors in the contemporary section of this anthology—E. E. Cummings, Karl Shapiro, and Jean-Claude van Itallie—are also fundamentally traditional in their approaches. "I Sing of Olaf" continues the antiwar sentiments expressed by Aristophanes, Erasmus, and Shakespeare. What is more, Cummings's moral outrage matches in vehemence Juvenal's upbraiding of Roman society. In contrast, Shapiro adopts in "The Humanities Building" an Horatian tone—witty, measured, urbane. Instead of bearing down and evoking indignation, he matter-of-factly details the scene with all of its cultural incongruities. The two moods are prevalent in every age and are equally effective. One does not laugh at suffering any more than one rails against a grotesque building and its misfits. Van Itallie's *Almost Like Being* is an hilarious burlesque of a movie script and its stereotyped characters. The posturing in public, the empty singing, the meaningless words all belong to various conventional satiric forms from the comedy of manners to parody.

The two remaining writers in the section on the contemporary scene find the old satiric forms and attitudes inadequate for their purposes. They exhibit the truth of what Auden wrote concerning the difficulty of satire today. They appeal to no clear moral and social norms that the reader can share. They find the evils in public life too overwhelming to attack in any standard way. As Bruce Jay Friedman, a writer in sympathy with their aims, observes: "What happened is that the satirist has had his ground usurped by the newspaper reporter." Actual life is so much more fantastic and ridiculous than anything he can think of. So with "no real territory of his own to roam" he sets out to discover "a new land, invent a new currency." He reaches "beyond satire" into the turbulent waters of black humor.

Ishmael Reed in "The Gangster's Death" and Donald Barthelme in "City Life" display various aspects of this black humor. Each dwells on the grim incoherence of the world in which he lives—its senseless violence, its lack of communication, its fragmentary nature—with varying degrees of intensity. Reed is the more savage and undisciplined, Barthelme the wittier and subtler. Both employ the fantastic and the nonsensical. Significantly both place greater emphasis on pity and despair than on ridicule and the rooting out of social ills. As one critic, disturbed by this interest in black humor, writes: "Satire, which we have thought of as fundamentally optimistic in the assumption that man is worth correcting, seems to have become in much current practice a way of dealing with hopelessness or cynicism—very different attitudes even from the bitterness which has often brought satire near to invective." And it is true that the literature of the absurd appears to be a new mode of writing, like satire in some of its techniques and thrusts, but different in tone and purpose. Samuel Beckett and Jean Genet in French drama and John Barth and Thomas Pynchon in the American novel are writers searching for a "new land" and a "new currency."

Whether satire will discard its traditional forms and objectives remains to be seen. Critics are always making gloomy pronouncements about the state of the great genres. The novel is dead. Tragedy can no longer be written. Romance is old-fashioned. And it is true that satire today rarely comes pure and unmixed with other modes. There is no homogeneous society on which many such as Auden believe it depends. The conventional ridicule of the fool or knave is not so widespread as the pity for the victim. Still, for all these handicaps, satire is alive and flourishing. As long as people laugh at others, see absurdities in the world, and seek to redress wrongs, they will respond to the satiric impulse no matter where it comes from—*Mad* magazine or *The New Yorker*, a political cartoon, an antiutopian novel like *1984*, or whatever form it takes.

The Contemporary Scene

E. E. Cummings

I Sing of Olaf

E. E. Cummings (1894–1963) is one of America's finest verse satirists. Son of a Cambridge, Massachusetts, Congregational minister, graduate of Harvard, and ambulance driver in World War I, he came to prominence in 1922 with *The Enormous Room* based on his experiences in a French detention camp. His first book of poems was *Tulips and Chimneys* (1923). In his work he attacks such traditional targets as war, conformity, science, phony patriotism, and bad art with savage wit and innovative typography and syntax. "I Sing of Olaf" is not only an indictment of war but also a highly skillful poem in its stucture (note the parallelism of the second and third sections, of the beginning and end) and in its martial rhythm. The first line is a parody of the opening verses of Virgil's *Aeneid*: "Arms and the man I sing."

i sing of Olaf glad and big
whose warmest heart recoiled at war;
a conscientious object-or

his well belovéd colonel (trig[1]
westpointer most succinctly bred)
took erring Olaf soon in hand;
but—though an host of overjoyed
noncoms (first knocking on the head
him) do through icy waters roll
that helplessness which others stroke   10
with brushes recently employed
anent this muddy toiletbowl,
while kindred intellects evoke
allegiance per blunt instruments—
Olaf (being to all intents
a corpse and wanting any rag
upon what God unto him gave)
responds, without getting annoyed
"I will not kiss your f.ing flag"

straightway the silver bird looked grave   20
(departing hurriedly to shave)

but—though all kinds of officers

---
[1] Trimly neat.

16

(a yearning nation's blueeyed pride)
their passive prey did kick and curse
until for wear their clarion
voices and boots were much the worse,
and egged the firstclassprivates on
his rectum wickedly to tease
by means of skilfully applied
bayonets roasted hot with heat—   30
Olaf (upon what were once knees)
does almost ceaselessly repeat
"there is some s. I will not eat"

our president, being of which
assertions duly notified
threw the yellowsonofabitch
into a dungeon, where he died

Christ (of His mercy infinite)
i pray to see; and Olaf, too

preponderatingly because   40
unless statistics lie he was
more brave than me: more blond than you.

Ishmael Reed

The Gangster's Death

Like E. E. Cummings, Ishmael Reed satirizes war, conformity, and
American culture with a mordant wit and fierce irony. His technique,
however, is quite different. Basically it is surrealistic. He moves rapidly
from one point to another and constantly mixes fantasy with reality,
illogic with logic to create a nightmare world. What he says about his
own fiction could apply equally to "The Gangster's Death": "I've
watched television all my life, and I think my way of editing, the speed
I bring to my books, the way the plot moves, is based upon some of the
television shows and cartoons I've seen." This is a particularly apt comment when one remembers that the Vietnam war was the first war the
American people saw on television. Born in Chattanooga, Tennessee, in
1938, son of an auto worker, the poet was educated at the State University of New York at Buffalo and now teaches at the University of California at Berkeley. He has written several novels as well as two books of
poetry.

how did he die/ O if i told you,
you would slap your hand against your forehead
and say good grief/ if i gripped you
by the lapel and told how they dumped
        thalidomide hand grenades
into his blood stream and/ how they injected
a cyst into his spirit the size of an egg
which grew and grew until floating
        gangrene encircled the globe
and/ how guerillas dropped from trees like   10
mean pythons and squeezed out his life/
so that jungle birds fled their perches/
so that hand clapping monkeys tumbled
        from branches and/
how twelve year olds snatched B 52's
        from the skies with their bare hands and/
how betty grable[1]/ couldn't open a hershey bar
        without the wrapper exploding and/
how thin bent women wrapped bicycle chains
        around their knuckles saying   20
        we will fight until the last bra or/
        give us bread or shoot us/ and/
how killing him became child's play

---

[1] Movie actress and pin-up girl popular in the 1940s.

in Danang in Mekong in Santo Domingo[2]

            and how rigor mortis was sprinkled
in boston soups
                giving rum running families
stiff back aches
so that they were no longer able to sit
at the elbows of the president
with turkey muskets   or/sit   30
on their behinds watching the boat races
off Massachusetts through field glasses but/
how they found their duck pants
       pulled off in the get-back-in-the-alleys
       of the world and/
how they were routed by the people
       spitting into their palms
       just waiting to use those lobster pinchers
       or smash that martini glass and/
how they warned him and gave him a chance   40
       with no behind the back dillinger[3]
       killing by flat headed dicks but/
how they held megaphones in their fists
       saying come out with your hands up and/
how refusing to believe the jig was up
       he accused them of apocalyptic barking
       saying out of the corner of his mouth
       come in and get me and/
how they snagged at his khaki legs
       until their mouths were full   50
       of ankles and calves and/
how they sank their teeth into his swanky jugular
       getting the sweet taste of max factor
       on their tongues and/
how his screams were so loud
       that the skins of eardrums blew off
       and blood trickled
               down the edges of mouths

---

[2] Danang and Mekong are references to the Vietnam war. President Johnson in April 1965 ordered American troops into Santo Domingo to prevent the spread of "Castroite Communism."

[3] The gangster John Dillinger was killed by FBI agents on July 22, 1934, as he came out of a Chicago movie theater.

and people got hip to his aliases/
                           i mean/
democracy and freedom began bouncing
all over the world
                    like bad checks   60
as people began scratching their heads
and stroking their chins
as his rhetoric stuck in his fat throat
               while he quoted
men with frills on their wrists
and fake moles on their cheeks
and swans on their snuff boxes
      who sit in Gilbert Stuart's⁴ portraits

      talking like baroque clocks/
      who sit talking turkey talk   70
   to people who say   we don't want
                          to hear it
as they lean over their plows reading Mao
wringing the necks of turkeys
         and making turkey talk gobble
         in upon itself
in Mekong and Danang and Santo Domingo
and

Che Guevara⁵ made personal appearances everywhere

Che Guevara in Macy's putting incendiary flowers   80
on marked down hats   and women
scratching out each other's eyes over ambulances
Che Guevara in Congress putting tnt shavings
in the ink wells   and politicians
tripped over their jowls trying to get away
Che Guevara in small towns and hamlets
where cans jump from the hands of stock clerks
   in flaming super markets/
where skyrocketing devil's food cakes
      contain the teeth of republican bankers/   90
where the steer of gentleman farmers
      shoot over the moon like beefy missiles

---

⁴ American portrait painter (1755–1828).
⁵ Communist revolutionary and friend of Castro, killed in Bolivia in 1967.

        while undeveloped people
stand in road shoulders saying
fly Che fly bop a few for us
     put cement on his feet
     and take him for a ride

O Walt Whitman
visionary of leaking faucets
great grand daddy of drips   100
   you said I hear america singing
but/ how can you sing when your throat is slit
and O/ how can you see when your head bobs
    in a sewer
in Danang and Mekong and Santo Domingo

and look at them weep for a stiff/
                       i mean
a limp dead hood
Bishops humping their backsides/
folding their hands in front of their noses
forming a human carpet for a zombie   110
men and women looking like sick dust mops/
   running their busted thumbs
   across whiskey headed guitars/
weeping into the evil smelling carnations
   of Baby Face McNamara
   and Killer Rusk[6]
whose arms are loaded with hijacked rest
in peace wreaths and/
look at them hump this stiff in harlem/
sticking out their lower lips/   120
and because he two timed them/
     midget manicheans shaking their fists
     in bullet proof telephone booths/
     dialing legbar on long distance
     receiving extra terrestrial sorry
              wrong number
seeing big nosed black people land in space ships/
seeing swamp gas/
shoving inauthentic fireballs down their throats/

---

   [6] Robert S. McNamara, secretary of defense, 1961–1968. Dean Rusk, secretary of
state,1961–1969. There was a gangster in the 1930s named Baby Face Nelson.

bursting their lungs on existentialist rope skipping/   130
    look at them mourn/
drop dead egalitarians and CIA polyglots
  crying into their bill folds
  we must love one another or die

while little boys wipe out whole regiments with bamboo
                                    sticks
while wrinkled face mandarins store 17 megatons in Haiku

for people have been holding his death birds
on their wrists and his death birds
make their arms sag with their filthy nests
and his death birds ate their baby's testicles   140
and they got sick and fed up
with those goddamn birds
and they brought their wrists together and blew/
                      i mean/
puffed their jaws and blew and shooed
  these death birds his way
and he is mourned by
drop dead egalitarians and CIA polyglots and
midget manicheans and Brooks Brothers Black People
  throwing valentines at crackers   150
  for a few spoons by Kirk's old Maryland engraved/
  for a look at Lassie's purple tongue/
  for a lock of roy roger's hair/
  for a Lawrence Welk champagne bubble

as for me/ like the man said
i'm always glad when the chickens come home to roost

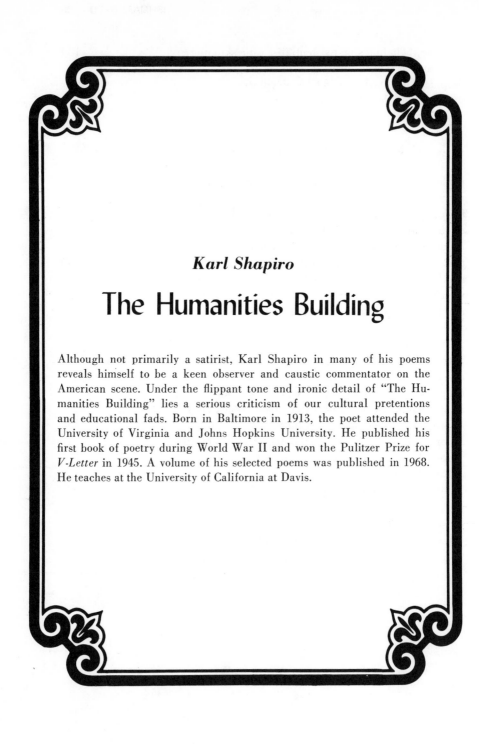

Karl Shapiro

The Humanities Building

Although not primarily a satirist, Karl Shapiro in many of his poems reveals himself to be a keen observer and caustic commentator on the American scene. Under the flippant tone and ironic detail of "The Humanities Building" lies a serious criticism of our cultural pretentions and educational fads. Born in Baltimore in 1913, the poet attended the University of Virginia and Johns Hopkins University. He published his first book of poetry during World War II and won the Pulitzer Prize for *V-Letter* in 1945. A volume of his selected poems was published in 1968. He teaches at the University of California at Davis.

All the bad Bauhaus[1] comes to a head
In this gray slab, this domino, this plinth
Standing among the olives or the old oak trees,
As the case may be and whatever the clime.
No bells, no murals, no gargoyles,
But rearing like a fort, with slits of eyes
Suspicious in the aggregate, its tons
Of concrete—glaciers of no known color—
Gaze down upon us. St. Thomas More,
Behold the Humanities Building!   10
                              On the top floor
Are one and a half professors of Greek,
Kicked upstairs but with the finest view,
Two philosophers, and assorted Slavics;
Then stacks of languages coming down,
Mainly the mother tongue and its dissident children
(History has a building all its own),
To the bottom level with its secretaries,
Advisers, blue-green photographic light
Of many precious copying machines;   20
All is bathed in cool fluorescence
From top to bottom, justly distributed:
Light, Innovation, Progress, Equity—

---

[1] A school of design and architecture established by Walter Gropius in Germany in
1919.

Though in my cell I hope and pray
Not to be confronted by
A student with a gun or a nervous breakdown,
Or a girl who closes the door as she comes in.

The Old Guard sits in judgment and wears ties,
Eying the New in proletarian drag,
And the Assistant with one lowered eyelid   30
Plots against Tenure, dreaming of getting it,

And in the lobby, under the bulletin boards,
The Baudelairean forest of posters[2]
For Transcendental Meditation, Audubon Group,
"The Hunchback of Notre Dame," Scientology,
Arab Students Co-op, "Case of the Curious Bride,"
Two students munch upon a single sandwich.

---

[2] See Baudelaire's line, "Man passes through forests of symbols," in his sonnet, "Correspondences."

Matthew Arnold

Dover Beach

Matthew Arnold (1822–1888), critic, scholar, inspector of schools, and poet, is as well known for his prose works such as *Essays on Criticism* and *Culture and Anarchy* as he is for his poetry. He devoted much of his life to improving education for the middle class in England and traveled widely both on the Continent and in America. "Dover Beach," his most famous poem, is one of the most moving expressions of doubt and pessimism in the Victorian era and points prophetically to the twentieth century.

The sea is calm tonight,
The tide is full, the moon lies fair
Upon the straits;—on the French coast the light
Gleams and is gone; the cliffs of England stand,
Glimmering and vast, out in the tranquil bay.
Come to the window, sweet is the night-air!
Only, from the long line of spray
Where the sea meets the moon-blanched land,
Listen! you hear the grating roar
Of pebbles which the waves draw back, and fling.   10
At their return, up the high strand,
Begin, and cease, and then again begin,
With tremulous cadence slow, and bring
The eternal note of sadness in.

Sophocles long ago
Heard it on the Aegean, and it brought
Into his mind the turbid ebb and flow
Of human misery;[1] we
Find also in the sound a thought,
Hearing it by this distant northern sea.   20

The Sea of Faith

---

[1] See Sophocles' *Antigone*, lines 583 ff.

Was once, too, at the full, and round earth's shore
Lay like the folds of a bright girdle furled.[2]
But now 1 only hear
Its melancholy, long, withdrawing roar,
Retreating, to the breath
Of the night-wind, down the vast edges drear
And naked shingles[3] of the world.

Ah, love, let us be true
To one another! for the world, which seems
To lie before us like a land of dreams,   30
So various, so beautiful, so new,
Hath really neither joy, nor love, nor light
Nor certitude, nor peace, nor help for pain;
And we are here as on a darkling plain
Swept with confused alarms of struggle and flight,
Where ignorant armies clash by night.

---

[2] At high tide the sea covers the land and at low tide it withdraws, spreads out, unfurls.
[3] Pebbled beach.

Anthony Hecht

The Dover Bitch,
A Criticism of Life

Anthony Hecht's parody of one of the most famous poems of the nineteenth century succeeds principally by its imitation of Arnold's form (the
dramatic monologue), speaker, situation, and tone. Nowhere is this more
apparent than in the last line where *"Nuit d'Amour"* parallels precisely
"ignorant armies clash by night." But the colloquialism and facetious-
ness not only mock the formality and solemnity of Arnold but also act as
a twentieth-century commentary on life as the poet sees it today in contrast to the Victorian's high seriousness or "criticism of life." Hecht was
born in New York in 1923. After graduating from Bard College in 1944,
he entered the army and served both in Europe and Japan. His second
book of poems, *The Hard Hours* (1968), won the Pulitzer Prize. He now
teaches at the University of Rochester.

So there stood Matthew Arnold and this girl
With the cliffs of England crumbling away behind them,
And he said to her, "Try to be true to me,
And I'll do the same for you, for things are bad
All over, etc., etc."
Well now, I knew this girl. It's true she had read
Sophocles in a fairly good translation
And caught that bitter allusion to the sea,
But all the time he was talking she had in mind
The notion of what his whiskers would feel like   10
On the back of her neck. She told me later on
That after a while she got to looking out
At the lights across the channel, and really felt sad,
Thinking of all the wine and enormous beds
And blandishments in French and the perfumes.
And then she got really angry. To have been brought
All the way down from London, and then be addressed
As a sort of mournful cosmic last resort
Is really tough on a girl, and she was pretty.
Anyway, she watched him pace the room   20
And finger his watch-chain and seem to sweat a bit,
And then she said one or two unprintable things.
But you mustn't judge her by that. What I mean to say is,
~~I'll eat him there in spite of every one."~~ '
She's really all right. I still see her once in a while
And she always treats me right. We have a drink

31

And I give her a good time, and perhaps it's a year
Before I see her again, but there she is,
Running to fat, but dependable as they come.
And sometimes I bring her a bottle of *Nuit d'Amour*.

Gore Vidal

Book Report

Gore Vidal was born at West Point in 1925, son of an army instructor of aeronautics. He wrote his first novel *Williwaw* at the age of 19. Subsequently he worked as an editor, actor, television host, critic, political columnist, and screen writer. He ran for Congress in 1960, inspired, he claims, by his political play *The Best Man*. In addition to novels he has written poetry, plays, and numerous literary and cultural essays. His best-known books are *Myra Breckinridge*, a parody of pornographic fiction, and two recent historical novels, *Burr* and *1876*. His skill as a wit and parodist is evident in "Book Report" where not only Warren's novel but also the language, tone, and form of an American cultural phenomenon are ridiculed with "fine raillery."

Can you hear me? Oh, good. Then I won't have to use this thing. It scares me to death! My husband always tells me, "Marian, you and your mother may not be very good but you're certainly loud enough when you give a book report." That's what he always says. Now then: the book I'm going to talk to you about today is by an American writer named Robert Penn Warren. Robert Penn Warren. He has written some poems, and of course most of us read his book a few years ago called *All the King's Men,* which they later made a movie out of and ruined, the way they always do. Mr. Warren's new book is a historical—*an* historical—novel *with a difference.* It begins with a beautiful quotation from a poem by A.E. Housman, the poet: "When shall I be dead and rid of the wrong my father did?"

And that's just what it's about. About Amantha Starr, a beautiful girl of sixteen, raised in Ohio, where she'd been sent to be educated by her father—sent by her father to be educated—a wealthy Kentucky plantation owner. When suddenly he dies, she comes home for his funeral, where she finds that not only did he die bankrupt, but that she is really a Negress, the daughter of one of his slaves, and she has to be sold to pay off these debts he left. Well, this is how the story starts. A really awful situation for a girl to be in. One day she had everything money and refinement could bring, and the next day she is a slave. The very first sentence of the book is filled with symbolism: "Oh, who am I? For so long that was, you might say, the cry of my heart." And then there follows a description of this wonderful house she lived in in Kentucky, south of Lexington, near Danville: a two-story brick house with a chimney at each end and a portico with pillars. The most beautiful house you could imagine! All of which she lost when she found she was colored and sold to a dealer who took her to New Orleans where she was put up for sale in the slave market as a slave.

Fortunately, she was bought by the most interesting person in the book, a fascinating older man with a lame leg who always walked with a heavy blackthorn stick with a great silver knob. His name was Hamish Bond, and he became her protector. Not until much later does she find out that he's really not named Bond but Hinks, that he was raised in Baltimore where he was a slave trader, going to Africa regularly and bringing back Negroes. He had some awful experiences in Africa. One in particular, a description of a massacre, is really gruesome where these Amazon women go through an entire village, slaughtering all the men, women and children because they're so enormous and bloodthirsty, much stronger than men. When Hamish, whose real name is Hinks, tries to keep one of the Amazons from killing a baby, this is what happens: "I just shoved her a little. It's very peculiar the way you have a habit. I just shoved her gentle because she was, in a way of speaking, a lady, and I had learned manners back in Baltimore. Here she was a crocodile-hided, blood-drinking old frau, who had been in her line of business for twenty years, and I caught myself making allowance for a lady." Well, he wished he hadn't, because right after he pushed her she slashed his leg with a big razor, making a long jagged cut which is what made him lame and why he had to always walk with that blackthorn cane with the silver knob.

Anyway, Hamish was kind in his brooding way to Amantha, and he treated her like she was really a lady which made her feel a bit better about being a slave. As somebody in the book says, the trouble with Hamish is he has "kindness like a disease." Another fascinating character Amantha meets is Hamish's *k'la* (meaning Negro best friend) Rau-ru, "whose eyes were wide, large and deepset, his nose wide but not flattened, the underlip full if not to the comic fullness favored in the minstrel shows of our day, and the corners of the mouth were drawn back so that the effect of that mouth was one of arrogant reserve and not blubbering docility."

Hamish was a very unusual man, especially after the Civil War started. One night there is a storm at Hamish's house—and Hamish takes Amantha in his arms while the rain blows in the window and she knows for the first time what love is. "With the hand of Hamish Bond laid to my side, and the spreading creep and prickle of sensation across the softness of my belly from the focus of Hamish Bond's sandpaper thumb, and the unplaiting and deliquescence of the deep muscles of thighs were as much History as any death-cry at the trenchlip or in the tangle of the abatis."

Can you still hear me? Well, that's how she feels as she discovers what love is and this maybe is the only serious fault in the book. I mean *would* a young girl like Amantha, even though she was well educated in Oberlin, Ohio, think thoughts quite like *that?* I mean, older more experienced women would, but would she? However, Mr. Warren writes poetic English and we can certainly excuse an occasional symbolic sentence like that. Well, there are many beautiful passages like this in the book, but the story never gets bogged down and the parts about the Civil War are really fascinating. Especially in New Orleans where she meets, completely by accident, Seth Parton, her girlhood sweetheart, who is now an officer in the Union Army, and also Tobias Sears, "the New England idealist to whom the butcheries of war must be justified by truth.'" I don't think it will spoil the book any if I tell you that everything ends all right with Tobias and Amantha . . . Miss Manty, as everybody calls her . . . together in quite a beautiful and touching ending.

I'd like to say something, by the way, if I may make a digression, about the much-maligned historical novel . . . the "bosom books" as they are disdainfully called by some critics, who think they know everything and can't keep from tearing apart books like Mr. Warren's. Now, I know and you know that maybe these books aren't *exactly* history, but they're awfully close, some of them, especially this one, and I can't help but think of Mrs. Gregg Henderson's fascinating report some meetings ago about the boys in Korea who were captured and tortured and brainwashed by the Chinese Communists who found that American boys were easy to break down BECAUSE THEY DID NOT KNOW ENOUGH ABOUT AMERICAN HISTORY AND WHY THEY WERE FIGHTING. Most of us here are mothers and we all know the trouble we have getting boys to read about history and all the things which don't seem important to them until they're caught by the enemy, when it's too late. So I don't think it's fair to make fun of novels that may be a little romantic but are still very useful ways of teaching what America is to people who are never going to read history or really deep things. I think Mr. Warren has done a wonderful job of bringing to life the Civil War and certain problems of that time—and frankly, I don't care a penny what the critics say about the book. After all, if people didn't want books like this, writers wouldn't write them and publishers wouldn't publish them. You can't argue with facts!

This book has been high on the best-seller list, and the movies have bought it, though they'll probably ruin it like they always do. A lot of people are going to be hearing about Amantha Starr and the Civil War. And they'll learn something. I firmly believe that these characters will stay with you for many a long day. Rau-ru, Miss Manty, the Amazons who go into that village killing all the men, Hamish Bond with his heavy blackthorn stick with the great silver knob—all these wonderful characters come alive for you in the pages of *Band of Angels* by Robert Penn Warren, published by Random House, three hundred and seventy-five pages long. Long? I wanted it to go on forever, and so will you!

Donald Barthelme

City Life

Like Ishmael Reed, Donald Barthelme satirizes American life by stressing its absurd and surrealistic aspects. Collage is his central principle. He makes this clear in an interview when he states that "New York is or can be regarded as a collage as opposed to say, a tribal village in which all of the huts are the same, duplicated. The point of collage is that unlike things are stuck together to make . . . a new reality. This new reality . . . may be or imply a comment on the other reality from which it came." He blends in his fictional collages clichés, puns, advertizing jargon, religious terminology, abstruse cultural allusions, and elements of pop art to produce a string of improbable scenes and wild characters who speak in non sequiturs. Born in Philadelphia in 1931, son of an architect, the author has lived in Texas, where he edited the magazine *Location*. Most of his volumes are collections of short stories that have appeared in *The New Yorker*. He has written two novels, *Snow White* (1967) and *Death of Father* (1976).

Elsa and Ramona entered the complicated city. They found an apartment without much trouble, several rooms on Porter Street. Curtains were hung. Bright paper things from a Japanese store were placed here and there.

—You'd better tell Charles that he can't come see us until everything is ready.

Ramona thought: I don't want him to come at all. He will go into a room with Elsa and close the door. I will be sitting outside reading the business news. Britain Weighs Economic Curbs. Bond Rate Surge Looms. Time will pass. Then, they will emerge. Acting as if nothing had happened. Elsa will make coffee. Charles will put brandy from his flat silver flask into the coffee. We will all drink the coffee with the brandy in it. Ugh!

—Where shall we put the telephone books?

—Put them over there, by the telephone.

Elsa and Ramona went to the $2 plant store. A man stood outside selling individual peacock feathers. Elsa and Ramona bought several hanging plants in white plastic pots. The proprietor put the plants in brown paper bags.

—Water them every day, girls. Keep them wet.

—We will.

Elsa uttered a melancholy reflection on life: It goes faster and faster! Ramona said: It's so difficult!

Charles accepted a position with greater responsibilities in another city.

—I'll be able to get in on weekends sometimes.

—Is this a real job?

—Of course, Elsa. You don't think I'd fool you, do you?

Clad in an extremely dark gray, if not completely black, suit he had shaved his mustache.

—This outfit doesn't let you wear them.

Ramona heard Elsa sobbing in the back bedroom. I suppose I should sympathize with her. But I don't.

2.

Ramona received the following letter from Charles:

Dear Ramona—

> Thank you, Ramona, for your interesting and curious letter. It is true that I have noticed you sitting there, in the living room, when I visit Elsa. I have many times made mental notes about your appearance, which I consider in no way inferior to that of Elsa herself. I get a pretty electric reaction to your taste in clothes, too. Those upper legs have not been lost on me. But the trouble is, when two girls are living together, one must make a choice. One can't have them both, in our society. This prohibition is enforced by you girls, chiefly, together with older ladies, who if the truth were known probably don't care, but nevertheless feel that standards must be upheld, somewhere. I have Elsa, therefore I can't have you. (I know that there is a philosophical problem about "being" and "having" but I can't discuss that now because I'm a little rushed due to the pressures of my new assignment.) So that's what obtains at the moment, most excellent Ramona. That's where we stand. Of course the future may be different. It not infrequently is.

> Hastily,
> Charles.

—What are you reading?
—Oh, it's just a letter.
—Who is it from?
—Oh, just somebody I know.
—Who?
—Oh, nobody.
—Oh.

Ramona's mother and father came to town from Montana. Ramona's thin father stood on the Porter Street sidewalk wearing a business suit and a white cowboy hat. He was watching his car. He watched from the steps of the house for a while, and then watched from the sidewalk a little, and then watched from the steps again. Ramona's mother looked in the suitcases for the present she had brought.

—Mother! You shouldn't have brought me such an expensive present!

—Oh, it wasn't all that expensive. We wanted you to have something for the new apartment.

—An original gravure by René Magritte!

—Well, it isn't very big. It's just a small one.

Whenever Ramona received a letter forwarded to her from her Montana home, the letter had been opened and the words "Oops! Opened by mistake!" written on the envelope. But she forgot that in gazing at the handsome new Magritte print, a picture of a tree with a crescent moon cut out of it.

—It's fantastically beautiful! Where shall we hang it?

—How about on the wall?

3.

At the University the two girls enrolled in the Law School.

—I hear the Law School's tough, Elsa stated, but that's what we want, a tough challenge.

—You are the only two girls ever to be admitted to our Law School, the Dean observed. Mostly, we have men. A few foreigners. Now I am going to tell you three things to keep an eye on: 1) Don't try to go too far too fast. 2) Wear plain clothes. And 3) Keep your notes clean. And if I hear the words "Yoo hoo" echoing across the quadrangle, you will be sent down instantly. We don't use those words in this school.

—I like what I already know, Ramona said under her breath.

Savoring their matriculation, the two girls wandered out to sample the joys of Pascin Street. They were closer together at this time than they had ever been. Of course, they didn't want to get too close together. They were afraid to get too close together.

Elsa met Jacques. He was deeply involved in the struggle.

—What is this struggle about, exactly, Jacques?

—My God, Elsa, your eyes! I have never seen that shade of umber in anyone's eyes before. Ever.

Jacques took Elsa to a Mexican restaurant. Elsa cut into her *cabrito con queso*.

—To think that this food was once a baby goat!

Elsa, Ramona, and Jacques looked at the dawn coming up over the hanging plants. Patterns of silver light and so forth.

—You're not afraid that Charles will bust in here unexpectedly and find us?

—Charles is in Cleveland. Besides, I'd say you were with Ramona. Elsa giggled.

Ramona burst into tears.

Elsa and Jacques tried to comfort Ramona.

—Why don't you take a 21-day excursion-fare trip to "preserves of nature"?

—If I went to a "preserve of nature," it would turn out to be nothing but a terrible fen!

Ramona thought: He will go into a room with Elsa and close the door. Time will pass. Then they will emerge, acting as if nothing had happened. Then the coffee. Ugh!

4.

Charles in Cleveland.

"Whiteness"

"Vital skepticism"

Charles advanced very rapidly in the Cleveland hierarchy. That sort of situation that develops sometimes wherein managers feel threatened by gifted subordinates and do not assign them really meaningful duties but instead shunt them aside into dead areas where their human potential is wasted did not develop in Charles' case. His devoted heart lifted him to the highest levels. It was Charles who pointed out that certain operations had been carried out more efficiently "when the cathedrals were white," and in time the entire Cleveland structure was organized around his notions: "whiteness," "vital skepticism."

Two men held Charles down on the floor and a third slipped a needle into his hip.

He awakened in a vaguely familiar room.

—Where am I? he asked the nurselike person who appeared to answer his ring.

—Porter Street, this creature said. Mlle. Ramona will see you shortly. In the meantime, drink some of this orange juice.

Well, Charles thought to himself, I cannot but admire the guts and address of this brave girl, who wanted me so much that she engineered this whole affair—my abduction from Cleveland and removal to these beloved rooms, where once I was entertained by the beautiful Elsa. And now I must see whether my key concepts can get me out of this "fix," for "fix" it is. I shouldn't have written that letter. Perhaps if I wrote another letter? A followup?

Charles formed the letter to Ramona in his mind.

Dear Ramona—

Now that I am back in your house, tied down to this bed with these steel bands around my ankles, I understand that perhaps my earlier letter to you was subject to misinterpretation etc. etc.

Elsa entered the room and saw Charles tied down on the bed.
—That's against the law!
—Sit down, Elsa. Just because you are a law student you want to proclaim the rule everywhere. But some things don't have to do with the law. Some things have to do with the heart. The heart, which was our great emblem and cockade, when the cathedrals were white.
—I'm worried about Ramona, Elsa said. She has been missing lectures. And she has been engaging in hilarity at the expense of the law.
—Jokes?
—Gibes. And now this extra-legality. Your sequestration.
Charles and Elsa looked out of the window at the good day.
—See that blue in the sky. How wonderful. After all the gray we've had.

5.

Elsa and Ramona watched the Motorola television set in their pajamas.
—What else is on? Elsa asked.
Ramona looked in the newspaper.
—On 7 there's "Johnny Allegro" with George Raft and Nina Foch. On 9 "Johnny Angel" with George Raft and Claire Trevor. On 11 there's "Johnny Apollo" with Tyrone Power and Dorothy Lamour. On 13 is "Johnny Concho" with Frank Sinatra and Phyllis Kirk. On 2 is "Johnny Dark" with Tony Curtis and Piper Laurie. On 4 is "Johnny Eager" with Dick Powell and Evelyn Keyes. On 31 is "Johnny Trouble" with Stuart Whitman and Ethel Barrymore.
—What's this one we're watching?

—What time is it?
—Eleven-thirty-five.
—"Johnny Guitar" with Joan Crawford and Sterling Hayden.

6.

Jacques, Elsa, Charles and Ramona sat in a row at the sun dance. Jacques was sitting next to Elsa and Charles was sitting next to Ramona. Of course Charles was also sitting next to Elsa but he was leaning toward Ramona mostly. It was hard to tell what his intentions were. He kept his hands in his pockets.
—How is the struggle coming, Jacques?
—Quite well, actually. Since the Declaration of Rye we have accumulated many hundreds of new members.
Elsa leaned across Charles to say something to Ramona.
—Did you water the plants?
The sun dancers were beating the ground with sheaves of wheat.
—Is that supposed to make the sun shine, or what? Ramona asked.
—Oh, I think it's just sort of to . . . honor the sun. I don't think it's supposed to make it do anything.
Elsa stood up.
—That's against the law!
—Sit down, Elsa.
Elsa became pregnant.

7.

"This young man, a man though only eighteen . . ."
A large wedding scene
Charles measures the church
Elsa and Jacques bombarded with flowers
Fathers and mothers riding on the city railway
The minister raises his hands
Evacuation of the sacristy: bomb threat
Black limousines with ribbons tied to their aerials
Several men on balconies who appear to be signalling, or applauding
Traffic lights
Pieces of blue cake
Champagne

8.

—Well, Ramona, I am glad we came to the city. In spite of everything.

—Yes, Elsa, it has turned out well for you. You are Mrs. Jacques Tope now. And soon there will be a little one.

—Not so soon. Not for eight months. I am sorry, though, about one thing. I hate to give up Law School.

—Don't be sorry. The Law needs knowledgeable civilians as well as practitioners. Your training will not be wasted.

—That's dear of you. Well, goodbye.

Elsa and Jacques and Charles went into the back bedroom. Ramona remained outside with the newspaper.

—Well, I suppose I might as well put the coffee on she said to herself. Rats!

9.

Laughing aristocrats moved up and down the corridors of the city.

Elsa, Jacques, Ramona and Charles drove out to the combined track and art gallery. Ramona had a Heineken and everyone else had one too. The tables were crowded with laughing aristocrats. More laughing aristocrats arrived in their carriages drawn by dancing matched pairs. Some drifted in from Flushing and São Paulo. Management of the funded indebtedness was discussed; the Queen's behavior was discussed. All of the horses ran very well, and the pictures ran well too. The laughing aristocrats sucked on the heads of their gold-headed canes some more.

Jacques held up his degrees from the New Yorker Theatre, where he had been buried in the classics, when he was twelve.

—I remember the glorious debris underneath the seats, he said, and I remember that I hated then, as I do now, laughing aristocrats.

The aristocrats heard Jacques talking. They all raised their canes in the air, in rage. A hundred canes shattered in the sun, like a load of anti-histamines falling out of an airplane. More laughing aristocrats arrived in phaetons and tumbrels.

As a result of absenting himself from Cleveland for eight months, Charles had lost his position there.

—It is true that I am part of the laughing-aristocrat structure, Charles said. I don't mean I am one of them. I mean I am their creature. They hold me in thrall.

Laughing aristocrats who invented the cost-plus contract . . .

Laughing aristocrats who invented the real estate broker . . .

Laughing aristocrats who invented Formica . . .
Laughing aristocrats wiping their surfaces clean with a damp cloth . . .
Charles poured himself another brilliant green Heineken.
—To the struggle!

10.

The Puerto Rican painters have come, as they do every three years, to
paint the apartment!
The painters, Emmanuel and Curtis, heaved their buckets, rollers, lad-
ders and drop cloths up the stairs into the apartment.
—What shade of white do you want this apartment painted?
A consultation.
—How about plain white?
—Fine, Emmanuel said. That's a mighty good-looking Motorola tele-
vision set you have there. Would you turn it to Channel 47, *por favor?*
There's a film we'd like to see. We can paint and watch at the same time.
—What's the film?
—"Victimas de Pecado," with Pedro Vargas and Ninon Sevilla.
Elsa spoke to her husband, Jacques.
—Ramona has frightened me.
—How?
—She said one couldn't sleep with someone more than four hundred
times without being bored.
—How does she know?
—She saw it in a book.
—Well, Jacques said, we only do what we really want to do about 11
per cent of the time. In our lives.
—11 per cent!
At the Ingres Gardens, the great singer Moonbelly sang a song of
rage.

11.

Vercingetorix, leader of the firemen, reached for his red telephone.
—Hello, is this Ramona?
—No, this is Elsa. Ramona's not home.
—Will you tell her that the leader of all the firemen called?
Ramona went out of town for a weekend with Vercingetorix. They went
to his farm, about eighty miles away. In the kitchen of the farm, bats
attacked them. Vercingetorix could not find his broom.

—Put a paper bag over them. Where is a paper bag?

—The groceries, Vercingetorix said.

Ramona dumped the groceries on the floor. The bats were zooming around the room uttering audible squeaks. With the large paper bag in his hands Vercingetorix made weak capturing gestures toward the bats.

—God, if one gets in my hair, Ramona said.

—They don't want to fly into the bag, Vercingetorix said.

—Give me the bag, if one gets in my hair I'll croak right here in front of you.

Ramona put the paper bag over her head just as a bat banged into her.

—What was that?

—A bat, Vercingetorix said, but it didn't get into your hair.

—Damn you, Ramona said, inside the bag, why can't you stay in the city like other men?

Moonbelly emerged from the bushes and covered her arms with kisses.

12.

Jacques persuaded Moonbelly to appear at a benefit for the signers of the Declaration of Rye, who were having a little legal trouble. Three hundred younger people sat in the church. Paper plates were passed up and down the rows. A number of quarters were collected.

Moonbelly sang a new song called "The System Cannot Withstand Close Scrutiny."

> The system cannot withstand close scrutiny
> The system cannot withstand close scrutiny
> The system cannot withstand close scrutiny
> The system cannot withstand close scrutiny
> Etc.

Jacques spoke briefly and well. A few more quarters showered down on the stage.

At the party after the benefit Ramona spoke to Jacques, because he was handsome and flushed with triumph.

—Tell me something.

—All right Ramona what do you want to know?

—Do you promise to tell me the truth?

—Of course. Sure.

—Can one be impregnated by a song?

—I think not. I would say no.

—While one is asleep, possibly?

—It's not very likely.

—What sort of people have hysterical pregnancies?

—Well, you know. Sort of nervous girls.

—If a hysterical pregnancy results in a birth, is it still considered hysterical?

—No.

—Rats!

13.

Charles and Jacques were trying to move a parked Volkswagen. When a Volkswagen is parked with its parking brake set you need three people to move it, usually.

A third person was sighted moving down the street.

—Say, buddy, could you give us a hand for a minute?

—Sure, the third person said.

Charles, Jacques, and the third person grasped the VW firmly in their hands and heaved. It moved forward opening up a new parking space where only half a space had been before.

—Thanks, Jacques said. Now would you mind helping us unload this panel truck here? It contains printed materials pertaining to the world-wide struggle for liberation from outmoded ways of thought that hold us in thrall.

—I don't mind.

Charles, Jacques, and Hector carried the bundles of printed material up the stairs into the Porter Street apartment.

—What does this printed material say, Jacques?

—It says that the government has promised to give us some of our money back if it loses the war.

—Is that true?

—No. And now, how about a drink?

Drinking their drinks they regarded the black trombone case which rested under Hector's coat.

—Is that a trombone case?

Hector's eyes glazed.

Moonbelly sat on the couch, his great belly covered with plants and animals.

—It's good to be what one is, he said.

14.

Ramona's child was born on Wednesday. It was a boy.

—But Ramona! Who is responsible? Charles? Jacques? Moonbelly? Vercingetorix?

—It was a virgin birth, unfortunately, Ramona said.

—But what does this imply about the child?

—Nothing, Ramona said. It was just an ordinary virgin birth. Don't bother your pretty head about it, Elsa dear.

However much Ramona tried to soft-pedal the virgin birth, people persisted in getting excited about it. A few cardinals from the Sacred Rota dropped by.

—What is this you're claiming here, foolish girl?

—I claim nothing, Your Eminence. I merely report.

—Give us the name of the man who has compromised you!

—It was a virgin birth, sir.

Cardinal Maranto frowned in several directions.

—There can't be another Virgin Birth!

Ramona modestly lowered her eyes. The child, Sam, was wrapped in a blanket with his feet sticking out.

—Better cover those feet.

—Thank you, Cardinal. I will.

15.

Ramona went to class at the Law School carrying Sam on her hip in a sling.

—What's that?

—My child.

—I didn't know you were married.

—I'm not.

—That's against the law! I think.

—What law is it against?

The entire class regarded the teacher.

Well there is a law against fornication on the books, but of course, it's not enforced very often ha ha. It's sort of difficult to enforce ha ha.

—I have to tell you, Ramona said, that this child is not of human man conceived. It was a virgin birth. Unfortunately.

A few waves of smickers washed across the classroom.

A law student named Harold leaped to his feet.

—Stop this smickering! What are we thinking of? To make mock of this fine girl! Rot me if I will permit it! Are we gentlemen? Is this lady our colleague? Or are we rather beasts of the field? This Ramona, this trull . . . No, that's not what I mean. I mean that we should think not upon her peculations but on our own peculations. For, as Augustine tells us, if for some error or sin of our own, sadness seizes us, let us not only bear in mind that an afflicted spirit is a sacrifice to God but also the words: for as water quencheth a flaming fire, so almsgiving quencheth sin; and for I desire, He says, mercy rather than sacrifice. As, therefore, if we were in danger from fire, we should, of course, run for water with which to extinguish it, and should be thankful if someone showed us water nearby, so if some flame of sin has arisen from the hay of our passions, we should take delight in this, that the ground for a work of great mercy is given to us. Therefore—

Harold collapsed, from the heat of his imagination.

A student in a neighboring seat looked deeply into Sam's eyes.

—They're brown.

16.

Moonbelly was fingering his axe.

—A birth hymn? Do I really want to write a birth hymn?

—What do I really think about this damn birth?

—Of course it's within the tradition.

—Is this the real purpose of cities? Is this why all these units have been brought together, under the red, white and blue?

—Cities are erotic, in a depressing way. Should that be my line?

—Of course I usually do best with something in the rage line. However—

—C . . . F . . . C . . . F . . . C . . . F . . . G7 . . .

Moonbelly wrote "Cities Are Centers of Copulation."

The recording company official handed Moonbelly a gold record marking the sale of a million copies of "Cities Are Centers of Copulation."

17.

Charles and Jacques were still talking to Hector Guimard, the former trombone player.

—Yours is not a modern problem, Jacques said. The problem today is not angst but lack of angst.

—Wait a minute, Jacques. Although I myself believe that there is nothing wrong with being a trombone player. I can understand Hector's feeling. I know a painter who feels the same way about being a painter. Every morning he gets up, brushes his teeth, and stands before the empty canvas. A terrible feeling of being *de trop* comes over him. So he goes to the corner and buys the Times, at the corner newsstand. He comes back home and reads the Times. During the period in which he's coupled with the Times he is all right. But soon the Times is exhausted. The empty canvas remains. So (usually) he makes a mark on it, some kind of mark that is not what he means. That is, any old mark, just to have something on the canvas. Then he is profoundly depressed because what is there is not what he meant. And it's time for lunch. He goes out and buys a pastrami sandwich at the deli. He comes back and eats the sandwich meanwhile regarding the canvas with the wrong mark on it out of the corner of his eye. During the afternoon, he paints out the mark of the morning. This affords him a measure of satisfaction. The balance of the afternoon is spent in deciding whether or not to venture another mark. The new mark, if one is ventured, will also, inevitably, be misconceived. He ventures it. It is misconceived It is, in fact, the worst kind of vulgarity. He paints out the second mark. Anxiety accumulates. However, the canvas is now, in and of itself, because of the wrong moves and the painting out, becoming rather interesting-looking. He goes to the A. & P. and buys a TV Mexican dinner and many bottles of Carta Blanca. He comes back to his loft and eats the Mexican dinner and drinks a couple of Carta Blancas, sitting in front of his canvas. The canvas is, for one thing, no longer empty. Friends drop in and congratulate him on having a not-empty canvas. He begins feeling better. A something has been wrested from the nothing. The quality of the something is still at issue—he is by no means home free. And of course all of painting—the whole art—has moved on somewhere else, it's not where his head is, and he knows that, but nevertheless he—

—How does this apply to trombone playing? Hector asked.

—I had the connection in my mind when I began, Charles said.

—As Goethe said, theory is gray, but the golden tree of life is green.

18.

Everybody in the city was watching a movie about an Indian village menaced by a tiger. Only Wendell Corey stood between the village and the tiger. Furthermore Wendell Corey had dropped his rifle—and was left with only his knife. In addition, the tiger had Wendell Corey's left arm in his mouth up to the shoulder.

Ramona thought about the city.

—I have to admit we are locked in the most exquisite mysterious muck. This muck heaves and palpitates. It is multi-directional and has a mayor.

To describe it takes many hundreds of thousands of words. Our muck is only a part of a much greater muck—the nation-state—which is itself the creation of that muck of mucks, human consciousness. Of course all these things also have a touch of sublimity—as when Moonbelly sings, for example, or all the lights go out. What a happy time that was, when all the electricity went away! If only we could re-create that paradise! By, for instance, all forgetting to pay our electric bills at the same time. All nine million of us. Then we'd all get those little notices that say unless we remit within five days the lights will go out. We all stand up from our chairs with the notice in our hands. The same thought drifts across the furrowed surface of nine million minds. We wink at each other, through the walls.

At the Electric Company, a nervousness appeared as Ramona's thought launched itself into parapsychological space.

Ramona arranged names in various patterns.

Vercingetorix
Moonbelly
Charles

Moonbelly
Charles
Vercingetorix

Charles
Vercingetorix
Moonbelly

—Upon me, their glance has fallen. The engendering force was, perhaps, the fused glance of all of them. From the millions of units crawling about on the surface of the city, their wavering desirous eye selected me. The pupil enlarged to admit more light: more me. They began dancing little dances of suggestion and fear. These dances constitute an invitation of unmistakable import—an invitation which, if accepted, leads one down many muddy roads. I accepted. What was the alternative?

Jean-Claude van Itallie

Almost Like Being

Almost Like Being is at once a burlesque of the American success story and a caricature of stars and "little" guys, leaders and humble servants in a movie script, how they talk and act for the camera. Great emphasis is placed on nonverbal communication and the striking of public poses. Although not as harsh in its satire of American life as the poems by Cummings and Reed, the play conceals beneath its vibrant foolishness a real concern for the sources of American hypocrisy and unhappiness. There is a constant reminder of the contrast between our mythical ideals and present realities. The playwright was born in Belgium in 1936, son of an investment banker, and became a naturalized citizen of the United States in 1952. He is a graduate of Harvard and has taught playwriting at various universities. His best-known work is *America Hurrah* (1966).

CHARACTERS

NARRATOR
DORIS
ROCK
BUD
KNOCKEFELLER
BILLY

This play is to be done as if it were a movie being shot by several cameras. When the individual actors are not, for a moment or two, on camera, their expression is deadpan and bored. They are "turned on" for their "bits." Often Doris will make a facial expression especially for the camera, or she will address it instead of another actor. The actors will always know exactly where the camera is at a given moment—sometimes a closeup, sometimes a two-shot, panning, etc. This technical device should serve as a comment on the action.

NARRATOR. (*Over the mike, under the movie music.*) A busy recording studio of one of the greatest companies in one of America's greatest cities. They are setting up for Miss Doris D. And yes, entering the room now in a small golf cart, is Miss D. herself. (*In comes Doris, wearing simple but gorgeous rehearsal clothes. She greets the few hundred people on the sound stage. Somehow when she greets one in particular, a certain Rock, there is a certain something deep in his voice, and a bell rings.*)
ROCK. Hello, Miss D. Hi there. (*The bell rings.*)
DORIS. Why hello to you.
ROCK. Miss D., I've set your levels at 440. Is that all right?

53

DORIS. Perfect.

NARRATOR: (*Over the mike.*) Miss D., we're ready when you are.

ROCK. 440?

DORIS. Ah, marvelous.

ROCK. 440, Bud.

BUD. Right, check, Rock. Here we go, Miss D. All America is waiting.

DORIS. I don't care how many times this happens. I'm always on my tippytoes, always. But I can only do my best, and with God's help, I'll get by.

NARRATOR. (*Over the mike.*) This is it, Doris. Sing. (*Doris sings a few lines from "When I Fall in Love, etc." Somehow her eyes seem constantly to stray to the control booth where a certain Rock is diddling the dials. Narrator, over the mike.*) Doris, Honey, perfect, just perfect.

DORIS. Oh, thank you, Mike. You really liked it? You're not just saying that? Thank you, Hal. It's so hard to tell yourself. Bill, thank you. I feel much better hearing that. Thank you, Stanley. Thanks Harris. Little Will. Oh Frank that's sweet of you to say. Chad when you're on the boom I simply trust, that's all, I *trust*. Thanks Charlie, you're the important one, keeping the studio in apple-pie order. Give my love to Oleander and the kids. Irving, I love you. Dear Chad. Godfrey, Harris, Bob, Dover, Port, Jeremy, Jonathan, Rhia, Gwenn, Fred, Joe, Tania dear, Lee, Jack, Jeff, Dwight, Paul, Sam, Kevin, Hiram, Sid, Earl, Robert, Alan, Arthur, Ray, Leonard, Asa, Jay, George, Llewellyn, Alexander, Larry, Caesar, Franz, Adolf, Hans, Wolfgang, Rolf, Henri, Pierre, Jean-Claude, Jean-Pierre, Jean-Paul, Charles, Ivan, Alyosha, Dmitri, Nicola, Boris.

BUD. (*Whispering to Rock.*) She never forgets a name.

ROCK. She is just the greatest.

DORIS. Paolo, Juan, Pietro, Giovanni, Nebuchadnezzar.

ROCK. I can't tell you what it does to me when she opens her mouth.

DORIS. And Bud, thanks a heap.

BUD. Thanks to *you*, Miss D.

DORIS. And thank *you*, Mr. uh uh uh uh . . .

DORIS. Uh uh . . . (*A bell rings.*)

ROCK. Rock. The name is Rock.

DORIS. Thank you, Mr. Rock.

ROCK. Just Rock is fine.

DORIS. Just Rock then.

NARRATOR. (*Over the mike.*) Lock it up, boys. (*Doris and Rock snap out of it.*)

DORIS. Goodbye, all. I wish I could kiss every one of you here.

(*She blows a little kiss. She leaves.*)

BUD. Hey, Man. Did she ever give you a tumble.

ROCK. (*Still in a daze.*) Yeah, yeah. What?

BUD. Some guys have all the luck. Now take me, the other day I was on the elevator and—

ROCK. Hey! Elevator!! Hold it!!! (*He rushes to the elevator and reaches it just in time to hold the door open and squeeze in scrunched right up nose-to-nose with . . .*) Oh. Hi.

DORIS. Hello, Just Rock.

ROCK. Almost didn't make it.

DORIS. (*Putting on her sexy face.*) Mmmmmmmmmmmmmm.

ROCK. Kind of crowded in here.

DORIS. (*Still with sexy face.*) Mmmmmmmmmmmmmm.

ROCK. Am I crowding you?

DORIS. (*Putting on her proper face.*) No. I'm fine.

ROCK. I could maybe move my arm a little down this way.

DORIS. (*Her very proper face.*) Don't bother, Mr. Rock.

ROCK. Just Rock.

DORIS. (*Her relenting face.*) Okay, Just Rock.

ROCK. Gee, I've never been so glad the studios are sixty-five floors up.

DORIS. (*Her coy face.*) Oh, and why's that, Rock?

ROCK. Well, it gives me a chance to talk to a star.

DORIS. (*Her simple face.*) Oh, Rock, I'm not a star. Sarah Bernhardt, now *that's* a star. I'm really nothing but a television, radio, theatre, and motion picture actress doing her best. And really underneath, well, I'm just *the* girl from Dubuque.

ROCK. Dubuque?

DORIS. Dubuque. *The* girl from Dubuque.

ROCK. Isn't that strange how some things, well . . . my mother was raised in Dubuque.

DORIS. Oh. Well then, do you know, maybe you know a little diner out there in the West called Mango Pete's?

ROCK. Mango Pete's? Do I know Mango Pete's?

DORIS. Oh my heavens you know Mango Pete's? Why I had chocolate—

ROCK. Banana vanilla pistachio triple frappes with cherries.

DORIS. And the sign over the counter said:

ROCK and DORIS. (*Together.*) "We don't serve anyone over twelve." (*They laugh together joyously.*)

DORIS. (Unnoticed.) Where am I? I feel sick . . . what a small world.

ROCK. It certainly is.

DORIS. (*Unnoticed.*) If I don't get some air I'm going to suffocate.

ROCK. (*Unnoticed.*) I get nervous on elevators. What if the cable broke.

DORIS. Small and funny and nice.

ROCK. Yeah nice. (*Unnoticed.*) What if it broke right now?

DORIS. (*Unnoticed.*) I think I'm going to puke.

DORIS and ROCK. (*Together.*) Small and funny and nice.

ROCK. (*Unnoticed.*) I can feel it breaking. Crashing downward. This is it. (*He closes his eyes.*)

DORIS. (*Unnoticed.*) I'm suffocating here. No more air. I can't breathe at all. (*There is a while of terror until they reach the bottom, during which she is suffocating and he is sure he is plunging toward death. As the elevator door opens, sprightly.*) Well, here we are.

ROCK. Yes. Well, well . . . could I ask you to lunch, Miss D.?

DORIS. (*Obviously in a quandary.*) Well, I'd love to. I'd really love it. But the fact is, well, someone is waiting for me.

ROCK. (*Devastated, but taking it like a man.*) You mean you have *Some*one?

DORIS. Well, not exactly *Some*one, but someone is waiting for me for lunch. As a matter of fact, it happens to be a certain Mr. Knockefeller.

ROCK. Well. I guess that's the breaks for the little guys like me.

DORIS. Oh, no, I didn't mean—

ROCK. Don't mention it. I'll be all right. There's only one place for the little guy.

DORIS: (*As a heavenly choir humming "This is the Army, Mr. Brown" swells under this tragic scene.*) One place?

ROCK. The khaki. It's the khaki for Rock. This is the army, Mr. Rock.

DORIS. Oh no. But let me explain.

ROCK. (*Trying his goddarndest to be brave.*) Don't bother yourself, Miss D.

DORIS. But I'm only going to see him for lunch.

ROCK. So long little patater. It's been keen. (*He sniffles only once and stalks off, scuffing his foot against a stone. She starts to run after him.*)

DORIS. Rock! (*She stops herself, putting her hand over her mouth.*) Darn. (*She stops in a very businesslike fashion and fixes her hair. Life must go on. But at the door of the restaurant she has one more uncontrolled outburst.*) Darn, darn, darn. (*Cocktail movie music. She enters the restaurant. Knockefeller, an older man with graying temples, is seated alone at the corner of the table, a solitary martini in front of him. Doris, very businesslike, pulling off her gloves.*) I need a drink. Order me a lemonade. (*She pulls out a hand-mirror and powders her nose. During the whole cocktail scene both she and Knockefeller smile and wave at various friends they see around the room.*)

KNOCKEFELLER. Do you realize . . . ?

DORIS. Order me a lemonade please.

KNOCKEFELLER. Waiter, a lemonade for the lady.

DORIS. Must you order so arrogantly?

KNOCKEFELLER. Arrogantly?

DORIS. Yes arrogantly. I said arrogantly.

KNOCKEFELLER. Do you know I've been waiting here two hours?

DORIS. I can't help that.

KNOCKEFELLER. Do you know what happens to the world bank while I'm here two hours?

DORIS. Oh I don't care a fig about the world bank.

KNOCKEFELLER. Now Doris, that's not very considerate.

DORIS. In fact I don't care a fig about . . .

KNOCKEFELLER. Go on. I can take it.

DORIS. Oh Barry, I'm sorry. You know I don't mean to be sharp. That's not the real me. What with my career and this whirl-a-gig life you're leading me it's too much. I'm under the heaviest pressure.

KNOCKEFELLER. It's okay, Dorrie. Drink your lemonade.

DORIS. I'm sick of lemonade.

KNOCKEFELLER. How about some champagne?

DORIS. At lunchtime? At lunchtime? Oh you and your big ways. I can't go on like this, Barry. I'm sorry. I'm simply not built that way I guess. You have to have had a coming-out cotillion I guess to get used to champagne at noon. I'm just the girl from Dubuque. *I* was raised on triple malted frappes at Mango Pete's.

KNOCKEFELLER. At Mango Pete's?

DORIS. Yes, darn it, at Mango Pete's. Oh you and your yachts. I can't give up my career for some old yachts.

KNOCKEFELLER. I never asked you to give up your career.

DORIS. You're from another world, Barry. We're from different worlds. An artist, a *real* artist is an *artist*. I can't give up my career. You mustn't ask me any more.

KNOCKEFELLER. But who's asking?

DORIS. Well, then. I've made my decision. Duty calls and I have much work to do before I sleep.

KNOCKEFELLER. Is this it?

DORIS. I'm sorry, Governor, but goodbye.

KNOCKEFELLER. Little Dorrie.

DORIS. (*Sincerely.*) I'm so sorry for you. (*She rushes out of the restaurant.*)

KNOCKEFELLER. Oh well, back to tired old whores.

DORIS. (*Alone for a moment outside the restaurant.*) I'm all alone. (*Cut to backstage that night at the nightclub. Doris' Negro maid Billy, dressed as a nun, is dressing Doris in her Madonna costume.*) I can't go on tonight.

I just can't go on. Not tonight.

BILLY. Miss D., Honey-lamb, is something the matter?

DORIS. Everything, Billy, everything. Sometimes life is like an angel-food cake that will never rise again.

BILLY. Is there anything I can do, Miss D.?

DORIS. Nothing, Honey, nothing. Just be your own sweet self. I don't know what I'd do without you.

BILLY. Oh Miss D. Honey you know I'll stand by even if you were starving and old and ugly and all your arms and legs were gone and you were blind and deaf and had warts all over your face and couldn't sing no more. I'd stand by. You know I would.

DORIS. I know it, Billy. You're my one friend in the world.

BILLY. Oh, Miss D. (*The applause having risen to a deafening pitch, out* that.

DORIS. Is my veil on straight?

BILLY. Just as straight as straight as straight as straight can be. You look just fine, Miss D. Just fine. I've never seen you look so fine.

DORIS. My crucifix.

BILLY. They're calling for you, Miss D. There must be thousands and thousands and thousands of people waiting for you, Honey, your public what you owe everything to. They love you, Miss D. Just think of that. How much they love you.

DORIS. Yes, yes I owe it to them. But thousands of pebbles don't make up for one Rock.

BILLY. Oh, Miss D. (*The applause having risen to a deafening pitch, out goes Miss D. to the footlights. They cheer and whistle. She manages a wee smile. The crowd is delirious. She holds her hand up for silence.*)

DORIS. My dear friends. My dear, dear friends. (*She holds up her hands in a plea for silence. The applause dies down just enough for her to be able to repeat her song. Doris sings same song as in studio, but with much more feeling now that she's been through so much.*) "When I fall in love . . ." (*After the first line, the public, in gratitude for having been given its favorite song, bursts into wild applause, and Doris once again is obliged to hold up her hand to keep them quiet.*) "It will be completely. Or I'll never fall in love. In this restless world we live in, life is ended before it's begun. And too many moonlight kisses dry in the warmth of the sun." (*Suddenly, behind her, who should appear, wounded and in uniform, but Rock. The Nun-Maid is overjoyed for Miss D.'s sake but Rock signals her to keep quiet until the song is over.*) "When I fall in love it will be completely or . . . I'll . . . never . . ." (*She sees Rock! She is so overcome she can hardly finish the song. She smiles at the audience, trying*

to keep up the show.) "... fall ... in ... I— ... love." (*At the end of the song, she rushes into Rock's arms. The audience, witness to all this, claps deliriously for both Doris and her boyfriend. She tries to pull him up to take a bow with her but he is shy. She finally succeeds. The audience goes wild. Doris and Rock join hands in what is to be the finale.*)
DORIS and ROCK. (*With gusto.*)

> An instant ago my feet were solid on the ground
> A moment ago I was sad but safe and sound ...
> But suddenly you're near
> And now you're really here
> And oh, *this* is the hour
> And *this* is the place
> And all at once the stars ...
> Are grinning at every soul alive!

(*On the words "every soul alive" Doris takes the Nun-Maid by the hand and she joins them in singing. Then Knockefeller appears on the sidelines. Doris beckons to him. He takes the Nun-Maid by the hand, and instantly you know these two were really meant for each other all along. Knockefeller also reaches over and shakes Rock's hand. Then all holding hands they step in rhythm toward the audience singing the last lines of the song. The song should sound like every popular movie joyous ending.*)
DORIS, ROCK, BILLY and KNOCKEFELLER.

> And me, well I'm grinning too,
> And me, well I'm feeling too
> Like it's nearly,
> Like it's almost,
> Like it's very nearly almost,
> Like it's almost like being—

(*On the last words—"it's almost like being"—they freeze in silence, wide smiles on their faces, and the lights black out.*)

The Tradition of Satire

Horace

The Town Mouse
and the Country Mouse

From *The Second Book of Satires*

ADAPTED FROM THE TRANSLATION BY SIR THEODORE MARTIN

Horace (65-8 B.C.), the son of a minor government official, was educated in Rome and Athens. Upon the death of Julius Caesar in 44 B.C., he joined the army of Junius Brutus to fight against Mark Antony and Octavius Caesar. After the war he became a clerk in Rome, where he started writing poetry and formed a friendship with Virgil. The great epic poet introduced him to the patron Maecenas, whose name became a symbol in literary history for a wealthy and sympathetic supporter of artists. Generously provided for, Horace wrote steadily in both the lyric and satiric forms and covered a wide range of subjects from the pleasures of living in the country to Roman history and the foibles of human nature. His satire is less severe than that of Juvenal, as the student may see by comparing "The Town Mouse and the Country Mouse" with Juvenal's Satire III.

My prayers with this I used to charge:
A piece of land not over large,
Wherein there should a garden be,
A clear spring flowing ceaselessly,
And where, to crown the whole, there should
Be found a patch of growing wood.
All this, and more, the gods have sent,
And I am heartily content.
    O son of Maia,[1] that I may
These blessings keep is all I pray.   10
If never by craft or base design
I've swelled what little store is mine,
Nor mean it ever shall be wrecked
Through my own failing or neglect;
If never from my lips a word
Shall drop of prayers so absurd
As, "Had I but that little nook,
Next to my field, that spoils its look!"
Or, "Would some lucky chance unfold
To me a crock of hidden gold,   20
As to the man, whom Hercules
Enriched and settled at his ease,
Who, with the treasure he had found,
Bought for himself the very ground

---

[1] Mercury, the god of gain, and the protector of poets.

Which he before for hire had tilled!"
If I with gratitude am filled
For what I have—by this I dare
Implore you to fulfil my prayer,
That you with fatness will endow
My little herd of cattle now,   30
And all things else their lord may own,
Except what wits he has alone,
And be, as heretofore, my chief
Protector, guardian, and relief!
   So, when from town and all its ills
I to my perch among the hills
Retreat, what better theme to choose
Than satire for my homely Muse?
No cruel ambition wastes me there,
No, nor the south wind's leaden air,   40
Nor Autumn's pestilential breath,
With victims feeding hungry death.
Sire of the morn, or if you prefer,
The name of Janus to your ear,[2]
Through whom whate'er to man is dear,
(So willed the gods for man's estate),
Do you my verse initiate!
At Rome you hurry me away
To bail my friend: "Quick, no delay,
Or some one—could worse luck befall you?—   50
Will in the kindly task forestall you."
So go I must, although the wind
Is north and killingly unkind,
Or snow, in thickly-falling flakes,
The wintry day more wintry makes.
And when, articulate and clear,
I've spoken what may cost me dear,
Elbowing the crowd that round me close,
I'm sure to crush somebody's toes.
"What's up, where are you pushing to?   60
What would you have, you madman, you?
You think that you, now, I daresay,

---

2 Janus, a divinity specially dear to the Latin race, presided over not only the opening of every year and every month, but also of every day. Prayers were offered to him
every morning.

May push whatever stops your way,
When you are to Maecenas bound!"[3]
Sweet, sweet, as honey is the sound,
I won't deny, of that last speech,
But then no sooner do I reach
The gloomy Esquiline,[4] than straight
Buzz, buzz around me runs the prate
Of people pestering me with cares,   70
All about other men's affairs.
"Roscius, according to report,
Expects by seven you'll be in court!"
"The scriveners, worthy Horace, pray,
You'll not forget they meet to-day,
Upon a point both grave and new,
One touching the whole body, too."[5]
"Do get Maecenas, do, to sign
This application here of mine!"
"Well, well, I'll try." "You can with ease   80
Arrange it, if you only please."
      Close on eight years it now must be,
Since first Maecenas numbered me
Among his friends, as one to take
Out driving with him, and to make
The confidant of trifles, say,
Like this, "What is the time of day?"
"The Thracian Bantam, would you bet
On him, or on the Syrian Pet?"[6]
"These chilly mornings will do harm,   90
If you don't mind to wrap up warm"
Such gossip as without a fear
One drops into the leakiest ear.
Yet all this time has envy's glance
On me looked more and more askance.
From mouth to mouth such comments run:
"Our friend indeed is Fortune's son.

---

[3] Horace's patron.
[4] Where Maecenas lived in Rome.
[5] Horace had belonged, if indeed he did not still belong, to the "*ordo*" or guild of "*Scribæ*," and, trusting to his influence in high quarters, they were anxious he should attend a meeting in which some matters of importance to the interests of the body were to be discussed.
[6] Gladiators.

Why, there he was, we all recall,
Beside Maecenas playing ball."
  Some chilling news through lane and street   100
Spreads from the Forum. All I meet
Accost me thus—"Dear friend, you're so
Close to the gods, that you must know:
About the Dacians, have you heard
Any fresh tidings?" "Not a word!"
"You're always jesting!" "Now may all
The gods confound me, great and small,
If I have heard one word!" "Well, well,
But you at any rate can tell
If Caesar means the lands, which he   110
Has promised to his troops, shall be
Selected from Italian ground,
Or in Sicily be found?"
And when I swear, as well I can,
That I know nothing, for a man
Of silence rare and most discreet
They cry me up to all the street.
  Thus do my wasted days slip by,
Not without many a wish and sigh.
Oh, when shall I the country see,   120
Its woodlands green? Oh, when be free,
With books of great old men, and sleep,
And hours of dreamy ease, to creep
Into oblivion sweet of life,
Its agitations and its strife?
When on my table shall be seen
Pythagoras's kin, the bean,[7]
And bacon, not too fat, embellish
My dish of greens, and give it relish?
Oh happy nights, oh feasts divine,   130
When, with the friends I love, I dine
At my own hearth-fire, and the meat
We leave gives my bluff slaves a treat!
No stupid laws our feasts control,
But each guest drains or leaves the bowl,
Precisely as he feels inclined.

---

[7] Referring to the popular opinion that Pythagoras and his disciples would not eat this vegetable, because in doing so they might be devouring their own flesh and blood—they believed in the transmigration of souls.

If he be strong, and have a mind
For seconds, good! if not, he's free
To sip his liquor leisurely.
And then the talk our banquet rouses!   140
Not gossip about our neighbours' houses,
Or if 'tis generally thought
That Lepos dances well or not?[8]
But what concerns us nearer, and
Is harmful not to understand,
Whether by wealth or worth, it's plain,
That men to happiness attain?
By what we're led to choose our friends,—
Regard for them, or our own ends?
In what does good consist, and what   150
Is the supremest form of that?
　　　My neighbor Cervius will strike in
With some old woman's tale, akin
To what we are discussing. Thus,
If some one recommends to us
Arellius' wealth, forgetting how
Much care it costs him, "Look you now,
Once on a time," he will begin,
"A country mouse received within
His humble cave a city brother,   160
As one old comrade would another.
A frugal mouse upon the whole,
But loved his friend, and had a soul,
And could be free and open-handed,
When hospitality demanded.
In brief, he did not spare his hoard
Of corn and peas, long carefully stored;
Raisins he brought, and scraps, to boot,
Half-gnawed, of bacon, which he put
With his own mouth before his guest,   170
In hopes, by offering his best
In such variety, he might
Persuade him to an appetite.
The city mouse, with languid eye,
Just picked a bit, then put it by;
Which with dismay the rustic saw,
As, stretched upon some stubbly straw,

---

[8] Lepos was a celebrated mime, and spoke and acted as well as danced.

He munched at bran and common grits,
Not venturing on the dainty bits.
At length the town mouse: 'What,' says he,   180
'My good friend, can the pleasure be
Of grubbing here, on the backbone
Of a great crag with trees o'ergrown?
Who'd not to these wild woods prefer
The city, with its crowds and stir?
Then come with me to town; you'll ne'er
Regret the hour that took you there.
All earthly things draw mortal breath;
Nor great nor little can from death
Escape, and therefore, friend, be gay,   190
Enjoy life's good things while you may,
Remembering how brief the space
Allowed to you in any case.'
        His words struck home; and, light of heart,
The rustic didn't wait to start,
Timing their journey so they might
Reach town beneath the cloud of night,
Which was at its high noon, when they
To a rich mansion found their way,
Where shining ivory couches vied   200
With coverlets in scarlet dyed,
And where in baskets were amassed
The ruins of a great repast,
Which some few hours before had closed.
There, having first his friend disposed
Upon a purple cover, straight
The city mouse began to wait
With scraps upon his country brother,
Each scrap more dainty than another,
And all a servant's duty proffered,   210
First tasting everything offered.
        The guest, reclining there in state,
Rejoiced now in his new-found fate,
Over each fresh tidbit smacked his lips,
And broke into the merriest quips,
When suddenly a banging door
Shook host and guest into the floor.
From room to room they rushed aghast,
And almost fell down dead at last,
When loud through all the house came sounds—   220
The barking of colossal hounds.

'Ho!' cried the country mouse. 'This kind
Of life is not for me, I find.
Give me my woods and cavern. There
At least I'm safe! And though both spare
And poor my food may be, rebel
I never will; so, fare you well!' "

Juvenal

Satire III

TRANSLATED BY ROLFE HUMPHRIES

Juvenal (circa 60–140), one of the three great verse satirists of Roman
literature (Horace and Persius are the other two), was known to Martial
and other poets during the reigns of Trajan and Hadrian, but little
verifiable information about him has come down to us. His 16 satires are
an impressive series of attacks on the abuses and follies of the Rome of
his age. He has been admired and imitated by a number of poets, including Marston and Donne in the Elizabethan period, Dryden and Johnson in the neoclassical period, and Robert Lowell in ours.

AGAINST THE CITY OF ROME

Troubled because my old friend is going, I still must commend him
For his decision to settle down in the ghost town of Cumae,
Giving the Sibyl one citizen more. That's the gateway to Baiae
There, a pleasant shore, a delightful retreat. I'd prefer
Even a barren rock in that bay to the brawl of Subura.[1]
Where have we ever seen a place so dismal and lonely
We'd not be better off there, than afraid, as we are here, of fires,
Roofs caving in, and the thousand risks of this terrible city
Where the poets recite all through the dog days of August?

While they are loading his goods on one little four-wheeled wagon,   10
Here he waits, by the old archways which the aqueducts moisten.
This is where Numa,[2] by night, came to visit his goddess.
That once holy grove, its sacred spring, and its temple,
Now are let out to the Jews, if they have some straw and a basket.
Every tree, these days, has to pay rent to the people.
Kick the Muses out; the forest is swarming with beggars.
So we go down to Egeria's vale, with its modern improvements.
How much more close the presence would be, were there lawns by the
        water,
Turf to the curve of the pool, not this unnatural marble!

Umbricius has much on his mind. "Since there's no place in the city,"   20
He says, "For an honest man, and no reward for his labors,

---

[1] A busy street in central Rome.
[2] An ancestral priest-king; *his goddess*, Egeria.

72

Since I have less today than yesterday, since by tomorrow
That will have dwindled still more, I have made my decision. I'm going
To the place where, I've heard, Daedalus put off his wings,
While my white hair is still new, my old age in the prime of its
    straightness,
While my fate spinner still has yarn on her spool, while I'm able
Still to support myself on two good legs, without crutches.
Rome, good-bye! Let the rest stay in the town if they want to,
Fellows like A, B, and C, who make black white at their pleasure,
Finding it easy to grab contracts for rivers and harbors,   30
Putting up temples, or cleaning out sewers, or hauling off corpses,
Or, if it comes to that, auctioning slaves in the market.
Once they used to be hornblowers, working the carneys;
Every wide place in the road knew their puffed-out cheeks and their
    squealing.
Now they give shows of their own. Thumbs up! Thumbs down! And
    the killers
Spare or slay, and then go back to concessions for private privies.
Nothing they won't take on. Why not?—since the kindness of Fortune
(Fortune is out for laughs) has exalted them out of the gutter.

"What should I do in Rome? I am no good at lying.
If a book's bad, I can't praise it, or go around ordering copies.   40
I don't know the stars; I can't hire out as assassin
When some young man wants his father knocked off for a price; I
    have never
Studied the guts of frogs, and plenty of others know better
How to convey to a bride the gifts of the first man she cheats with.
I am no lookout for thieves, so I cannot expect a commission
On some governor's staff. I'm a useless corpse, or a cripple.
Who has a pull these days, except your yes men and stooges
With blackmail in their hearts, yet smart enough to keep silent?
No honest man feels in debt to those he admits to his secrets,
But your Verres[3] must love the man who can tattle on Verres   50
Any old time that he wants. Never let the gold of the Tagus,
Rolling under its shade, become so important, so precious
You have to lie awake, take bribes that you'll have to surrender,
Tossing in gloom, a threat to your mighty patron forever.

"Now let me speak of the race that our rich men dote on most fondly.
These I avoid like the plague, let's have no coyness about it.

---

[3] A politician in the old Republic, more than a century earlier.

Citizens, I can't stand a Greekized Rome. Yet what portion
Of the dregs of our town comes from Achaia[4] only?
Into the Tiber pours the silt, the mud of Orontes,[5]
Bringing its babble and brawl, its dissonant harps and its timbrels,   60
Bringing also the tarts who display their wares at the Circus.
Here's the place, if your taste is for hat-wearing whores, brightly
      colored!
What have they come to now, the simple souls from the country
Romulus used to know? They put on the *trechedipna*
(That might be called, in our tongue, their running-to-dinner outfit),
Pin on their *niketeria* (medals), and smell *ceromatic*
(Attar of wrestler). They come, trooping from Samos and Tralles,
Andros, wherever that is, Azusa and Cucamonga,[6]
Bound for the Esquiline or the hill we have named for the vineyard,
Termites, into great halls where they hope, some day, to be tyrants.   70
Desperate nerve, quick wit, as ready in speech as Isaeus,
Also a lot more long-winded. Look over there! See that fellow?
What do you take him for? He can be anybody he chooses,
Doctor of science or letters, a vet or a chiropractor,
Orator, painter, masseur, palmologist, tightrope walker.
If he is hungry enough, your little Greek stops at nothing.
Tell him to fly to the moon, and he runs right off for his space ship.
Who flew first? Some Moor, some Turk, some Croat, or some Slovene?
Not on your life, but a man from the very center of Athens.

"Should I not run away from these purple-wearing freeloaders?   80
Must I wait while they sign their names? Must their couches always be
      softer?
Stowaways, that's how they got here, in the plums and figs from
      Damascus.
I was here long before they were: my boyhood drank in the sky
Over the Aventine hill; I was nourished by Sabine olives.
Agh, what lackeys they are, what sycophants! See how they flatter
Some ignoramus's talk, or the looks of some horrible eyesore,
Saying some Ichabod Crane's long neck reminds them of muscles
Hercules strained when he lifted Antaeus aloft on his shoulders,
Praising some cackling voice that really sounds like a rooster's
When he's pecking a hen. We can praise the same objects that they do,   90
Only, they are believed. Does an actor do any better

---

[4] Greece.
[5] The river which flows through Antioch in the Near East.
[6] *Samos . . . Cucamonga*, places in Greece.

Mimicking Thais, Alcestis, Doris without any clothes on?
It seems that a woman speaks, not a mask; the illusion is perfect
Down to the absence of bulge and the little cleft under the belly.
Yet they win no praise at home, for all of their talent.
Why?—Because Greece is a stage, and every Greek is an actor.
Laugh, and he splits his sides; weep, and his tears flow in torrents
Though he's not sad; if you ask for a little more fire in the winter
He will put on his big coat; if you say 'I'm hot,' he starts sweating.
We are not equals at all; he always has the advantage,   100
Able, by night or day, to assume, from another's expression,
This or that look, prepared to throw up his hands, to cheer loudly
If his friend gives a good loud belch or doesn't piss crooked,
Or if a gurgle comes from his golden cup when inverted
Straight up over his nose—a good deep swig, and no heeltaps!

"Furthermore, nothing is safe from his lust, neither matron nor virgin,
Not her affianced spouse, or the boy too young for the razor.
If he can't get at these, he would just as soon lay his friend's grandma.
(Anything, so he'll get in to knowing the family secrets!)
Since I'm discussing the Greeks, let's turn to their schools and
     professors,   110
The crimes of the hood and gown. Old Dr. Egnatius, informant,
Brought about the death of Barea, his friend and his pupil,
Born on that riverbank where the pinion of Pegasus landed.
No room here, none at all, for any respectable Roman
Where a Protogenes rules, or a Diphilus, or a Hermarchus,
Never sharing their friends—a racial characteristic!
Hands off! He puts a drop of his own, or his countryside's poison
Into his patron's ear, an ear which is only too willing
And I am kicked out of the house, and all my years of long service
Count for nothing. Nowhere does the loss of a client mean less.   120

"Let's not flatter ourselves. What's the use of our service?
What does a poor man gain by hurrying out in the nighttime,
All dressed up before dawn, when the praetor nags at his troopers
Bidding them hurry along to convey his respects to the ladies,
Barren, of course, like Albina, before any others can get there?
Sons of men freeborn give right of way to a rich man's
Slave; a crack, once or twice, at Calvina or Catiena[7]
Costs an officer's pay, but if you like the face of some floozy

---

[7] Prostitutes.

You hardly have money enough to make her climb down from her
    high chair.
Put on the stand, at Rome, a man with a record unblemished,   130
No more a perjurer than Numa was, or Metellus,
What will they question? His wealth, right away, and possibly, later,
(Only possibly, though) touch on his reputation.
'How many slaves does he feed? What's the extent of his acres?
How big are his platters? How many? What of his goblets and wine
    bowls?'
His word is as good as his bond—if he has enough bonds in his
    strongbox.
But a poor man's oath, even if sworn on all altars
All the way from here to the farthest Dodecanese island,
Has no standing in court. What has he to fear from the lightnings
Of the outraged gods? He has nothing to lose; they'll ignore him.   140

"If you're poor, you're a joke, on each and every occasion.
What a laugh, if your cloak is dirty or torn, if your toga
Seems a little bit soiled, if your shoe has a crack in the leather,
Or if more than one patch attests to more than one mending!
Poverty's greatest curse, much worse than the fact of it, is that
It makes men objects of mirth, ridiculed, humbled, embarrassed.
'Out of the front-row seats!' they cry when you're out of money,
Yield your place to the sons of some pimp, the spawn of some cathouse,
Some slick auctioneer's brat, or the louts some trainer has fathered
Or the well-groomed boys whose sire is a gladiator.   150
Such is the law of place, decreed by the nitwitted Otho:[8]
All the best seats are reserved for the classes who have the most
    money.
Who can marry a girl if he has less money than she does?
What poor man is an heir, or can hope to be? Which of them ever
Rates a political job, even the meanest and lowest?
Long before now, all poor Roman descendants of Romans
Ought to have marched out of town in one determined migration.
Men do not easily rise whose poverty hinders their merit.
Here it is harder than anywhere else: the lodgings are hovels,
Rents out of sight; your slaves take plenty to fill up their bellies   160
While you make do with a snack. You're ashamed of your earthenware
    dishes—
Ah, but that wouldn't be true if you lived content in the country,

---

[8] A Roman emperor.

Wearing a dark-blue cape, and the hood thrown back on your
    shoulders.

"In a great part of this land of Italy, might as well face it,
No one puts on a toga unless he is dead. On festival days
Where the theater rises, cut from green turf, and with great pomp
Old familiar plays are staged again, and a baby,
Safe in his mother's lap, is scared of the grotesque mask,
There you see all dressed alike, the balcony and the front rows,
Even His Honor content with a tunic of simple white.   170
Here, beyond our means, we have to be smart, and too often
Get our effects with too much, an elaborate wardrobe, on credit!
This is a common vice; we must keep up with the neighbors,
Poor as we are. I tell you, everything here costs you something.
How much to give Cossus the time of day, or receive from Veiento
One quick glance, with his mouth buttoned up for fear he might greet
    you?
One shaves his beard, another cuts off the locks of his boy friend,
Offerings fill the house, but these, you find, you will pay for.
Put this in your pipe and smoke it—we have to pay tribute
Giving the slaves a bribe for the prospect of bribing their masters.   180

"Who, in Praeneste's cool, or the wooded Volsinian uplands,
Who, on Tivoli's heights, or a small town like Gabii, say,
Fears the collapse of his house? But Rome is supported on pipestems,
Matchsticks; it's cheaper, so, for the landlord to shore up his ruins,
Patch up the old cracked walls, and notify all the tenants
They can sleep secure, though the beams are in ruins above them.
No, the place to live is out there, where no cry of *Fire!*
Sounds the alarm of the night, with a neighbor yelling for water,
Moving his chattels and goods, and the whole third story is smoking.
This you'll never know: for if the ground is scared first,   190
You are the last to burn, up there where the eaves of the attic
Keep off the rain, and the doves are brooding over their nest eggs.
Codrus owned one bed, too small for a midget to sleep on,
Six little jugs he had, and a tankard adorning his sideboard,
Under whose marble (clay), a bust or a statute of Chiron,
Busted, lay on its side; an old locker held Greek books
Whose divinest lines were gnawed by the mice, those vandals.
Codrus had nothing, no doubt, and yet he succeeded, poor fellow,
Losing that nothing, his all. And this is the very last straw—

No one will help him out with a meal or lodging or shelter.   200
Stripped to the bone, begging for crusts, he still receives nothing.

"Yet if Asturicus' mansion burns down, what a frenzy of sorrow!
Mothers dishevel themselves, the leaders dress up in black,
Courts are adjourned. We groan at the fall of the city, we hate
The fire, and the fire still burns, and while it is burning,
Somebody rushes up to replace the loss of the marble,
Some one chips in toward a building fund, another gives statues,
Naked and shining white, some masterpiece of Euphranor
Or Polyclitus' chef d'oeuvre; and here's a fellow with bronzes
Sacred to Asian gods. Books, chests, a bust of Minerva,   210
A bushel of silver coins. *To him that hath shall be given!*
This Persian, childless, of course, the richest man in the smart set,
Now has better things, and more, than before the disaster.
How can we help but think he started the fire on purpose?

"Tear yourself from the games, and get a place in the country!
One little Latian town, like Sora, say, or Frusino,
Offers a choice of homes, at a price you pay here, in one year,
Renting some hole in the wall. Nice houses, too, with a garden,
Springs bubbling up from the grass, no need for a windlass or bucket,
Plenty to water your flowers, if they need it, without any trouble.   220
Live there, fond of your hoe, an independent producer,
Willing and able to feed a hundred good vegetarians.
Isn't it something, to feel, wherever you are, how far off,
You are a monarch? At least, lord of a single lizard.

"Here in town the sick die from insomnia mostly.
Undigested food, on a stomach burning with ulcers,
Brings on listlessness, but who can sleep in a flophouse?
Who but the rich can afford sleep and a garden apartment?
That's the source of infection. The wheels creak by on the narrow
Streets of the wards, the drivers squabble and brawl when they're
        stopped,   230
More than enough to frustrate the drowsiest son of a sea cow.
When his business calls, the crowd makes way, as the rich man,
Carried high in his car, rides over them, reading or writing,
Even taking a snooze, perhaps, for the motion's composing.
Still, he gets where he wants before we do; for all of our hurry
Traffic gets in our way, in front, around and behind us.
Somebody gives me a shove with an elbow, or two-by-four scantling.

One clunks my head with a beam, another cracks down with a beer
    keg.
Mud is thick on my shins, I am trampled by somebody's big feet.
Now what?—a soldier grinds his hobnails into my toes.   240

"Don't you see the mob rushing along to the handout?
There are a hundred guests, each one with his kitchen servant.
Even Samson himself could hardly carry those burdens,
Pots and pans some poor little slave tries to keep on his head, while
    he hurries
Hoping to keep the fire alive by the wind of his running.
Tunics, new-darned, are ripped to shreds; there's the flash of a fir
    beam
Huge on some great dray, and another carries a pine tree,
Nodding above our heads and threatening death to the people.
What will be left of the mob, if that cart of Ligurian marble
Breaks its axle down and dumps its load on these swarms?   250
Who will identify limbs or bones? The poor man's cadaver,
Crushed, disappears like his breath. And meanwhile, at home, his
    household
Washes the dishes, and puffs up the fire, with all kinds of a clatter
Over the smeared flesh-scrapers, the flasks of oil, and the towels.
So the boys rush around, while their late master is sitting,
Newly come to the bank of the Styx, afraid of the filthy
Ferryman there, since he has no fare, not even a copper
In his dead mouth to pay for the ride through that muddy whirlpool.

"Look at other things, the various dangers of nighttime.
How high it is to the cornice that breaks, and a chunk beats my
    brains out,   260
Or some slob heaves a jar, broken or cracked, from a window.
Bang! It comes down with a crash and proves its weight on the side-
    walk.
You are a thoughtless fool, unmindful of sudden disaster,
If you don't make your will before you go out to have dinner.
There are as many deaths in the night as there are open windows
Where you pass by; if you're wise, you will pray, in your wretched
    devotions,
People may be content with no more than emptying slop jars.
"There your hell-raising drunk, who has had the bad luck to kill no
    one,
Tosses in restless rage, like Achilles mourning Patroclus,

Turns from his face to his back, can't sleep, for only a fracas   270
Gives him the proper sedation. But any of these young hoodlums,
All steamed up on wine, watches his step when the crimson
Cloak goes by, a lord, with a long, long line of attendants,
Torches and brazen lamps, warning him, *Keep your distance!*
Me, however, whose torch is the moon, or the feeblest candle
Fed by a sputtering wick, he absolutely despises.
Here is how it all starts, the fight, if you think it is fighting
When he throws all the punches, and all I do is absorb them.
He stops. He tells me to stop. I stop. I have to obey him.
What can you do when he's mad and bigger and stronger than you
     are?   280
'Where do you come from?' he cries, 'you wino, you bean-bloated
     bastard?
Off what shoemaker's dish have you fed on chopped leeks and boiled
     lamb-lip?
What? No answer? Speak up, or take a swift kick in the rear.
Tell me where you hang out—in some praying-house with Jewboys?'
If you try to talk back, or sneak away without speaking,
All the same thing: you're assaulted, and then put under a bail bond
For committing assault. This is a poor man's freedom.
Beaten, cut up by fists, he begs and implores his assailant,
Please, for a chance to go home with a few teeth left in his mouth.

"This is not all you must fear. Shut up your house or your store, 290
Bolts and padlocks and bars will never keep out all the burglars,
Or a holdup man will do you in with a switch blade.
If the guards are strong over Pontine marshes and pinewoods
Near Volturno, the scum of the swamps and the filth of the forest
Swirl into Rome, the great sewer, their sanctuary, their haven.
Furnaces blast and anvils groan with the chains we are forging:
What other use have we for iron and steel? There is danger
We will have little left for hoes and mattocks and ploughshares.
Happy the men of old, those primitive generations
Under the tribunes and kings, when Rome had only one jailhouse!   300

"There is more I could say, I could give you more of my reasons,
But the sun slants down, my oxen seem to be calling,
My man with the whip is impatient, I must be on my way.
So long! Don't forget me. Whenever you come to Aquino
Seeking relief from Rome, send for me. I'll come over
From my bay to your hills, hiking along in my thick boots
Toward your chilly fields. What's more, I promise to listen
If your satirical verse esteems me worthy the honor."

Lucian

Hermes and Charon

From *Dialogues of the Dead*

TRANSLATED BY M. D. MACLEOD

Lucian (circa 115–200) was a Greek rhetorician who traveled in various
parts of the Roman empire, earning his living by declamations. Eventually
he settled in Athens to study with the Stoic philosophers. It was in that
period that he wrote serious dialogues in a tradition that descended
from Plato, but later he renounced philosophy and began his famous
satirical dialogues, a form which he virtually invented. In these he attacks the old myths and philosophies that still prevailed in the Mediterranean world. "Hermes and Charon" is one of the *Dialogues of the
Dead* which are set in the lower world where the spirits of the heroes are
sent.

HERMES. If you don't mind, ferryman, let's work out how much you owe me at the moment, so that we won't quarrel about it later.

CHARON. Let's do that, Hermes. It's better to have this settled, and it'll save trouble.

HERMES: I brought you an anchor as you ordered; five drachmae.

CHARON. That's dear.

HERMES: By Hades, that's what I paid for it, and a thong for an oar cost me two obols.

CHARON. Put down five drachmae and two obols.

HERMES. And a darning-needle for your sail. Five obols it cost me.

CHARON. Put that down too.

HERMES. And wax to plug up the leaks in your boat, and nails, and a bit of rope which you made into a brace, costing two drachmae in all.

CHARON. You got these cheap too!

HERMES. That's all, unless we've forgotten something in our calculations. Well, when do you say that you are going to pay me?

CHARON. For the moment, Hermes, it's impossible, but if an epidemic or a war sends me down a large batch, I can then make a profit, by overcharging on the fares in the rush.

HERMES. So, for the present, I'll have to sit down and pray for the worst to happen so that I may be paid?

CHARON. It can't be helped, Hermes. We get few coming here at the moment, as you can see. It's peacetime.

HERMES. Better so, even if you do keep me waiting for what you owe me. Ah, but in the old days, Charon, you know what men they were that came, all of them brave, and most of them covered with blood and wounded; but now we get a few poisoned by a wife or a son, or with their legs and bellies all puffed out with rich living, a pale miserable lot, all of them, quite unlike the old ones. Most of them have money to thank for their coming here; they scheme against each other for it, apparently.

CHARON. Yes, it's the grand passion.

HERMES. Then you won't think it wrong of me if I dun you for my debt.

Erasmus

Charon

From *The Colloquies*

<small>TRANSLATED BY C. R. THOMPSON</small>

Desiderius Erasmus (circa 1466–1536) was born in the Netherlands; he was the son of a priest. He became a priest himself in 1492, but the constraints of monastic life were not to his liking. He had already read the classics, Greek as well as Latin, and he soon went to Paris, where he met the new Humanist group. Later he made many friends in England, especially Sir Thomas More, who, like himself, admired Lucian. (Martin Luther once denounced Erasmus as a modern Lucian.) It was in More's house in London that he wrote his most famous work in satire, *The Praise of Folly* (1511), a mock argument in self-defense delivered by Folly (a personified figure). Here the excesses of the learned professions—law, science, and theology—are held up to ridicule. Erasmus adopted the dialogue form in his *Colloquies*, which began appearing in 1518, as an informal way to deal with such subjects as war, marriage, government, and theology. He thought of them as literary exercises. "Charon," a dialogue that was first printed in 1529, is directed against war and warmongers, and its descent from Lucian's "Hermes and Charon" should be clear to the reader.

CHARON: Why the hustle and bustle, Alastor?

ALASTOR: Well met, Charon! I was speeding to you.

CHARON. What's new?

ALASTOR. I bring news that will delight you and Proserpina.

CHARON. Out with it, then. Unload it.

ALASTOR. The Furies have done their work with as much zeal as success. Not a corner of the earth have they left unravaged by their hellish dissensions—wars, robberies, plagues: so much so that now, with their snakes let loose, they're completely bald.[1] Drained of poisons, they roam about, looking for whatever vipers and asps they can find, since they're as smooth-headed as an egg—not a hair on their crowns, nor a drop of good poison in their breasts. So get your boat and oars ready, for there'll soon be such a crowd of shades coming that I fear you can't ferry them all.

CHARON. No news to me.

ALASTOR. Where did you learn it?

CHARON. Ossa[2] brought it more than two days ago.

ALASTOR. Can't get ahead of that goddess! But why are you loitering here without your boat, then?

CHARON. Business trip: I came here to get a good, strong trireme ready. My galley's so rotten with age and so patched up that it won't do for

---

[1] The Furies had poisonous snakes for hair. These they sent to torment the consciences of the wicked.

[2] The goddess Rumor.

this job, if what Ossa told me is true. Though what need was there of Ossa? The plain fact of the matter demands it: I've had a shipwreck.

ALASTOR. You *are* dripping wet, undoubtedly. I thought you were coming back from a bath.

CHARON. Oh, no, I've been swimming out of the Stygian swamp.

ALASTOR. Where have you left the shades?

CHARON. Swimming with the frogs.

ALASTOR. But what did Ossa report?

CHARON. That the three rulers[3] of the world, in deadly hatred, clash to their mutual destruction. No part of Christendom is safe from the ravages of war, for those three have dragged all the rest into alliance. They're all in such a mood that none of them is willing to yield to another. Neither Dane nor Pole nor Scot nor Turk, in fact, is at peace; catastrophes are building up; the plague rages everywhere, in Spain, Britain, Italy, France. In addition, there's a new épidemic,[4] born of difference of opinion. It has so corrupted everybody's mind that sincere friendship exists nowhere, but brother distrusts brother, and husband and wife disagree. I have hopes of a splendid slaughter in the near future, too, if the war of tongues and pens comes to actual blows.

ALASTOR. Ossa reported all this quite correctly, for I've seen more than this with my own eyes; I, the constant attendant and assistant of the Furies, who have never shown themselves more deserving of their name.

CHARON. But there's danger that some devil may turn up and preach peace all of a sudden—and mortal minds are fickle. I hear there's a certain Polygraphus[5] up there who's incessantly attacking war with his pen and urging men to peace.

ALASTOR. He's sung to deaf ears this long while. He once wrote a "Complaint of Peace O'erthrown"; now he's written the epitaph of peace dead and buried. On the other hand, there are some who are as helpful to our cause as the Furies themselves.

CHARON. Who are those?

ALASTOR. Certain creatures in black and white cloaks and ash gray tunics,

---

[3] Charles V, Holy Roman Emperor, aligned against Francis I, king of France, and later against Henry VIII, king of England, in wars over Italian territory, and especially Rome. The papacy suffered a disaster in 1527, the sack of Rome by Charles's undisciplined troops; the wars ended in Charles's favor in 1529, shortly after this colloquy appeared.

[4] Lutheranism.

[5] Erasmus.

adorned with plumage of various kinds. They never leave the courts
of princes. They instill into their ears a love of war; they incite
rulers and populace alike; they proclaim in their evangelical sermons that war is just, holy, and right. And—to make you marvel
more at the audacity of the fellows—they proclaim the very same
thing on both sides. To the French they preach that God is on the
French side: he who has God to protect him cannot be conquered!
To the English and Spanish they declare this war is not the emper-
or's but God's: only let them show themselves valiant men and
victory is certain! But if anyone *does* get killed, he doesn't perish
utterly but flies straight up to heaven, armed just as he was.

CHARON. And people believe these men?

ALASTOR. What can a pretense of religion not achieve? Youth, inexperi-
ence, thirst for glory, anger, and natural human inclination swallow
this whole. People are easily imposed upon. And it's not hard to
upset a cart that's ready to collapse of its own accord.

CHARON. I'll be glad to reward these creatures!

ALASTOR. Give them a fine dinner. They like nothing better.

CHARON. A dinner of mallows, lupines, and leeks. That's the only fare
we have, as you know.

ALASTOR. Oh, no, it must be partridges, capons, and pheasants if you wish
to be an acceptable host.

CHARON. But what makes them such warmongers? Or what advantage are
they afraid of losing?

ALASTOR. They make more profit from the dying than from the living.
There are wills, masses for kinsmen, bulls, and many other sources
of revenue not to be despised. In short, they prefer to buzz in camp
rather than in their own hives. War spawns many bishops who in
peacetime weren't worth a penny.

CHARON. They're smart.

ALASTOR. But why do you need a trireme?

CHARON. I don't, if I want to be shipwrecked in the middle of the swamp
again.

ALASTOR. On account of the crowd?

CHARON. Of course.

ALASTOR. But you haul shades, not bodies. Just how light are shades?

CHARON. They may be water skippers, but enough water skippers could
sink a boat. Then, you know, the boat is unsubstantial, too.

ALASTOR. But sometimes, I remember, when there was a crowd so large
the boat couldn't hold them all, I saw three thousand shades hanging
from your rudder, and you didn't feel any weight.

CHARON. I grant there are such souls, which departed little by little from

bodies worn away by consumption or hectic fever. But those plucked
on the sudden from heavy bodies bring a good deal of bodily sub
stance along with them. Apoplexy, quinsy, plague, but especially
war, send this kind.

ALASTOR. Frenchmen or Spaniards don't weigh much, I suppose.

CHARON. Much less than others, though even their souls are not exactly
featherweight. But from well-fed Britons and Germans such shades
come at times that lately I've hardly dared to ferry even ten, and
unless I'd thrown them overboard I'd have gone down with
boat, rowers, and passage money.

ALASTOR. A terrible risk!

CHARON. Meanwhile what do you think is going to happen when heavy
lords, Thrasos,[6] and swashbucklers come along?

ALASTOR. None of those who die in a just war come to you, I believe. For
these, they say, fly straight to heaven.

CHARON. Where they fly to, I don't know. I do know one thing: that whenever a war's on, so many come to me wounded and cut up that I'd
be surprised if any had been left on earth. They come loaded not
only with debauchery and gluttony but even with bulls, benefices,
and many other things.

ALASTOR. But they don't bring these along with them. The souls come to
you naked.

CHARON. True, but newcomers bring along dreams of such things.

ALASTOR. So dreams are heavy?

CHARON. They weigh down my boat. Weigh down, did I say? They've
already sunk it! Finally, do you imagine so many odols weigh
nothing?

ALASTOR. Well, I suppose they do, if it's brass ones they bring.

CHARON. So I've decided to look out for a vessel strong enough for the
load.

ALASTOR. Lucky you!

CHARON. How so?

ALASTOR. Because you'll soon grow rich.

CHARON. From a lot of shades?

ALASTOR. Of course.

CHARON. If only they'd bring their riches with them! As it is, those in the
boat who lament the kingdoms, prelacies, abbacies, and countless
talents of gold they left up there bring me nothing but an obol. And
so everything I've scraped together in three thousand years has t
be laid out for one trireme.

---

[6] Plural of Thraso, the name of a boastful soldier in Terence's *Eunuch*.

ALASTOR. If you want to make money, you have to spend money.

CHARON. Yet mortals, as I hear, do business better: with Mercury's help they grow rich within three years.

ALASTOR. But sometimes those same mortals go broke. Your profit is less, but it's more certain.

CHARON. How certain I can't tell. If some god should turn up now and settle the affairs of princes, my whole fortune would be lost.

ALASTOR. Don't give the matter a thought; just leave it to me.[7] You've no reason to fear a peace within ten whole years. Only the Roman pontiff is zealous in urging peace, but his efforts are wasted. Cities, too, weary of their troubles, complain bitterly. People—I don't know who they are—mutter that it's outrageous for human affairs to be turned topsy-turvy on account of the personal grudges or ambitions of two or three men. But the Furies, believe me, will defeat counsel, no matter how good it is.—Yet what need was there for you to ask this favor of those above? Haven't we workmen of our own? We have Vulcan, surely.

CHARON. Fine—if I wanted a bronze ship.

ALASTOR. Labor's cheap.

CHARON. Yes, but we're short of timber.

ALASTOR. What, aren't there any forests here?

CHARON. Even the groves in the Elysian fields have been used up.

ALASTOR. What for?

CHARON. For burning shades of heretics. So that we've been forced of late to mine coal from the depths of the earth.

ALASTOR. What, can't those shades be punished at less expense?

CHARON. This was the decision of Rhadamanthus.[8]

ALASTOR. When you've bought your trireme, where will you get rowers?

CHARON. My job is to hold the tiller; the shades must row if they want passage.

ALASTOR. But some haven't learned how to handle an oar.

CHARON. No distinction of persons with me: monarchs row and cardinals row, each in their turn, no less than common folk, whether they've learned or not.

ALASTOR: Good luck in getting a trireme at a bargain. I won't hold you up any longer. I'll take the good news to Orcus.[9] But say, Charon—

CHARON. What?

---

[7] Alastor, an "avenging spirit" and ally of the Furies, means that vicious men will not be permitted to "cool down" now and get off from their carnage lightly.

[8] One of the three Judges of the Dead.

[9] Death himself.

ALASTOR. Hurry back, so the crowd won't quickly overwhelm you.

CHARON. Oh, you'll meet over two hundred thousand on the bank already, besides those swimming in the swamp. But I'll hurry as much as I can. Tell 'em I'll be there right away.

Geoffrey Chaucer

The Nun's Priest's Tale

TRANSLATED INTO MODERN ENGLISH BY NEVILL COGHILL

Geoffrey Chaucer (circa 1343–1400) was born in London, the son of a prosperous middle-class wine merchant. He spent most of his life in aristocratic and court circles and held a number of positions including that of page in one of the great households of England, soldier in France, envoy for the king to Italy and France, controller of the Customs and Subsidies on Wool for the Port of London, justice of the peace and member of Parliament for the county of Kent, and clerk of the King's Works. His two most important works are *Troilus and Criseyde* and *The Canterbury Tales*. In "The Nun's Priest's Tale" the beast fable and the mock-epic combine to ridicule the pretentious dignity of man, reducing human beings to animals and an epic hero to a rooster in a barnyard. Pompous rhetoric and excessive pedantry add to the deflation of Chanticleer's sense of self-importance and to the delightful humor and satire of the tale.

Once, long ago, there dwelt a poor old widow
In a small cottage, by a little meadow
Beside a grove and standing in a dale.
This widow-woman of whom I tell my tale
Since the sad day when last she was a wife
Had led a very patient, simple life.
Little she had in capital or rent,
But still, by making do with what God sent,
She kept herself and her two daughters going.
Three hefty sows—no more—were all her showing,   10
Three cows as well; there was a sheep called Molly.
    Sooty her hall, her kitchen melancholy,
And there she ate full many a slender meal;
There was no *sauce piquante* to spice her veal,
No dainty morsel ever passed her throat,
According to her cloth she cut her coat.
Repletion never left her in disquiet
And all her physic was a temperate diet,
Hard work for exercise and heart's content.
And rich man's gout did nothing to prevent   20
Her dancing, apoplexy struck her not;
She drank no wine, nor white nor red had got.
Her board was mostly served with white and black,
Milk and brown bread, in which she found no lack;
Broiled bacon or an egg or two were common,
She was in fact a sort of dairy-woman.

She had a yard that was enclosed about
By a stockade and a dry ditch without,
In which she kept a cock called Chanticleer.
In all the land for crowing he'd no peer;   30
His voice was jollier than the organ blowing
In church on Sundays, he was great at crowing.
Far, far more regular than any clock
Or abbey bell the crowing of this cock.
The equinoctial wheel and its position[1]
At each ascent he knew by intuition;
At every hour—fifteen degrees of movement—
He crowed so well there could be no improvement.
His comb was redder than fine coral, tall
And battlement like a castle wall,   40
His bill was black and shone as bright as jet,
Like azure were his legs and they were set
On azure toes with nails of lily white,
Like burnished gold his feather, flaming bright.
   This gentlecock was master in some measure
Of seven hens, all there to do his pleasure.
They were his sisters and his paramours,
Coloured like him in all particulars;
She with the loveliest dyes upon her throat
Was known as gracious Lady Pertelote.   50
Courteous she was, discrete and debonair,
Companionable too, and took such care
In her deportment, since she was seven days old
She held the heart of Chanticleer controlled,
Locked up securely in her every limb;
O such happiness his love to him!
And such a joy it was to hear them sing,
As when the glorious sun began to spring,
In sweet accord *My Love is far from land*[2]
—For in those far off days I understand   60
All birds and animals could speak and sing.
   Now it befell, as dawn began to spring,
When Chanticleer and Pertelote and all
His wives were perched in this poor widow's hall

---

[1] The celestial equator was believed to make a complete rotation of the earth every 24 hours at the rate of 15 degrees every hour.

[2] Refrain of a popular song: My Love has gone away into a foreign land.

(Fair Pertelote was next him on the perch),
This Chanticleer began to groan and lurch
Like someone sorely troubled by a dream,
And Pertelote who heard him roar and scream
Was quite aghast and said, 'O dearest heart,
What's ailing you? Why do you groan and start?   70
Fie, what a sleeper! What a noise to make!'
'Madam,' he said, 'I beg you not to take
Offense, but by the Lord I had a dream
So terrible just now I had to scream;
I still can feel my heart racing from fear.
God turn my dream to good and guard all here,
And keep my body out of durance vile!
I dreamt that roaming up and down a while
Within our yard I saw a kind of beast,
A sort of hound that tried or seemed at least   80
To try and seize me . . . would have killed me dead!
His colour was a blend of yellow and red,
His ears and tail were tipped with sable fur
Unlike the rest; he was a russet cur.
Small was his snout, his eyes were glowing bright.
It was enough to make one die of fright.
That was no doubt what made me groan and swoon.'
     'For shame,' she said, 'you timorous poltroon!
Alas, what cowardice! By God above,
You've forfeited my heart and lost my love.   90
I cannot love a coward, come what may.
For certainly, whatever we may say,
All women long—and O that it might be!—
For husbands tough, dependable and free,
Secret, discreet, no niggard, not a fool
That boasts and then will find his courage cool
At every trifling thing. By God above,
How dare you say for shame, and to your love,
That anything at all was to be feared?
Have you no manly heart to match your beard?   100
And can a dream reduce you to such terror?
Dreams are a vanity, God knows, pure error.
Dreams are engendered in the too-replete
From vapours in the belly, which compete
With others, too abundant, swollen tight.
     'No doubt the redness in your dream to-night

Comes from the superfluity and force
Of the red choler in your blood.[3] Of course.
That is what puts a dreamer in the dread
Of crimsoned arrows, fires flaming red,   110
Of great red monsters making as to fight him,
And big red whelps and little ones to bite him;
Just so the black and melancholy vapours
Will set a sleeper shrieking, cutting capers
And swearing that black bears, black bulls as well,
Or blackest fiends are haling him to Hell.
And there are other vapours that I know
That on a sleeping man will work their woe,
But I'll pass on as lightly as I can.
    'Take Cato[4] now, that was so wise a man,   120
Did he not say, "Take no account of dreams"?
Now, sir,' she said, 'on flying from these beams,
For love of God do take some laxative;
Upon my soul that's the advice to give
For melancholy choler; let me urge
You free yourself from vapours with a purge.
And that you may have no excuse to tarry
By saying this town has no apothecary,
I shall myself instruct you and prescribe
Herbs that will cure all vapours of that tribe,   130
Herbs from our very farmyard! You will find
Their natural property is to unbind
And purge you well beneath and well above.
Now don't forget it, dear, for God's own love!
Your face is choleric and shows distension;
Be careful lest the sun in his ascension
Should catch you full of humours, hot and many.
And if he does, my dear, I'll lay a penny
It means a bout of fever or a breath
Of tertian ague. You may catch your death.   140
    'Worms for a day or two I'll have to give
As a digestive, then your laxative.
Centaury, fumitory, caper-spurge
And hellebore will make a splendid purge;[5]

---

[3] Choler is the humor of anger and thus leads to violent dreams.
[4] Dionysius Cato, fourth-century author of a volume of moral maxims.
[5] Herbs used as cathartics.

And then there's laurel or the blackthorn berry,
Ground-ivy too that makes our yard so merry;
Peck them right up, my dear, and swallow whole.
Be happy, husband, by your father's soul!
Don't be afraid of dreams. I'll say no more.'
   'Madam,' he said, 'I thank you for your lore,   150
But with regard to Cato all the same,
His wisdom has, no doubt, a certain fame,
But though he said that we should take no heed
Of dreams, by God, in ancient books I read
Of many a man of more authority
Than ever Cato was, believe you me,
Who say the very opposite is true
And prove their theories by experience too.
Dreams have quite often been significations
As well of triumphs as of tribulations   160
That people undergo in this our life.
This needs no argument at all, dear wife,
The proof is all too manifest indeed.
   'One of the greatest authors one can read
Says thus: there were two comrades once who went
On pilgrimage, sincere in their intent.
And as it happened they had reached a town
Where such a throng was milling up and down
And yet so scanty the accommodation,
They could not find themselves a habitation,   170
No, not a cottage that could lodge them both.
And so they separated, very loath,
Under constraint of this necessity
And each went off to find some hostelry,
And lodge whatever way his luck might fall.
   'The first of them found refuge in a stall
Down in a yard with oxen and a plough.
His friend found lodging for himself somehow
Elsewhere, by accident or destiny,
Which governs all of us and equally.   180
   'Now it so happened, long ere it was day,
This fellow had a dream, and as he lay
In bed it seemed he heard his comrade call,
"Help! I am lying in an ox's stall
And shall to-night be murdered as I lie.
Help me, dear brother, help or I shall die!

Come in all haste!" Such were the words he spoke;
The dreamer, lost in terror, then awoke.
But once awake he paid it no attention,
Turned over and dismissed it as invention,   190
It was a dream, he thought, a fantasy.
And twice he dreamt this dream successively.
  'Yet a third time his comrade came again,
Or seemed to come, and said, "I have been slain
Look, look! my wounds are bleeding wide and deep.
Rise early in the morning, break your sleep
And go to the west gate. You there shall see
A cart all loaded up with dung," said he,
"And in that dung my body has been hidden.
Boldly arrest that cart as you are bidden.   200
It was my money that they killed me for."
  'He told him every detail, sighing sore,
And pitiful in feature, pale of hue.
This dream, believe me, Madam, turned out true;
For in the dawn, as soon as it was light,
He went to where his friend had spent the night
And when he came upon the cattle-stall
He looked about him and began to call.
  'The innkeeper, appearing thereupon,
Quickly gave answer, "Sir, your friend has gone.   210
He left the town a little after dawn."
The man began to feel suspicious, drawn
By memories of his dream—the western gate,
The dung-cart—off he went, he would not wait,
Towards the western entry. There he found,
Seemingly on its way to dung some ground,
A dung-cart loaded on the very plan
Described so closely by the murdered man.
So he began to shout courageously
For right and vengeance on the felony,   220
"My friend's been killed! There's been a foul attack,
He's in that cart and gaping on his back!
Fetch the authorities, get the sheriff down
—Whosever job it is to run the town—
Help! My companion's murdered, sent to glory!"
  'What need I add to finish off the story?
People ran out and cast the cart to ground,
And in the middle of the dung they found

The murdered man. The corpse was fresh and new.
   'O blessed God, that art so just and true,   230
Thus thou revealest murder! As we say,
"Murder will out." We see it day by day.
Murder's a foul, abominable treason,
So loathsome to God's justice, to God's reason,
He will not suffer its concealment. True,
Things may lie hidden for a year or two,
But still "Murder will out", that's my conclusion.
   'All the town officers in great confusion
Seized on the carter and they gave him hell,
And then they racked the innkeeper as well,   240
And both confessed. And then they took the wrecks
And there and then they hanged them by their necks.
   'By this we see that dreams are to be dreaded.
And in the self-same book I find embedded,
Right in the very chapter after this
(I'm not inventing, as I hope for bliss)
The story of two men who started out
To cross the sea—for a merchandise no doubt—
But as the winds were contrary they waited.
It was a pleasant town, I should have stated,   250
Merrily grouped about the haven-side.
A few days later with the evening tide
The wind veered round so as to suit them best;
They were delighted and they went to rest
Meaning to sail next morning. Well,
To one of them a miracle befell.
   'This man as he lay sleeping, it would seem,
Just before dawn had an astounding dream.
He thought a man was standing by his bed
Commanding him to wait, and thus he said: 260
"If you set sail to-morrow as you intend
You will be drowned. My tale is at an end."
   'He woke and told his friend what had occurred
And begged him that the journey be deferred
At least a day, implored him not to start.
But his companion, lying there apart,
Began to laugh and treat him to derision.
"I'm not afraid," he said, "of any vision,
To let it interfere with my affairs;
A straw for all your dreamings and your scares.   270

Dreams are just empty nonsense, merest japes;
Why, people dream all day of owls and apes,
All sorts of trash that can't be understood,
Things that have never happened and never could.
But as I see you mean to stay behind
And miss the tide for wilful sloth of mind
God knows I'm sorry for it, but good day!"
And so he took his leave and went his way.
    'And yet, before they'd covered half the trip
—I don't know what went wrong—there was a rip   280
And by some accident the ship went down,
Her bottom rent, all hands aboard to drown
In sight of all the vessels at her side,
That had put out upon the self-same tide.
    'So, my dear Pertelote, if you discern
The force of these examples, you may learn
One never should be careless about dreams,
For, undeniably, I say it seems
That many are a sign of trouble breeding.
    'Now, take St Kenelm's life which I've been reading;   290
He was Kenulphus' son, the noble King
Of Mercia. Now, St Kenelm dreamt a thing
Shortly before they murdered him one day.
He saw his murder in a dream, I say.
His nurse expounded it and gave her reasons
On every point and warned him against treasons
But as the saint was only seven years old
All that she said about it left him cold.
He was so holy how could visions hurt?
    'By God, I willingly would give my shirt   300
To have you read his legend as I've read it;
And, Madam Pertelote, upon my credit,
Macrobius[6] wrote of dreams and can explain us
The vision of young Scipio Africanus,
And he affirms that dreams can give a due
Warning of things that later on come true.
    'And then there's the Old Testament—a manual
Well worth your study; see the *Book of Daniel.*

---

[6] Macrobius wrote a commentary on Cicero's account in *De Republica* of the dreams of Scipio Africanus Minor concerning his grandfather Scipio, the conqueror of Hannibal.

Did Daniel think a dream was vanity?
Read about Joseph too and you will see   310
That many dreams—I do not say that all—
Give cognizance of what is to befall.
      'Look at Lord Pharaoh, king of Egypt! Look
At what befell his butler and his cook.
Did not their visions have a certain force?
But those who study history of course
Meet many dreams that set them wondering.
      'What about Croesus too, the Lydian king,
Who dreamt that he was sitting in a tree,
Meaning he would be hanged? It had to be.   320
      'Or take Andromache, great Hector's wife;
The day on which he was to lose his life
She dreamt about, the very night before,
And realized that if Hector went to war
He would be lost that very day in battle.
She warned him; he dismissed it all as prattle
And sailed forth to fight, being self-willed,
And there he met Achilles and was killed.
The tale is long and somewhat overdrawn,
And anyhow it's very nearly dawn,   330
So let me say in very brief conclusion
My dream undoubtedly fortells confusion,
It bodes me ill, I say. And, furthermore,
Upon your laxatives I set no store,
For they are venomous. I've suffered by them
Often enough before and I defy them.
      'And now, let's talk of fun and stop all this.
Dear Madam, as I hope for Heaven's bliss,
Of one thing God has sent me plenteous grace,
For when I see the beauty of your face,   340
That scarlet loveliness about your eyes,
All thought of terror and confusion dies.
For it's as certain as the Creed, I know,
Mulier est hominis confusio
(A Latin tag, dear Madam, meaning this:
"Women is man's delight and all his bliss"),
For when at night I feel your feathery side,
Although perforce I cannot take a ride
Because, alas, our perch was made too narrow,
Delight and solace fill me to the marrow   350
And I defy all visions and all dreams!'

And with that word he flew down from the beams,
For it was day, and down his hens flew all,
And with a chuck he gave the troupe a call
For he had found a seed upon the floor.
Royal he was, he was afraid no more.
He feathered Pertelote in wanton play
And trod her twenty times ere prime of day.
Grim as a lion's was his manly frown
As on his toes he sauntered up and down;   360
He scarcely deigned to set his foot to ground
And every time a seed of corn was found
He gave a chuck, and up his wives ran all.
Thus royal as a prince who strides his hall
Leave we this Chanticleer engaged on feeding
And pass to the adventure that was breeding.

   Now when the month in which the world began,
March, the first month, when God created man,
Was over, and the thirty-second day
Thereafter ended, on the third of May   370
It happened that Chanticleer in all his pride,
His seven wives attendant at his side,
Cast his eyes upward to the blazing sun,
Which in the sign of *Taurus* then had run
His twenty-one degrees and somewhat more,[7]
And knew by nature and no other lore
That it was nine o'clock. With blissful voice
He crew triumphantly and said, 'Rejoice,
Behold the sun! The sun is up, my seven.
Look, it has climbed forty degrees in heaven,   380
Forty degrees and one in fact, by this.
Dear Madam Pertelote, my earthly bliss,
Hark to those blissful birds and how they sing!
Look at those pretty flowers, how they spring!
Solace and revel fill my heart!' He laughed.

   But in that moment Fate let fly her shaft;
Ever the latter end of joy is woe,
God knows that worldly joy is swift to go.
A rhetorician with a flair for style
Could chronicle this maxim in his file   390
Of Notable Remarks with safe conviction.

---

[7] On May 3 the sun would have passed about 21 degrees through Taurus, the Bull, the second sign of the zodiac. It would be about 41 degrees from the horizon at 9 A.M.

Then let the wise give ear; this is no fiction
My story is as true, I undertake,
As that of good Sir Lancelot du Lake
Who held all women in such high esteem.
Let me return full circle to my theme.
   A coal-tipped fox of sly iniquity
That had been lurking round the grove for three
Long years, that very night burst through and passed
Stockade and hedge, as Providence forecast,   400
Into the yard where Chanticleer the Fair
Was wont, with all his ladies, to repair.
Still, in a bed of cabbages, he lay
Until about the middle of the day
Watching the cock and waiting for his cue,
As all these homicides so gladly do
That lie about in wait to murder men.
O false assassin, lurking in thy den!
O new Iscariot, new Ganelon!
And O Greek Sinon, thou whose treachery won   410
Troy town and brought it utterly to sorrow![8]
O Chanticleer, accursed be that morrow
That brought thee to the yard from thy high beams!
Thou hadst been warned, and truly, by thy dreams
That this would be a perilous day for thee.
   But that which God's foreknowledge can foresee
Must needs occur, as certain men of learning
Have said. Ask any scholar of discerning;
He'll say the Schools are filled with altercation
On this vexed matter of predestination   420
Long bandied by a hundred thousand men.
How can I sift it to the bottom then?
The Holy Doctor St Augustine shines
In this, and there is Bishop Bradwardine's
Authority, Boethius'[9] too, decreeing
Whether the fact of God's divine foreseeing
Constrains me to perform a certain act

---

[8] Ganelon, the betrayer who caused the defeat of Charlemagne and the death of Roland. Sinon, the Greek who tricked King Priam into letting the Wooden Horse into Troy.

[9] Thomas Bradwardine, archbishop of Canterbury who died in 1349. Boethius, the sixth-century author of *The Consolation of Philosophy*. Both authors were concerned with the relationship between freedom of the will and predestination.

—And by 'constraint' I mean the simple fact
Of mere compulsion by necessity—
Or whether a free choice is granted me   430
To do a given act or not to do it
Though, ere it was accomplished, God foreknew it,
Or whether Providence is not so stringent
And merely makes necessity contingent.
 But I decline discussion of the matter;
My tale is of a cock and of the clatter
That came of following his wife's advice
To walk about his yard on the precise
Morning after the dream of which I told.
 O woman's counsel is so often cold!   440
A woman's counsel brought us first to woe,
Made Adam out of Paradise to go
Where he had been so merry, so well at ease.
But, for I know not whom it may displease
If I suggest that women are to blame,
Pass over that; I only speak in game.
Read the authorities to know about
What has been said of women; you'll find out.
These are the cock's words, and not mine, I'm giving;
I think no harm of any woman living.   450
 Merrily in her dust-bath in the sand
Lay Pertelote. Her sisters were at hand
Basking in sunlight. Chanticleer sang free,
More merrily than a mermaid in the sea
(For *Physiologus* reports the thing[10]
And says how well and merrily they sing).
And so it happened as he cast his eye
Towards the cabbage at a butterfly
It fell upon the fox there, lying low.
Gone was all inclination then to crow,   460
'Cok cok,' he cried, giving a sudden start,
As one who feels a terror at his heart,
For natural instinct teaches beasts to flee
The moment they perceive an enemy,
Though they had never met with it before.
 This Chanticleer was shaken to the core

---

[10] A bestiary first written in Greek in the second century and translated into Latin in the fourth and fifth centuries. It involves moralized accounts of real and fabulous creatures.

And would have fled. The fox was quick to say
However, 'Sir! Whither so fast away?
Are you afraid of me, that am your friend?
A fiend, or worse, I should be, to intend   470
You harm, or practise villainy upon you;
Dear sir, I was not even spying on you!
Truly I came to do no other thing
Than just to lie and listen to you sing.
You have as merry a voice as God has given
To any angel in the courts of Heaven;
To that you add a musical sense as strong
As had Boethius who was skilled in song.
My Lord your Father (God receive his soul!),
Your mother too—how courtly, what control!—   480
Have honoured my poor house, to my great ease;
And you, sir, too, I should be glad to please.
For, when it comes to singing, I'll say this
(Else may these eyes of mine be barred from bliss),
There never was a singer I would rather
Have heard at dawn than your respected father.
All that he sang came welling from his soul
And how he put his voice under control!
The pains he took to keep his eyes tight shut
In concentration—then the tip-toe strut,   490
The slender neck stretched out, the delicate beak!
No singer could approach him in technique
Or rival him in song, still less surpass.
I've read the story in *Burnel the Ass*,[11]
Among some other verses, of a cock
Whose leg in youth was broken by a knock
A clergyman's son had given him, and for this
He made the father lose his benefice.
But certainly there's no comparison
Between the subtlety of such a one   500
And the discretion of your father's art
And wisdom. Oh, for charity of heart,
Can you not emulate your sire and sing?'

----

[11] A satirical poem by the twelfth-century poet Nigel Wireker. The tale is about a priest's son who breaks a cock's leg by throwing a stone at it. In revenge, the bird refuses to crow in the morning of the day the priest is to be ordained and receive a benefice. Thus he fails to wake up in time and as the result of being late for the ceremony loses his preferment.

This Chanticleer began to beat a wing
As one incapable of smelling treason,
So wholly had this flattery ravished reason.
Alas, my lords! there's many a sycophant
And flatterer that fill your courts with cant
And give more pleasure with zeal forsooth
Than he who speaks in soberness and truth.   510
Read what *Ecclesiasticus* records
Of flatterers. 'Ware treachery, my lords!
   This Chanticleer stood high upon his toes,
He stretched his neck, his eyes began to close,
His beak to open; with his eyes shut tight
He then began to sing with all his might.
   Sir Russel Fox then leapt to the attack,
Grabbing his gorge he flung him o'er his back
And off he bore him to the woods, the brute,
And for the moment there was no pursuit.   520
   O Destiny that may not be evaded!
Alas that Chanticleer had so paraded!
Alas that he had flown down from the beams!
O that his wife took no account of dreams!
And on a Friday too to risk their necks![12]
O Venus, goddess of the joys of sex,
Since Chanticleer thy mysteries professed
And in thy service always did his best,
And more for pleasure than to multiply
His kind, on thine own day is he to die?   530
   O Geoffrey, thou my dear and sovereign master[13]
Who, when they brought King Richard to disaster
And shot him dead, lamented so his death,
Would that I had thy skill, thy gracious breath,
To chide a Friday half so well as you!
(For he was killed upon a Friday too.)
Then I could fashion you a rhapsody
For Chanticleer in dread and agony.
   Sure never such a cry or lamentation
Was made by ladies of high Trojan station,   540
When Ilium fell and Pyrrhus with his sword

---

[12] Friday is Venus' day.

[13] Geoffrey de Vinsauf, a twelfth-century rhetorician who lamented the passing of Richard I on Friday. He chided the day for the king's death.

Grabbed Priam by the beard, their king and lord,
And slew him there as the *Aeneid* tells,
As what was uttered by those hens. Their yells
Surpassed them all in palpitating fear
When they beheld the rape of Chanticleer.
Dame Pertelote emitted sovereign shrieks
That echoed up in anguish to the peaks
Louder than those extorted from the wife
Of Hasdrubal,[14] when he had lost his life   550
And Carthage all in flame and ashes lay.
She was so full of torment and dismay
That in the very flames she chose her part
And burnt to ashes with a steadfast heart.
O woeful hens, louder your shrieks and higher
Than those of Roman matrons when the fire
Consumed their husbands, senators of Rome,
When Nero burnt their city and their home,
Beyond a doubt that Nero was their bale!

    Now let me turn again to tell my tale;   560
This blessed widow and her daughters two
Heard all these hens in clamour and halloo
And, rushing to the door at all this shrieking,
They saw the fox towards the covert streaking
And, on his shoulder, Chanticleer stretched flat.
'Look, look!' they cried, 'O mercy, look at that!
Ha! Ha! the fox!' and after him they ran,
And stick in hand ran many a serving man,
Ran Coll our dog, ran Talbot, Bran and Shaggy,
And with a distaff in her hand ran Maggie,   570
Ran cow and calf and ran the very hogs
In terror at the barking dogs;
The men and women shouted, ran and cursed,
They ran so hard they thought their hearts would burst,
They yelled like fiends in Hell, ducks left the water
Quacking and flapping as on point of slaughter,
Up flew the geese in terror over the trees,
Out of the hive came forth the swarm of bees;
So hideous was the noise—God bless us all,
Jack Straw[15] and all his followers in their brawl   580

---

[14] King of Carthage who committed suicide when the city was destroyed by the Romans in 146 B.C.

[15] A leader of the Peasants' Revolt in 1389 that was directed in part against the Flemings living in London.

Were never half so shrill, for all their noise,
When they were murdering those Flemish boys,
As that day's hue and cry upon the fox.
They grabbed up trumpets made of brass and box,
Of horn and bone, on which they blew and pooped,
And therewithal they shouted and they whooped
So that it seemed the very heavens would fall.
    And now, good people, pay attention all.
See how Dame Fortune quickly changes side
And robs her enemy of hope and pride!   590
This cock that lay upon the fox's back
In all his dread contrived to give a quack
And said, 'Sir Fox, if I were you, as God's
My witness, I would round upon these clods
And shout, "Turn back, you saucy bumpkins all!
A very pestilence upon you fall!
Now that I have in safety reached the wood
Do what you like, the cock is mine for good;
I'll eat him there in spite of every one." '
    The fox replying, 'Faith, it shall be done!'   600
Opened his mouth and spoke. The nimble bird,
Breaking away upon the uttered word,
Flew high into the tree-tops on the spot.
And when the fox perceived where he had got,
'Alas,' he cried, 'alas, my Chanticleer,
I've done you grievous wrong, indeed I fear
I must have frightened you; I grabbed too hard
When I caught hold and took you from the yard,
But, sir, I meant no harm, don't be offended,
Come down and I'll explain what I intended;   610
So help me God I'll tell the truth—on oath!'
'No,' said the cock, 'and curses on us both,
And first on me if I were such a dunce
As let you fool me oftener than once.
Never again, for all your flattering lies,
You'll coax a song to make me blink my eyes;
And as for those who blink when they should look,
God blot them from his everlasting Book!'
'Nay, rather,' said the fox, 'his plagues be flung
On all who chatter that should hold their tongue.'   620
    Lo, such it is not to be on your guard
Against the flatterers of the world, or yard,
And if you think my story is absurd,

A foolish trifle of a beast and bird,
A fable of a fox, a cock, a hen,
Take hold upon the moral, gentlemen.
   St Paul himself, a saint of great discerning;
Says that all things are written for our learning;
So take the grain and let the chaff be still.
And, gracious Father, if it be thy will   630
As saith my Saviour, make us all good men,
And bring us to his heavenly bliss.
                      Amen.

Sir Walter Raleigh

The Lie

Sir Walter Raleigh (1552–1618) was a soldier, courtier, and explorer as well as a poet, and he was often involved in the public life of the Elizabethan age. Much of his poetry, however, was lost, including most of the long poem called *Cynthia* that was written to the queen. His vigorous and passionate career ended in 1618, when he was executed after having been imprisoned in the Tower of London for many years by James I. "The Lie," which was written around 1592, must have been well known in some circles, because this attack on the world's vanities and institutions provoked several replies. Allen Tate in his essay on Elizabethan satire mentions the strain of medieval allegory that lingers in Raleigh's poetry, and "The Lie" might be regarded as a transmutation of the old "complaint."

Go, soul, the body's guest,
Upon a thankless errand;
Fear not to touch the best;
The truth shall be thy warrant.
Go, since I needs must die,
And give the world the lie.

Say to the court, it glows
And shines like rotten wood;
Say to the church, it shows
What's good, and doth no good.   10
If church and court reply,
Then give them both the lie.

Tell potentates, they live
Acting by others' action;
Not loved unless they give,
Not strong but by a faction.
If potentates reply,
Give potentates the lie.

Tell men of high condition,
That manage the estate,   20
Their purpose is ambition,
Their practice only hate.

And if they once reply,
Then give them all the lie.

Tell them that brave it most,[1]
They beg for more by spending,
Who, in their greatest cost,
Seek nothing but commending.
And if they make reply,
Then give them all the lie.   30

Tell zeal it wants devotion;
Tell love it is but lust;
Tell time it is but motion;
Tell flesh it is but dust.
And wish them not reply,
For thou must give the lie.

Tell age it daily wasteth;
Tell honor how it alters;
Tell beauty how she blasteth;
Tell favor how it falters.   40
And as they shall reply,
Give every one the lie.

Tell wit how much it wrangles
In tickle[2] points of niceness;
Tell wisdom she entangles
Herself in overwiseness.
And when they do reply,
Straight give them both the lie.

Tell physic of her boldness;
Tell skill it is pretension;   50
Tell charity of coldness;
Tell law it is contention.
And as they do reply,
So give them still the lie.

---

[1] Waste money on clothes.
[2] Delicate.

Tell fortune of her blindness;
Tell nature of decay;
Tell friendship of unkindness;
Tell justice of delay.
And if they will reply,
Then give them all the lie.   60

Tell arts they have no soundness,
But vary by esteeming;
Tell schools they want profoundness,
And stand too much on seeming.
If arts and schools reply,
Give arts and schools the lie.

Tell faith it's fled the city;
Tell how the country erreth;
Tell manhood shakes off pity;
Tell virtue least preferreth.   70
And if they do reply,
Spare not to give the lie.

So when thou hast, as I
Commanded thee, done blabbing—
Although to give the lie
Deserves no less than stabbing—
Stab at thee he that will,
No stab the soul can kill.

William Shakespeare

Sonnet 66

William Shakespeare (1564–1616) was apparently affected by the general interest in satire that prevailed among the literary men of his generation. Although he wrote no formal satires, two of his plays, *Troilus and Cressida* (1601–1602) and *Timon of Athens* (1605–1608), the latter based on a dialogue by Lucian, are satirical in their effect. Indeed *Hamlet* has certain affinities with *Troilus and Cressida*. (Oscar J. Campbell, in *Shakespeare's Satire*, has explored this phase of the dramatist's work.) The satirical impulse likewise operates at times in the sequence of 154 sonnets, and, in Sonnet 66, the cataloguing of the world's failures is reminiscent of the medieval "complaint" that we find in Raleigh's "The Lie." The end of the sonnet, however, moves out of the satirical framework.

Tired with all these, for restful death I cry,
As, to behold desert[1] a beggar born,
And needy nothing[2] trimm'd in jollity,[3]
And purest faith unhappily forsworn,
And gilded honour shamefully misplaced,
And maiden virtue rudely strumpeted,
And right perfection wrongfully disgraced,
And strength by limping sway disabled,[4]
And art made tongue-tied by authority,
And folly doctor-like[5] controlling skill,
And simple truth miscall'd simplicity,[6]
And captive good attending captain ill:
Tired with all these, from these would I be gone,
Save that, to die, I leave my love alone.

---

[1] Those who possess merit in contrast with "needy nothing" in the next line.
[2] Moral and mental emptiness.
[3] Finery.
[4] Four syllables.
[5] Like a learned person.
[6] Silliness.

Christopher Marlowe

The Passionate Shepherd
to His Love

Christopher Marlowe (1564–1593), son of a Canterbury shoemaker, went to Cambridge University on a scholarship to prepare for the ministry. Instead of taking holy orders, however, he began writing plays. He completed the first of his famous tragedies, *Tamburlaine*, at the age of 23. The last six years of his brief life were violent ones. He was involved in a murder and jailed. Charges of atheism and treason were hurled at him. He died in an inn during an argument over a bill.

It was during this turbulent period that he composed his most important play, *Dr. Faustus*. He is also the author of one of the most significant long poems of the English Renaissance, *Hero and Leander*. His lyric, "The Passionate Shepherd to His Love," is typical of the pastoral poetry of the period in its idyllic picture of nature and young lovers.

Come live with me and be my Love,
And we will all the pleasures prove[1]
That hills and valleys, dales and fields,
Or woods or steepy mountain yields.

And we will sit upon the rocks
And see the shepherds feed their flocks
By shallow rivers, to whose falls
Melodious birds sing madrigals.

And I will make thee beds of roses
And a thousand fragrant posies;
A cap of flowers, and a kirtle[2]
Embroidered all with leaves of myrtle;[3]

A gown made of the finest wool
Which from our pretty lambs we pull;
Fair-linéd slippers for the cold,
With buckles of the purest gold;

A belt of straw and ivy buds
With coral clasps and amber studs—

10

---

[1] Experience or test.
[2] Dress or gown.
[3] An evergreen shrub sacred to Venus and a symbol of love.

And if these pleasures may thee move,
Come live with me and be my Love.   20

The shepherd swains shall dance and sing
For thy delight each May morning—
If these delights thy mind may move,
Then live with me and be my Love.

John Donne

The Baite

The witty parody of Marlowe's "The Passionate Shepherd to His Love" by John Donne (1572–1631) is typical of his early poetry when he wrote satires on London life, bawdy elegies, and cynical songs about women and love and was considered by his contemporaries as "a great visitor of Ladies, a great frequenter of Playes, a great writer of conceited Verses." With his marriage to Ann More in 1601 his poetry became more serious and complex. He later composed a number of religious sonnets and devotional poems as well as two long elegies on the death of his patron's daughter that are his most intellectually ambitious poetic works. It was during this period he left the Catholic Church and became a convert to Anglicanism. After he took holy orders in 1615, he wrote little poetry. He became dean of St. Paul's in 1621. His satirical verse is marked by a jaunty, colloquial tone, far-fetched images or conceits, clever wordplay, and a brilliant display of paradox and irony.

Come live with me, and be my love,
And we will some new pleasures prove,
Of golden sands, and crystal brooks,
With silken lines, and silver hooks.

There will the river whispering run,
Warmed by thy eyes more than the sun,
And there the enamored fish will stay,
Begging themselves they may betray.

When thou wilt swim in that live bath,
Each fish, which every channel hath,   10
Will amorously to thee swim,
Gladder to catch thee, than thou him.

If thou, to be seen, beest loth,
By sun or moon, thou darkenest both;
And if myself have leave to see,
I need not their light, having thee.

Let others freeze with angling reeds,[1]
And cut their legs with shells and weeds,

---

[1] Rods made out of reeds.

Or treacherously poor fish beset
With strangling snare, or windowy net.   20

Let coarse bold hands from slimy nest
The bedded fish in banks out-wrest,
Or curious[2] traitors, sleave-silk[3] flies,
Bewitch poor fishes' wand'ring eyes.

For thee, thou need'st no such deceit,
For thou thyself art thine own bait;
The fish that is not catched thereby,
Alas, is wiser far than I.

---

[2] Artfully made.
[3] Artificial flies woven from threads of unravelled silk.

Molière

The Misanthrope

ENGLISH VERSION BY RICHARD WILBUR

Molière (1622–1673) was born and died in Paris. His real name was Jean-Baptiste Poquelin. Although the family was bourgeois, his father held a post in the royal household and thus secured certain advantages for his children. Molière's education was classical and included a study of the Roman comic playwrights Terence and Plautus. Like Shakespeare, he was an actor-manager; his mastery of the stage was won out of experience. His success in Paris was immense, but he frequently had to defend himself from those who felt attacked, and undoubtedly his friendship with Louis XIV gave him an assurance about these matters. Among his most important plays are *The Misanthrope* (1666), *Tartuffe* (1667), *The Miser* (1668), and *The Would-Be Gentleman* (1671). Although *The Misanthrope* is one of the supreme examples of the comedy of manners, it is an interesting fact that some readers in the past, for example the German poet Goethe, have regarded Alceste as a tragic figure. But Robert C. Elliott, in *The Power of Satire*, sees him as "the satirist satirized," and for most readers his uncompromising attitude is finally ridiculous.

CHARACTERS

ALCESTE, in love with Célimène
PHILINTE, Alceste's friend
ORONTE, in love with Célimène
CÉLIMÈNE, Alceste's beloved
ELIANTE, Célimène's cousin
ARSINOÉ, a friend of Célimène's
ACASTE

CLITANDRE } Marquesses

BASQUE, Célimène's servant
A GUARD of the Marshalsea
DUBOIS, Alceste's valet

The Scene throughout is in Célimène's house at Paris.

ACT I

SCENE 1. (PHILINTE, ALCESTE)

PHILINTE. Now, what's got into you?
ALCESTE (seated).   Kindly leave me alone.
PHILINTE. Come, come, what is it?   This lugubrious tone . . .
ALCESTE. Leave me, I said; you spoil my solitude.
PHILINTE. Oh, listen to me, now, and don't be rude.
ALCESTE. I choose to be rude, Sir, and to be hard of hearing.
PHILINTE. These ugly moods of yours are not endearing;
  Friends though we are, I really must insist . . .
ALCESTE (*abruptly rising*). Friends? Friends, you say? Well, cross me
    off your list.
  I've been your friend till now, as you well know;
  But after what I saw a moment ago   10
  I tell you flatly that our ways must part.
  I wish no place in a dishonest heart.
PHILINTE. Why, what have I done, Alceste? Is this quite just?
ALCESTE. My God, you ought to die of self-disgust.
  I call your conduct inexcusable, Sir,
  And every man of honor will concur.
  I see you almost hug a man to death,
  Exclaim for joy until you're out of breath,
  And supplement these loving demonstrations
  With endless offers, vows, and protestations;   20
  Then when I ask you "Who was that?" I find
  That you can barely bring his name to mind!
  Once the man's back is turned, you cease to love him,
  And speak with absolute indifference of him!
  By God, I say it's base and scandalous
  To falsify the heart's affections thus;
  If I caught myself behaving in such a way,
  I'd hang myself for shame, without delay.
PHILINTE. It hardly seems a hanging matter to me;
  I hope that you will take it graciously   30
  If I extend myself a slight reprieve,
  And live a little longer, by your leave.
ALCESTE. How dare you joke about a crime so grave?
PHILINTE. What crime? How else are people to behave?
ALCESTE. I'd have them be sincere, and never part
  With any word that isn't from the heart.
PHILINTE. When someone greets us with a show of pleasure,

It's but polite to give him equal measure,
Return his love the best that we know how,
And trade him offer for offer, vow for vow.   40
ALCESTE. No, no, this formula you'd have me follow,
However fashionable, is false and hollow,
And I despise the frenzied operations
Of all these barterers of protestations,
These lavishers of meaningless embraces,
These utterers of obliging commonplaces,
Who court and flatter everyone on earth
And praise the fool no less than the man of worth.
Should you rejoice that someone fondles you,
Offers his love and service, swears to be true,   50
And fills your ears with praises of your name,
When to the first damned fop he'll say the same?
No, no: no self-respecting heart would dream
Of prizing so promiscuous an esteem;
However high the praise, there's nothing worse
Than sharing honors with the universe.
Esteem is founded on comparison:
To honor all men is to honor none.
Since you embrace this indiscriminate vice,
Your friendship comes at far too cheap a price;   60
I spurn the easy tribute of a heart
Which will not set the worthy man apart:
I choose, Sir, to be chosen; and in fine,
The friend of mankind is no friend of mine.
PHILINTE. But in polite society, custom decrees
That we show certain outward coutesies. . . .
ALCESTE. Ah, no! we should condemn with all our force
Such false and artificial intercourse.
Let men behave like men; let them display
Their inmost hearts in everything they say;   70
Let the heart speak, and let our sentiments
Not mask themselves in silly compliments.
PHILINTE. In certain cases it would be uncouth
And most absurd to speak the naked truth;
With all respect for your exalted notions,
It's often best to veil one's true emotions.
Wouldn't the social fabric come undone
If we were wholly frank with everyone?
Suppose you met with someone you couldn't bear;

Would you inform him of it then and there?   80
ALCESTE. Yes.
PHILINTE.   Then you'd tell old Emilie it's pathetic
   The way she daubs her features with cosmetic
   And plays the gay coquette at sixty-four?
ALCESTE. I would.
PHILINTE.   And you'd call Dorilas a bore,
   And tell him every ear at court is lame
   From hearing him brag about his noble name?
ALCESTE. Precisely.
PHILINTE.   Ah, you're joking.
ALCESTE.   *Au contraire:*
   In this regard there's none I'd choose to spare.
   All are corrupt; there's nothing to be seen
   In court or town but aggravates my spleen.   90
   I fall into deep gloom and melancholy
   When I survey the scene of human folly,
   Finding on every hand base flattery,
   Injustice, fraud, self-interest, treachery. . . .
   Ah, it's too much; mankind has grown so base,
   I mean to break with the whole human race.
PHILINTE. This philosophic rage is a bit extreme;
   You've no idea how comical you seem;
   Indeed, we're like those brothers in the play
   Called *School for Husbands*, one of whom was prey . . .   100
ALCESTE. Enough, now! None of your stupid similes.
PHILINTE. Then let's have no more tirades, if you please.
   The world won't change, whatever you say or do;
   And since plain speaking means so much to you,
   I'll tell you plainly that by being frank
   You've earned the reputation of a crank,
   And that you're thought ridiculous when you rage
   And rant against the manners of the age.
ALCESTE. So much the better; just what I wish to hear.
   No news could be more grateful to my ear.   110
   All men are so destestable in my eyes,
   I should be sorry if they thought me wise.
PHILINTE. Your hatred's very sweeping, is it not?
ALCESTE. Quite right: I hate the whole degraded lot.
PHILINTE. Must all poor human creatures be embraced,
   Without distinction, by your vast distaste?
   Even in these bad times, there are surely a few . . .

ALCESTE. No, I include all men in one dim view:
    Some men I hate for being rogues: the others
    I hate because they treat the rogues like brothers,   120
    And, lacking a virtuous scorn for what is vile,
    Receive the villain with a complaisant smile,
    Notice how tolerant people choose to be
    Toward that bold rascal who's at law with me.
    His social polish can't conceal his nature;
    One sees at once that he's a treacherous creature;
    No one could possibly be taken in
    By those soft speeches and that sugary grin.
    The whole world knows the shady means by which
    The low-brow's grown so powerful and rich,   130
    And risen to a rank so bright and high
    That virtue can but blush, and merit sigh.
    Whenever his name comes up in conversation,
    None will defend his wretched reputation;
    Call him knave, liar, scoundrel, and all the rest,
    Each head will nod, and no one will protest.
    And yet his smirk is seen in every house,
    He's greeted everywhere with smiles and bows,
    And when there's any honor that can be got
    By pulling strings, he'll get it, like as not.   140
    My God! It chills my heart to see the ways
    Men come to terms with evil nowadays;
    Sometimes, I swear, I'm moved to flee and find
    Some desert land unfouled by humankind.
PHILINTE. Come, let's forget the follies of the times
    And pardon mankind for its petty crimes;
    Let's have an end of rantings and of railings,
    And show some leniency toward human failings.
    This world requires a pliant rectitude;
    Too stern a virtue makes one stiff and rude;   150
    Good sense views all extremes with detestation,
    And bids us to be noble in moderation.
    The rigid virtues of the ancient days
    Are not for us; they jar with all our ways
    And ask of us too lofty a perfection.
    Wise men accept their times without objection,
    And there's no greater folly, if you ask me,
    Than trying to reform society.

Like you, I see each day a hundred and one
Unhandsome deeds that might be better done, 160
But still, for all the faults that meet my view,
I'm never known to storm and rave like you.
I take men as they are, or let them be,
And teach my soul to bear their frailty;
And whether in court or town, whatever the scene,
My phlegm's as philosophic as your spleen.
ALCESTE. This phlegm which you so eloquently commend,
Does nothing ever rile it up, my friend?
Suppose some man you trust should treacherously
Conspire to rob you of your property, 170
And do his best to wreck your reputation?
Wouldn't you feel a certain indignation?
PHILINTE. Why, no. These faults of which you so complain
Are part of human nature, I maintain,
And it's no more a matter for disgust
That men are knavish, selfish and unjust,
Than that the vulture dines upon the dead,
And wolves are furious, and apes ill-bred.
ALCESTE. Shall I see myself betrayed, robbed, torn to bits,
And not . . . Oh, let's be still and rest our wits. 180
Enough of reasoning, now. I've had my fill.
PHILINTE. Indeed, you would do well, Sir, to be still.
Rage less at your opponent, and give some thought
To how you'll win this lawsuit that he's brought.
ALCESTE. I assure you I'll do nothing of the sort.
PHILINTE. Then who will plead your case before the court?
ALCESTE. Reason and right and justice will plead for me.
PHILINTE. Oh, Lord. What judges do you plan to see?
ALCESTE. Why, none. The justice of my cause is clear.
PHILINTE. Of course, man; but there's politics to fear. . . . 190
ALCESTE. No, I refuse to lift a hand. That's flat.
  I'm either right, or wrong.
PHILINTE.   Don't count on that.
ALCESTE. No, I'll do nothing.
PHILINTE.   Your enemy's influence
  Is great, you know . . .
ALCESTE.   That makes no difference.
PHILINTE. It will; you'll see.
ALCESTE.   Must honor bow to guile?

If so, I shall be proud to lose the trial.
PHILINTE. Oh, really . . . ˙
ALCESTE.   I'll discover by this case
   Whether or not men are sufficiently base
   And impudent and villainous and perverse
   To do me wrong before the universe.   200
PHILINTE. What a man!
ALCESTE.   Oh, I could wish, whatever the cost,
   Just for the beauty of it, that my trial were lost.
PHILINTE. If people heard you talking so, Alceste,
   They'd split their sides. Your name would be a jest.
ALCESTE. So much the worse for jesters.
PHILINTE.   May I enquire
   Whether this rectitude you so admire,
   And these hard virtues you're enamored of
   Are qualities of the lady whom you love?
   It much surprises me that you, who seem
   To view mankind with furious disesteem,   210
   Have yet found something to enchant your eyes
   Amidst a species which you so despise.
   And what is more amazing, I'm afraid,
   Is the most curious choice your heart has made.
   The honest Éliante is fond of you,
   Arsinoé, the prude, admires you too;
   And yet your spirit's been perversely led
   To choose the flighty Célimène instead,
   Whose brittle malice and coquettish ways
   So typify the manners of our days.   220
   How is it that the traits you most abhor
   Are bearable in this lady you adore?
   Are you so blind with love that you can't find them?
   Or do you contrive, in her case, not to mind them?
ALCESTE. My love for that young widow's not the kind
   That can't perceive defects; no, I'm not blind.
   I see her faults, despite my ardent love,
   And all I see I fervently reprove.
   And yet I'm weak; for all her falsity,
   That woman knows the art of pleasing me,   230
   And though I never cease complaining of her,
   I swear I cannot manage not to love her.
   Her charm outweighs her faults; I can but aim
   To cleanse her spirit in my love's pure flame.

PHILINTE. That's no small task; I wish you all success.
　You think then that she loves you?
ALCESTE. 　　　　　　　　　　Heavens, yes!
　I wouldn't love her did she not love me.
PHILINTE. Well, if her taste for you is plain to see,
　Why do these rivals cause you such despair?
ALCESTE. True love, Sir, is possessive, and cannot bear　　　240
　To share with all the world. I'm here today
　To tell her she must send that mob away.
PHILINTE. If I were you, and had your choice to make,
　Éliante, her cousin, would be the one I'd take;
　That honest heart, which cares for you alone,
　Would harmonize far better with your own.
ALCESTE. True, true: each day my reason tells me so;
　But reason doesn't rule in love, you know.
PHILINTE. I fear some bitter sorrow is in store;
　This love . . .　　　　　　　　　　　　　　　　　250

SCENE 2. (ORONTE, ALCESTE, PHILINTE)

ORONTE (to Alceste). The servants told me at the door
　That Éliante and Célimène were out,
　But when I heard, dear Sir, that you were about,
　I came to say, without exaggeration,
　That I hold you in the vastest admiration,
　And that it's always been my dearest desire
　To be the friend of one I so admire.
　I hope to see my love of merit requited,
　And you and I in friendship's bond united.
　I'm sure you won't refuse—if I may be frank—　　　10
　A friend of my devotedness—and rank.

(*During this speech of* ORONTE'S, ALCESTE *is abstracted, and seems unaware that he is being spoken to. He only breaks off his reverie when* ORONTE *says:*)

It was for you, if you please, that my words were intended.
ALCESTE. For me, Sir?
ORONTE. 　　　　　Yes, for you. You're not offended?
ALCESTE. By no means. But this much surprises me. . . .

The honor comes most unexpectedly. . . .
ORONTE. My high regard should not astonish you;
   The whole world feels the same. It is your due.
ALCESTE. Sir . . .
ORONTE.   Why, in all the State there isn't one
   Can match your merits; they shine, Sir, like the sun.
ALCESTE. Sir . . .
ORONTE.   You are higher in my estimation   20
   Than all that's most illustrious in the nation.
ALCESTE. Sir . . .
ORONTE.   If I lie, may heaven strike me dead!
   To show you that I mean what I have said,
   Permit me, Sir, to embrace you most sincerely,
   And swear that I will prize our friendship dearly.
   Give me your hand. And now, Sir, if you choose,
   We'll make our vows.
ALCESTE.   Sir . . .
ORONTE.   What! You refuse?
ALCESTE. Sir, it's a very great honor you extend:
   But friendship is a sacred thing, my friend;
   It would be profanation to bestow   30
   The name of friend on one you hardly know.
   All parts are better played when well-rehearsed;
   Let's put off friendship, and get acquainted first.
   We may discover it would be unwise
   To try to make our natures harmonize.
ORONTE. By heaven! You're sagacious to the core;
   This speech has made me admire you even more.
   Let time, then, bring us closer day by day;
   Meanwhile, I shall be yours in every way.
   If, for example, there should be anything   40
   You wish at court, I'll mention it to the King.
   I have his ear, of course; it's quite well known
   That I am much in favor with the throne.
   In short, I am your servant. And now, dear friend,
   Since you have such fine judgment, I intend
   To please you, if I can, with a small sonnet
   I wrote not long ago. Please comment on it,
   And tell me whether I ought to publish it.
ALCESTE. You must excuse me, Sir; I'm hardly fit
   To judge such matters.
ORONTE.   Why not?

ALCESTE.   I am, I fear,   50
  Inclined to be unfashionably sincere.
ORONTE. Just what I ask; I'd take no satisfaction
  In anything but your sincere reaction.
  I beg you not to dream of being kind.
ALCESTE. Since you desire it, Sir, I'll speak my mind.
ORONTE. *Sonnet.* It's a sonnet.... *Hope*... The poem's addressed
  To a lady who wakened hopes within my breast.
  Hope... this is not the pompous sort of thing,
  Just modest little verses, with a tender ring.
ALCESTE. Well, we shall see.
ORONTE.   *Hope*... I'm anxious to hear   60
  Whether the style seems properly smooth and clear,
  And whether the choice of words is good or bad.
ALCESTE. We'll see, we'll see.
ORONTE.   Perhaps I ought to add
  That it took me only a quarter-hour to write it,
ALCESTE. The time's irrelevant, Sir: kindly recite it.
ORONTE (*reading*). *Hope comforts us awhile, 'tis true,*
           Lulling our cares with careless laughter,
           And yet such joy is full of rue,
           My Phyllis, if nothing follows after.
PHILINTE. I'm charmed by this already; the style's delightful.   70
ALCESTE (*sotto voce, to Philinte*). How can you say that? Why, the thing
  is frightful.
ORONTE.   *Your fair face smiled on me awhile,*
           But was it kindness so to enchant me?
           'Twould have been fairer not to smile,
           If hope was all you meant to grant me.
PHILINTE. What a clever thought! How handsomely you phrase it!
ALCESTE (*sotto voce, to Philinte*). You know the thing is trash.
  How dare you praise it?
ORONTE.   *If it's to be my passion's fate*
           Thus everlastingly to wait,   80
           Then death will come to set me free:
           For death is fairer than the fair;
           Phyllis, to hope is to despair
           When one must hope eternally.
PHILINTE. The close is exquisite—full of feeling and grace.
ALCESTE (*sotto voce, aside*). Oh, blast the close; you'd better close your
  face
  Before you send your lying soul to hell.

PHILINTE. I can't remember a poem I've liked so well.

ALCESTE (*sotto voce, aside*). Good Lord!

ORONTO (*to Philinte*).   I fear you're flattering me
    a bit.

PHILINTE. Oh, no!

ALCESTE (*sotto voce, aside*). What else d'you call it, you hypocrite?   90

ORONTE (*to Alceste*). But you, Sir, keep your promise now: don't shrink
    From telling me sincerely what you think.

ALCESTE. Sir, these are delicate matters; we all desire
    To be told that we've the true poetic fire.
    But once, to one whose name I shall not mention,
    I said, regarding some verse of his invention,
    That gentleman should rigorously control
    That itch to write which often afflicts the soul;
    That one should curb the heady inclination
    To publicize one's little avocation;   100
    And that in showing off one's works of art
    One often plays a very clownish part.

ORONTE. Are you suggesting in a devious way
    That I ought not . . .

ALCESTE.   Oh, that I do not say.
    Further, I told him that no fault is worse
    Than that of writing frigid, lifeless verse,
    And that the merest whisper of such a shame
    Suffices to destroy a man's good name.

ORONTE. D'you mean to say my sonnet's dull and trite?

ALCESTE. I don't say that. But I went on to cite   110
    Numerous cases of once-respected men
    Who came to grief by taking up the pen.

ORONTE. And am I like them? Do I write so poorly?

ALCESTE. I don't say that. But I told this person, "Surely
    You're under no necessity to compose;
    Why you should wish to publish, heaven knows.
    There's no excuse for printing tedious rot
    Unless one writes for bread, as you do not.
    Resist temptation, then, I beg of you;
    Conceal your pastimes from the public view;   120
    And don't give up, on any provocation,
    Your present high and courtly reputation,
    To purchase at a greedy printer's shop
    The name of silly author and scribbling fop."
    These were the points I tried to make him see.

ORONTE. I sense that they are also aimed at me;
    But now—about my sonnet—I'd like to be told . . .
ALCESTE. Frankly, that sonnet should be pigeonholed.
    You've chosen the worst models to imitate.
    The style's unnatural. Let me illustrate: 130
            For example, *Your fair face smiled on me awhile,*
            Followed by, *'Twould have been fairer not to smile!*
            Or this: *such joy is full of rue;*
            Or this: *For death is fairer than the fair;*
            Or, *Phyllis, to hope is to despair*
                When one must hope eternally!
    This artificial style, that's all the fashion,
    Has neither taste, nor honesty, nor passion;
    It's nothing but a sort of wordy play,
    And nature never spoke in such a way.   140
    What, in this shallow age, is not debased?
    Our fathers, though less refined, had better taste;
    I'd barter all that men admire today
    For one old love song I shall try to say:
            If the King had given me for my own
            Paris, his citadel,
            And I for that must leave alone
            Her whom I love so well,
            I'd say then to the Crown,
            Take back your glittering town;   150
            My darling is more fair, I swear,
            My darling is more fair.
    The rhyme's not rich, the style is rough and old,
    But don't you see that it's the purest gold
    Beside the tinsel nonsense now preferred,
    And that there's passion in its every word?
            If the King had given me for my own
            Paris, his citadel,
            And I for that must leave alone
            Her whom I love so well,   160
            I'd say then to the Crown,
            Take back your glittering town;
            My darling is more fair, I swear,
            My darling is more fair.
    There speaks a loving heart. (*To Philinte.*) You're laughing, eh?
    Laugh on, my precious wit. Whatever you say,
    I hold that song's worth all the bibelots

That people hail today with ah's and oh's.
ORONTE. And I maintain my sonnet's very good.
ALCESTE. It's not at all surprising that you should.   170
    You have your reasons; permit me to have mine
    For thinking that you cannot write a line.
ORONTE. Others have praised my sonnet to the skies.
ALCESTE. I lack their art of telling pleasant lies.
ORONTE. You seem to think you've got no end of wit.
ALCESTE. To praise your verse, I'd need still more of it.
ORONTE. I'm not in need of your approval, Sir.
ALCESTE. That's good; you couldn't have it if you were.
ORONTE. Come now, I'll lend you the subject of my sonnet;
    I'd like to see you try to improve upon it.   180
ALCESTE. I might, by chance, write something just as shoddy;
    But then I wouldn't show it to everybody.
ORONTE. You're most opinionated and conceited.
ALCESTE. Go find your flatterers, and be better treated.
ORONTE. Look here, my little fellow, pray watch your tone.
ALCESTE. My great big fellow, you'd better watch your own.
PHILINTE (*stepping between them*). Oh, please, please, gentlemen!
    This will never do.
ORONTE. The fault is mine, and I leave the field to you.
    I am your servant, Sir, in every way.   190
ALCESTE. And I, Sir, am your most abject valet.

SCENE 3. (PHILINTE, ALCESTE)

PHILINTE. Well, as you see, sincerity in excess
    Can get you into a very pretty mess;
    Oronte was hungry for appreciation. . . .
ALCESTE. Don't speak to me.
PHILINTE.   What?
ALCESTE.   No more conversation.
PHILINTE. Really, now . . .
ALCESTE.   Leave me alone.
PHILINTE.   If I . . .
ALCESTE.   Out of my sight!
PHILINTE. But what . . .
ALCESTE.   I won't listen.
PHILINTE.   But . . .
ALCESTE.   Silence!

PHILINTE.   Now, is it polite . . .
ALCESTE. By heaven, I've had enough. Don't follow me.
PHILINTE. Ah, you're just joking. I'll keep you company.

ACT II

SCENE 1. (ALCESTE, CÉLIMÈNE)

ALCESTE. Shall I speak plainly, Madam? I confess
   Your conduct gives me infinite distress,
   And my resentment's grown too hot to smother.
   Soon, I foresee, we'll break with one another.
   If I said otherwise, I should deceive you;
   Sooner or later, I shall be forced to leave you,
   And if I swore that we shall never part,
   I should misread the omens of my heart.
CÉLIMÈNE. You kindly saw me home, it would appear,
   So as to pour invectives in my ear.   10
ALCESTE. I've no desire to quarrel. But I deplore
   Your inability to shut the door
   On all these suitors who beset you so.
   There's what annoys me, if you care to know.
CÉLIMÈNE. Is it my fault that all these men pursue me?
   Am I to blame if they're attracted to me?
   And when they gently beg an audience,
   Ought I to take a stick and drive them hence?
ALCESTE. Madam, there's no necessity for a stick;
   A less responsive heart would do the trick.   20
   Of your attractiveness I don't complain;
   But those your charms attract, you then detain
   By a most melting and receptive manner,
   And so enlist their hearts beneath your banner.
   It's the agreeable hopes which you excite
   That keep these lovers round you day and night;
   Were they less liberally smiled upon,
   That sighing troop would very soon be gone.
   But tell me, Madam, why it is that lately
   This man Clitandre interests you so greatly?   30
   Because of what high merits do you deem

Him worthy of the honor of your esteem?
Is it that your admiring glances linger
On the splendidly long nail of his little finger?
Or do you share the general deep respect
For the blond wig he chooses to affect?
Are you in love with his embroidered hose?
Do you adore his ribbons and his bows?
Or is it that this paragon bewitches
Your tasteful eye with his vast German breeches?   40
Perhaps his giggle, or his falsetto voice,
Makes him the latest gallant of your choice?
CÉLIMÈNE. You're much mistaken to resent him so.
Why I put up with him you surely know:
My lawsuit's very shortly to be tried,
And I must have his influence on my side.
ALCESTE. Then lose your lawsuit, Madam, or let it drop;
Don't torture me by humoring such a fop.
CÉLIMÈNE. You're jealous of the whole world, Sir.
ALCESTE.   That's true,
Since the whole world is well-received by you.   50
CÉLIMÈNE. That my good nature is so unconfined
Should serve to pacify your jealous mind;
Were I to smile on one, and scorn the rest,
Then you might have some cause to be distressed.
ALCESTE. Well, if I mustn't be jealous, tell me, then,
Just how I'm better treated than other men.
CÉLIMÈNE. You know you have my love. Will that not do?
ALCESTE. What proof have I that what you say is true?
CÉLIMÈNE. I would expect, Sir, that my having said it
Might give the statement sufficient credit.   60
ALCESTE. But how can I be sure that you don't tell
The selfsame thing to other men as well?
CÉLIMÈNE. What a gallant speech! How flattering to me!
What a sweet creature you make me out to be!
Well, then to save you from the pangs of doubt,
All that I've said I hereby cancel out;
Now, none but yourself shall make a monkey of you:
Are you content?
ALCESTE.   Why, why am I doomed to love you?
I swear that I shall bless the blissful hour
When this poor heart's no longer in your power!   70
I make no secret of it: I've done my best

To exorcise this passion from my breast;
But thus far all in vain; it will not go;
It's for my sins that I must love you so.
CÉLIMÈNE. Your love for me is matchless, Sir; that's clear.
ALCESTE. Indeed, in all the world it has no peer;
  Words can't describe the nature of my passion,
  And no man ever loved in such a fashion.
CÉLIMÈNE. Yes, it's a brand-new fashion, I agree:
  You show your love by castigating me,
  And all your speeches are enraged and rude.   80
  I've never been so furiously wooed.
ALCESTE. Yet you could calm that fury, if you chose.
  Come, shall we bring our quarrels to a close?
  Let's speak with open hearts, then, and begin . . .

SCENE 2. (CÉLIMÈNE, ALCESTE, BASQUE)

CÉLIMÈNE. What is it?
BASQUE.   Acaste is here.
CÉLIMÈNE.   Well, send him in.

SCENE 3. (CÉLIMÈNE, ALCESTE)

ALCESTE. What! Shall we never be alone at all?
  You're always ready to receive a call,
  And you can't bear, for ten ticks of the clock,
  Not to keep open house for all who knock.
CÉLIMÈNE. I couldn't refuse him: he'd be most put out.
ALCESTE. Surely that's not worth worrying about.
CÉLIMÈNE. Acaste would never forgive me if he guessed
  That I consider him a dreadful pest.
ALCESTE. If he's a pest, why bother with him then?
CÉLIMÈNE. Heavens! One can't antagonize such men;   10
  Why, they're the chartered gossips of the court,
  And have a say in things of every sort.
  One must receive them, and be full of charm;
  They're no great help, but they can do you harm,
  And though your influence be ever so great,
  They're hardly the best people to alienate.
ALCESTE. I see, dear lady, that you could make a case

For putting up with the whole human race;
These friendships that you calculate so nicely . . .

SCENE 4. (ALCESTE, CÉLIMÈNE, BASQUE)

BASQUE. Madam, Clitandre is here as well.
ALCESTE.   Precisely.
CÉLIMÈNE. Where are you going?
ALCESTE.   Elsewhere.
CÉLIMÈNE.   Stay.
ALCESTE.   No, no.
CÉLIMÈNE. Stay, Sir.
ALCESTE.   I can't.
CÉLIMÈNE.   I wish it.
ALCESTE.   No, I must go.
  I beg you, Madam, not to press the matter;
You know I have no taste for idle chatter.
CÉLIMÈNE. Stay. I command you.
ALCESTE.   No, I cannot stay.
CÉLIMÈNE. Very well; you have my leave to go away.

SCENE 5. (ÉLIANTE, PHILINTE, ACASTE, CLITANDRE,
ALCESTE, CÉLIMÈNE, BASQUE)

ÉLIANTE (*to Célimène*). The Marquesses have kindly come to call.
  Were they announced?
CÉLIMÈNE.   Yes, Basque, bring chairs for all.

(*Basque provides the chairs, and exits.*)

(*To Alceste.*) You haven't gone?
ALCESTE.   No; and I shan't depart
  Till you decide who's foremost in your heart.
CÉLIMÈNE. Oh, hush.
ALCESTE.   It's time to choose; take them, or me.
CÉLIMÈNE. You're mad.
ALCESTE.   I'm not, as you shall shortly see.
CÉLIMÈNE. Oh?
ALCESTE.   You'll decide.
CÉLIMÈNE.   You're joking now, dear friend.

ALCESTE. No, no; you'll choose; my patience is at an end.
CLITANDRE. Madam, I come from court, where poor Cléonte
    Behaved like a perfect fool, as is his wont.   10
    Has he no friend to counsel him, I wonder,
    And teach him less unerringly to blunder?
CÉLIMÈNE. It's true, the man's a most accomplished dunce;
    His gauche behavior charms the eye at once;
    And every time one sees him, on my word,
    His manner's grown a trifle more absurd.
ACASTE. Speaking of dunces, I've just now conversed
    With old Damon, who's one of the very worst;
    I stood a lifetime in the broiling sun
    Before his dreary monologue was done.   20
CÉLIMÈNE. Oh, he's a wondrous talker, and has the power
    To tell you nothing hour after hour:
    If, by mistake, he ever came to the point,
    The shock would put his jawbone out of joint.
ÉLIANTE (*to Philinte*). The conversation takes its usual turn,
    And all our dear friends' ears will shortly burn.
CLITANDRE. Timante's a character, Madam.
CÉLIMÈNE.   Isn't he, though?
    A man of mystery from top to toe,
    Who moves about in a romantic mist   30
    On secret missions which do not exist.
    His talk is full of eyebrows and grimaces;
    How tired one gets of his momentous faces;
    He's always whispering something confidential
    Which turns out to be quite inconsequential;
    Nothing's too slight for him to mystify;
    He even whispers when he says "good-by."
ACASTE. Tell us about Géralde.
CÉLIMÈNE.   That tiresome ass.
    He mixes only with the titled class,
    And fawns on dukes and princes, and is bored
    With anyone who's not at least a lord.   40
    The man's obsessed with rank, and his discourses
    Are all of hounds and carriages and horses;
    He uses Christian names with all the great,
    And the word Milord, with him, is out of date.
CLITANDRE. He's very taken with Bélise, I hear.
CÉLIMÈNE. She is the dreariest company, poor dear.
    Whenever she comes to call, I grope about

To find some topic which will draw her out,
But, owing to her dry and faint replies,
The conversation wilts, and droops, and dies.   50
In vain one hopes to animate her face
By mentioning the ultimate commonplace;
But sun or shower, even hail or frost
Are matters she can instantly exhaust.
Meanwhile her visit, painful though it is,
Drags on and on through mute eternities,
And though you ask the time, and yawn, and yawn,
She sits there like a stone and won't be gone.

ACASTE. Now for Adraste.
CÉLIMÈNE.   Oh, that conceited elf
Has a gigantic passion for himself;   60
He rails against the court, and cannot bear it
That none will recognize his hidden merit;
All honors given to others give offense
To his imaginary excellence.

CLITANDRE. What about young Cléon? His house, they say,
Is full of the best society, night and day.
CÉLIMÈNE. His cook has made him popular, not he:
It's Cléon's table that people come to see.
ÉLIANTE. He gives a splendid dinner, you must admit.
CÉLIMÈNE. But must he serve himself along with it?   70
For my taste, he's a most insipid dish
Whose presence sours the wine and spoils the fish.
PHILINTE. Damis, his uncle, is admired no end.
What's your opinion, Madam?
CÉLIMÈNE.   Why, he's my friend.
PHILINTE. He seems a decent fellow, and rather clever.
CÉLIMÈNE. He works too hard at cleverness, however.
I hate to see him sweat and struggle so
To fill his conversation with bons mots.
Since he's decided to become a wit
His taste's so pure that nothing pleases it;   80
He scolds at all the latest books and plays,
Thinking that wit must never stoop to praise,
That finding fault's a sign of intellect,
That all appreciation is abject,
And that by damning everything in sight
One shows oneself in a distinguished light.
He's scornful even of our conversations:

Their trivial nature sorely tries his patience;
He folds his arms, and stands above the battle,
And listens sadly to our childish prattle.   90
ACASTE. Wonderful, Madam! You've hit him off precisely.
CLITANDRE. No one can sketch a character so nicely.
ALCESTE. How bravely, Sirs, you cut and thrust at all
    These absent fools, till one by one they fall:
    But let one come in sight, and you'll at once
    Embrace the man you lately called a dunce,
    Telling him in a tone sincere and fervent
    How proud you are to be his humble servant.
CLITANDRE. Why pick on us? *Madame's* been speaking, Sir.
    And you should quarrel, if you must, with her.   100
ALCESTE. No, no, by God, the fault is yours, because
    You lead her on with laughter and applause,
    And make her think that she's the more delightful
    The more her talk is scandalous and spiteful.
    Oh, she would stoop to malice far, far less
    If no such claque approved her cleverness.
    It's flatterers like you whose foolish praise
    Nourishes all the vices of these days.
PHILINTE. But why protest when someone ridicules
    Those you'd condemn, yourself, as knaves or fools?   110
CÉLIMÈNE. Why, Sir? Because he loves to make a fuss.
    You don't expect him to agree with us,
    When there's an opportunity to express
    His heaven-sent spirit of contrariness?
    What other people think, he can't abide;
    Whatever they say, he's on the other side;
    He lives in deadly terror of agreeing;
    'Twould make him seem an ordinary being.
    Indeed, he's so in love with contradiction,
    He'll turn against his most profound conviction   120
    And with a furious eloquence deplore it,
    If only someone else is speaking for it.
ALCESTE. Go on, dear lady, mock me as you please;
    You have your audience in ecstasies.
PHILINTE. But what she says is true: you have a way
    Of bridling at whatever people say;
    Whether they praise or blame, your angry spirit
    Is equally unsatisfied to hear it.
ALCESTE. Men, Sir, are always wrong, and that's the reason

That righteous anger's never out of season; 130
All that I hear in all their conversation
Is flattering praise or reckless condemnation.
CÉLIMÈNE. But . . .
ALCESTE.   No, no, Madam, I am forced to state
That you have pleasures which I deprecate,
And that these others, here, are much to blame
For nourishing the faults which are your shame.
CLITANDRE. I shan't defend myself, Sir; but I vow
I'd thought this lady faultless until now.
ACASTE. I see her charms and graces, which are many;
But as for faults, I've never noticed any. 140
ALCESTE. I see them, Sir; and rather than ignore them,
I strenuously criticize her for them.
The more one loves, the more one should object
To every blemish, every least defect.
Were I this lady, I would soon get rid
Of lovers who approved of all I did,
And by their slack indulgence and applause
Endorsed my follies and excused my flaws.
CÉLIMÈNE. If all heart beat according to your measure,
The dawn of love would be the end of pleasure; 150
And love would find its perfect consummation
In ecstasies of rage and reprobation.
ÉLIANTE. Love, as a rule, affects men otherwise,
And lovers rarely love to criticize.
They see their lady as a charming blur,
And find all things commendable in her.
If she has any blemish, fault, or shame,
They will redeem it by a pleasing name.
The pale-faced lady's lily-white, perforce;
The swarthy one's a sweet brunette, of course; 160
The spindly lady has a slender grace;
The fat one has a most majestic pace;
The plain one, with her dress in disarray,
They classify as *beauté négligée;*
The hulking one's a goddess in their eyes,
The dwarf, a concentrate of Paradise;
The haughty lady has a noble mind;
The mean one's witty, and the dull one's kind;
The chatterbox has liveliness and verve,
The mute one has a virtuous reserve. 170

So lovers manage, in their passion's cause,
To love their ladies even for their flaws.
ALCESTE. But I still say . . .
CÉLIMÉNE.   I think it would be nice
To stroll around the gallery once or twice.
What! You're not going, Sirs?
CLITANDRE AND ACASTE.   No, Madam, no.
ALCESTE. You seem to be in terror lest they go.
Do what you will, Sirs; leave, or linger on,
But I shan't go till after you are gone.
ACASTE. I'm free to linger, unless I should perceive
Madame is tired, and wishes me to leave.   180
CLITANDRE. And as for me, I needn't go today
Until the hour of the King's *coucher.*
CÉLIMÈNE (*to Alceste*). You're joking, surely?
ALCESTE.   Not in the least; we'll see
Whether you'd rather part with them, or me.

SCENE 6. (ALCESTE, CÉLIMÈNE, ÉLIANTE, ACASTE,
PHILINTE, CLITANDRE, BASQUE)

BASQUE (*to Alceste*). Sir, there's a fellow here who bids me state
That he must see you, and that it can't wait.
ALCESTE. Tell him that I have no such pressing affairs.
BASQUE. It's a long tailcoat that this fellow wears,
With gold all over.
CÉLIMÈNE (*to Alceste*). You'd best go down and see.
Or—have him enter.

SCENE 7. (ALCESTE, CÉLIMÈNE, ÉLIANTE, ACASTE,
PHILINTE, CLITANDRE, GUARD)

ALCESTE (*confronting the Guard*). Well, what do you want with me?
Come in, Sir.
GUARD.   I've a word, Sir, for your ear.
ALCESTE. Speak it aloud, Sir; I shall strive to hear.
GUARD. The Marshals have instructed me to say
You must report to them without delay.
ALCESTE. Who? Me, Sir?
GUARD.   Yes, Sir; you.

ALCESTE.   But what do they want?

PHILINTE (*to Alceste*). To scotch your silly quarrel with Oronte.

CÉLIMÈNE (*to Philinte*). What quarrel?

PHILINTE.   Oronte and he have fallen out
>Over some verse he spoke his mind about;
>The Marshals wish to arbitrate the matter.   1G

ALCESTE. Never shall I equivocate or flatter!

PHILINTE. You'd best obey their summons; come, let's go.

ALCESTE. How can they mend our quarrel, I'd like to know?
>Am I to make a cowardly retraction,
>And praise those jingles to his satisfaction?
>I'll not recant; I've judged that sonnet rightly.
>It's bad.

PHILINTE. But you might say so more politely. . . .

ALCESTE. I'll not back down; his verses make me sick.

PHILINTE. If only you could be more politic!   20
>But come, let's go.

ALCESTE.   I'll go, I won't unsay
>A single word.

PHILINTE.   Well, let's be on our way.

ALCESTE. Till I am ordered by my lord the King
>To praise that poem, I shall say the thing
>Is scandalous, by God, and that the poet
>Ought to be hanged for having the nerve to show it.

            (*To Clitandre and Acaste, who are laughing.*)

>By heaven, Sirs, I really didn't know
>That I was being humorous.

CÉLIMÈNE.   Go, Sir, go;
>Settle your business.

ALCESTE.   I shall, and when I'm through,
>I shall return to settle things with you.   30

ACT III

SCENE 1. (CLITANDRE, ACASTE)

CLITANDRE. Dear Marquess, how contented you appear;
>All things delight you, nothing mars your cheer.
>Can you, in perfect honesty, declare
>That you've a right to be so debonair?

ACASTE. By Jove, when I survey myself, I find
  No cause whatever for distress of mind.
  I'm young and rich; I can in modesty
  Lay claim to an exalted pedigree;
  And owing to my name and my condition
  I shall not want for honors and position.   10
  Then as to courage, that most precious trait,
  I seem to have it, as was proved of late
  Upon the field of honor, where my bearing,
  They say, was very cool and rather daring.
  I've wit, of course; and taste in such perfection
  That I can judge without the least reflection,
  And at the theater, which is my delight,
  Can make or break a play on opening night,
  And lead the crowd in hisses or bravos,
  And generally be known as one who knows.   20
  I'm clever, handsome, gracefully polite;
  My waist is small, my teeth are strong and white;
  As for my dress, the world's astonished eyes
  Assure me that I bear away the prize.
  I find myself in favor everywhere,
  Honored by men, and worshipped by the fair;
  And since these things are so, it seems to me
  I'm justified in my complacency.
CLITANDRE. Well, if so many ladies hold you dear,
  Why do you press a hopeless courtship here?   30
ACASTE. Hopeless, you say? I'm not the sort of fool
  That likes his ladies difficult and cool.
  Men who are awkward, shy, and peasantish
  May pine for heartless beauties, if they wish,
  Grovel before them, bear their cruelties,
  Woo them with tears and sighs and bended knees,
  And hope by dogged faithfulness to gain
  What their poor merits never could obtain.
  For men like me, however, it makes no sense
  To love on trust, and foot the whole expense.   40
  Whatever any lady's merits be,
  I think, thank God, that I'm as choice as she;
  That if my heart is kind enough to burn
  For her, she owes me something in return;
  And that in any proper love affair
  The partners must invest an equal share.
CLITANDRE. You think, then, that our hostess favors you?

ACASTE. I've reason to believe that that is true.
CLITANDRE. How did you come to such a mad conclusion?
  You're blind, dear fellow. This is sheer delusion.   50
ACASTE. All right, then: I'm deluded and I'm blind.
CLITANDRE. Whatever put the notion in your mind?
ACASTE. Delusion.
CLITANDRE.   What persuades you that you're right?
ACASTE. I'm blind.
CLITANDRE.   But have you any proofs to cite?
ACASTE. I tell you I'm deluded.
CLITANDRE.   Have you, then,
  Received some secret pledge from Célimène?
ASCASTE. Oh, no: she scorns me.
CLITANDRE.   Tell me the truth, I beg.
ACASTE. She just can't bear me.
CLITANDRE.   Ah, don't pull my leg.
  Tell me what hope she's given you, I pray.
ACASTE. I'm hopeless, and it's you who win the day.   60
  She hates me thoroughly, and I'm so vexed
  I mean to hang myself on Tuesday next.
CLITANDRE. Dear Marquess, let us have an armistice
  And make a treaty. What do you say to this?
  If ever one of us can plainly prove
  That Célimène encourages his love,
  The other must abandon hope, and yield,
  And leave him in possession of the field.
ACASTE. Now, there's a bargain that appeals to me;
  With all my heart, dear Marquess, I agree.   70
  But hush.

SCENE 2. (CÉLIMÈNE, ACASTE, CLITANDRE)

CÉLIMÈNE. Still here?
CLITANDRE.   'Twas love that stayed our feet.
CÉLIMÈNE. I think I heard a carriage in the street.
  Whose is it? D'you know?

SCENE 3. (CÉLIMÈNE, ACASTE, CLITANDRE, BASQUE)

BASQUE.   Arsinoé is here,
  Madame.

CÈLIMÉNE. Arsinoé, you say? Oh, dear.

BASQUE. Éliante is entertaining her below.

CÉLIMÈNE. What brings the creature here, I'd like to know?

ACASTE. They say she's dreadfully prudish, but in fact
 I think her piety . . .

CÉLIMÈNE.   It's all an act.
 At heart she's worldly, and her poor success
 In snaring men explains her prudishness.
 It breaks her heart to see the beaux and gallants   10
 Engrossed by other women's charms and talents,
 And so she's always in a jealous rage
 Against the faulty standards of the age.
 She lets the world believe that she's a prude
 To justify her loveless solitude,
 And strives to put a brand of moral shame
 On all the graces that she cannot claim.
 But still she'd love a lover; and Alceste
 Appears to be the one she'd love the best.
 His visits here are poison to her pride;   20
 She seems to think I've lured him from her side;
 And everywhere, at court or in the town,
 The spiteful, envious woman runs me down.
 In short, she's just as stupid as can be,
 Vicious and arrogant in the last degree,
 And . . .

SCENE 4. (ARSINOÉ, CÉLIMÈNE, CLITANDRE, ACASTE)

CÉLIMÈNE. Ah! What happy chance has brought you here?
 I've thought about you ever so much, my dear.

ARSINOÉ. I've come to tell you something you should know.

CÉLIMÈNE. How good of you to think of doing so!

(Clitandre and Acaste go out, laughing.)

SCENE 5. (ARSINOÉ, CÉLIMÈNE)

ARSINOÉ. It's just as well those gentlemen didn't tarry.

CÉLIMÈNE. Shall we sit down?

ARSINOÉ.   That won't be necessary.
Madam, the flame of friendship ought to burn

Brightest in matters of the most concern,
And as there's nothing which concerns us more
Than honor, I have hastened to your door
To bring you, as your friend, some information
About the status of your reputation.
I visited, last night, some virtuous folk,
And, quite by chance, it was of you they spoke; 10
There was, I fear, no tendency to praise
Your light behavior and your dashing ways.
The quantity of gentlemen you see
And your by now notorious coquetry
Were both so vehemently criticized
By everyone, that I was much surprised.
Of course, I needn't tell you where I stood;
I came to your defense as best I could,
Assured them you were harmless, and declared
Your soul was absolutely unimpaired. 20
But there are some things, you must realize,
One can't excuse, however hard one tries,
And I was forced at last into conceding
That your behavior, Madam, is misleading,
That it makes a bad impression, giving rise
To ugly gossip and obscene surmise,
And that if you were more *overtly* good,
You wouldn't be so much misunderstood.
Not that I think you've been unchaste—no! no!
The saints preserve me from a thought so low! 30
But mere good conscience never did suffice:
One must avoid the outward show of vice.
Madam, you're too intelligent, I'm sure,
To think my motives anything but pure
In offering you this counsel—which I do
Out of a zealous interest in you.
CÉLIMÈNE. Madam, I haven't taken you amiss;
I'm very much obliged to you for this;
And I'll at once discharge the obligation
By telling you about *your* reputation. 40
You've been so friendly as to let me know
What certain people say of me, and so
I mean to follow your benign example
By offering you a somewhat similar sample.
The other day, I went to an affair
And found some most distinguished people there
Discussing piety, both false and true.

The conversation soon came round to you.
Alas! Your prudery and bustling zeal
Appeared to have a very slight appeal.   50
Your affectation of a grave demeanor,
Your endless talk of virtue and of honor,
The aptitude of your suspicious mind
For finding sin where there is none to find,
Your towering self-esteem, that pitying face
With which you contemplate the human race,
Your sermonizings and your sharp aspersions
On people's pure and innocent diversions—
All these were mentioned, Madam, and, in fact,
Were roundly and concertedly attacked.   60
"What good," they said, "are all these outward shows,
When everything belies her pious pose?
She prays incessantly; but then, they say,
She beats her maids and cheats them of their pay;
She shows her zeal in every holy place,
But still she's vain enough to paint her face;
She holds that naked statues are immoral,
But with a naked *man* she'd have no quarrel."
Of course, I said to everybody there
That they were being viciously unfair;   70
But still they were disposed to criticize you,
And all agreed that someone should advise you
To leave the morals of the world alone,
And worry rather more about your own.
They felt that one's self-knowledge should be great
Before one thinks of setting others straight;
That one should learn the art of living well
Before one threatens other men with hell,
And that the Church is best equipped, no doubt,
To guide our souls and root our vices out.   80
Madam, you're too intelligent, I'm sure,
To think my motives anything but pure
In offering you this counsel—which I do
Out of a zealous interest in you.
ARSINOÉ. I dared not hope for gratitude, but I
    Did not expect so acid a reply;
    I judge, since you've been so extremely tart,
    That my good counsel pierced you to the heart.
CÉLIMÈNE. Far from it, Madam. Indeed, it seems to me
    We ought to trade advice more frequently.   90
    One's vision of oneself is so defective

That it would be an excellent corrective.
If you are willing. Madam, let's arrange
Shortly to have another frank exchange
In which we'll tell each other, *entre nous,*
What you've heard tell of me, and I of you.
ARSINOÉ. Oh, people never censure you, my dear;
 It's me they criticize. Or so I hear.
CÉLIMÈNE. Madam, I think we either blame or praise
 According to our taste and length of days.   100
 There is a time of life for coquetry,
 And there's a season, too, for prudery.
 When all one's charms are gone, it is, I'm sure,
 Good strategy to be devout and pure:
 It makes one seem a little less forsaken.
 Some day, perhaps, I'll take the road you've taken:
 Time brings all things. But I have aplenty,
 And see no cause to be a prude at twenty.
ARSINOÉ. You give your age in such a gloating tone
 That one would think I was an ancient crone;   110
 We're not so far apart, in sober truth,
 That you can mock me with a boast of youth!
 Madam, you baffle me. I wish I knew
 What moves you to provoke me as you do.
CÉLIMÈNE. For my part, Madam, I should like to know
 Why you abuse me everywhere you go.
 Is it my fault, dear lady, that your hand
 Is not, alas, in very great demand?
 If men admire me, if they pay me court
 And daily make me offers of the sort   120
 You'd dearly love to have them make to you,
 How can I help it? What would you have me do?
 If what you want is lovers, please feel free
 To take as many as you can from me.
ARSINOÉ. Oh, come. D'you think the world is losing sleep
 Over the flock of lovers which you keep,
 Or that we find it difficult to guess
 What price you pay for their devotedness?
 Surely you don't expect us to suppose
 Mere merit could attract so many beaux?   130
 It's not your virtue that they're dazzled by;
 Nor is it virtuous love for which they sigh.
 You're fooling no one, Madam; the world's not blind;
 There's many a lady heaven has designed

To call men's noblest, tenderest feelings out,
Who has no lovers dogging her about;
From which it's plain that lovers nowadays
Must be acquired in bold and shameless ways,
And only pay one court for such reward
As modesty and virtue can't afford.   140
Then don't be quite so puffed up, if you please,
About your tawdry little victories;
Try, if you can, to be a shade less vain,
And treat the world with somewhat less disdain.
If one were envious of your amours,
One soon could have a following like yours;
Lovers are no great trouble to collect
If one prefers them to one's self-respect.
CÉLIMÈNE. Collect them then, my dear; I'd love to see
You demonstrate that charming theory;   150
Who knows, you might . . .
ARSINOÉ.   Now, Madam, that will do;
It's time to end this trying interview.
My coach is late in coming to your door,
Or I'd have taken leave of you before.
CÉLIMÈNE. Oh, please don't feel that you must rush away;
I'd be delighted, Madam, if you'd stay.
However, lest my conversation bore you,
Let me provide some better company for you;
This gentleman, who comes most apropos,
Will please you more than I could do, I know.   160

SCENE 6. (ALCESTE, CÉLIMÈNE, ARSINOÉ)

CÉLIMÈNE. Alceste, I have a little note to write
Which simply must go out before tonight;
Please entertain *Madame;* I'm sure that she
Will overlook my incivility.

SCENE 7. (ALCESTE, ARSINOÉ)

ARSINOÉ. Well, Sir, our hostess graciously contrives
For us to chat until my coach arrives;
And I shall be forever in her debt
For granting me this little tête-à-tête.

We women very rightly give our hearts
To men of noble character and parts,
And your especial merits, dear Alceste,
Have roused the deepest sympathy in my breast.
Oh, how I wish they had sufficient sense
At court, to recognize your excellence!   10
They wrong you greatly, Sir. How it must hurt you
Never to be rewarded for your virtue!

ALCESTE. Why, Madam, what cause have I to feel aggrieved?
What great and brilliant thing have I achieved?
What service have I rendered to the King
That I should look to him for anything?

ARSINOÉ. Not everyone who's honored by the State
Has done great services. A man must wait
Till time and fortune offer him the chance.
Your merit, Sir, is obvious at a glance,   20
And . . .

ALCESTE. Ah, forget my merit; I am not neglected.
The court, I think, can hardly be expected
To mine men's souls for merit, and unearth
Our hidden virtues and our secret worth.

ARSINOÉ. *Some* virtues, though, are far too bright to hide;
Yours are acknowledged, Sir, on every side.
Indeed, I've heard you warmly praised of late
By persons of considerable weight.

ALCESTE. This fawning age has praise for everyone,   30
And all distinctions, Madam, are undone.
All things have equal honor nowadays,
And no one should be gratified by praise.
To be admired, one only need exist,
And every lackey's on the honors list.

ARSINOÉ. I only wish, Sir, that you had your eye
On some position at court, however high;
You'd only have to hint at such a notion
For me to set the proper wheels in motion;
I've certain friendships I'd be glad to use   40
To get you any office you might choose.

ALCESTE. Madam, I fear that any such ambition
Is wholly foreign to my disposition.
The soul God gave me isn't of the sort
That prospers in the weather of a court.
It's all too obvious that I don't possess
The virtues necessary for success.

My one great talent is for speaking plain;
I've never learned to flatter or to feign;
And anyone so stupidly sincere   50
Had best not seek a courtier's career.
Outside the court, I know, one must dispense
With honors, privilege, and influence;
But still one gains the right, foregoing these,
Not to be tortured by the wish to please.
One needn't live in dread of snubs and slights,
Nor praise the verse that every idiot writes,
Nor humor silly Marquesses, nor bestow
Politic sighs on Madam So-and-So.
ARSINOÉ. Forget the court, then; let the matter rest.   60
But I've another cause to be distressed
About your present situation, Sir.
It's to your love affair that I refer.
She whom you love, and who pretends to love you,
Is, I regret to say, unworthy of you.
ALCESTE. Why, Madam? Can you seriously intend
To make so grave a charge against your friend?
ARSINOÉ. Alas, I must. I've stood aside too long
And let that lady do you grievous wrong;
But now my debt to conscience shall be paid: 70
I tell you that your love has been betrayed.
ALCESTE. I thank you, Madam; you're extremely kind.
Such words are soothing to a lover's mind.
ARSINOÉ. Yes, though she *is* my friend, I say again
You're very much too good for Célimène.
She's wantonly misled you from the start.
ALCESTE. You may be right; who knows another's heart?
But ask yourself if it's the part of charity
To shake my soul with doubts of her sincerity.
ARSINOÉ. Well, if you'd rather be a dupe than doubt her,   80
That's your affair. I'll say no more about her.
ALCESTE. Madam, you know that doubt and vague suspicion
Are painful to a man in my position;
It's most unkind to worry me this way
Unless you've some real proof of what you say.
ARSINOÉ. Sir, say no more: all doubts shall be removed,
And all that I've been saying shall be proved.
You've only to escort me home, and there
We'll look into the heart of this affair.
I've ocular evidence which will persuade you   90

Beyond a doubt, that Célimène's betrayed you.
Then, if you're saddened by that revelation,
Perhaps I can provide some consolation.

ACT IV

SCENE 1. (ÉLIANTE, PHILINTE)

PHILINTE. Madam, he acted like a stubborn child;
   I thought they never would be reconciled;
   In vain we reasoned, threatened, and appealed;
   He stood his ground and simply would not yield.
   The Marshals, I feel sure, have never heard
   An argument so splendidly absurd.
   "No gentlemen," said he, "I'll not retract.
   His verse is bad: extremely bad, in fact.
   Surely it does the man no harm to know it.
   Does it disgrace him, not to be a poet?   10
   A gentleman may be respected still,
   Whether he writes a sonnet well or ill.
   That I dislike his verse should not offend him;
   In all that touches honor, I commend him;
   He's noble, brave, and virtuous—but I fear
   He can't in truth be called a sonneteer.
   I'll gladly praise his wardrobe; I'll endorse
   His dancing, or the way he sits a horse;
   But, gentlemen, I cannot praise his rhyme.
   In fact, it ought to be a capital crime   20
   For anyone so sadly unendowed
   To write a sonnet, and read the thing aloud."
   At length he fell into a gentler mood
   And, striking a concessive attitude,
   He paid Oronte the following courtesies:
   "Sir, I regret that I'm so hard to please,
   And I'm profoundly sorry that your lyric
   Failed to provoke me to a panegyric."
   After these curious words, the two embraced,
   And then the hearing was adjourned—in haste.   30
ÉLIANTE. His conduct has been very singular lately;
   Still, I confess that I respect him greatly.

The honesty in which he takes such pride
Has—to my mind—it's noble, heroic side.
In this false age, such candor seems outrageous;
But I could wish that it were more contagious.
PHILINTE. What most intrigues me in our friend Alceste
Is the grand passion that rages in his breast.
The sullen humors he's compounded of
Should not, I think, dispose his heart to love;   40
But since they do, it puzzles me still more
That he should choose your cousin to adore.
ÉLIANTE. It does, indeed, belie the theory
That love is born of gentle sympathy,
And that the tender passion must be based
On sweet accords of temper and of taste.
PHILINTE. Does she return his love, do you suppose?
ÉLIANTE. Ah, that's a difficult question, Sir. Who knows?
How can we judge the truth of her devotion?
Her heart's a stranger to its own emotion.   50
Sometimes it thinks it loves, when no love's there;
At other times it loves quite unaware.
PHILINTE. I rather think Alceste is in for more
Distress and sorrow than he's bargained for;
Were he of my mind, Madam, his affection
Would turn in quite a different direction,
And we would see him more responsive to
The kind regard which he receives from you.
ÉLIANTE. Sir, I believe in frankness, and I'm inclined,
In matters of the heart, to speak my mind.   60
I don't oppose his love for her; indeed,
I hope with all my heart that he'll succeed,
And were it in my power, I'd rejoice
In giving him the lady of his choice.
But if, as happens frequently enough
In love affairs, he meets with a rebuff—
If Célimène should grant some rival's suit—
I'd gladly play the role of substitute;
Nor would his tender speeches please me less
Because they'd once been made without success.   70
PHILINTE. Well, Madam, as for me, I don't oppose
Your hopes in this affair; and heaven knows
That in my conversations with the man
I plead your cause as often as I can.
But if those two should marry, and so remove

All chance that he will offer you his love,
Then I'll declare my own, and hope to see
Your gracious favor pass from him to me.
In short, should you be cheated of Alceste,
I'd be most happy to be second best.   80
ÉLIANTE. Philinte, you're teasing.
PHILINTE.   Ah, Madam, never fear;
   No words of mine were ever so sincere,
   And I shall live in fretful expectation
   Till I can make a fuller declaration.

SCENE 2. (ALCESTE, ÉLIANTE, PHILINTE)

ALCESTE. Avenge me, Madam! I must have satisfaction,
   Or this great wrong will drive me to distraction!
ÉLIANTE. Why, what's the matter? What's upset you so?
ALCESTE. Madam, I've had a mortal, mortal blow.
   If Chaos repossessed the universe,
   I'd swear I'd not be shaken any worse.
   I'm ruined. . . . I can say no more. . . . My soul . . .
ÉLIANTE. Do try, Sir, to regain your self-control.
ALCESTE. Just heaven! Why were so much beauty and grace
   Bestowed on one so vicious and so base?   10
ÉLIANTE. Once more, Sir, tell us. . . .
ALCESTE.   My world has gone to wrack;
   I'm—I'm betrayed; she's stabbed me in the back:
   Yes, Célimène (who would have thought it of her?)
   Is false to me, and has another lover.
ÉLIANTE. Are you quite certain? Can you prove these things?
PHILINTE. Lovers are prey to wild imaginings
   And jealous fancies. No doubt there's some mistake. . . .
ALCESTE. Mind your own business, Sir, for heaven's sake.

(*To Éliante.*)

   Madam, I have the proof that you demand
   Here in my pocket, penned by her own hand.   20
   Yes, all the shameful evidence one could want
   Lies in this letter written to Oronte—
   Oronte! whom I felt sure she couldn't love,
   And hardly bothered to be jealous of.
PHILINTE. Still, in a letter, appearances may deceive;
   This may not be so bad as you believe.

ALCESTE. Once more I beg you, Sir, to let me be;
  Tend to your own affairs; leave mine to me.
ÉLIANTE. Compose yourself; this anguish that you feel . . .
ALCESTE. Is something, Madam, you alone can heal.   30
  My outraged heart, beside itself with grief,
  Appeals to you for comfort and relief.
  Avenge me on your cousin, whose unjust
  And faithless nature has deceived my trust;
  Avenge a crime your pure soul must detest.
ÉLIANTE. But how, Sir?
ALCESTE.   Madam, this heart within my breast
  Is yours; pray take it; redeem my heart from her,
  And so avenge me on my torturer.
  Let her be punished by the fond emotion,
  The ardent love, the bottomless devotion,   40
  The faithful worship which this heart of mine
  Will offer up to yours as to a shrine.
ÉLIANTE. You have my sympathy, Sir, in all you suffer;
  Nor do I scorn the noble heart you offer;
  But I suspect you'll soon be mollified,
  And this desire for vengeance will subside.
  When some belovèd hand has done us wrong
  We thirst for retribution—but not for long;
  However dark the deed that she's committed,
  A lovely culprit's very soon acquitted.   50
  Nothing's so stormy as an injured lover,
  And yet no storm so quickly passes over.
ALCESTE. No, Madam, no— this is no lovers' spat;
  I'll not forgive her; it's gone too far for that;
  My mind's made up; I'll kill myself before
  I waste my hopes upon her any more.
  Ah, here she is. My wrath intensifies.
  I shall confront her with her tricks and lies,
  And crush her utterly, and bring you then
  A heart no longer slave to Célimène.   60

SCENE 3. (CÉLIMÈNE, ALCESTE)

ALCESTE (*aside*). Sweet heaven, help me to control my passion.
CÉLIMÈNE (*aside*). Oh, Lord.
  (*To Alceste.*)
              Why stand there staring in that fashion?
  And what d'you mean by those dramatic sighs,

And that malignant glitter in your eyes?
ALCESTE. I mean that sins which cause the blood to freeze
    Look innocent beside your treacheries;
    That nothing Hell's or Heaven's wrath could do
    Ever produced so bad a thing as you.
CÉLIMÈNE. Your compliments were always sweet and pretty.
ALCESTE. Madam, it's not the moment to be witty.   10
    No, blush and hang your head; you've ample reason,
    Since I've the fullest evidence of your treason.
    Ah, this is what my sad heart prophesied;
    Now all my anxious fears are verified;
    My dark suspicion and my gloomy doubt
    Divined the truth, and now the truth is out.
    For all your trickery, I was not deceived;
    It was my bitter stars that I believed.
    But don't imagine that you'll go scot-free;
    You shan't misuse me with impunity.   20
    I know that love's irrational and blind;
    I know the heart's not subject to the mind,
    And can't be reasoned into beating faster;
    I know each soul is free to choose its master;
    Therefore had you but spoken from the heart,
    Rejecting my attentions from the start,
    I'd have no grievance, or at any rate
    I could complain of nothing but my fate.
    Ah, but so falsely to encourage me—
    That was a treason and a treachery   30
    For which you cannot suffer too severely,
    And you shall pay for that behavior dearly.
    Yes, now I have no pity, not a shred;
    My temper's out of hand; I've lost my head;
    Shocked by the knowledge of your double-dealings,
    My reason can't restrain my savage feelings;
    A righteous wrath deprives me of my senses,
    And I won't answer for the consequences.
CÉLIMÈNE. What does this outburst mean? Will you please explain?
    Have you, by any chance, gone quite insane?   40
ALCESTE. Yes, yes, I went insane the day I fell
    A victim to your black and fatal spell,
    Thinking to meet with some sincerity
    Among the treacherous charms that beckoned me.
CÉLIMÈNE. Pooh. Of what treachery can you complain?
ALCESTE. How sly you are, how cleverly you feign!
    But you'll not victimize me any more.

Look: here's a document you've seen before.
This evidence, which I acquired today,
Leaves you, I think, without a thing to say.   50
CÉLIMÈNE. Is this what sent you into such a fit?
ALCESTE. You should be blushing at the sight of it.
CÉLIMÈNE. Ought I to blush? I truly don't see why.
ALCESTE. Ah, now you're being bold as well as sly;
    Since there's no signature, perhaps you'll claim . . .
CÉLIMÈNE. I wrote it, whether or not it bears my name.
ALCESTE. And you can view with equanimity
    This proof of your disloyalty to me!
CÉLIMÈNE. Oh, don't be so outrageous and extreme.
ALCESTE. You take this matter lightly, it would seem.   60
    Was it no wrong to me, no shame to you,
    That you should send Oronte this billet-doux?
CÉLIMÈNE. Oronte! Who said it was for him?
ALCESTE.   Why, those
    Who brought me this example of your prose.
    But what's the difference? If you wrote the letter
    To someone else, it pleases me no better.
    My grievance and your guilt remain the same.
CÉLIMÈNE. But need you rage, and need I blush for shame,
    If this was written to a *woman* friend?
ALCESTE. Ah! Most ingenious. I'm impressed no end;   70
    And after that incredible evasion
    Your guilt is clear. I need no more persuasion.
    How dare you try so clumsy a deception?
    D'you think I'm wholly wanting in perception?
    Come, come, let's see how brazenly you'll try
    To bolster up so palpable a lie:
    Kindly construe this ardent closing section
    As nothing more than sisterly affection!
    Here, let me read it. Tell me, if you dare to,
    That this is for a woman . . .
CÉLIMÈNE.   I don't care to.   80
    What right have you to badger and berate me,
    And so highhandedly interrogate me?
ALCESTE. Now, don't be angry; all I ask of you
    Is that you justify a phrase or two . . .
CÉLIMÈNE. No, I shall not. I utterly refuse,
    And you may take those phrases as you choose.
ALCESTE. Just show me how this letter could be meant
    For a woman's eyes, and I shall be content.
CÉLIMÈNE. No, no, it's for Oronte; you're perfectly right.

I welcome his attentions with delight,   90
I prize his character and his intellect,
And everything is just as you suspect.
Come, do your worst now; give your rage free rein;
But kindly cease to bicker and complain.
ALCESTE (*aside*). Good God! Could anything be more inhuman?
  Was ever a heart so mangled by a woman?
  When I complain of how she has betrayed me,
  She bridles, and commences to upbraid me!
  She tries my tortured patience to the limit;
  She won't deny her guilt; she glories in it!   100
  And yet my heart's too faint and cowardly
  To break these chains of passion, and be free
  To scorn her as it could, and rise above
  This unrewarded, mad, and bitter love.

(*To Célimène.*)

  Ah, traitress, in how confident a fashion
  You take advantage of my helpless passion,
  And use my weakness for your faithless charms
  To make me once again throw down my arms!
  But do at least deny this black transgression;
  Take back that mocking and perverse confession;   110
  Defend this letter and your innocence,
  And I, poor fool, will aid in your defense.
  Pretend, pretend, that you are just and true,
  And I shall make myself believe in you.
CÉLIMÈNE. Oh, stop it. Don't be such a jealous dunce,
  Or I shall leave off loving you at once.
  Just why should I *pretend?* What could impel me
  To stoop so low as that? And kindly tell me
  Why, if I loved another, I shouldn't merely
  Inform you of it, simply and sincerely!   120
  I've told you where you stand, and that admission
  Should altogether clear me of suspicion;
  After so generous a guarantee,
  What right have you to harbor doubts of me?
  Since women are (from natural reticence)
  Reluctant to declare their sentiments,
  And since the honor of our sex requires
  That we conceal our amorous desires,
  Ought any man for whom such laws are broken

To question what the oracle has spoken? 130
Should he not rather feel an obligation
To trust that most obliging declaration?
Enough, now. Your suspicions quite disgust me;
Why should I love a man who doesn't trust me?
I cannot understand why I continue,
Fool that I am, to take an interest in you.
I ought to choose a man less prone to doubt,
And give you something to be vexed about.
ALCESTE. Ah, what a poor enchanted fool I am;
These gentle words, no doubt, were all a sham, 140
But destiny requires me to entrust
My happiness to you, and so I must.
I'll love you to the bitter end, and see
How false and treacherous you dare to be.
CÉLIMÈNE. No, you don't really love me as you ought.
ALCESTE. I love you more than can be said or thought;
Indeed, I wish you were in such distress
That I might show my deep devotedness.
Yes, I could wish that you were wretchedly poor,
Unloved, uncherished, utterly obscure; 150
That fate had set you down upon the earth
Without possessions, rank, or gentle birth;
Then, by the offer of my heart, I might
Repair the great injustice of your plight;
I'd raise you from the dust, and proudly prove
The purity and vastness of my love.
CÉLIMÈNE. This is a strange benevolence indeed!
God grant that I may never be in need. . . .
Ah, here's Monsieur Dubois, in quaint disguise.

SCENE 4. (CÉLIMÈNE, ALCESTE, DUBOIS)

ALCESTE. Well, why this costume? Why those frightened eyes?
What ails you?
DUBOIS.   Well, Sir, things are most mysterious.
ALCESTE. What do you mean?
DUBOIS.   I fear they're very serious.
ALCESTE. What?
DUBOIS.   Shall I speak more loudly?
ALCESTE.   Yes; speak out.
DUBOIS. Isn't there someone here, Sir?

ALCESTE.   Speak, you lout!
  Stop wasting time.
DUBOIS.   Sir, we must slip away.
ALCESTE. How's that?
DUBOIS.   We must decamp without delay.
ALCESTE. Explain yourself.
DUBOIS.   I tell you we must fly.
ALCESTE. What for?
DUBOIS.   We mustn't pause to say good-by.
ALCESTE. Now what d'you mean by all of this, you clown?   10
DUBOIS. I mean, Sir, that we've got to leave this town.
ALCESTE. I'll tear you limb from limb and joint from joint
  If you don't come more quickly to the point.
DUBOIS. Well, Sir, today a man in a black suit,
  Who wore a black and ugly scowl to boot,
  Left us a document scrawled in such a hand
  As even Satan couldn't understand.
  It bears upon your lawsuit, I don't doubt;
  But all hell's devils couldn't make it out.
ALCESTE. Well, well, go on. What then? I fail to see   20
  How this event obliges us to flee.
DUBOIS. Well, Sir, an hour later, hardly more,
  A gentleman who's often called before
  Came looking for you in an anxious way.
  Not finding you, he asked me to convey
  (Knowing I could be trusted with the same)
  The following message. . . . Now, what *was* his name?
ALCESTE. Forget his name, you idiot. What did he say?
DUBOIS. Well, it was one of your friends, Sir, anyway.
  He warned you to begone, and he suggested   30
  That if you stay, you may well be arrested.
ALCESTE. What? Nothing more specific? Think, man, think!
DUBOIS. No, Sir. He had me bring him pen and ink,
  And dashed you off a letter which, I'm sure,
  Will render things distinctly less obscure.
ALCESTE. Well—let me have it!
CÉLIMÈNE.   What *is* this all about?
ALCESTE. God knows; but I have hopes of finding out.
  How long am I to wait, you blitherer?
DUBOIS. (*after a protracted search for the letter*). I must have left it
  on your table, Sir.
ALCESTE. I ought to . . .
CÉLIMÈNE.   No, no, keep your self-control;   40
  Go find out what's behind his rigmarole.

ALCESTE. It seems that fate, no matter what I do,
    Has sworn that I may not converse with you;
    But, Madam, pray permit your faithful lover
    To try once more before the day is over.

ACT V

SCENE 1. (ALCESTE, PHILINTE)

ALCESTE. No, it's too much. My mind's made up, I tell you.
PHILINTE. Why should this blow, however hard, compel you . . .
ALCESTE. No, no, don't waste your breath in argument;
    Nothing you say will alter my intent;
    This age is vile, and I've made up my mind
    To have no further commerce with mankind.
    Did not truth, honor, decency, and the laws
    Oppose my enemy and approve my cause?
    My claims were justified in all men's sight;
    I put my trust in equity and right;   10
    Yet, to my horror and the world's disgrace,
    Justice is mocked, and I have lost my case!
    A scoundrel whose dishonesty is notorious
    Emerges from another lie victorious!
    Honor and right condone his brazen fraud,
    While rectitude and decency applaud!
    Before his smirking face, the truth stands charmed,
    And virtue conquered, and the law disarmed!
    His crime is sanctioned by a court decree!
    And not content with what he's done to me,   20
    The dog now seeks to ruin me by stating
    That I composed a book now circulating,
    A book so wholly criminal and vicious
    That even to speak its title is seditious!
    Meanwhile Oronte, my rival, lends his credit
    To the same libelous t.. ., and helps to spread it!
    Oronte! a man of honor and of rank,
    With whom I've been entirely fair and frank;
    Who sought me out and forced me, willy-nilly,
    To judge some verse I found extremely silly;   30
    And who, because I properly refused
    To flatter him, or see the truth abused,
    Abets my enemy in a rotten slander!

There's the reward of honesty and candor!
The man will hate me to the end of time
For failing to commend his wretched rhyme!
And not this man alone, but all humanity
Do what they do from interest and vanity;
They prate of honor, truth, and righteousness,
But lie, betray, and swindle nonetheless.⁣   40
Come then: man's villainy is too much to bear;
Let's leave this jungle and this jackal's lair.
Yes! treacherous and savage race of men,
You shall not look upon my face again.
PHILINTE. Oh, don't rush into exile prematurely;
Things aren't as dreadful as you make them, surely.
It's rather obvious, since you're still at large,
That people don't believe your enemy's charge.
Indeed, his tale's so patently untrue
That it may do more harm to him than you.   50
ALCESTE. Nothing could do that scoundrel any harm:
His frank corruption is his greatest charm,
And, far from hurting him, a further shame
Would only serve to magnify his name.
PHILINTE. In any case, his bald prevarication
Has done no injury to your reputation,
And you may feel secure in that regard.
As for your lawsuit, it should not be hard
To have the case reopened, and contest
This judgment . . .
ALCESTE.   No, no, let the verdict rest.   60
Whatever cruel penalty it may bring,
I wouldn't have it changed for anything.
It shows the times' injustice with such clarity
That I shall pass it down to our posterity
As a great proof and signal demonstration
Of the black wickedness of this generation.
It may cost twenty thousand francs; but I
Shall pay their twenty thousand, and gain thereby
The right to storm and rage at human evil,
And send the race of mankind to the devil.   70
PHILINTE. Listen to me . . .
ALCESTE.   Why? What can you possibly say?
Don't argue, Sir; your labor's thrown away.
Do you propose to offer lame excuses
For men's behavior and the times' abuses?

PHILINTE. No, all you say I'll readily concede:
  This is a low, conniving age indeed;
  Nothing but trickery prospers nowadays,
  And people ought to mend their shabby ways.
  Yes, man's a beastly creature; but must we then
  Abandon the society of men?   80
  Here in the world, each human frailty
  Provides occasion for philosophy,
  And that is virtue's noblest exercise;
  If honesty shone forth from all men's eyes,
  If every heart were frank and kind and just.
  What could our virtues do but gather dust
  (Since their employment is to help us bear
  The villainies of men without despair)?
  A heart well-armed with virtue can endure. . . .
ALCESTE. Sir, you're a matchless reasoner, to be sure;   90
  Your words are fine and full of cogency;
  But don't waste time and eloquence on me.
  My reason bids me go, for my own good.
  My tongue won't lie and flatter as it should;
  God knows what frankness it might next commit,
  And what I'd suffer on account of it.
  Pray let me wait for Célimène's return
  In peace and quiet. I shall shortly learn,
  By her response to what I have in view,
  Whether her love for me is feigned or true.   100
PHILINTE. Till then, let's visit Éliante upstairs.
ALCESTE. No, I am too weighed down with somber cares.
  Go to her, do; and leave me with my gloom
  Here in the darkened corner of this room.
PHILINTE. Why, that's no sort of company, my friend;
  I'll see if Éliante will not descend.

SCENE 2. (CÉLIMÈNE, ORONTE, ALCESTE)

ORONTE. Yes, Madam, if you wish me to remain
  Your true and ardent lover, you must deign
  To give me some more positive assurance.
  All this suspense is quite beyond endurance.
  If your heart shares the sweet desires of mine,
  Show me as much by some convincing sign;
  And here's the sign I urgently suggest:

That you no longer tolerate Alceste,
But sacrifice him to my love, and sever
All your relations with the man forever.   10
CÉLIMÈNE. Why do you suddenly dislike him so?
   You praised him to the skies not long ago.
ORONTE. Madam, that's not the point. I'm here to find
   Which way your tender feelings are inclined.
   Choose, if you please, between Alceste and me,
   And I shall stay or go accordingly.
ALCESTE. (*emerging from the corner*). Yes, Madam, choose; this gentle-
      man's demand
   Is wholly just, and I support his stand.

   I too am true and ardent; I too am here
   To ask you that you make your feelings clear.   20
   No more delays, now; no equivocation;
   The time has come to make your declaration.
ORONTE. Sir, I've no wish in any way to be
   An obstacle to your felicity.
ALCESTE. Sir, I've no wish to share her heart with you;
   That may sound jealous, but at least it's true.
ORONTE. If, weighing us, she leans in your direction . . .
ALCESTE. If she regards you with the least affection . . .
ORONTE. I swear I'll yield her to you there and then.
ALCESTE. I swear I'll never see her face again.   30
ORONTE. Now, Madam, tell us what we've come to hear.
ALCESTE. Madam, speak openly and have no fear.
ORONTE. Just say which one is to remain your lover.
ALCESTE. Just name one name, and it will all be over.
ORONTE. What! Is it possible that you're undecided?
ALCESTE. What! Can your feelings possibly be divided?
CÉLIMÈNE. Enough: this inquisition's gone too far:
   How utterly unreasonable you are!
   Not that I couldn't make the choice with ease;
   My heart has no conflicting sympathies;   40
   I know full well which one of you I favor,
   And you'd not see me hesitate or waver.
   But how can you expect me to reveal
   So cruelly and bluntly what I feel?
   I think it altogether too unpleasant
   To choose between two men when both are present;
   One's heart has means more subtle and more kind
   Of letting its affections be divined,
   Nor need one be uncharitably plain
   To let a lover know he loves in vain.   50

ORONTE. No, no, speak plainly; I for one can stand it.
  I beg you to be frank.
ALCESTE.   And I demand it.
  The simple truth is what I wish to know,
  And there's no need for softening the blow.
  You've made an art of pleasing everyone,
  But now your days of coquetry are done:
  You have no choice now, Madam, but to choose,
  For I'll know what to think if you refuse;
  I'll take your silence for a clear admission
  That I'm entitled to my worst suspicion.   60
ORONTE. I thank you for this ultimatum, Sir,
  And I may say I heartily concur.
CÉLIMÈNE. Really, this foolishness is very wearing:
  Must you be so unjust and overbearing?
  Haven't I told you why I must demur?
  Ah, here's Éliante; I'll put the case to her.

SCENE 3. (ÉLIANTE, PHILINTE, CÉLIMÈNE, ORONTE,
         ALCESTE)

CÉLIMÈNE. Cousin, I'm being persecuted here
  By these two persons, who, it would appear,
  Will not be satisfied till I confess
  Which one I love the more, and which the less,
  And tell the latter to his face that he
  Is henceforth banished from my company.
  Tell me, has ever such a thing been done?
ÉLIANTE. You'd best not turn to me; I'm not the one
  To back you in a matter of this kind:
  I'm all for those who frankly speak their mind.
ORONTE. Madam, you'll search in vain for a defender.
ALCESTE. You're beaten, Madam, and may as well surrender.
ORONTE. Speak, speak, you must; and end this awful strain.
ALCESTE. Or don't, and your position will be plain.
ORONTE. A single word will close this painful scene.
ALCESTE. But if you're silent, I'll know what you mean.

SCENE 4. (ARSINOÉ, CÉLIMÈNE, ÉLIANTE, ALCESTE,
         PHILINTE, ACASTE, CLITANDRE, ORONTE)

ACASTE (*to Célimène*). Madam, with all due deference, we two
  Have come to pick a little bone with you.

CLITANDRE (*to Oronte and Alceste*). I'm glad you're present, Sirs, as
  you'll soon learn,
  Our business here is also your concern.
ARSINOÉ (*to Célimène*). Madam, I visit you so soon again
  Only because of these two gentlemen,
  Who came to me indignant and aggrieved
  About a crime too base to be believed.
  Knowing your virtue, having such confidence in it,
  I couldn't think you guilty for a minute,   10
  In spite of all their telling evidence;
  And, rising above our little difference,
  I've hastened here in friendship's name to see
  You clear yourself of this great calumny.
ACASTE. Yes, Madam, let us see with what composure
  You'll manage to respond to this disclosure.
  You lately sent Clitandre this tender note.
CLITANDRE. And this one, for Acaste, you also wrote.
ACASTE (*to Oronte and Alceste*). You'll recognize this writing, Sirs, I
  think;
  The lady is so free with pen and ink   20
  That you must know it all too well, I fear.
  But listen: this is something you should hear.

  "How absurd you are to condemn my lightheartedness in society, and to accuse me of being happiest in the company of others.
Nothing could be more unjust; and if you do not come to me
instantly and beg pardon for saying such a thing, I shall never
forgive you as long as I live. Our big bumbling friend the
Viscount . . ."
  What a shame that he's not here.

  "Our big bumbling friend the Viscount, whose name stands   30
first in your complaint, is hardly a man to my taste; and ever
since the day I watched him spend three-quarters of an hour
spitting into a well, so as to make circles in the water, I have been
unable to think highly of him. As for the little Marquess . . ."
  In all modesty, gentlemen, that is I.

  "As for the little Marquess, who sat squeezing my hand for such
a long while yesterday, I find him in all respects the most trifling
creature alive; and the only things of value about him are his cape
and his sword. As for the man with the green ribbons . . ."
  (*To Alceste.*) It's your turn now, Sir.   40

  "As for the man with the green ribbons, he amuses me now and
then with his bluntness and his bearish ill-humor; but there are
many times indeed when I think him the greatest bore in the world.

And as for the sonneteer . . ."
(*To Oronte.*) Here's your helping.
    "And as for the sonneteer, who has taken it into his head to be
witty, and insists on being an author in the teeth of opinion, I
simply cannot be bothered to listen to him, and his prose wearies
me quite as much as his poetry. Be assured that I am not always
so well-entertained as you suppose; that I long for your company,   50
more than I dare to say, at all these entertainments to which people
drag me; and that the presence of those one loves is the true and
perfect seasoning to all one's pleasures."
CLITANDRE. And now for me.
    "Clitandre, whom you mention, and who so pesters me with his
saccharine speeches, is the last man on earth for whom I could
feel any affection. He is quite mad to suppose that I love him, and
so are you, to doubt that you are loved. Do come to your senses;
exchange your suppositions for his; and visit me as often as possible, to help me bear the annoyance of his unwelcome attentions."   60
It's sweet character that these letters show,
And what to call it, Madam, you well know.
Enough. We're off to make the world acquainted
With this sublime self-portrait that you've painted.
ACASTE. Madam, I'll make you no farewell oration;
    No, you're not worthy of my indignation.
    Far choicer hearts than yours, as you'll discover,
    Would like this little Marquess for a lover.

SCENE 5. (CÉLIMÈNE, ÉLIANTE, ARSINOÉ, ALCESTE,
                    ORONTE, PHILINTE)

ORONTE. So! After all those loving letters you wrote,
    You turn on me like this, and cut my throat!
    And your dissembling, faithless heart, I find,
    Has pledged itself by turns to all mankind!
    How blind I've been! But now I clearly see;
    I thank you, Madam, for enlightening me.
    My heart is mine once more, and I'm content;
    The loss of it shall be your punishment.

(*To Alceste.*)

Sir, she is yours; I'll seek no more to stand
Between your wishes and this lady's hand.

SCENE 6. (CÉLIMÈNE, ÉLIANTE, ARSINOÉ, ALCESTE, PHILINTE)

ARSINOÉ (*to Célimène*). Madam, I'm forced to speak. I'm far too stirred
  To keep my counsel, after what I've heard.
  I'm shocked and staggered by your want of morals.
  It's not my way to mix in others' quarrels;
  But really, when this fine and noble spirit,
  This man of honor and surpassing merit,
  Laid down the offering of his heart before you,
  How *could* you . . .
ALCESTE.   Madam, permit me, I implore you,
  To represent myself in this debate.
  Don't bother, please, to be my advocate.   10
  My heart, in any case, could not afford
  To give your services their due reward;
  And if I chose, for consolation's sake,
  Some other lady, 'twould not be you I'd take.
ARSINOÉ. What makes you think you could, Sir? And how dare you
  Imply that I've been trying to ensnare you?
  If you can for a moment entertain
  Such flattering fancies, you're extremely vain.
  I'm not so interested as you suppose
  In Célimène's discarded gigolos.   20
  Get rid of that absurd illusion, do.
  Women like me are not for such as you.
  Stay with this creature, to whom you're so attached;
  I've never seen two people better matched.

SCENE 7. (CÉLIMÈNE, ÉLIANTE, ALCESTE, PHILINTE)

ALCESTE (*to Célimène*). Well, I've been still throughout this exposé,
  Till everyone but me has said his say.
  Come, have I shown sufficient self-restraint?
  And may I now . . .
CÉLIMÈNE.   Yes, make your just complaint.
  Reproach me freely, call me what you will;
  You've every right to say I've used you ill.
  I've wronged you, I confess it; and in my shame
  I'll make no effort to escape the blame.
  The anger of those others I could despise;
  My guilt toward you I sadly recognize.   10

Your wrath is wholly justified, I fear;
I know how culpable I must appear,
I know all things bespeak my treachery,
And that, in short, you've grounds for hating me.
Do so; I give you leave.
ALCESTE.   Ah, traitress—how,
How should I cease to love you, even now?
Though mind and will were passionately bent
On hating you, my heart would not consent.

(To Éliante and Philinte.)

Be witness to my madness, both of you;
See what infatuation drives one to;   20
But wait; my folly's only just begun,
And I shall prove to you before I'm done
How strange the human heart is, and how far
From rational we sorry creatures are.

To Célimène.)

Woman, I'm willing to forget your shame,
And clothe your treacheries in a sweeter name;
I'll call them youthful errors, instead of crimes,
And lay the blame on these corrupting times.
My one condition is that you agree
To share my chosen fate, and fly with me   30
To that wild, trackless, solitary place
In which I shall forget the human race.
Only by such a course can you atone
For those atrocious letters; by that alone
Can you remove my present horror of you,
And make it possible for me to love you.
CÉLIMÈNE. What! I renounce the world at my young age,
And die of boredom in some hermitage?
ALCESTE. Ah, if you really loved me as you ought,
You wouldn't give the world a moment's thought;   40
Must you have me, and all the world beside?
CÉLIMÈNE. Alas, at twenty one is terrified
Of solitude. I fear I lack the force
And depth of soul to take so stern a course.
But if my hand in marriage will content you,

Why, there's a plan which I might well consent to,
And . . .
ALCESTE. No, I detest you now. I could excuse
Everything else, but since you thus refuse
To love me wholly, as a wife should do,
And see the world in me, as I in you,   50
Go! I reject your hand, and disenthrall
My heart from your enchantments, once for all.

SCENE 8. (ÉLIANTE, ALCESTE, PHILINTE)

ALCESTE (*to Éliante*). Madam, your virtuous beauty has no peer;
Of all this world you only are sincere;
I've long esteemed you highly, as you know;
Permit me ever to esteem you so,
And if I do not now request your hand,
Forgive me, Madam, and try to understand.
I feel unworthy of it; I sense that fate
Does not intend me for the married state,
That I should do you wrong by offering you
My shattered heart's unhappy residue,   10
And that in short . . .
ÉLIANTE.   Your argument's well taken:
Nor need you fear that I shall feel forsaken.
Were I to offer him this hand of mine,
Your friend Philinte, I think, would not decline.
PHILINTE. Ah, Madam, that's my heart's most cherished goal,
For which I'd gladly give my life and soul.
ALCESTE (*to Éliante and Philinte*). May you be true to all you now profess,
And so deserve unending happiness.
Meanwhile, betrayed and wronged in everything,
I'll flee this bitter world where vice is king,   20
And seek some spot unpeopled and apart
Where I'll be free to have an honest heart.
PHILINTE. Come, Madam, let's do everything we can
To change the mind of this unhappy man.

Alexander Pope

The Rape of the Lock

Alexander Pope (1688–1744) is the outstanding verse satirist in English. A friend of Swift and John Gay, and heir to Dryden, he was successful almost from the beginning. His age was the high moment of satire in English literary history. Aside from *The Rape of the Lock* (the second version of 1714 is included here), we should note his other work in this mode. His most ambitious poem, the mock-epic *Dunciad* (second version, 1743), attains a kind of grandeur in its vision of intellectual corruption. The later personal satires and the imitations of Horace show Pope writing with a new colloquial ease. *The Rape of the Lock* is discussed at some length in the introduction to this anthology.

CANTO I

What dire offense from am'rous causes springs,
What mighty contests rise from trivial things,
I sing—This verse to CARYL,[1] Muse! is due:
This, even Belinda may vouchsafe to view:
Slight is the subject, but not so the praise,
If she inspire, and he approve my lays.
    Say what strange motive, Goddess! could compel
A well-bred lord t' assault a gentle belle?
O say what stranger cause, yet unexplored,
Could make a gentle belle reject a lord?   10
In tasks so bold, can little men engage,
And in soft bosoms dwells such mighty rage?
    Sol through white curtains shot a tim'rous ray,
And oped those eyes that must eclipse the day:
Now lap-dogs give themselves the rousing shake,
And sleepless lovers, just at twelve, awake:
Thrice rung the bell, the slipper knocked the ground,
And the pressed watch[2] returned a silver sound.
Belinda still her downy pillow prest,
Her guardian sylph[3] prolonged the balmy rest: 20

---

    [1] John Caryll. He suggested that Pope write *The Rape of the Lock* in order to alleviate the conflict between the two families involved in the actual incident in which Lord Petre snipped a lock of hair from Arabella Fermor.

    [2] A repeater watch. It rang the hour when pressed by a finger.

    [3] According to the Rosicrucians the four elements of air, earth, water, and fire are inhabited respectively by Sylphs, Gnomes, Nymphs, and Salamanders. Sylphs also protected a woman's chastity.

'Twas he had summoned to her silent bed
The morning-dream that hovered o'er her head;
A youth more glitt'ring than a Birth-night beau,[4]
(That even in slumber caused her cheek to glow)
Seemed to her ear his winning lips to lay,
And thus in whispers said, or seemed to say:
    Fairest of mortals, thou distinguished care
Of thousand bright inhabitants of air!
If e'er one vision touched thy infant thought;
Of all the nurse and all the priest have taught;   30
Of airy elves by moonlight shadows seen,
The silver token, and the circled green,[5]
Or virgins visited by angel-powers,
With golden crowns and wreaths of heav'nly flowers;
Hear and believe! thy own importance know,
Nor bound thy narrow views to things below.
Some secret truths, from learned pride concealed,
To maids alone and children are revealed:
What though no credit doubting wits may give?
The fair and innocent shall still believe.   40
Know, then, unnumbered spirits round thee fly,
The light militia of the lower sky:
These, though unseen, are ever on the wing,
Hang o'er the box, and hover round the ring.[6]
Think what an equipage thou hast in air.
And view with scorn two pages and a chair.[7]
As now your own, our beings were of old,
And once inclosed in woman's beauteous mould;
Thence, by a soft transition, we repair
From earthly vehicles to these of air.   50
Think not, when woman's transient breath is fled,
That all her vanities at once are dead;
Succeeding vanities she still regards,
And though she plays no more, o'erlooks the cards.
Her joy in gilded chariot, when alive,
And love of ombre[8] after death survive.
For when the fair in all their pride expire,

---

[4] A gentleman dressed in a splendid way for a ball at court to celebrate a royal birthday.

[5] A coin or circle left by the fairies in the grass.

[6] The "box" in the theater and the fashionable "ring" or drive in Hyde Park.

[7] Sedan chair.

[8] A fashionable card game.

To their first elements their souls retire:[9]
The sprites of fiery termagants in flame
Mount up, and take a salamander's name.   60
Soft yielding minds to water glide away,
And sip, with nymphs, their elemental tea.
The graver prude sinks downward to a gnome,
In search of mischief still on earth to roam.
The light coquettes in sylphs aloft repair,
And sport and flutter in the fields of air.
   Know further yet; whoever fair and chaste
Rejects mankind, is by some sylph embraced:
For spirits, freed from mortal laws, with ease
Assume what sexes and what shapes they please.   70
What guards the purity of melting maids,
In courtly balls, and midnight masquerades,
Safe from the treach'rous friend, the daring spark,[10]
The glance by day, the whisper in the dark,
When kind occasion prompts their warm desires,
When music softens, and when dancing fires?
'Tis but their sylph, the wise celestials know,
Though honor is the word with men below.
   Some nymphs there are, too conscious of their face,
For life predestined to the gnomes' embrace.   80
These swell their prospects and exalt their pride,
When offers are disdained, and love denied:
Then gay ideas crowd the vacant brain,
While Peers, and Dukes, and all their sweeping train,
And Garters, Stars, and Coronets appear,[11]
And in soft sounds, "Your Grace" salutes their ear.
'Tis these that early taint the female soul,
Instruct the eyes of young coquettes to roll,
Teach infant-cheeks a bidden blush to know,
And little hearts to flutter at a beau.   90
   Oft, when the world imagine women stray,
The sylphs through mystic mazes guide their way,
Through all the giddy circle they pursue,
And old impertinence expel by new.
What tender maid but must a victim fall
To one man's treat, but for another's ball?
When Florio speaks what virgin could withstand,

---

[9] See note 3.

[10] A derogatory name for a showy or lively man about town.

[11] Symbols of noble rank.

If gentle Damon[12] did not squeeze her hand?
With varying vanities, from every part,
They shift the moving toyshop of their heart;   100
Where wigs with wigs, with sword-knots sword-knots strive,
Beaux banish beaux, and coaches coaches drive.
This erring mortals levity may call;
Oh blind to truth! the sylphs contrive it all.
  Of these am I, who thy protection claim,
A watchful sprite, and Ariel is my name.
Late, as I ranged the crystal wilds of air,
In the clear mirror of thy ruling star,
I saw, alas! some dread event impend,
Ere to the main this morning sun descend,   110
But heaven reveals not what, or how, or where:
Warned by the sylph, oh pious maid, beware!
This to disclose is all thy guardian can:
Beware of all, but most beware of man!
  He said; when Shock,[13] who thought she slept too long,
Leaped up, and waked his mistress with his tongue.
'Twas then, Belinda, if report say true,
Thy eyes first opened on a billet-doux,[14]
Wounds, charms, and ardors were no sooner read,
But all the vision vanished from thy head.   120
  And now, unveiled, the toilet[15] stands displayed,
Each silver vase in mystic order laid.
First, robed in white, the nymph intent adores,
With head uncovered, the cosmetic powers.
A heav'nly image in the glass appears,
To that she bends, to that her eyes she rears;
Th' inferior priestess, at her altar's side,
Trembling begins the sacred rites of Pride.
Unnumbered treasures ope at once, and here
The various off'rings of the world appear;   130
From each she nicely culls with curious toil,
And decks the goddess with the glitt'ring spoil.
This casket India's glowing gems unlocks,
And all Arabia breathes from yonder box.
The tortoise here and elephant unite,
Transformed to combs, the speckled, and the white.

---

12 Conventional names for characters in pastoral love poems.
13 A lapdog.
14 A love letter.
15 A dressing table.

Here files of pins extend their shining rows,
Puffs, powders, patches,[16] Bibles, billet-doux.
Now awful Beauty puts on all its arms;
The fair each moment rises in her charms,   140
Repairs her smiles, awakens every grace,
And calls forth all the wonders of her face;
Sees by degrees a purer blush arise,
And keener lightnings quicken in her eyes.
The busy sylphs surround their darling care,
These set the head, and those divide the hair,
Some fold the sleeve, whilst others plait the gown;
And Betty's[17] praised for labors not her own.

CANTO II

Not with more glories, in th' ethereal plain,
The Sun first rises o'er the purpled main,
Than issuing forth, the rival of his beams
Launched on the bosom of the silver Thames.
Fair nymphs, and well-drest youths around her shone,
But every eye was fixed on her alone.
On her white breast a sparkling cross she wore,
Which Jews might kiss, and infidels adore.
Her lively looks a sprightly mind disclose,
Quick as her eyes, and as unfixed as those: 10
Favors to none, to all she smiles extends;
Oft she rejects, but never once offends.
Bright as the sun, her eyes the gazers strike,
And, like the sun, they shine on all alike.
Yet graceful ease, and sweetness void of pride,
Might hide her faults, if belles had faults to hide:
If to her share some female errors fall,
Look on her face, and you'll forget 'em all.
   This nymph, to the destruction of mankind,
Nourished two locks, which graceful hung behind   20
In equal curls, and well conspired to deck
With shining ringlets the smooth iv'ry neck.
Love in these labyrinths his slaves detains,
And mighty hearts are held in slender chains.
With hairy springes[1] we the birds betray,

----

16 Beauty patches worn on the face.
17 Conventional name for a lady's maid.
 1 Snares.

Slight lines of hair surprise the finny prey,[2]
Fair tresses man's imperial race ensnare,
And beauty draws us with a single hair.
    Th' advent'rous baron the bright locks admired;
He saw, he wished, and to the prize aspired.   30
Resolved to win, he meditates the way,
By force to ravish, or by fraud betray;
For when success a lover's toil attends,
Few ask, if fraud or force attained his ends.
    For this, ere Phœbus rose, he had implored
Propitious heaven, and every power adored,
But chiefly Love—to Love an altar built,
Of twelve vast French romances, neatly gilt.
There lay three garters, half a pair of gloves;
And all the trophies of his former loves;   40
With tender billet-doux he lights the pyre,
And breathes three am'rous sighs to raise the fire.
Then prostrate falls, and begs with ardent eyes
Soon to obtain, and long possess the prize:
The powers gave ear, and granted half his prayer,
The rest, the winds dispersed in empty air.
    But now secure the painted vessel glides,
The sun-beams trembling on the floating tides:
While melting music steals upon the sky,
And softened sounds along the waters die;   50
Smooth flow the waves, the zephyrs gently play,
Belinda smiled, and all the world was gay.
All but the sylph—with careful thoughts opprest,
Th' impending woe sat heavy on his breast.
He summons strait his denizens of air;
The lucid squadrons round the sails repair:
Soft o'er the shrouds aërial whispers breathe,
That seemed but zephyrs to the train beneath.
Some to the sun their insect-wings unfold,
Waft on the breeze, or sink in clouds of gold;   60
Transparent forms, too fine for mortal sight,
Their fluid bodies half dissolved in light,
Loose to the wind their airy garments flew,
Thin glitt'ring textures of the filmy dew,
Dipt in the richest tincture of the skies,
Where light disports in ever-mingling dyes,
While every beam new transient colors flings,

---

[2] Fish.

Colors that change when'er they wave their wings.
Amid the circle on the gilded mast,
Superior by the head, was Ariel placed;   70
His purple pinions opening to the sun,
He raised his azure wand, and thus begun:
     Ye sylphs and sylphids, to your chief give ear!
Fays, fairies, genii, elves, and dæmons, hear!
Ye know the spheres and various tasks assigned
By laws eternal to th' aërial kind.
Some in the fields of purest æther play,
And bask and whiten in the blaze of day.
Some guide the course of wand'ring orbs on high,
Or roll the planets through the boundless sky.   80
Some less refined, beneath the moon's pale light
Pursue the stars that shoot athwart the night,
Or suck the mists in grosser air below,
Or dip their pinions in the painted bow,[3]
Or brew fierce tempests on the wintry main,
Or o'er the glebe[4] distil the kindly rain.
Others on earth o'er human race preside,
Watch all their ways, and all their actions guide:
Of these the chief the care of nations own,
And guard with arms divine the British throne.   90
     Our humbler province is to tend the fair,
Not a less pleasing, though less glorious care;
To save the powder from too rude a gale,
Nor let th' imprisoned essences exhale;
To draw fresh colors from the vernal flowers;
To steal from rainbows, e'er they drop in showers,
A brighter wash;[5] to curl their waving hairs,
Assist their blushes, and inspire their airs;
Nay, oft, in dreams, invention we bestow,
To change a flounce, or add a furbelow.   100
     This day, black omens threat the brightest fair,
That e'er deserved a watchful spirit's care;
Some dire disaster, or by force, or slight;
But what, or where, the fates have wrapt in night.
Whether the nymph shall break Diana's law,[6]
Or some frail china jar receive a flaw;

---

[3] Rainbow.
[4] Cultivated field.
[5] Cosmetic lotion.
[6] Diana was the goddess of chastity.

Or stain her honor, or her new brocade;
Forget her prayers, or miss a masquerade;
Or lose her heart, or necklace, at a ball;
Or whether heaven has doomed that Shock must fall.   110
Haste, then, ye spirits! to your charge repair:
The flutt'ring fan be Zephyretta's care;
The drops[7] to thee, Brillante, we consign;
And, Momentilla, let the watch be thine;
Do thou, Crispissa,[8] tend her fav'rite lock;
Ariel himself shall be the guard of Shock.
    To fifty chosen sylphs, of special note,
We trust th' important charge, the petticoat:
Oft have we known that seven-fold fence to fail,
Though stiff with hoops, and armed with ribs of whale,   120
Form a strong line about the silver bound,
And guard the wide circumference around.
    Whatever spirit, careless of his charge,
His post neglects, or leaves the fair at large,
Shall feel sharp vengeance soon o'ertake his sins,
Be stopped in vials, or transfixed with pins;
Or plunged in lakes of bitter washes lie,
Or wedged whole ages in a bodkin's eye:[9]
Gums and pomatums shall his flight restrain,
While clogged he beats his silken wings in vain;   130
Or alum styptics[10] with contracting power
Shrink his thin essence like a riveled[11] flower:
Or, as Ixion[12] fixed, the wretch shall feel
The giddy motion of the whirling mill,
In fumes of burning chocolate shall glow,
And tremble at the sea that froths below!
    He spoke; the spirits from the sails descend;
Some, orb in orb, around the nymph extend;
Some thrid the mazy ringlets of her hair;
Some hang upon the pendants of her ear: 140
With beating hearts the dire event they wait,
Anxious, and trembling for the birth of fate.

---

[7] Earrings.
[8] From Latin *crispere*, meaning to cut.
[9] Needle with a large eye.
[10] Astringents.
[11] Shrivelled.
[12] In Greek myth Ixion was tortured in the underworld by being bound on an ever-turning wheel.

CANTO III

Close by those meads, forever crowned with flowers,
Where Thames with pride surveys his rising towers,
There stands a structure of majestic frame,
Which from the neighb'ring Hampton[1] takes its name.
Here Britain's statesmen oft the fall foredoom
Of foreign tyrants and of nymphs at home;
Here thou, great ANNA! whom three realms obey,[2]
Dost sometimes counsel take—and sometimes tea.
    Hither the heroes and the nymphs resort,
To taste awhile the pleasures of a court;   10
In various talk th' instructive hours they past,
Who gave the ball, or paid the visit last;
One speaks the glory of the British Queen,
And one describes a charming Indian screen;
A third interprets motions, looks, and eyes;
At every word a reputation dies.
Snuff, or the fan, supply each pause of chat,
With singing, laughing, ogling, *and all that.*
    Meanwhile, declining from the noon of day,
The sun obliquely shoots his burning ray;   20
The hungry judges soon the sentence sign,
And wretches hang that jury-men may dine;
The merchant from th' Exchange returns in peace,
And the long labors of the toilet cease.
Belinda now, whom thirst of fame invites,
Burns to encounter two advent'rous knights,
At ombre singly to decide their doom;
And swells her breast with conquests yet to come.
Straight the three bands prepare in arms to join,
Each band the number of the sacred nine.   30
Soon as she spreads her hand, th' aërial guard
Descend, and sit on each important card:
First Ariel perched upon a Matadore,[3]
Then each, according to the rank they bore;
For sylphs, yet mindful of their ancient race,

---

[1] Hampton Court Palace outside of London.

[2] Queen of England (1702-1714). The English maintained their foolish claim to rule France as well as Great Britain and Ireland.

[3] Matadors are the three cards of highest value in ombre. They are the Spadillio (ace of spades), Manillio (deuce of spades), Basto (the ace of clubs).

Are, as when women, wondrous fond of place.
   Behold, four Kings in majesty revered,
With hoary whiskers and a forky beard;
And four fair Queens whose hands sustain a flower,
Th' expressive emblem of their softer power;   40
Four Knaves in garbs succinct,[4] trusty band,
Caps on their heads, and halberts in their hand;
And particolored troops, a shining train,
Draw forth to combat on the velvet plain.
   The skilful nymph reviews her force with care:
Let Spades be trumps! she said, and trumps they were.
   Now move to war her sable Matadores,
In show like leaders of the swarthy Moors.
Spadillio first, unconquerable lord!
Led off two captive trumps, and swept the board.   50
As many more Manillio forced to yield,
And marched a victor from the verdant field.
Him Basto followed, but his fate more hard
Gained but one trump and one plebeian card.
With his broad sabre next, a chief in years,
The hoary Majesty of Spades appears,
Puts forth one manly leg, to sight revealed,
The rest, his many-colored robe concealed.
The rebel Knave, who dares his prince engage,
Proves the just victim of his royal rage.   60
Even mighty Pam,[5] that kings and queens o'erthrew
And mowed down armies in the fights of loo,
Sad chance of war! now destitute of aid,
Falls undistinguished by the victor spade!
   Thus far both armies to Belinda yield;
Now to the Baron fate inclines the field.
His warlike Amazon her host invades,
Th' imperial consort of the crown of Spades.
The Club's black tyrant first her victim died,
Spite of his haughty mien, and barb'rous pride: 70
What boots the regal circle on his head,
His giant limbs, in state unwieldy spread;
That long behind he trails his pompous robe,
And, of all monarchs, only grasps the globe?
   The Baron now his Diamonds pours apace;

---

4 Girded up.
5 The knave of clubs. It is the highest trump card in the game of loo.

Th' embroidered King who shows but half his face,
And his refulgent Queen, with powers combined
Of broken troops an easy conquest find.
Clubs, Diamonds, Hearts, in wild disorder seen,
With throngs promiscuous strow the level green.   80
Thus when dispersed a routed army runs,
Of Asia's troops, and Afric's sable sons,
With like confusion different nations fly,
Of various habit, and of various dye,
The pierced battalions of dis-united fall,
In heaps on heaps; one fate o'erwhelms them all.
    The Knave of Diamonds tries his wily arts,
And wins (oh shameful chance!) the Queen of Hearts.
At this, the blood the virgin's cheek forsook,
A livid paleness spreads o'er all her look;   90
She sees, and trembles at th' approaching ill,
Just in the jaws of ruin, and codille.[6]
And now (as oft in some distempered State)
On one nice Trick depends the general fate.
An Ace of Hearts steps forth: The King unseen
Lurked in her hand, and mourned his captive Queen:
He springs to vengeance with an eager pace,
And falls like thunder on the prostrate Ace.
The nymph exulting fills with shouts the sky;
The walls, the woods, and long canals reply.   100
    Oh thoughtless mortals! ever blind to fate,
Too soon dejected, and too soon elate.
Sudden, these honors shall be snatched away,
And cursed for ever this victorious day.
    For lo! the board with cups and spoons is crowned,
The berries crackle, and the mill turns round;[7]
On shining altars of Japan[8] they raise
The silver lamp; the fiery spirits blaze:
From silver spouts the grateful liquors glide,
While China's earth receives the smoking tide: 110
At once they gratify their scent and taste,
And frequent cups prolong the rich repast.
Straight hover round the fair her airy band;
Some, as she sipped, the fuming liquor fanned,

---

[6] Codille is the word signifying the main player's losing hand in the game of ombre.
[7] Coffee is roasted and ground.
[8] Lacquered tables.

Some o'er her lap their careful plumes displayed,
Trembling, and conscious of the rich brocade.
Coffee (which makes the politician wise,
And see through all things with his half-shut eyes)
Sent up in vapors to the Baron's brain
New stratagems, the radiant lock to gain.   120
Ah cease, rash youth! desist ere 'tis too late,
Fear the just Gods, and think of Scylla's fate!
Changed to a bird, and sent to flit in air,
She dearly pays for Nisus[9] injured hair!
    But when to mischief mortals bend their will,
How soon they find fit instruments of ill!
Just then, Clarissa drew with tempting grace
A two-edged weapon from her shining case:
So ladies in romance assist their knight,
Present the spear, and arm him for the fight.   130
He takes the gift with rev'rence, and extends
The little engine on his fingers' ends;
This just behind Belinda's neck he spread,
As o'er the fragrant steams she bends her head.
Swift to the lock a thousand sprites repair,
A thousand wings, by turns, blow back the hair;
And thrice they switched the diamond in her ear;
Thrice she looked back, and thrice the foe drew near.
Just in that instant, anxious Ariel sought
The close recesses of the virgin's thought;   140
As on the nosegay in her breast reclined,
He watched th' ideas rising in her mind,
Sudden he viewed, in spite of all her art,
An earthly lover lurking at her heart.
Amazed, confused, he found his power expired,
Resigned to fate, and with a sigh retired.
    The Peer now spreads the glitt'ring forfex[10] wide,
T' inclose the lock; now joins it, to divide.
Even then, before the fatal engine closed,
A wretched sylph too fondly interposed;   150
Fate urged the shears, and cut the sylph in twain,
(But airy substance soon unites again)

---

[9] Scylla, daughter of Nisus, betrayed her father by cutting from his head a lock on which the whole kingdom depended and giving it to her lover, Minos. He was shocked at her deed and left her. She was turned into a bird.
[10] Scissors.

The meeting points the sacred hair dissever
From the fair head, forever, and forever!
    Then flashed the living lightning from her eyes,
And screams of horror rend th' affrighted skies.
Not louder shrieks to pitying heaven are cast,
When husbands, or when lap-dogs breathe their last;
Or when rich china vessels fall'n from high,
In glitt'ring dust and painted fragments lie!   160
Let wreaths of triumph now my temples twine,
(The victor cried) the glorious prize is mine!
While fish in streams, or birds delight in air,
Or in a coach and six the British fair,
As long as *Atalantis*[11] shall be read,
Or the small pillow grace a lady's bed,
While visits shall be paid on solemn days,
When num'rous wax-lights in bright order blaze,
While nymphs take treats, or assignations give,
So long my honor, name, and praise shall live!   170
What Time would spare, from steel receives its date,
And monuments, like men, submit to fate!
Steel could the labor of the Gods destroy,
And strike to dust th' imperial towers of Troy;
Steel could the works of mortal pride confound,
And hew triumphal arches to the ground.
What wonder then, fair nymph! thy hairs should feel,
The conq'ring force of unresisted steel?

CANTO IV

But anxious cares the pensive nymph oppressed,
And secret passions labored in her breast.
Not youthful kings in battle seized alive,
Not scornful virgins who their charms survive,
Not ardent lovers robbed of all their bliss,
Not ancient ladies when refused a kiss,
Not tyrants fierce that unrepenting die,
Not Cynthia[1] when her manteau's pinned awry,
E'er felt such rage, resentment, and despair,
As thou, sad virgin! for thy ravished hair.   10

---

11 A notorious novel concerning contemporary court scandal written by Mrs. Manley (1709).
1 Diana, goddess of the hunt and chastity. A manteau is a loose fitting robe.

For, that sad moment, when the sylphs withdrew
And Ariel weeping from Belinda flew,
Umbriel, a dusky, melancholy sprite,
As ever sullied the fair face of light,
Down to the central earth, his proper scene,
Repaired to search the gloomy Cave of Spleen.[2]
  Swift on his sooty pinions flits the gnome,
And in a vapour reached the dismal dome.
No cheerful breeze this sullen region knows,
The dreaded East is all the wind that blows.   20
Here in a grotto, sheltered close from air,
And screened in shades from day's detested glare,
She sighs forever on her pensive bed,
Pain at her side, and megrim[3] at her head.
  Two handmaids wait the throne: alike in place,
But diff'ring far in figure and in face.
Here stood Ill-nature like an ancient maid,
Her wrinkled form in black and white arrayed;
With store of prayers, for mornings, nights, and noons,
Her hand is filled; her bosom with lampoons.   30
  There Affectation, with a sickly mien,
Shows in her cheek the roses of eighteen,
Practised to lisp, and hang the head aside,
Faints into airs, and languishes with pride,
On the rich quilt sinks with becoming woe,
Wrapt in a gown, for sickness, and for show.
The fair ones feel such maladies as these,
When each new night-dress gives a new disease.
  A constant vapor[4] o'er the palace flies;
Strange phantoms rising as the mists arise;   40
Dreadful, as hermit's dreams in haunted shades,
Or bright, as visions of expiring maids.
Now glaring fiends, and snakes on rolling spires,
Pale specters, gaping tombs, and purple fires:
Now lakes of liquid gold, Elysian scenes,
And crystal domes, and angels in machines.[5]
  Unnumbered throngs on every side are seen,

---

2 Ill humor.
3 Headache.
4 Referring to "The Vapors," the affectation of peevishness or petulance on the part
of fashionable women.
5 Mechanical devices used in the theater to create sensational stage effects.

Of bodies changed to various forms of Spleen.
Here living tea-pots stand, one arm held out,
One bent; the handle this, and that the spout: 50
A pipkin[6] there, like Homer's tripod walks;[7]
Here sighs a jar, and there a goose-pie talks,[8]
Men prove with child, as powerful fancy works,
And maids turned bottles, call aloud for corks.
   Safe past the gnome through this fantastic band,
A branch of healing spleenwort in his hand.
Then thus addressed the power: "Hail, wayward Queen!
Who rule the sex to fifty from fifteen:
Parent of vapors and of female wit,
Who give th' hysteric or poetic fit,   60
On various tempers act by various ways,
Make some take physic, others scribble plays;
Who cause the proud their visits to delay,
And send the godly in a pet to pray.
A nymph there is, that all thy power disdains,
And thousands more in equal mirth maintains.
But oh! if e'er thy gnome could spoil a grace,
Or raise a pimple on a beauteous face,
Like citron-waters[9] matrons' cheeks inflame,
Or change complexions at a losing game;   70
If e'er with airy horns I planted heads,[10]
Or rumpled petticoats, or tumbled beds,
Or caus'd suspicion when no soul was rude,
Or discomposed the head-dress of a prude,
Or e'er to costive[11] lap-dog gave disease,
Which not the tears of brightest eyes could ease:
Hear me, and touch Belinda with chagrin,
That single act gives half the world the spleen."
   The goddess with a discontented air
Seems to reject him, though she grants his prayer.   80
A wondrous bag with both her hands she binds,
Like that where once Ulysses held the winds;
There she collects the force of female lungs,
Sighs, sobs, and passions, and the war of tongues.

---

6 Earthen pot.
7 In the *Iliad* Vulcan provides mobile three-legged stools for the gods.
8 Pope noted that "a Lady of distinction imagin'd herself in this condition."
9 Flavored brandy.
10 I made men believe they had horns on their heads, that is, had unfaithful wives.
11 Constipated.

A vial next she fills with fainting fears,
Soft sorrows, melting griefs, and flowing tears.
The gnome rejoicing bears her gifts away,
Spreads his black wings and slowly mounts to day.
    Sunk in Thalestris'[12] arms the nymph he found,
Her eyes dejected and her hair unbound.   90
Full o'er their heads the swelling bag he rent,
And all the Furies issued at the vent.
Belinda burns with more than mortal ire,
And fierce Thalestris fans the rising fire.
"Oh wretched maid!" she spreads her hands, and cried,
(While Hampton's echoes, "Wretched maid!" replied)
"Was it for this you took such constant care
The bodkin, comb, and essence to prepare?
For this your locks in paper durance bound,
For this with torturing irons[13] wreathed around?   100
For this with fillets[14] trained your tender head,
And bravely bore the double loads of lead?
Gods! shall the ravisher display your hair,
While the fops envy, and the ladies stare!
Honor forbid! at whose unrivaled shrine
Ease, pleasure, virtue, all our sex resign.
Methinks already I your tears survey,
Already hear the horrid things they say,
Already see you a degraded toast,
And all your honor in a whisper lost!   110
How shall I, then, your helpless fame defend?
'Twill then be infamy to seem your friend!
And shall this prize, th' inestimable prize,
Exposed through crystal to the gazing eyes,
And heightened by the diamond's circling rays,
On that rapacious hand forever blaze?
Sooner shall grass in Hyde Park Circus grow,
And wits take lodgings in the sound of Bow,[15]
Sooner let earth, air, sea, to chaos fall,
Men, monkeys, lap-dogs, parrots, perish all!"   120
    She said; then raging to Sir Plume repairs,
And bids her beau demand the precious hairs:

---

[12] The name stems from a queen of the Amazons and suggests one who is warlike.
[13] Curlers with lead strips.
[14] Bands for confining the hair somewhat like a hair net.
[15] No fashionable wit would live within the sound of the bells of St. Mary-le-Bow, a cockney area.

(Sir Plume of amber snuff-box justly vain,
And the nice conduct of a clouded cane)
With earnest eyes, and round unthinking face,
He first the snuff-box opened, then the case,
And thus broke out—"My Lord, why, what the devil?
Z—ds! damn the lock! 'fore Gad, you must be civil!
Plague on't! tis past a jest—nay prithee, pox!
Give her the hair"—he spoke, and rapped his box.   130
    "It grieves me much" (replied the Peer again)
"Who speaks so well should ever speak in vain.
But by this lock, this sacred lock I swear,
(Which never more shall join its parted hair;
Which never more its honors shall renew,
Clipped from the lovely head where late it grew)
That while my nostrils draw the vital air,
This hand, which won it, shall for ever wear."
He spoke, and speaking, in proud triumph spread
The long-contended honours of her head.   140
    But Umbriel, hateful gnome! forbears not so;
He breaks the vial whence the sorrows flow.
Then see! the nymph in beauteous grief appears,
Her eyes half-languishing, half-drowned in tears;
On her heaved bosom hung her drooping head,
Which, with a sigh, she raised; and thus she said.
    "Forever cursed be this detested day,
Which snatched my best, my fav'rite curl away!
Happy! ah ten times happy had I been,
If Hampton Court these eyes had never seen!   150
Yet am not I the first mistaken maid,
By love of courts to numerous ills betrayed.
Oh had I rather un-admired remained
In some lone isle, or distant Northern land;
Where the gilt chariot never marks the way,
Where none learn ombre, none e'er taste bohea!¹⁶
There kept my charms concealed from mortal eye,
Like roses, that in deserts bloom and die.
What moved my mind with youthful lords to roam?
Oh had I stayed, and said my prayers at home!   160
'Twas this, the morning omens seemed to tell,
Thrice from my trembling hand the patch-box fell;

---

¹⁶ Expensive tea.

The tott'ring china shook without a wind,
Nay, Poll sat mute, and Shock was most unkind!
A sylph too warned me of the threats of fate,
In mystic visions, now believed too late!
See the poor remnants of these slighted hairs!
My hands shall rend what even thy rapine spares:
These in two sable ringlets taught to break,
Once gave new beauties to the snowy neck;   170
The sister-lock now sits uncouth, alone,
And in its fellow's fate foresees its own;
Uncurled it hangs, the fatal shears demands,
And tempts once more, thy sacrilegious hands.
Oh hadst thou, cruel! been content to seize
Hairs less in sight, or any hairs but these!"

CANTO V

She said: the pitying audience melt in tears.
But Fate and Jove had stopped the Baron's ears.
In vain Thalestris with reproach assails,
For who can move when fair Belinda fails?
Not half so fixed the Trojan[1] could remain,
While Anna begged and Dido raged in vain.
Then grave Clarissa graceful waved her fan;
Silence ensued, and thus the nymph began.
    "Say why are beauties praised and honored most,
The wise man's passion, and the vain man's toast?   10
Why decked with all that land and sea afford,
Why angels called, and angel-like adored?
Why round our coaches crowd the white-gloved beaux,
Why bows the side-box from its inmost rows;
How vain are all these glories, all our pains,
Unless good sense preserve what beauty gains:
That men may say, when we the front-box grace:
'Behold the first in virtue as in face!'
Oh! if to dance all night, and dress all day,
Charmed the small-pox, or chased old-age away;   20
Who would not scorn what housewife's cares produce,
Or who would learn one earthly thing of use?

---

[1] In the *Aeneid* (IV. 9-34) Dido and her sister Anna beseech Aeneas not to leave
Carthage.

To patch, nay ogle, might become a saint,
Nor could it sure be such a sin to paint.
But since, alas! frail beauty must decay,
Curled or uncurled, since locks will turn to grey;
Since painted, or not painted, all shall fade,
And she who scorns a man, must die a maid;
What then remains but well our power to use,
And keep good-humor still whate'er we lose?   30
And trust me, dear! good-humor can prevail,
When airs, and flights, and screams, and scolding fail.
Beauties in vain their pretty eyes may roll;
Charms strike the sight, but merit wins the soul."
    So spoke the Dame, but no applause ensued;
Belinda frowned, Thalestris called her prude.
"To arms, to arms!" the fierce virago[2] cries,
And swift as lightning to the combat flies.
All side in parties, and begin th' attack;
Fans clap, silks rustle, and tough whalebones crack;   40
Heroes' and heroines' shouts confus'dly rise,
And bass and treble voices strike the skies.
No common weapons in their hands are found,
Like gods they fight, nor dread a mortal wound.
    So when bold Homer makes the gods engage,
And heavenly breasts with human passions rage;
'Gainst Pallas, Mars; Latona, Hermes arms;
And all Olympus rings with loud alarms:
Jove's thunder roars, heaven trembles all around,
Blue Neptune storms, the bellowing deeps resound: 50
Earth shakes her nodding towers, the ground gives way,
And the pale ghosts start at the flash of day!
    Triumphant Umbriel on a sconce's[3] height
Clapped his glad wings, and sat to view the fight:
Propped on their bodkin spears, the sprites survey
The growing combat, or assist the fray,
    While through the press enraged Thalestris flies,
And scatters death around from both her eyes.
A beau and witling perished in the throng,
One died in metaphor, and one in song.   60
"O cruel nymph! a living death I bear,"
Cried Dapperwit, and sunk beside his chair.

---

[2] A turbulent woman, a female warrior.
[3] Candlestick holder.

A mournful glance Sir Fopling upwards cast,
"Those eyes are made so killing"—was his last.
Thus on Maeander's flowery margin lies
Th' expiring swan, and as he sings he dies.
    When bold Sir Plume had drawn Clarissa down,
Chloe stepped in, and killed him with a frown;
She smiled to see the doughty hero slain,
But, at her smile, the beau revived again.   70
    Now Jove suspends his golden scales in air,
Weighs the men's wits against the lady's hair;
The doubtful beam long nods from side to side;
At length the wits mount up, the hairs subside.
    See, fierce Belinda on the Baron flies,
With more than usual lightning in her eyes:
Nor feared the chief th' unequal fight to try,
Who sought no more than on his foe to die.
    But this bold lord with manly strength endued,
She with one finger and a thumb subdued: 80
Just where the breath of life his nostrils drew,
A charge of snuff the wily virgin threw;
The gnomes direct, to every atom just,
The pungent grains of titillating dust.
Sudden, with starting tears each eye o'erflows,
And the high dome re-echoes to his nose.
    "Now meet thy fate," insensed Belinda cried,
And drew a deadly bodkin⁴ from her side.
(The same, his ancient personage to deck,
Her great great grandsire wore about his neck,   90
In three seal-rings; which after, melted down,
Formed a vast buckle for his widow's gown:
Her infant grandame's whistle next it grew,
The bells she jingled, and the whistle blew;
Then in a bodkin graced her mother's hairs,
Which long she wore, and now Belinda wears.)
    "Boast not my fall" (he cried) "insulting foe!
Thou by some other shalt be laid as low,
Nor think, to die dejects my lofty mind:
All that I dread is leaving you behind!
Rather than so, ah let me still survive,
And burn in Cupid's flames—but burn alive."

----

⁴ A pin shaped like a dagger.

"Restore the lock!" she cries; and all around,
"Restore the lock!" the vaulted roofs rebound.
Not fierce Othello in so loud a strain
Roared for the handkerchief that caused his pain.
But see how oft ambitious aims are crossed,
And chiefs contend till all the prize is lost!
The lock, obtained with guilt, and kept with pain,
In every place is sought, but sought in vain: 110
With such a prize no mortal must be blest,
So heaven decrees! with heaven who can contest?
    Some thought it mounted to the lunar sphere,
Since all things lost on earth are treasured there.
There heroes' wits are kept in pond'rous vases,
And beaux in snuff-boxes and tweezer-cases.
There broken vows and death-bed alms are found,
And lovers' hearts with ends of riband bound,
The courtier's promises, and sick man's prayers,
The smiles of harlots, and the tears of heirs,   120
Cages for gnats, and chains to yoke a flea,
Dried butterflies, and tomes of casuistry.[5]
    But trust the Muse—she saw it upward rise,
Though marked by none but quick, poetic eyes:
(So Rome's great founder[6] to the heavens withdrew,
To Proculus alone confessed in view)
A sudden star, it shot through liquid air,
And drew behind a radiant trail of hair.
Not Berenice's locks[7] first rose so bright,
The heavens bespangling with disheveled light.   130
The sylphs behold it kindling as it flies,
And pleased pursue its progress through the skies.
    This the beau monde[8] shall from the Mall[9] survey,
And hail with music its propitious ray.
This the blest lover shall for Venus take,
And send up vows from Rosamonda's lake.
This Partridge[10] soon shall view in cloudless skies,
When next he looks through Galileo's eyes;[11]

[5] Books of arguments concerning right and wrong conduct.
[6] Romulus.
[7] Berenice, the wife of Ptolemy III, gave a lock of her hair to the gods to ensure her husband's return from war and it turned into a constellation.
[8] The fashionable world.
[9] The Mall is a promenade in St. James' Park.
[10] A London astrologer often satirized for his ridiculous predictions.
[11] The telescope.

And hence th' egregious wizard shall foredoom
The fate of Louis, and the fall of Rome.   140
    Then cease, bright nymph! to mourn thy ravished hair,
Which adds new glory to the shining sphere!
Not all the tresses that fair head can boast,
Shall draw such envy as the lock you lost.
For, after all the murders of your eye,
When, after millions slain, yourself shall die:
When those fair suns shall set, as set they must,
And all those tresses shall be laid in dust,
This lock, the Muse shall consecrate to fame,
And 'midst the stars inscribe Belinda's name.   150

Jonathan Swift

A Modest Proposal

Jonathan Swift (1677–1745), the son of English parents, was born in Dublin a few months after the death of his father and was educated at Trinity College. After serving as secretary to Sir William Temple, he entered a varied career both as an Anglican clergyman and a political polemicist. His first important satirical works, *The Tale of a Tub* and *The Battle of the Books*, appeared in 1704. After serving first the Whig and then the Tory parties, he left the political scene in 1713 to become dean of St. Patrick's Cathedral in Dublin. There he lived the rest of his life. *Gulliver's Travels* was published in 1726. "A Modest Proposal" (1729) is the best example in English literature of sustained irony, an irony that begins with the word "Modest" in the title and continues to increase in subtlety and intensity right up to the very last sentence. Swift parodies the naive, logical humanitarian speaker intent on alleviating poverty in Ireland and attacks English absentee landlords who strip the Irish of their wealth, their self-respect, and their independence and leave them an oppressed and hungry people.

FOR PREVENTING THE CHILDREN OF POOR PEOPLE IN IRE-LAND FROM BEING A BURDEN TO THEIR PARENTS OR COUNTRY, AND FOR MAKING THEM BENEFICIAL TO THE PUBLIC

It is a melancholy object to those who walk through this great town[1] or travel in the country, when they see the streets, the roads, and cabin doors crowded with beggars of the female sex, followed by three, four, or six children, all in rags, and importuning every passenger for an alms. These mothers, instead of being able to work for their honest livelihood, are forced to employ all their time in strolling to beg sustenance for their helpless infants, who as they grow up, either turn thieves for want of work, or leave their dear native country, to fight for the Pretender in Spain,[2] or sell themselves to the Barbadoes.[3]

I think it is agreed by all parties, that this prodigious number of children in the arms, or on the backs, or at the heels of their mothers, and frequently of their fathers, is in the present deplorable state of the kingdom a very great additional grievance; and therefore whoever could find out a fair, cheap, and easy method of making these children sound and useful members of the common-wealth, would deserve so well of the public as to have his statue set up for a preserver of the nation.

---

[1] Dublin.

[2] The Pretender is James Francis Edward Stuart (1688-1766), son of King James II, who claimed the throne of England after his father was deposed during the Bloodless Revolution of 1688. His followers, known as Jacobites, were involved in an intrigue with the Spanish prime minister.

[3] They become indentured servants in Barbadoes, a British colony in the West Indies.

But my intention is very far from being confined to provide only for the children of professed beggars; it is of a much greater extent, and shall take in the whole number of infants at a certain age, who are born of parents in effect as little able to support them, as those who demand our charity in the streets.

As to my own part, having turned my thoughts, for many years, upon this important subject, and maturely weighed the several schemes of other projectors,[4] I have always found them grossly mistaken in their computation. It is true, a child just dropt from its dam may be supported by her milk for a solar year with little other nourishment, at most not above the value of two shillings, which the mother may certainly get, or the value in scraps, by her lawful occupation of begging; and it is exactly at one year old that I propose to provide for them in such a manner, as, instead of being a charge upon their parents, or the parish, or wanting food and raiment for the rest of their lives, they shall, on the contrary, contribute to the feeding and partly to the clothing of many thousands.

There is likewise another great advantage in my scheme, that it will prevent those voluntary abortions, and that horrid practice of women murdering their bastard children, alas! too frequent among us—sacrificing the poor innocent babes, I doubt, more to avoid the expense than the shame—which would move tears and pity in the most savage and inhuman breast.

The number of souls in this kingdom[5] being usually reckoned one million and a half, of these I calculate there may be about two hundred thousand couples whose wives are breeders; from which number I subtract thirty thousand couples, who are able to maintain their own children, although I apprehend there cannot be so many, under the present distresses of the kingdom; but this being granted, there will remain an hundred and seventy thousand breeders. I again subtract fifty thousand, for those women who miscarry, or whose children die by accident or disease within the year. There only remain an hundred and twenty thousand children of poor parents annually born: The question therefore is, How this number shall be reared, and provided for? which, as I have already said, under the present situation of affairs, is utterly impossible by all the methods hitherto proposed; for we can neither employ them in handicraft or agriculture; we neither build houses, (I mean in the country) nor cultivate land: They can very seldom pick up a livelihood by stealing till they arrive at six years old, except where they are of towardly parts, although, I confess, they learn the rudiments much earlier; during which time they can however be properly looked upon only as probationers; as I have been informed by a principal gentleman in the county of Cavan, who protested to me, that he never knew

---

4 Devisers of schemes.
5 Ireland.

above one or two instances under the age of six, even in a part of the kingdom so renowned for the quickest proficiency in that art.

I am assured by our merchants, that a boy or girl before twelve years old, is no saleable commodity, and even when they come to this age, they will not yield above three pounds, or three pounds and half a crown at most, on the exchange; which cannot turn to account either to the parents or kingdom, the charge of nutrient and rags having been at least four times that value.

I shall now therefore humbly propose my own thoughts, which I hope will not be liable to the least objection.

I have been assured by a very knowing American of my acquaintance in London, that a young healthy child well nursed is at a year old a most delicious nourishing and wholesome food, whether stewed, roasted, baked, or boiled; and I make no doubt that it will equally serve in a fricassee, or a ragout.[6]

I do therefore humbly offer it to publick consideration, that of the hundred and twenty thousand children, already computed, twenty thousand may be reserved for breed, whereof only one fourth part to be males; which is more than we allow to sheep, black cattle, or swine; and my reason is that these children are seldom the fruits of marriage, a circumstance not much regarded by our savages; therefore one male will be sufficient to serve four females. That the remaining hundred thousand may, at a year old, be offered in sale to the persons of quality and fortune through the kingdom; always advising the mother to let them suck plentifully in the last month, so as to render them plump and fat for a good table. A child will make two dishes at an entertainment for friends; and when the family dines alone, the fore or hind quarter will make a reasonable dish, and seasoned with a little pepper or salt will be very good boiled on the fourth day, especially in winter.

I have reckoned upon a medium that a child just born will weigh twelve pounds, and in a solar year, if tolerably nursed, increaseth to twenty-eight pounds.

I grant this food will be somewhat dear, and therefore very proper for landlords, who, as they have already devoured most of the parents, seem to have the best title to the children.

Infant's flesh will be in season throughout the year, but more plentiful in March, and a little before and after; for we are told by a grave author, an eminent French physician,[7] that fish being a prolific diet, There are more children born in Roman Catholic countries about nine months after Lent, than at any other season; therefore, reckoning a year after Lent, the markets will be more glutted than usual because the number of popish

---

[6] Meat stew.

[7] François Rabelais (ca. 1494-1553). He was a writer of comedy and satire.

infants is at least three to one in this kingdom, and therefore it will have one other collateral advantage, by lessening the number of papists among us.

I have already computed the charge of nursing a beggar's child (in which list I reckon all cottagers, laborers, and four-fifths of the farmers) to be about two shillings per annum, rags included; and I belive no gentleman would repine to give ten shillings for the carcass of a good fat child, which, as I have said, will make four dishes of excellent nutritive meat, when he hath only some particular friend or his own family to dine with him. Thus the squire will learn to be a good landlord, and grow popular among his tenants; the mother will have eight shillings net profit, and be fit for work till she produces another child.

Those who are more thrifty (as I must confess the times require) may flay the carcass, the skin of which, artificially[8] dressed, will make admirable gloves for ladies, and summer boots for fine gentlemen.

As to our city of Dublin, shambles[9] may be appointed for this purpose in the most convenient parts of it, and butchers we may be assured will not be wanting; although I rather recommend buying the children alive and dressing them hot from the knife, as we do roasting pigs.

A very worthy person, a true lover of his country, and whose virtues I highly esteem, was lately pleased in discoursing on this matter to offer a refinement upon my scheme. He said that many gentlemen of this kingdom, having of late destroyed their deer, he conceived that the want of venison might be well supplied by the bodies of young lads and maidens, not exceeding fourteen years of age nor under twelve; so great a number of both sexes in every country being now ready to starve for want of work and service; and these to be disposed of by their parents if alive, or otherwise by their nearest relations. But with due deference to so excellent a friend, and so deserving a patriot, I cannot be altogether in his sentiments; for as to the males, my American acquaintance assured me from frequent experience that their flesh was generally tough and lean, like that of our schoolboys, by continual exercise, and their taste disagreeable; and to fatten them would not answer the charge. Then as to the females, it would, I think with humble submission, be a loss to the publick, because they soon would become breeders themselves: and besides it is not improbable that some scrupulous people might be apt to censure such a practice (although indeed very unjustly) as a little bordering upon cruelty, which, I confess, hath always been with me the strongest objection against any project, how well soever intended.

But in order to justify my friend, he confessed that this expedient was put

---

8 Skillfully.
9 Slaughterhouses.

into his head by the famous Psalmanazar,[10] a native of the island Formosa, who came from thence to London, above twenty years ago, and in conversation told my friend that in his country when any young person happened to be put to death, the executioner sold the carcass to persons of quality, as a prime dainty, and that, in his time, the body of a plump girl of fifteen, who was crucified for an attempt to poison the Emperor, was sold to his Imperial Majesty's prime minister of state, and other great mandarins of the court, in joints from the gibbet, at four hundred crowns. Neither indeed can I deny, that if the same use were made of several plump young girls in this town, who, without one single groat to their fortunes, cannot stir abroad without a chair, and appear at a play-house and assemblies in foreign fineries which they never will pay for, the kingdom would not be the worse.

Some persons of a desponding spirit are in great concern about that vast number of poor people, who are aged, diseased, or maimed, and I have been desired to employ my thoughts what course may be taken, to ease the nation of so grievous an encumbrance. But I am not in the least pain upon that matter, because it is very well known, that they are every day dying, and rotting, by cold, and famine, and filth, and vermin, as fast as can be reasonably expected. And as to the younger laborers, they are now in almost as hopeful a condition. They cannot get work, and consequently pine away for want of nourishment, to a degree, that if at any time they are accidentally hired to common labour, they have not strength to perform it, and thus the country and themselves are happily delivered from the evils to come.

I have too long digressed, and therefore shall return to my subject. I think the advantages by the proposal which I have made are obvious and many, as well as of the highest importance.

For *first*, as I have already observed, it would greatly lessen the number of Papists, with whom we are yearly over-run, being the principal breeders of the nation, as well as our most dangerous enemies, and who stay at home on purpose with a design to deliver the kingdom to the Pretender, hoping to take their advantage by the absence of so many good Protestants, who have chosen rather to leave their country, than stay at home, and pay tithes against their conscience to an Episcopal curate.

Secondly, the poorer tenants will have something valuable of their own, which by law may be made liable to distress[11] and help to pay their landlord's rent, their corn and cattle being already seized, and money a thing unknown.

Thirdly, whereas the maintenance of an hundred thousand children, from two years old and upward, cannot be computed at less than ten shillings

---

10 George Psalmanazar (ca. 1679-1763) was a Frenchman who wrote a fictitious account of Formosa and was considered an imposter.

11 The seizure of goods or property for the payment of debts or other obligations.

apiece per annum, the nation's stock will be thereby increased fifty thousand pounds per annum, besides the profit of a new dish introduced to the tables of all gentlemen of fortune in the kingodm who have any refinement in taste. And the money will circulate among ourselves, the goods being entirely of our own growth and manufacture.

Fourthly, the constant breeders, beside the gain of eight shillings sterling per annum by the sale of their children, will be rid of the charge of maintaining them after the first year.

Fifthly, this food would likewise bring great custom to taverns, where the vintners will certainly be so prudent as to produce the best receipts for dressing it to perfection, and consequently have their houses frequented by all the fine gentlemen who justly value themselves upon their knowledge in good eating; and a skillful cook, who understands how to oblige his guests, will contrive to make it as expensive as they please.

Sixthly, this would be a great inducement to marriage, which all wise nations have either encouraged by rewards or enforced by laws and penalties. It would increase the care and the tenderness of mothers toward their children, when they were sure of a settlement for life to the poor babes, provided in some sort by the public, to their annual profit instead of expense. We should soon see an honest emulation among the married women, which of them could bring the fattest child to the market. Men would become as fond of their wives during the time of their pregnancy as they are now of their mares in foal, their cows in calf, their sows when they are ready to farrow; nor offer to beat or kick them (as is too frequent a practice) for fear of a miscarriage.

Many other advantages might be enumerated. For instance, the addition of some thousand carcasses in our exportation of barreled beef, the propagation of swine's flesh, and improvement in the art of making good bacon, so much wanted among us by the great destruction of pigs too frequent at our tables; which are no way comparable in taste or magnificence to a well-grown, fat, yearling child, which roasted whole will make a considerable figure at a lord mayor's feast or any other public entertainment. But this and many others I omit, being studious of brevity.

Supposing that one thousand families in this city would be constant customers for infants' flesh, besides others who might have it at merry meetings, particularly at weddings and christenings, I compute that Dublin would take off annually about twenty thousand carcasses; and the rest of the kingdom (where probably they will be sold somewhat cheaper) the remaining eighty thousand.

I can think of no one objection that will possibly be raised against this proposal, unless it should be urged that the number of people will be thereby much lessened in the kingdom. This I freely own, and 'twas indeed one principal design in offering it to the world. I desire the reader will observe that I calculate my remedy for this one individual kingdom of Ireland, and for no other that ever was, is, or, I think, ever can be upon earth. Therefore let no man talk to me of other expedients: of taxing our absentees at five shillings a pound; of using neither clothes, nor household furniture, except what is of our own growth and manufacture; of utterly rejecting the materials and instruments that promote foreign luxury; of curing the expensiveness of pride, vanity, idleness, and gaming in our women; of introducing a vein of parsimony, prudence and temperance; of learning to love our country, wherein we differ from Laplanders, and the inhabitants of Topinamboo;[12] of quitting our animosities, and factions, nor act any longer like the Jews, who were murdering one another at the very moment their city was taken;[13] of being a little cautious not to sell our country and consciences for nothing; of teaching landlords to have at least one degree of mercy towards their tenants; lastly, of putting a spirit of honesty, industry, and skill into our shopkeepers, who, if a resolution could now be taken to buy only our native goods, would immediately unite to cheat and exact upon us in the price, the measure, and the goodness, nor could ever yet be brought to make one fair proposal of just dealing, though often and earnestly invited to it.

Therefore I repeat, let no man talk to me of these and the like expedients, till he hath at least some glimpse of hope, that there will ever be some hearty and sincere attempt to put them in practice.

But as to my self, having been wearied out for many years with offering vain, idle, visionary thoughts, and at length utterly despairing of success, I fortunately fell upon this proposal, which as it is wholly new, so it hath something solid and real, of no expense and little trouble, full in our own power, and whereby we can incur no danger in disobliging England. For this kind of commodity will not bear exportation, the flesh being of too tender a consistence, to admit a long continuance in salt, although perhaps I could name a country,[14] which would be glad to eat up our whole nation without it.

After all, I am not so violently bent upon my own opinion as to reject any offer proposed by wise men, which shall be found equally innocent, cheap, easy, and effectual. But before something of that kind shall be advanced in contradiction to my scheme, and offering a better, I desire the author or authors will be pleased maturely to consider two points. First, as things now stand, how they will able to find food and raiment for a hundred thousand useless mouths and backs. And secondly, there being a

---

[12] The Laplanders love their cold country and the savages of Brazil their jungles more than the English in Ireland love that country.
[13] The siege of Jerusalem by the Romans in A.D. 70.
[14] England.

round million of creatures in human figure throughout this kingdom, whose whole subsistence put into a common stock would leave them in debt two millions of pounds sterling, adding those who are beggars by profession, to the bulk of farmers, cottagers and labourers, with their wives and children, who are beggars in effect; I desire those politicians, who dislike my overture, and may perhaps be so bold to attempt an answer, that they will first ask the parents of these mortals, whether they would not at this day think it a great happiness to have been sold for food at a year old, in the manner I prescribe, and thereby have avoided such a perpetual scene of misfortunes as they have since gone through, by the oppression of landlords, the impossibility of paying rent without money or trade, the want of common sustenance, with neither house nor clothes to cover them from the inclemencies of the weather, and the most inevitable prospect of entailing the like or greater miseries upon their breed for ever.

I profess, in the sincerity of my heart, that I have not the least personal interest in endeavoring to promote this necessary work, having no other motive than the public good of my country, by advancing our trade, providing for infants, relieving the poor, and giving some pleasure to the rich. I have no children by which I can propose to get a single penny; the youngest being nine years old, and my wife past child-bearing.

Voltaire

Candide or the Optimist

ADAPTED FROM THE TRANSLATION BY WILLIAM F. FLEMING

Voltaire (1694–1778), whose real name was François-Marie Arouet, was educated at a Jesuit school in Paris and later studied law. He attained success early with a tragedy, *Oedipe* (1718), an epic, *La Henriade* (1723), and various political satires, one of which resulted in an 11-month imprisonment. After another term in prison he spent 3 years in England, where he was impressed by the more tolerant system of government. His criticism of the French government and church was far-reaching and made prolonged residence in France difficult. At one point he lived at the court of Frederick the Great of Prussia, but eventually he settled down in Switzerland and wrote *Candide* (1759). The tale is a reaction to the optimistic philosophy of his youth, which he abandoned after the Lisbon earthquake of 1755. The form is the travel romance parodied by introducing ridiculous coincidences and situations. Despite the loose narrative structure, the plan of the book is quite rigid: 10 chapters are given to the Old World, 10 to the New, and the last 10 to the Continent again and Asia Minor. There is also the unifying device of characters turning up who seem to have vanished forever, an ironic comment since in real life those who disappear rarely return. Few satires are so devastating in their depiction of naive idealism or resist so convincingly an easy cynicism. In a letter written the same year as *Candide* Voltaire remarked that although he found the world full of "uncertainties, lies, fanaticism," he preferred "to plant, to sow, to build, and above all to be free."

Chapter I.

In the country of Westphalia, in the castle of the baron of Thunder-ten-tronckh, lived a youth whom nature had endowed with a most sweet disposition. His face was the true index of his mind. He had a solid judgment joined to the most unaffected simplicity; and hence, I presume, he had his name of Candide. The old servants of the house suspected him to have been the son of the baron's sister, by a very good sort of a gentleman of the neighborhood, whom that young lady refused to marry, because he could produce no more than seventy-one quarterings in his arms;[1] the rest of the genealogical tree belonging to the family having been lost through the injuries of time.

The baron was one of the most powerful lords in Westphalia; for his castle had not only a gate, but even windows; and his great hall was hung with tapestry. He used to hunt with his mastiffs and spaniels instead of greyhounds; his groom served him for huntsman; and the parson of the parish officiated as his grand almoner[2] He was called My Lord by all his people, and he never told a story but every one laughed at it.

My lady baroness weighed three hundred and fifty pounds and, consequently, was a person of no small consideration. She did the honors of the house with a dignity that commanded universal respect. Her daughter

---

[1] Divisions on a coat of arms to indicate the degrees of nobility.

[2] Distributor of alms at the court.

Cunégonde[3] was about seventeen years of age, fresh colored, comely, plump, and desirable. The baron's son seemed to be a youth in every respect worthy of his father. Pangloss, the tutor, was the oracle of the family, and little Candide listened to his instructions with all the simplicity natural to his age and disposition.

Master Pangloss[4] taught metaphysico-theologo-cosmolo-nigology.[5] He could prove to admiration that there is no effect without a cause; and, that in this best of all possible worlds, the baron's castle was the most magnificent of all castles, and my lady the best of all possible baronesses.

It is demonstrable, said he, that things cannot be otherwise than as they are; for as all things have been created for some end, they must necessarily be created for the best end. Observe, for instance, the nose is formed for spectacles, therefore we wear spectacles. The legs are visibly designed for stockings, accordingly we wear stockings. Stones were made to be hewn, and to construct castles, therefore My Lord has a magnificent castle; for the greatest baron in the province ought to be the best lodged. Swine were intended to be eaten, therefore we eat pork all the year round: and they, who assert that everything is *right*, do not express themselves correctly; they should say that everything is *best*.

Candide listened attentively, and believed implicitly; for he thought Cunégonde excessively handsome, though he never had the courage to tell her so. He concluded that next to the happiness of being baron of Thunder-ten-tronckh, the next was that of being Cunégonde, the next that of seeing her every day, and the last that of hearing the doctrine of Master Pangloss, the greatest philosopher of the whole province, and consequently of the whole world.

One day when Cunégonde went to take a walk in a little neighboring wood which was called a park, she saw, through the bushes, the sage Doctor Pangloss giving a lecture in experimental philosophy to her mother's chambermaid, a little brunette, very pretty, and very obedient. As Cunégonde had a great disposition for the sciences, she observed with the utmost attention the experiments, which were repeated before her eyes; she perfectly well understood the force of the doctor's reasoning upon causes and effects. She retired greatly flurried, quite pensive and filled with the desire of knowledge, imagining that she might be a *sufficient reason* for young Candide, and he for her.

On her way back, she happened to meet the young man; she blushed, he

---

[3] The name is from Kunigunde, wife of Emperor Henry II. She walked barefoot on hot irons to show her chastity.

[4] The word means literally "all-tongue."

[5] A caricature of the philosophy of Leibnitz (1646–1716) whose ideas were made popular by Alexander Pope in his *Essay on Man* and Christian Wolff (1679–1754). It stresses determinism and optimism.

blushed also; she wished him a good morning in a flattering tone, he returned the salute, without knowing what he said. The next day, as they were rising from dinner, Cunégonde and Candide slipped behind the screen. She dropped her handkerchief, the young man picked it up. She innocently took hold of his hand, and he as innocently kissed hers with a warmth, a sensibility, a grace—all very particular; their lips met; their eyes sparkled; their knees trembled; their hands strayed. The baron chanced to come by; he beheld the cause and effect, and, without hesitation, saluted Candide with some notable kicks in the behind, and drove him out of doors. Cunégonde fainted away, and as soon as she came to herself, the baroness boxed her ears. Thus a general consternation was spread over this most magnificent and most agreeable of all possible castles.

Chapter II.

WHAT BEFELL CANDIDE AMONG THE BULGARIANS.[1]

Candide, thus driven out of this terrestrial paradise, rambled a long time without knowing where he went; sometimes he raised his weeping eyes towards heaven, and sometimes he cast a melancholy look towards the magnificent castle, where dwelt the fairest of young baronesses. He laid himself down to sleep in a furrow, heartbroken and supperless. The snow fell in great flakes, and, in the morning when he awoke, he was almost frozen to death; however, he crawled to the next town, which was called Wald-berghoff-trarbkdikdorff, without a penny in his pocket, and half dead with hunger and fatigue. He took up his stand at the door of an inn. He had not been long there, before two men dressed in blue, fixed their eyes steadfastly upon him. "Comrade," said one of them to the other, "yonder is a well made young fellow, and of the right size." Upon which they made up to Candide, and with the greatest civility and politeness invited him to dine with them. "Gentlemen," replied Candide, with a most engaging modesty, "you do me much honor, but upon my word I have no money." "Money, sir!" said one of the blues to him,[2] "young persons of your appearance and merit never pay anything; why, are not you five feet five inches high?" "Yes, gentlemen, that is really my size," replied he, with a low bow. "Come then, sir, sit down along with us; we will not only pay your reckoning, but will never suffer such a clever young fellow as you to want money. Men were born to assist one another." "You are perfectly right, gentlemen," said Candide, "this is precisely the doctrine of Master

[1] Prussian troops of Frederick the Great. The word comes from the French *bougre* and the English *bugger* and suggests the pederasty of the emperor and his troops.

[2] The recruiting officers of Frederick the Great wore blue.

Pangloss; and I am convinced that everything is for the best." His generous companions next entreated him to accept a few crowns, which he readily complied with, at the same time offering them his note for the payment, which they refused, and sat down to table. "Have you not a great affection for—" "O yes! I have a great affection for the lovely Cunégonde." "Maybe so," replied one of the blues, "but that is not the question! We ask you whether you have not a great affection for the king of the Bulgarians?"[3] "For the king of the Bulgarians?" said Candide, "oh Lord! not at all, why I never saw him in my life." "Is it possible! oh, he is a most charming king! Come, we must drink his health." "With all my heart, gentlemen," says Candide, and off he tossed his glass. "Bravo!" cry the blues; "you are now the support, the defender, the hero of the Bulgarians; your fortune is made; you are in the high road to glory." So saying, they handcuffed him and carried him away to the regiment. There he was made to wheel about to the left, to draw his ramrod, to return his ramrod, to present, to fire, to march, and they gave him thirty blows with a cane; the next day he performed his exercise a little better, and they gave him but twenty; the day following he came off with ten, and was looked upon as a young fellow of surprising genius by all his comrades.

Candide was struck with amazement, and could not conceive how he came to be a hero. One fine spring morning he took it into his head to take a walk, and he marched straight forward, conceiving it to be a privilege of the human species, as well as of the brute creation, to make use of their legs how and when they pleased. He had not gone above two leagues when he was overtaken by four other heroes, six feet high, who bound him neck and heels, and carried him to a dungeon. A court-martial sat upon him, and he was asked which he liked better, to run the gauntlet thirty-six times through the whole regiment, or to have his brains blown out with a dozen musket-balls? In vain did he remonstrate to them that the human will is free, and that he chose neither; they obliged him to make a choice, and he determined, in virtue of that divine gift called free will, to run the gauntlet thirty-six times. He had gone through this discipline twice, and the regiment being composed of 2,000 men, they composed for him exactly 4,000 strokes, which laid bare all his muscles and nerves from the nape of his neck to his stern. As they were preparing to make him set out the third time, our young hero, unable to support it any longer, begged as a favor that they would be so obliging as to shoot him through the head; the favor being granted, a bandage was tied over his eyes, and he was made to kneel down. At that very instant, his Bulgarian majesty happening to pass by made a stop, and inquired into the delinquent's crime, and being a prince of great penetration, he found, from what he heard of Candide, that he was a young meta-

[3] Frederick the Great of Prussia whom Voltaire visited in 1750.

physician, entirely ignorant of the world; and therefore, out of his great
clemency, he condescended to pardon him, for which his name will be
celebrated in every journal, and in every age. A skillful surgeon cured
Candide in three weeks by means of emollients prescribed by Dioscorides.[4]
His sores were now skinned over and he was able to march, when the king
of the Bulgarians gave battle to the king of the Abarians.[5]

Chapter III.

HOW CANDIDE ESCAPED FROM THE BULGARIANS, AND
WHAT BEFELL HIM AFTERWARDS.

Never was anything so gallant, so well turned out, so brilliant, and so
finely disposed as the two armies. The trumpets, fifes, oboes, drums, and
cannon made such harmony as never was heard in hell itself. The entertainment began by a discharge of cannon, which, in the twinkling of an eye,
laid flat about six thousand men on each side. The musket bullets swept
away, out of the best of all possible worlds, nine or ten thousand scoundrels
that infested its surface. The bayonet was next the sufficient reason of the
deaths of several thousands. The whole might amount to thirty thousand
souls. Candide trembled like a philosopher, and concealed himself as well
as he could during this heroic butchery.

At length, while the two kings were causing *Te Deums* to be sung in their
camps, Candide took a resolution to go and reason somewhere else upon
causes and effects. After passing over heaps of dead or dying men, the first
place he came to was a neighboring village, in the Abarian territories,
which had been burned to the ground by the Bulgarians, according to the
laws of war. Here lay a number of old men covered with wounds, who beheld their wives dying with their throats cut, and hugging their children
to their breasts, all stained with blood. There several young virgins, whose
bodies had been ripped open, after they had satisfied the natural necessities
of the Bulgarian heroes, breathed their last; while others, half burned
in the flames, begged to be despatched out of the world. The ground about
them was covered with the brains, arms, and legs of dead men.

Candide made all the haste he could to another village, which belonged
to the Bulgarians, and there he found the heroic Abares had enacted the
same tragedy. Continuing to walk over palpitating limbs or through ruined
buildings, at length he arrived beyond the theatre of war, with a little provision in his budget and Cunégonde's image in his heart. When he arrived

---

[4] Greek physician of the first century A.D.
[5] The French, who fought the Prussians in the Seven Years' War (1756-1763).

in Holland his provision failed him; but having heard that the inhabitants
of that country were all rich and Christians, he made himself sure of being
treated by them in the same manner as at the baron's castle, before he had
been driven from there through the power of Cunégonde's bright eyes.

He asked charity of several grave-looking people, who one and all
answered him, that if he continued to follow this trade they would have him
sent to the house of correction, where he should be taught to get his bread.

He next addressed himself to a person who had just come from harangu-
ing a numerous assembly for a whole hour on the subject of charity. The
orator, squinting at him under his broad-brimmed hat, asked him sternly,
what brought him thither and whether he was for the good old cause?
"Sir," said Candide, in a submissive manner, "I conceive there can be no
effect without a cause; everything is linked together by necessity and arranged for the best. It was necessary that I should be banished from the
presence of Cunégonde; that I should afterwards run the gauntlet; and it
is necessary I should beg my bread, till I am able to get it: all this could
not have been otherwise." "Friend," said the orator, "do you hold the pope
to be Antichrist?" "Truly, I never heard anything about it," said Candide,
"but whether he is or not, I am in want of something to eat." "You deserve
neither to eat nor to drink," replied the orator, "wretch, monster, that you
are! hence! avoid my sight, nor ever come near me again while you live."
The orator's wife happened to put her head out of the window at that
instant, when, seeing a man who doubted whether the pope was Antichrist,
she discharged upon his head a pot full of . . . Good heavens, to what excess does religious zeal transport womankind!

A man who had never been christened, an honest Anabaptist[1] named
James, was witness to the cruel and ignominious treatment showed to one
of his brethren, a rational being with two feet and no wings.[2] Moved with
pity he carried him to his own house, washed him, gave him meat and
drink, and made him a present of two florins, at the same time proposing
to instruct him in his own trade of weaving Persian silks, which are fabri-
cated in Holland. Candide, filled with so much goodness, threw himself at
his feet, crying, "Now I am convinced that my Master Pangloss told me
truth when he said that everything was for the best in this world; for I am
infinitely more affected with your extraordinary generosity than with the
inhumanity of that gentleman in the black cloak, and his wife." The next
day, as Candide was walking out, he met a beggar all covered with scabs,
his eyes sunk in his head, the end of his nose eaten off, his mouth drawn

---

[1] Anabaptists were religious radicals unpopular in the sixteenth century. They settled in a free and tolerant Holland and became respectable citizens.

[2] Plato's definition of man to which he added a soul to distinguish him from a
plucked chicken.

on one side, his teeth as black as a cloak, snuffling and coughing most violently, and every time he attempted to spit dropping a tooth.

[In Chapter 4, Candide discovers that the beggar is Pangloss. The Bulgarians, he tells Candide, assaulted Cunégonde and the other members of the family and destroyed the castle. Pangloss has contracted a disease from Paquette, the Baroness' maid, but he insists that the malady is "indispensable in this best of worlds." Candide, Pangloss, and James sail for Lisbon; they arrive as a storm and an earthquake begin.]

Chapter V.

A TEMPEST, A SHIPWRECK, AN EARTHQUAKE; AND WHAT ELSE BEFELL DR. PANGLOSS, CANDIDE, AND JAMES THE ANABAPTIST.

Half the passengers, weakened and half-dead with the inconceivable anxiety and sickness which the rolling of a vessel at sea occasions through the whole human frame, were lost to all sense of the danger that surrounded them. The others made loud outcries, or went to their prayers; the sails were blown into shreds, and the masts were brought by the board. The vessel was a total wreck. Every one was busily employed, but nobody could be either heard or obeyed. The Anabaptist, being upon deck, lent a helping hand as well as the rest, when a brutish sailor gave him a blow and laid him speechless; but, with the violence of the blow the sailor himself tumbled headlong overboard, and fell upon a piece of the broken mast, which he immediately grasped. Honest James, forgetting the injury he had so lately received from him, flew to his assistance, and, with great difficulty, hauled him in again, but, in the attempt, was, by a sudden jerk of the ship, thrown overboard himself, in sight of the very fellow whom he had risked his life to save, and who took not the least notice of him in this distress. Candide, who beheld all that passed and saw his benefactor one moment rising above water, and the next swallowed up by the merciless waves, was preparing to jump after him, but was prevented by the philosopher Pangloss, who demonstrated to him that the roadstead of Lisbon had been made on purpose for the Anabaptist to be drowned there. While he was proving his argument *a priori*, the ship foundered and the whole crew perished, except Pangloss, Candide, and the sailor who had been the means of drowning the good Anabaptist. The villain swam ashore; but Pangloss and Candide reached the land upon a plank.

As soon as they had recovered from their surprise and fatigue they walked towards Lisbon; with what little money they had left they thought to save themselves from starving after having escaped drowning.

Scarcely had they ceased to lament the loss of their benefactor and set foot in the city, when they perceived that the earth trembled under their feet, and the sea, swelling and foaming in the harbor, was dashing in pieces the vessels that were riding at anchor. Large sheets of flames and cinders covered the streets and public places; the houses tottered and were tumbled topsy-turvy even to their foundations, which were themselves destroyed, and thirty thousand inhabitants of both sexes, young and old, were buried beneath the ruins.[1] The sailor, whistling and swearing, cried, "Damn it, there's something to be got here." "What can be the *sufficient reason* for this phenomenon?" said Pangloss. "It is certainly the day of judgment," said Candide. The sailor, defying death in the pursuit of plunder, rushed into the midst of the ruin, where he found some money, with which he got drunk, and, after he had slept himself sober he purchased the favors of the first good-natured wench that came in his way, amidst the ruins of demolished houses and the groans of half-buried and expiring persons. Pangloss pulled him by the sleeve; "Friend," said he, "this is not right, you trespass against the *universal reason*, and have mistaken your time." "Go to hell!" answered the other, "I am a sailor and was born at Batavia, and have trampled four times upon the crucifix in as many voyages to Japan;[2] you have come to a good hand with your *universal reason*."

In the meantime, Candide, who had been wounded by some pieces of stone that fell from the houses, lay stretched in the street, almost covered with rubbish. "For God's sake," said he to Pangloss, "get me a little wine and oil! I am dying." "This concussion of the earth is no new thing," said Pangloss, "the city of Lima in South America, experienced the same last year; the same cause, the same effects; there is certainly a train of sulphur all the way underground from Lima to Lisbon." "Nothing is more probable," said Candide; "but for the love of God a little oil and wine." "Probable!" replied the philosopher, "I maintain that the thing is demonstrable." Candide fainted away, and Pangloss fetched him some water from a neighboring spring.

The next day, in searching among the ruins, they found something to

---

[1] The Lisbon earthquake occurred on November 1, 1755. It provoked Voltaire into satirizing the doctrine of optimism held by Leibnitz. In a letter on the disaster Voltaire wrote: "One will find it difficult to divine how the laws of motion bring about such terrible disasters in *the best of all possible worlds*." Leibnitz's philosophy was an attempt "to reconcile a mechanistic interpretation of the universe with belief in a God whose ends are just and good."

[2] The Japanese forced Europeans trading with them to perform this sacrilegious act in order to discourage Christians from doing business in Japan.

eat with which they replenished their exhausted strength. After this they assisted the inhabitants in relieving the distressed and wounded. Some, whom
they had humanely assisted, gave them as good a dinner as could be expected under such terrible circumstances. The meal, indeed, was mournful,
and the company moistened their bread with their tears; but Pangloss
endeavored to comfort them under this affliction by affirming that things
could not be otherwise than they were: "For," said he, "all this is for the
very best end, for if there is a volcano at Lisbon it could be in no other spot;
and it is impossible but things should be as they are, for everything is for
the best."

By the side of the tutor sat a little man dressed in black, who was one of the
familiars[3] of the Inquisition. This person, taking him up with great complai-
sance, said, "Possibly, my good sir, you do not believe in original sin; for, if
everything is best, there could have been no such thing as the fall or punishment of man."

"I humbly ask your excellency's pardon," answered Pangloss, still more
politely; "for the fall of man and the curse consequent thereupon necessarily
entered into the system of the best of worlds." "That is as much as to say,
sir," rejoined the *familiar*, "you do not believe in free will." "Your
excellency will be so good as to excuse me," said Pangloss, "free will is
consistent with absolute necessity; for it was necessary we should be free,
for in that the will—"

Pangloss was in the midst of his proposition, when the inquisitor beckoned
to his attendant to help him to a glass of port wine.

Chapter VI.

HOW THE PORTUGUESE MADE A SUPERB AUTO-DA-FÉ
TO PREVENT ANY FUTURE EARTHQUAKES, AND
HOW CANDIDE UNDERWENT PUBLIC
FLAGELLATION

After the earthquake, which had destroyed three-fourths of the city of
Lisbon, the sages of that country could think of no means more effectual
to preserve the kingdom from utter ruin than to entertain the people with
an *auto-da-fé*,[1] it having been decided by the University of Coimbra that
the burning of a few people alive by a slow fire, and with great ceremony,
is an infallible preventive of earthquakes.

---

[3] Officers of the Inquisition.

[1] "Act of faith." Reference to a sentence imposed by the Inquisition that resulted
in the burning of a heretic at the stake.

In consequence thereof they had seized on a Biscayan for marrying his godmother, and on two Portuguese for taking out the bacon of a chicken they were eating;[2] after dinner they came and secured Doctor Pangloss, and his pupil Candide, the one for speaking his mind, and the other for seeming to approve what he had said. They were conducted to separate apartments, extremely cool, where they were never uncomfortable with the sun. Eight days afterwards they were each dressed in a *sanbenito*,[3] and their heads were adorned with paper mitres. The mitre and *sanbenito* worn by Candide were painted with flames reversed and with devils that had neither tails nor claws; but Doctor Pangloss's devils had both tails and claws, and his flames were upright. In these habits they marched in procession, and heard a very pathetic sermon, which was followed by an anthem, accompanied by bagpipes. Candide was flogged to some tune, while the anthem was being sung; the Biscayan and the two men who would not eat bacon were burned, and Pangloss was hanged, which is not a common custom at these solemnities. The same day there was another earthquake, which made most dreadful havoc.

Candide, amazed, terrified, confounded, astonished, all bloody, and trembling from head to foot, said to himself, "If this is the best of all possible worlds what are the others? If I had only been whipped, I could have put up with it, as I did among the Bulgarians; but oh my dear Pangloss! my beloved master! you greatest of philosophers! that ever I should live to see you hanged, without knowing for what! O my dear Anabaptist, you best of men, that it should be your fate to be drowned in the very harbor! O Cunégonde, you mirror of young ladies! that it should be your fate to have your body ripped open!"

He was making the best of his way from the place where he had been preached to, whipped, absolved and blessed, when he was accosted by an old woman, who said to him: "Take courage, child, and follow me."

[In Chapter 7, a strange old woman takes care of Candide. She brings him to Cunégonde, who tells him that she has survived being raped and disembowelled.]

Chapter VIII.

CUNÉGONDE'S STORY.

"I was in bed, and fast asleep, when it pleased heaven to send the Bulgarians to our delightful castle of Thunder-ten-tronckh, where they mur-

---

[2] An indication they were still faithful to Judaism.

[3] The robe of a heretic condemned to die by the Inquisition.

dered my father and brother, and cut my mother in pieces. A tall Bulgarian soldier, six feet high, perceiving that I had fainted away at this sight,
attempted to ravish me; the operation brought me to my senses. I cried, I
struggled, I bit, I scratched, I would have torn the tall Bulgarian's eyes
out, not knowing that what had happened at my father's castle was a
customary thing. The brutal soldier, enraged at my resistance, gave me a
wound in my left leg with his dagger, the mark of which I still carry."
"I long to see it," said Candide, with all imaginable simplicity. "You
shall," said Cunégonde, "but let me proceed." "Pray do," replied Candide.

She continued. "A Bulgarian captain came in, and saw me covered with
blood, and the soldier still as busy as if no one had been present. The
officer, enraged at the fellow's want of respect to him, killed him with one
stroke of his sabre as he lay upon me. This captain took care of me, had
me cured, and carried me as a prisoner of war to his quarters. I washed
what little linen he possessed and cooked his meals: he was very fond of
me, that was certain; neither can I deny that he was well made, and had
a soft, white skin, but he was very stupid, and knew nothing of philosophy: it might plainly be perceived that he had not been educated under
Doctor Pangloss. In three months, having gambled away all his money,
and having grown tired of me, he sold me to a Jew, named Don Issachar,
who traded in Holland and Portugal, and was passionately fond of women.
This Jew showed me great kindness, in hopes of gaining favors; but he
never could prevail on me to yield. A modest woman may be once
ravished; but her virtue is greatly strengthened thereby. In order to
make sure of me, he brought me to this country-house you now see. I
had hitherto believed that nothing could equal the beauty of the castle of
Thunder-ten-tronckh; but I found I was mistaken.

"The Grand Inquisitor saw me one day at Mass, eyed me all through the
service, and when it was over, sent to let me know he wanted to speak
with me about some private business. I was conducted to his palace,
where I told him all my story; he represented to me how much it was
beneath a person of my birth to belong to a circumcised Israelite. He
caused a proposal to be made to Don Issachar, that he should resign me
to his lordship. Don Issachar, being the court banker, and a man of
credit, was not easy to be prevailed upon. His lordship threatened him
with an *auto-da-fé*; in short, my Jew was frightened into a compromise, and
it was agreed between them, that the house and myself belong to both
in common; that the Jew should have Monday, Wednesday, and the
Sabbath to himself; and the inquisitor the other four days of the week.
This agreement has subsisted almost six months; but not without several
contests, whether the space from Saturday night to Sunday morning
belonged to the old or the new law. For my part, I have hitherto with-

stood them both, and truly I believe this is the very reason why they are both so fond of me.

"At length to turn aside the scourge of earthquakes, and to intimidate Don Issachar, my lord inquisitor was pleased to celebrate an *auto-da-fé*. He did me the honor to invite me to the ceremony. I had a very good seat; and refreshments of all kinds were offered the ladies between mass and the execution. I was dreadfully shocked at the burning of the two Jews, and the honest Biscayan who married his godmother; but how great was my surprise, my consternation, and concern, when I beheld a figure so like Pangloss, dressed in a *sanbenito* and mitre! I rubbed my eyes, I looked at him attentively. I saw him hanged, and I fainted away: scarce had I recovered my senses, when I saw you stripped of clothing; this was the height of horror, grief, and despair. I must confess to you for a truth, that your skin is whiter and more blooming that that of the Bulgarian captain. This spectacle worked me up to a pitch of distraction. I screamed out, and would have said, 'hold, barbarian!' but my voice failed me; and indeed my cries would have signified nothing. After you had been severely whipped, how is it possible, I said to myself, that the lovely Candide and the sage Pangloss should be at Lisbon, the one to receive a hundred lashes, and the other to be hanged by order of my lord inquisitor, of whom I am so great a favorite? Pangloss deceived me most cruelly in saying that everything is for the best.

"Thus agitated and perplexed, now distracted and lost, now half dead with grief, I revolved in my mind the murder of my father, mother, and brother, committed before my eyes; the insolence of the rascally Bulgarian soldier; the wound he gave me in the groin; my servitude; my being a cook-wench to my Bulgarian captain; my subjection to the hateful Jew, and my cruel inquisitor; the hanging of Doctor Pangloss; the *Miserere* sung while you were being whipped; and particularly the kiss I gave you behind the screen, the last day I ever beheld you. I returned thanks to God for having brought you to the place where I was, after so many trials. I charged the old woman who attends me to bring you here as soon as was convenient. She has punctually executed my orders, and I now enjoy the inexpressible satisfaction of seeing you, hearing you, and speaking to you. But you must certainly be half dead with hunger; I myself have a great inclination to eat, and so let us sit down to supper."

Upon this the two lovers immediately placed themselves at table, and, after having supped, they returned to seat themselves again on the magnificent sofa already mentioned, when Señor Don Issachar, one of the masters of the house, entered unexpectedly; it was the Sabbath day, and he came to enjoy his privilege, and sigh forth his passion at the feet of the fair Cunégonde.

[In Chapter 9, Candide kills Don Issachar, but in self-defense. Soon the Inquisitor enters and Candide likewise kills him. Candide, Cunégonde, and the old woman escape to Avecena in the mountains.]

Chapter X.

IN WHAT DISTRESS CANDIDE, CUNÉGONDE, AND THE
OLD WOMAN ARRIVE AT CADIZ; AND OF THEIR
EMBARKATION.

"Who could it be that has robbed me of my gold coins and jewels?" exclaimed Cunégonde, all bathed in tears. "How shall we live? What shall we do? Where shall I find inquisitors and Jews who can give me more?" "Alas!" said the old woman, "I have a shrewd suspicion of a reverend father, who lay last night in the same inn with us at Badajoz; God forbid I should condemn any one wrongfully, but he came into our room twice, and he set off in the morning long before us." "Alas!" said Candide, "Pangloss has often demonstrated to me that the goods of this world are common to all men and that everyone has an equal right to the enjoyment of them; but, according to these principles, the father ought to have left us enough to carry us to the end of our journey. Have you nothing at all left, my dear Cunégonde?" "Not a maravedi," replied she. "What is to be done then?" said Candide. "Sell one of the horses," replied the old woman, "I will get up behind Cunégonde, though I have only one cushion to ride on, and we shall reach Cadiz."

In the same inn there was a Benedictine friar, who bought the horse very cheap. Candide, Cunégonde, and the old woman, after passing through Lucina, Chellas, and Lebrixa, arrived at length at Cadiz. A fleet was then getting ready, and troops were assembling in order to induce the reverend fathers, Jesuits of Paraguay, who were accused of having excited one of the Indian tribes in the neighborhood of the town of the Holy Sacrament, to revolt against the kings of Spain and Portugal. Candide, having been in the Bulgarian service, performed the military exercise of that nation before the general of this little army with so intrepid an air and with such agility and expedition that he received the command of a company of infantry. Being now made a captain, he embarked with Cunégonde, the old woman, two valets, and the two Andalusian horses, which had belonged to the Grand Inquisitor of Portugal.

During their voyage they amused themselves with many profound reasonings on poor Pangloss's philosophy. "We are now going into another world, and surely it must be there that everything is for the best; for I must confess that we have had some little reason to complain of what passes in ours, both as to the physical and moral part. Though I have a sincere love for you," said Cunégonde, "yet I still shudder at the reflection of what I have seen and experienced." "All will be well," replied Candide, "the sea of this new world is already better than our European seas: it is smoother, and the winds blow more regularly." "God grant it," said Cunégonde, "but I have met with such terrible treatment in this world that I have almost lost all hopes of a better one." Cried the old woman: "If you had suffered half what I have, there might be some reason for complaining." Cunégonde could scarce refrain from laughing at the good old woman, and thought it droll enough to pretend to a greater share of misfortunes than her own. "Alas! my good dame," said she, "unless you had been ravished by two Bulgarians, had received two deep wounds in your belly, had seen two of your own castles demolished, had lost two fathers, and two mothers, and seen both of them barbarously murdered before your eyes, and to sum up all, had two lovers whipped at an *auto-da-fé*, I cannot see how you could be more unfortunate than I. Add to this, though born a baroness, and bearing seventy-two quarterings, I have been reduced to the station of a cook-wench." "Miss," replied the old woman, "you do not know my family as yet; but if I were to show you my rear end, you would not talk in this manner, but suspend your judgment." This speech raised an extreme curiosity in Candide and Cunégonde; and the old woman continued as follows:

Chapter XI.

THE HISTORY OF THE OLD WOMAN.

"I have not always been blear-eyed. My nose did not always touch my chin; nor was I always a servant. You must know that I am the daughter of Pope Urban X[1] and of the princess of Palestrina. Till the age of fourteen I was brought up in a castle, compared with which all the castles of the German barons would not have been fit for stabling, and one of my robes would have bought half the province of Westphalia. I grew up and improved in beauty, wit, and every graceful accomplishment; and in the midst of pleasures, homage, and the highest expectations. I already began to inspire the men with love. My breast began to take its right form, and such a breast! white, firm, and formed like that of Venus of Medici; my

---

[1] Voltaire's posthumous note: "Behold the author's extreme discretion. Up to now there has never been a Pope called Urban X. The author fears to present a known Pope with a bastard daughter. What circumspection! What delicacy of conscience."

eyebrows were as black as jet, and as for my eyes, they darted flames and eclipsed the lustre of the stars, as I was told by the poets of our part of the world. My maids, when they dressed and undressed me, used to fall into an ecstasy in viewing me before and behind: and all the men longed to be in their places.

"I was contracted in marriage to a sovereign prince of Massa Carara. Such a prince! as handsome as myself, sweet-tempered, agreeable, witty, and madly in love with me. I loved him, too, as our sex generally do for the first time, with rapture and idolatry. The nuptials were prepared with surprising pomp and magnificence; the ceremony was attended with feasts, tournaments, and comic operas: all Italy composed sonne's in my praise, though not one of them was tolerable. I was on the point of reaching the summit of bliss, when an old marchioness, who had been mistress to the prince, my husband, invited him to drink chocolate. In less than two hours after he returned from the visit, he died of most terrible convulsions. But this is a mere trifle. My mother, distracted to the highest degree, and yet less afflicted than I, determined to leave for some time so fatal a place. As she had a very fine estate in the neighborhood of Gaeta, we embarked on board a galley, which was gilded like the high altar of St. Peter's at Rome. In our passage we were boarded by a Salé rover. Our men defended themselves like true Pope's soldiers; they flung themselves upon their knees, laid down their arms, and begged the corsair to give them absolution *in articulo mortis*.[2]

"The Moors presently stripped us as bare as ever we were born. My mother, my maids of honor, and myself, were treated in the same manner. It is amazing how quick these gentry are at undressing people. But what surprised me most was that they made a rude sort of surgical examination of parts of the body which are sacred to the functions of nature. I thought it a very strange kind of ceremony; for thus we are generally apt to judge of things when we have not seen the world. I afterwards learned that it was to discover if we had any diamonds concealed. This practice has been established since time immemorial among those civilized nations that sail the seas. I was informed that the religious knights of Malta never fail to make this search whenever any Moors of either sex fall into their hands. It is a part of the law of nations from which they never deviate.

"I need not tell you how great a hardship it was for a young princess and her mother to be made slaves and carried to Morocco. You may easily imagine what we must have suffered on board a corsair. My mother was still extremely handsome, our maids of honor, and even our common waiting-women, had more charms than were to be found in all Africa. As for myself, I was enchanting; I was beauty itself, and then I had my virginity.

---

[2] At the point of death.

But, alas! I did not retain it long; this precious flower, which had been reserved for the lovely prince of Massa Carara, was cropped by the captain of the Moorish vessel, who was a hideous Negro, and thought he did me infinite honor. Indeed, both the princess of Palestrina and I must have had very strong constitutions to undergo all the hardships and violences we suffered before our arrival at Morocco. But I will not detain you any longer with such common things; they are hardly worth mentioning.

"Upon our arrival at Morocco we found that kingdom deluged with blood. Fifty sons of the emperor Muley Ishmael[3] were each at the head of a party. This produced fifty civil wars of blacks against blacks, of tawnies against tawnies, and of mulattoes against mulattoes. In short, the whole empire was one continual scene of carnage.

"No sooner were we landed than a party of blacks, of a contrary faction to that of my captain, came to rob him of his booty. Next to the money and jewels, we were the most valuable things he had. I witnessed on this occasion such a battle as you never beheld in your cold European climates. The northern nations have not that fermentation in their blood, nor that raging lust for women that is so common in Africa. The natives of Europe seem to have their veins filled with milk only; but fire and vitriol circulate in those of the inhabitants of Mount Atlas and the neighboring provinces. They fought with the fury of the lions, tigers, and serpents of their country, to decide who should have us. A Moor seized my mother by the right arm, while my captain's lieutenant held her by the left; another Moor laid hold of her by the right leg, and one of our corsairs led her by the other. In this manner almost all of our women were dragged by four soldiers. My captain kept me concealed behind him, and with his drawn scimitar cut down everyone who opposed him; at length I saw all our Italian women and my mother mangled and torn in pieces by the monsters who contended for them. The captives, my companions, the Moors who took us, the soldiers, the sailors, the blacks, the whites, the mulattoes, and lastly, my captain himself, were all slain, and I remained alone expiring upon a heap of dead bodies. Similar barbarous scenes were transacted every day over the whole country, which is of three hundred leagues in extent, and yet they never missed the five stated times of prayer enjoined by their prophet Mahomet.

"I disengaged myself with great difficulty from such a heap of corpses, and crawled to a large orange-tree that stood on the bank of a neighboring brook, where I fell down exhausted with fatigue, and overwhelmed with horror, despair, and hunger. My senses being overpowered, I fell asleep, or rather seemed to be in a trance. Thus I lay in a state of weakness and insensibility between life and death, when I felt myself pressed

---

[3] The tyrannical sultan of Morocco who died in 1762.

by something that moved up and down upon my body. This brought me to myself. I opened my eyes, and saw a white man, who sighed and muttered these words between his teeth, *O che sciagura d'essere senza coglioni!*[4]

Chapter XII.

THE ADVENTURES OF THE OLD WOMAN CONTINUED.

"Astonished and delighted to hear my native language, and no less surprised at the young man's words, I told him that there were far greater misfortunes in the world than what he complained of. And to convince him of it, I gave him a short history of the horrible disasters that had happened to me; and as soon as I had finished, I fainted again. He carried me in his arms to a neighboring cottage, where he had me put to bed, procured me something to eat, waited on me with the greatest attention, comforted me, caressed me, told me that he had never seen anything so perfectly beautiful as myself, and that he had never so much regretted the loss of what no one could restore to him. 'I was born at Naples,' said he, 'where they make eunuchs of thousands of children every year; some die of the operation; some acquire voices far beyond the most tuneful of your ladies; and others are sent to govern states and empires. I underwent this operation very successfully, and was one of the singers in the princess of Palestrina's chapel.' 'How,' cried I, 'in my mother's chapel!' 'The princess of Palestrina, your mother!' cried he, bursting into a flood of tears. 'Is it possible you should be the beautiful young princess whom I had the care of bringing up till she was six years old, and who at that tender age promised to be as fair as I now behold you?' 'I am the same,' I replied. 'My mother lies about a hundred yards from here cut in pieces and buried under a heap of dead bodies.'

"I then related to him all that had happened to me, and he in return acquainted me with all his adventures, and how he had been sent to the court of the king of Morocco by a Christian prince to conclude a treaty with that monarch; in consequence of which he was to be furnished with military stores and ships to enable him to destroy the commerce of other Christian governments. 'I have executed my commission,' said the eunuch; 'I am going to take ship at Ceuta, and I'll take you along with me to Italy. *Ma che sciagura d'essere senza coglioni!*'

"I thanked him with tears of joy, but, instead of taking me with him into Italy, he carried me to Algiers, and sold me to the dey[1] of that prov-

---

[4] "Oh, what an affliction to be a eunuch!"
[1] Governor.

ince. I had not been long a slave when the plague, which had made the tour of Africa, Asia, and Europe, broke out at Algiers with redoubled fury. You have seen an earthquake; but tell me, Miss, have your ever had the plague?"

"Never," answered the young baroness.

"If you had ever had it," continued the old woman, "you would own an earthquake was a trifle to it. It is very common in Africa; I was seized with it. Figure to yourself the distressed condition of the daughter of a pope, only fifteen years old, and who in less than three months had felt the miseries of poverty and slavery; had been debauched almost every day; had beheld her mother cut into four quarters; had experienced the scourges of famine and war; and was now dying of the plague at Algiers. I did not, however, die of it; but my eunuch, and the dey, and almost the whole seraglio of Algiers, were swept off.

"As soon as the first fury of this dreadful pestilence was over, a sale was made of the dey's slaves. I was purchased by a merchant who carried me to Tunis. This man sold me to another merchant, who sold me again to another at Tripoli; from Tripoli I was sold to Alexandria, from Alexandria to Smyrna, and from Smyrna to Constantinople. After many changes, I at length became the property of an aga of the janizaries,[2] who, soon after I came into his possession, was ordered away to the defence of Azov,[3] then besieged by the Russians.

"The aga, being very fond of women, took his whole seraglio with him, and lodged us in a small fort, with two black eunuchs and twenty soldiers for our guard. Our army made a great slaughter among the Russians; but they soon returned us the compliment. Azov was taken by storm, and the enemy spared neither age, sex, nor condition, but put all to the sword, and laid the city in ashes. Our little fort alone held out; they resolved to reduce us by famine. The twenty janizaries, who were left to defend it, had bound themselves by an oath never to surrender the place. Being reduced to the extremity of famine, they found themselves obliged to kill our two eunuchs, and eat them rather than violate their oath. But this horrible repast soon failing them, they next determined to devour the women.

"We had a very pious and humane man, who gave them a most excellent sermon on this occasion, exhorting them not to kill us all at once. 'Cut off a single rumpsteak from each of these ladies,' said he, 'and you will fare extremely well; if you are under the necessity of having recourse to the same expedient again, you will find the like supply a few days hence. Heaven will approve of so charitable an action, and work your deliverance.'

"By the force of this eloquence he easily persuaded them, and all of us

---

[2] Bodyguards of the Turkish sultan.
[3] A town at the mouth of the Don River in Russia.

underwent the operation. The man applied the same balsam as they do to children after circumcision. We were all ready to give up the ghost.

"The janizaries had scarcely time to finish the meal with which we had supplied them, when the Russians attacked the place by means of flat-bottom boats, and not a single janizary escaped. The Russians paid no regard to the condition we were in; but there are French surgeons in all parts of the world, and one of them took us under his care and cured us. I shall never forget, while I live, that as soon as my wounds were perfectly healed he made me certain proposals. In general, he desired us all to be of good cheer, assuring us that the like had happened in many sieges; and that it was perfectly agreeable to the laws of war.

"As soon as my companions were in a condition to walk, they were sent to Moscow. As for me, I fell to the lot of a boyar,[4] who put me to work in his garden, and gave me twenty lashes a day. But this nobleman having about two years afterwards been broken alive upon the wheel, with about thirty others, for some court intrigues, I took advantage of the event, and made my escape. I travelled over a great part of Russia. I was a long time an inn-keeper's servant at Riga, then at Rostock, Wismar, Leipzig, Cassel, Utrecht, Leyden, The Hague, and Rotterdam: I have grown old in misery and disgrace living with only one buttock, and having in perpetual remembrance that I am a Pope's daughter. I have been a hundred times upon the point of killing myself, but still I was fond of life. This ridiculous weakness is, perhaps, one of the dangerous principles implanted in our nature. For what can be more absurd than to persist in carrying a burden of which we wish to be eased? to detest, and yet to strive to preserve our existence? In a word, to caress the serpent that devours us and hug him close to our bosoms till he has gnawed into our hearts?

"In the different countries which it has been my fate to traverse, and at the many inns where I have been a servant, I have observed a prodigious number of people who held their existence in abhorrence, and yet I never knew more than twelve who voluntarily put an end to their misery; namely, three Negroes, four Englishmen, as many Genevese, and a German professor, named Robek.[5] My last place was with a Jew, Don Issachar, who placed me near your person, my fair lady; to whose fortunes I have attached myself, and have been more concerned with your adventures than with my own. I should never have even mentioned the latter to you had you not irked me with an account of sufferings; and if it was not customary to tell stories on board a ship in order to pass away the time. In short, my dear Miss, I have a great deal of knowledge and experience in the world;

---

[4] Russian nobleman.

[5] John Robek (1672–1739) wrote a defense of suicide and drowned himself at the age of sixty-seven.

therefore take my advice: divert yourself, and prevail upon each passenger to tell his story, and if there is one of them all that has not cursed his existence many times, and said to himself over and over again that he was the most wretched of mortals, I give you leave to throw me head long into the sea."

[In Chapter 13, after their arrival at Buenos Aires they call on the governor. He proposes to Cunégonde and the old woman tells her to accept. Candide must leave, because it is known that he killed the Inquisitor.]

Chapter XIV.

THE RECEPTION CANDIDE AND CACAMBO MET WITH AMONG THE JESUITS IN PARAGUAY.

Candide had brought with him from Cadiz such a footman as one often meets with on the coasts of Spain and in the colonies. He was the fourth part of a Spaniard, of a mongrel breed, and born in Tucuman.[1] He had successively gone through the profession of a singing boy, sexton, sailor, monk, peddler, soldier, and lackey. His name was Cacambo; he had a great affection for his master, because his master was a very good man. He immediately saddled the two Andalusian horses. "Come my good master, let us follow the old woman's advice, and make all the haste we can from this place without staying to look behind us." Candide burst into a flood of tears: "O, my dear Cunégonde, must I then be compelled to quit you just as the governor was going to honor us with his presence at our wedding! Cunégonde, so long lost and found again, what will now become of you?" "Lord!" said Cacambo, "she must do as well as she can; women are never at a loss. God takes care of them, and so let us make the best of our way." "But where will you carry me? where can we go? what can we do without Cunégonde?" cried the disconsolate Candide. "By St. James of Compostella," said Cacambo, "you were going to fight against the Jesuits of Paraguay; now let us go and fight for them; I know the road perfectly well; I'll conduct you to their kingdom; they will be delighted with a captain that understands the Bulgarian drill; you will certainly make a prodigious fortune. If we cannot succeed in this world we may in another. It is a great pleasure to see new objects and perform new exploits."

"Then you have been in Paraguay?" asked Candide. "Indeed I have," replied Cacambo; "I was a servant in the college of the Assumption, and

---

[1] Argentine province.

am as well acquainted with the new government of Los Padres[2] as I am with the streets of Cadiz. Oh, it is an admirable government, that is most certain! The kingdom is at present upwards of three hundred leagues in diameter, and divided into thirty provinces; the fathers there are masters of everything, and the people have no money at all; this you must allow is the masterpiece of justice and reason. For my part, I see nothing so divine as the good fathers, who wage war in this part of the world against the troops of Spain and Portugal, at the same time that they hear the con- fessions of those very princes in Europe; who kill Spaniards in America and send them to heaven in Madrid. This pleases me exceedingly, but let us push forward; you are going to see the happiest and most fortunate of all mortals. How charmed will those fathers be to hear that a captain who understands the Bulgarian military drill is coming among them."

As soon as they reached the first barrier, Cacambo called to the advance guard, and told them that a captain wanted to speak to my lord, the general. Notice was given to the main guard, and immediately a Paraguayan officer ran to throw himself at the feet of the commandant to impart this news to him. Candide and Cacambo were immediately disarmed, and their two Andalusian horses were seized. The two strangers were conducted between two files of musketeers; the commandant was at the further end with a three-cornered cap on his head, his gown tucked up, a sword by his side, and a half-pike in his hand; he made a sign, and instantly twenty-four soldiers drew up round the newcomers. A sergeant told them that they must wait, the commandant could not speak to them; and that the reverend father provincial did not suffer any Spaniard to open his mouth but in his presence, or to stay above three hours in the province. "And where is the reverend father provincial?" said Cacambo. "He has just come from Mass and is at the parade," replied the sergeant, "and in about three hours' time you may possibly have the honor to kiss his spurs." "But," said Cacambo, "the captain, who, as well as myself, is perishing of hunger, is no Spaniard, but a German; therefore, pray, might we not be permitted to break our fast till we can be introduced to his reverence?"

The sergeant immediately went and acquainted the commandant with what he heard. "God be praised," said the reverend commandant, "since he is a German I will hear what he has to say; let him be brought to my arbor."

Immediately they conducted Candide to a beautiful pavilion adorned with a colonade of green and gold marble, and with trellises which served as a kind of cage for parrots, humming-birds, guinea-hens, and all other curious kinds of birds. An excellent breakfast was provided in vessels of gold; and while the Paraguayans were eating coarse Indian corn out of

---

[2] The Jesuits.

wooden dishes in the open air, and exposed to the burning heat of the sun, the reverend father commandant retired to his cool arbor.

He was a very handsome young man, round-faced, fair, and fresh-colored, his eyebrows were finely arched, he had a piercing eye, the tips of his ears were red, his lips vermilion, and he had a bold and commanding air; but such a boldness as neither resembled that of a Spaniard nor of a Jesuit. He ordered his men to give back to Candide and Cacambo their arms, together with their two Andalusian horses. Cacambo gave the poor beasts some oats to eat close by the arbor, keeping a strict eye upon them all the while for fear of surprise.

Candide having kissed the hem of the commandant's robe, they sat down to table. "It seems you are a German," said the Jesuit to him in that language. "Yes, reverend father," answered Candide. As they pronounced these words they looked at each other with great amazement and with an emotion that neither could conceal.

"From what part of Germany do you come?" said the Jesuit.

"From the dirty province of Westphalia," answered Candide. "I was born in the castle of Thunder-ten-tronckh."

"Oh heavens! is it possible?" said the commandant.

"What a miracle!" cried Candide.

"Can it be you?" said the commandant.

On this they both drew a few steps backwards, then running into each other's arms, embraced, and wept profusely. "Is it you then, reverend father? You are the brother of the fair Cunégonde? You who were slain by the Bulgarians! You the baron's son! You a Jesuit in Paraguay! I must confess this is a strange world we live in. O Pangloss! Pangloss! what joy this would have given you if you had not been hanged."

The commandant dismissed the Negro slaves, and the Paraguayans who presented them with liquor in crystal goblets. He returned thanks to God and St. Ignatius[3] a thousand times; he clasped Candide in his arms, and both their faces were bathed in tears. "You will be more surprised, more affected, more excited," said Candide, "when I tell you that Cunégonde, your sister, whose belly was supposed to have been ripped open, is in perfect health."

"Where?"

"In your neighborhood, with the governor of Buenos Aires; and I myself was going to fight against you." Every word they uttered during this long conversation was productive of some new matter of astonishment. Their souls fluttered on their tongues, listened in their ears, and sparkled in their eyes. Like true Germans, they continued a long while at table, waiting for

---

[3] St. Ignatius Loyola founded the Jesuit order.

the reverend father; and the commandant spoke to his dear Candide as follows:

Chapter XV.

HOW CANDIDE KILLED THE BROTHER OF HIS DEAR CUNÉGONDE.

"Never while I live shall I lose the memory of that horrible day on which I saw my father and mother barbarously butchered before my eyes and my sister ravished. When the Bulgarians retired we searched in vain for my dear sister. She was nowhere to be found; but the bodies of my father, mother, and myself, with two servant maids and three little boys, all of whom had been murdered by the remorseless enemy, were thrown into a cart to be buried in a chapel belonging to the Jesuits, within two leagues of our family seat. A Jesuit sprinkled us with some holy water, which was very salty, and a few drops of it went into my eyes; the father perceived that my eyelids stirred a little; he put his hand upon my breast and felt my heart beat; upon which he gave me proper assistance, and at the end of three weeks I was perfectly recovered. You know, my dear Candide, I was very handsome; I became still more so, and the reverend father Croust, superior of that house, took a great fancy to me; he gave me the habit of the order, and some years afterwards I was sent to Rome. Our general stood in need of new recruits of young German Jesuits. The sovereigns of Paraguay admit as few Spanish Jesuits as possible; they prefer those of other nations, as being more obedient to command. The reverend father-general looked upon me as a proper person to work in that vineyard. I set out in company with a Polander and a Tyrolese. Upon my arrival I was honored with a subdeaconship and a lieutenancy. Now I am colonel and priest. We shall give a warm reception to the king of Spain's troops; I can assure you they will be well excommunicated and beaten. Providence has sent you hither to assist us. But is it true that my dear sister Cunégonde is in the neighborhood with the governor of Buenos Aires?"

Candide swore that nothing could be more true; and the tears began to trickle down their cheeks. The baron knew no end of embracing Candide, he called him his brother, his deliverer.

"Perhaps," said he, "my dear Candide, we shall be fortunate enough to enter the town, sword in hand, and recover my sister Cunégonde."

"Ah! that would crown my wishes," replied Candide; "for I intended to marry her; and I hope I shall still be able to do it."

"Insolent fellow!" cried the baron. "You! you have the impudence to marry my sister, who bears seventy-two quarterings! Really, I think you have an insufferable degree of assurance to dare so much as to mention such an audacious design to me."

Candide, thunderstruck at the oddness of this speech, answered: "Reverend father, all the quarterings in the world are of no meaning. I have delivered your sister from a Jew and an inquisitor; she is under many obligations to me, and she is resolved to give me her hand. My master, Pangloss, always told me that mankind are by nature equal. Therefore, you may depend upon it that I will marry your sister."

"We shall see to that, villain!" said the Jesuit baron of Thunder-ten-tronckh, and struck him across the face with the flat side of his sword. Candide in an instant drew his rapier and plunged it up to the hilt in the Jesuit's body; but in pulling it out reeking hot, he burst into tears.

"Good God!" cried he, "I have killed my old master, my friend, my brother-in-law; I am the best man in the world, and yet I have already killed three men; and of these three two were priests."

Cacambo, who was standing sentry near the door of the arbor, instantly ran up.

"Nothing remains," said his master, "but to sell our lives as dearly as possible; they will undoubtedly look into the arbor; we must die sword in hand."

Cacambo, who had seen many of this kind of adventures, was not discouraged. He stripped the baron of his Jesuit's habit and put it upon Candide, then gave him the dead man's three-cornered cap and made him mount on horseback. All this was done as quick as thought.

"Gallop, master," cried Cacambo; "everybody will take you for a Jesuit going to give orders; and we shall have passed the frontiers before they will be able to overtake us." He flew as he spoke these words, crying out loudly in Spanish, "Make way; make way for the reverend father-colonel."

Chapter XVI.

WHAT HAPPENED TO OUR TWO TRAVELLERS WITH TWO GIRLS, TWO MONKEYS, AND THE SAVAGES, CALLED OREILLONS.[1]

Candide and his valet had already passed the frontiers before it was known that the German Jesuit was dead. The wary Cacambo had taken care to fill

---

[1] From the Spanish *Orejones*, connoting "pierced ears" or "big ears." The savages wore ornaments in their ears.

his bag with bread, chocolate, some ham, some fruit, and a few bottles of wine. They penetrated with their Andalusian horses into a strange country, where they could discover no beaten path. At length a beautiful meadow, crossed with streams, opened to their view. Cacambo proposed to his master to take some nourishment, and he set him an example.

"How can you desire me to feast upon ham when I have killed the baron's son and am doomed never more to see the beautiful Cunégonde? What will it avail me to prolong a wretched life that must be spent far from her in remorse and despair? And then what will the *Journal of Trévoux*[2] say?" was Candide's reply.

While he was making these reflections he still continued eating. The sun was now on the point of setting when the ears of our two wanderers were assailed with cries which seemed to be uttered by a female voice. They could not tell whether these were cries of grief or of joy; however, they instantly started up, full of that inquietude and apprehension which a strange place naturally inspires. The cries proceeded from two young women who were tripping disrobed along the mead, while two monkeys followed close at their heels biting at their limbs. Candide was touched with compassion; he had learned to shoot while he was among the Bulgarians, and he could hit a nut in a hedge without touching a leaf. Accordingly he took up his double-barrelled Spanish gun, pulled the trigger, and laid the two monkeys lifeless on the ground.

"God be praised, my dear Cacambo, I have rescued two poor girls from a most perilous situation; if I have committed a sin in killing an inquisitor and a Jesuit, I have made ample amends by saving the lives of these two girls. Who knows but they may be young ladies of a good family, and that the assistance I have been so happy to give them may procure us great advantage in this country?"

He was about to continue when he felt himself struck speechless at seeing the two girls embracing the dead bodies of the monkeys in the tenderest manner, bathing their wounds with their tears, and rending the air with the most doleful lamentations.

"Really," said he to Cacambo, "I should not have expected to see such a prodigious share of good nature."

"Master," replied the knowing valet, "you have made a precious piece of work of it; do you know that you have killed the lovers of these two ladies?"

"Their lovers! Cacambo, you are jesting! It cannot be! I can never believe it."

"Dear sir," replied Cacambo, "you are surprised at everything; why

---

[2] A French Jesuit journal founded in 1701 and hostile to Voltaire.

should you think it so strange that there should be a country where monkeys insinuate themselves into the good graces of the ladies? They are the fourth part of a man as I am the fourth part of a Spaniard."

"Alas!" replied Candide, "I remember to have heard my master Pangloss say that such accidents as these frequently came to pass in former times, and that these mixtures produce centaurs, fauns, and satyrs; and that many of the ancients had seen such monsters; but I looked upon the whole as fabulous."

"Now you are convinced," said Cacambo, "that it is very true, and you see what use is made of those creatures by persons who have not had a proper education; all I am afraid of is that these same ladies may play us some ugly trick."

These judicious reflections operated so far on Candide as to make him quit the meadow and strike into a thicket. There he and Cacambo supped, and after heartily cursing the grand inquisitor, the governor of Buenos Aires, and the baron, they fell asleep on the ground. When they awoke they were surprised to find that they could not move; the reason was that the Oreillons who inhabit that country, and to whom the ladies had given information of these two strangers, had bound them with cords made of the bark of trees. They saw themselves surrounded by fifty naked Oreillons armed with bows and arrows, clubs, and hatchets of flint; some were making a fire under a large caldron; and others were preparing spits, crying out one and all, "A Jesuit! a Jesuit! we shall be revenged; we shall have excellent cheer; let us eat this Jesuit; let us eat him up."

"I told you, master," cried Cacambo, mournfully, "that these two wenches would play us some scurvy trick."

Candide, seeing the cauldron and the spits, cried out, "I suppose they are going either to boil or roast us. Ah! what would Pangloss say if he were to see how pure nature is formed? Everything is right; it may be so; but I must confess it is something hard to be bereft of dear Cunégonde and to be spitted like a rabbit by these barbarous Oreillons."

Cacambo, who never lost his presence of mind in distress, said to the disconsolate Candide: "Do not despair; I understand a little of the jargon of these people; I will speak to them."

"Please do," said Candide, "and be sure you remind them of the horrid barbarity of boiling and roasting human creatures, and how little of Christianity there is in such practices."

"Gentlemen," said Cacambo, "you think perhaps you are going to feast upon a Jesuit; if so, it is mighty well; nothing can be more agreeable to justice than thus to treat your enemies. Indeed the law of nature teaches us to kill our neighbor, and accordingly we find this practised all over the world; and if we do not indulge ourselves in eating human flesh, it is because we have much better fare; but for you, who have not such resources as we, it is certainly much better to feast upon your enemies than to throw their bodies to the fowls of the air, and thus lose all the fruits of your victory. But surely, gentlemen, you would not choose to eat your friends. You imagine you are going to roast a Jesuit, whereas my master is your friend, your defender, and you are going to spit the very man who has been destroying your enemies; as to myself, I am your countryman; this gentleman is my master, and so far from being a Jesuit, give me leave to tell you he has very lately killed one of that order, whose spoils he now wears, and which have probably occasioned your mistake. To convince you of the truth of what I say, take the habit he has on and carry it to the first barrier of the Jesuits' kingdom, and inquire whether my master did not kill one of their officers. There will be little or no time lost by this, and you may still reserve our bodies in your power to feast on if you should find what we have told you to be false. But, on the contrary, if you find it to be true, I am persuaded you are too well acquainted with the principles of the laws of society, humanity, and justice, not to use us courteously, and let us depart unhurt."

This speech appeared very reasonable to the Oreillons; they deputed two of their people with all diligence to inquire into the truth of this affair and acquit themselves of their commission like men of sense. The two soon returned with good tidings for our distressed adventurers. Upon this they were loosed, and those who were so lately going to roast and boil them now showed them all sorts of civilities; offered them girls, gave them refreshments, and reconducted them to the confines of their country, crying before them all the way, in token of joy: "He is no Jesuit, he is no Jesuit."

Candide could not help admiring the cause of his deliverance. "What men! what manners!" cried he; "if I had not fortunately run my sword up to the hilt in the body of Cunégonde's brother, I should have certainly been eaten alive. But, after all, pure nature is an excellent thing; since these people, instead of eating me, showed me a thousand civilities as soon as they knew I was not a Jesuit."

Chapter XVII.

CANDIDE AND HIS VALET ARRIVED IN THE COUNTRY OF EL DORADO[1] WHAT THEY SAW THERE.

When they got to the frontiers of the Oreillons, "You see," said Cacambo to Candide, "this hemisphere is not better than the other; now take my advice and let us return to Europe by the shortest way possible."

---

[1] The famous mythical country of gold that so many explorers sought in the New World.

"But how can we get back?" said Candide; "and where shall we go? To my own country? The Bulgarians and the Abares are laying that waste with fire and sword; or shall we go to Portugal? There I shall be burned; and if we abide here we are every moment in danger of being spitted. But how can I bring myself to quit that part of the world where my dear Cunégonde has her residence?"

"Let us return towards Cayenne," said Cacambo; "there we shall meet with some Frenchmen; for you know those gentry ramble all over the world; perhaps they will assist us, and God will look with pity on our distress."

It was not so easy to get to Cayenne. They knew pretty nearly whereabouts it lay; but the mountains, rivers, precipices, robbers, savages, were dreadful obstacles in the way. Their horses died with fatigue and their provisions were at an end. They subsisted a whole month on wild fruit, till at length they came to a little river bordered with cocoa trees; the sight of which at once revived their drooping spirits and furnished nourishment for their enfeebled bodies.

Cacambo, who was always giving as good advice as the old woman herself, said to Candide: "You see there is no holding out any longer; we have travelled enough on foot. I spy an empty canoe near the river side; let us fill it with cocoanuts, get into it, and go down with the stream; a river always leads to some inhabited place. If we do not meet with agreeable things, we shall at least meet with something new."

"Agreed," replied Candide; "let us recommend ourselves to Providence."

They rowed a few leagues down the river, the banks of which were in some places covered with flowers; in others barren; in some parts smooth and level, and in others steep and rugged. The stream widened as they went further on, till at length it passed under one of the frightful rocks, whose summits seemed to reach the clouds. Here our two travellers had the courage to commit themselves to the stream, which, contracting in this part, hurried them along with a dreadful noise and rapidity. At the end of twenty-four hours they saw daylight again; but their canoe was dashed to pieces against the rocks. They were obliged to creep along, from rock to rock, for the space of a league, till at length a spacious plain presented itself to their sight. This place was bounded by a chain of inaccessible mountains. The country appeared cultivated equally for pleasure and to produce the necessaries of life. The useful and agreeable were here equally blended. The roads were covered, or rather adorned, with carriages formed of glittering materials, in which were men and women of a surprising beauty, drawn with great rapidity by red sheep of a very large size; which far surpassed the finest coursers of Andalusia, Tetuan, or Mecquinez.

"Here is a country, however," said Candide, "preferable to Westphalia."

He and Cacambo landed near the first village they saw, at the entrance of which they perceived some children covered with tattered garments of the richest brocade, playing at quoits. Our two inhabitants of the other hemisphere amused themselves greatly with what they saw. The quoits were large, round pieces, yellow, red, and green, which cast a most glorious lustre. Our travellers picked some of them up, and they proved to be gold, emeralds, rubies and diamonds; the least of which would have been the greatest ornament to the superb throne of the Great Mogul.

"Without doubt," said Cacambo, "those children must be the king's sons that are playing at quoits." As he was uttering these words the schoolmaster of the village appeared, who came to call the children to school.

"There," said Candide, "is the tutor of the royal family."

The little ragamuffins immediately left their diversion, leaving the quoits on the ground with all their other playthings. Candide gathered them up, ran to the schoolmaster, and, with a most respectful bow, presented them to him, giving him to understand by signs that their royal highnesses had forgot their gold and precious stones. The schoolmaster, with a smile, flung them upon the ground, then examining Candide from head to foot with an air of admiration, he turned his back and went on his way.

Our travellers took care, however, to gather up the gold, the rubies, and the emeralds.

"Where are we?" cried Candide. "The king's children in this country must have an excellent education, since they are taught to show such a contempt for gold and precious stones."

Cacambo was as much surprised as his master. They then drew near the first house in the village, which was built after the manner of a European palace. There was a crowd of people about the door, and a still greater number in the house. The sound of the most delightful instruments of music was heard, and the most agreeable smell came from the kitchen. Cacambo went up to the door and heard those within talking in the Peruvian language, which was his mother tongue; for every one knows that Cacambo was born in a village of Tucuman, where no other language is spoken.

"I will be your interpreter here," said he to Candide. "Let us go in; this is an inn."

Immediately two waiters and two servant-girls, dressed in cloth of gold, and their hair braided with ribbons of tissue, accosted the strangers and invited them to sit down to the table. Their dinner consisted of four dishes of different soups, each garnished with two young paroquets, a large dish of bouillé that weighed two hundred pounds, two roasted monkeys of a delicious flavor, three hundred humming-birds in one dish, and six hundred fly-birds in another; some excellent ragouts, delicate tarts, and the whole served up in dishes of rock-crystal. Several sorts of liquors, extracted from the sugar-cane, were handed about by the servants who attended.

Most of the company were tradesmen and coachmen, all extremely polite; they asked Cacambo a few questions with the utmost discretion and circumspection; and replied to his in a most obliging and satisfactory manner.

As soon as dinner was over, both Candide and Cacambo thought they should pay very handsomely for their entertainment by laying down two of those large gold pieces which they had picked off the ground; but the landlord and landlady burst into a fit of laughing and held their sides for some time. When the fit was over, "Gentlemen," said the landlord, "I plainly perceive you are strangers, and such we are not accustomed to charge; pardon us, therefore, for laughing when you offered us the common pebbles of our highways for payment of your reckoning. To be sure, you have none of the coin of this kingdom; but there is no necessity of having any money at all to dine in this house. All the inns, which are established for the convenience of those who carry on the trade of this nation, are maintained by the government. You have found but very indifferent entertainment here, because this is only a poor village; but in almost every other of these public houses you will meet with a reception worthy of persons of your merit." Cacambo explained the whole of this speech of the landlord to Candide, who listened to it with the same astonishment with which his friend communicated it.

"What sort of a country is this," said the one to the other, "that is unknown to all the world; and in which Nature has everywhere so different an appearance to what she has in ours? Possibly this is the part of the globe where everything is right, for there must certainly be some such place. And, for all that Master Pangloss could say, I often perceived that things went very ill in Westphalia."

Chapter XVIII.

WHAT THEY SAW IN THE COUNTRY OF EL DORADO.

Cacambo revealed his curiosity to his landlord by a thousand different questions; the honest man answered him thus: "I am very ignorant, sir, but I am contented with my ignorance; however, we have in this neighborhood an old man retired from court, who is the most learned and communicative person in the whole kingdom." He then conducted Cacambo to the old man; Candide acted now only a second character, and attended his valet. They entered a very plain house, for the door was nothing but silver, and the ceiling was only of beaten gold, but wrought in such elegant taste as to vie with the richest. The antechamber, indeed, was only incrusted with rubies and emeralds; but the order in which everything was disposed made amends for this great simplicity.

The old man received the strangers on his sofa, which was stuffed with humming-birds' feathers; and ordered his servants to present them with liquors in golden goblets, after which he satisfied their curiosity in the following terms:

"I am now one hundred and seventy-two years old, and I learned of my late father, who was equerry to the king, the amazing revolutions of Peru, to which he had been an eye-witness. This kingdom is the ancient patrimony of the Incas, who very imprudently quitted it to conquer another part of the world, and were at length conquered and destroyed themselves by the Spaniards.

"Those princes of their family who remained in their native country acted more wisely. They ordained, with the consent of their whole nation, that none of the inhabitants of our little kingdom should ever quit it; and to this wise ordinance we owe the preservation of our innocence and happiness. The Spaniards had some confused notion of this country, to which they gave the name of *El Dorado;* and Sir Walter Raleigh, an Englishman, actually came very near it about three hundred years ago; but the inaccessible rocks and precipices with which our country is surrounded on all sides has hitherto secured us from the rapacious fury of the people of Europe, who have an unaccountable fondness for the pebbles and dirt of our land, for the sake of which they would murder us all to the very last man."

The conversation lasted some time and turned chiefly on the form of government, their manners, their women, their public diversions, and the arts. At length, Candide, who had always had a taste for metaphysics, asked whether the people of that country had any religion.

The old man reddened a little at this question.

"Can you doubt it?" said he; "do you take us for wretches lost to all sense of gratitude?"

Cacambo asked in a respectful manner what was the established religion of El Dorado. The old man blushed again, and said: "Can there be two religions, then? Ours, I apprehend, is the religion of the whole world; we worship God from morning till night."

"Do you worship but one God?" said Cacambo, who still acted as the interpreter of Candide's doubts.

"Certainly," said the old man; "there are not two, nor three, nor four Gods. I must confess the people of your world ask very extraordinary questions."

However, Candide could not refrain from making more inquiries of the old man; he wanted to know in what manner they prayed to God in El Dorado.

"We do not pray to him at all," said the reverend sage; "we have nothing to ask of Him. He has given us all we want, and we give Him thanks incessantly." Candide had a curiosity to see some of their priests, and desired Cacambo to ask the old man where they were. At which he smiling said:

"My friends, we are all of us priests; the king and all the heads of families sing solemn hymns of thanksgiving every morning, accompanied by five or six thousand musicians."

"What!" said Cacambo, "have you no monks among you to dispute, to govern, to intrigue, and to burn people who are not of the same opinion with themselves?"

"Do you take us for fools?" said the old man. "Here we are all of one opinion, and know not what you mean by your monks."

During the whole of this discourse Candide was in raptures, and he said to himself, "What a prodigious difference is there between this place and Westphalia; and this house and the baron's castle. Ah, Master Pangloss! had you ever seen El Dorado, you would no longer have maintained that the castle of Thunder-ten-tronckh was the finest of all possible edifices; there is nothing like seeing the world, that's certain."

This long conversation being ended, the old man ordered six sheep to be harnessed and put to the coach, and sent twelve of his servants to escort the travellers to court.

"Excuse me," said he, "for not waiting on you in person, my age deprives me of that honor. The king will receive you in such a manner that you will have no reason to complain; and doubtless you will make a proper allowance for the customs of the country if they should not happen altogther to please you."

Candide and Cacambo got into the coach, the six sheep flew, and, in less than a quarter of an hour, they arrived at the king's palace, which was situated at the further end of the capital. At the entrance was a portal two hundred and twenty feet high and one hundred wide; but it is impossible for words to express the materials of which it was built. The reader, however, will readily conceive that they must have a prodigious superiority over the pebbles and sand, which we call gold and precious stones.

Twenty beautiful young virgins in waiting received Candide and Cacambo on their alighting from the coach, conducted them to the bath and clad them in robes woven of the down of humming-birds; after which they were introduced by the great officers of the crown of both sexes to the king's apartment, between two files of musicians, each file consisting of a thousand, agreeable to the custom of the country. When they drew near to the presence-chamber, Cacambo asked one of the officers in what manner they were to pay their obeisance to his majesty; whether it was the custom to fall upon their knees, or to prostrate themselves upon the ground; whether they were to put their hands upon their heads, or behind their backs; whether they were to lick the dust off the floor; in short, what was the ceremony usual on such occasions.

"The custom," said the great officer, "is to embrace the king and kiss him on each cheek."

Candide and Cacambo accordingly threw their arms round his majesty's neck, who received them in the most gracious manner imaginable, and very politely asked them to sup with him.

While supper was preparing orders were given to show them the city, where they saw public structures that reared their lofty heads to the clouds; the market-places decorated with a thousand columns, fountains of spring water, of rose water, and of liquors drawn from the sugarcane, incessantly flowing in the great squares, which were paved with a kind of precious stones that emitted an odor like that of cloves and cinnamon. Candide asked to see the high court of justice, the parliament, but was answered that they had none in that country, being utter strangers to lawsuits. He then inquired if they had any prisons; they replied none. But what gave him at once the greatest surprise and pleasure was the palace of sciences, where he saw a gallery two thousand feet long, filled with the various apparatus in mathematics and natural philosophy.

After having spent the whole afternoon in seeing only about the thousandth part of the city, they were brought back to the king's palace. Candide sat down at the table with his majesty, his valet Cacambo, and several ladies of the court. Never was entertainment more elegant, nor could any one possibly show more wit than his majesty displayed while they were at supper. Cacambo explained all the king's *bons mots* to Candide, and, although they were translated, they still appeared to be *bons mots*. Of all the things that surprised Candide, this was not the least. They spent a whole month in this hospitable place, during which time Candide was continually saying to Cacambo:

"I own, my friend, once more, that the castle where I was born is a mere nothing in comparison to the place where we now are; but still Cunégonde is not here, and you yourself have doubtless some fair one in Europe for whom you sigh. If we remain here we shall only be as others are; whereas, if we return to our own world with only a dozen of El Dorado sheep, loaded with the pebbles of this country, we shall be richer than all the kings in Europe; we shall no longer need to stand in awe of the inquisitors; and we may easily recover Cunégonde."

This speech was perfectly agreeable to Cacambo. A fondness for roving, for making a figure in their own country, and for boasting of what they had seen in their travels, was so powerful in our two wanderers that they resolved to be no longer happy; and demanded permission of the king to quit the country.

"You are about to do a rash and silly action," said the king. "I am sensible my kingdom is an inconsiderable spot; but when people are tolerably at their ease in any place, I should think it would be to their interest to remain there. Most assuredly, I have no right to detain you, or any strangers, against your wills; this is an act of tyranny to which our manners and our laws are equally repugnant; all men are by nature free; you have therefore an undoubted liberty to depart whenever you please, but you will have many and great difficulties to encounter in passing the frontiers. It is impossible to ascend that rapid river which runs under high and vaulted rocks, and by which you were conveyed hither by a kind of miracle. The mountains by which my kingdom are hemmed in on all sides, are ten thousand feet high, and perfectly perpendicular; they are above ten leagues across, and the descent from them is one continued precipice. However, since you are determined to leave us, I will immediately give orders to the superintendent of my carriages to cause one to be made that will convey you very safely. When they have conducted you to the back of the mountains, nobody can attend you farther; for my subjects have made a vow never to quit the kingdom, and they are too prudent to break it. Ask me whatever else you please."

"All we shall ask of your majesty," said Cacambo, "is only a few sheep laden with provisions, pebbles, and the clay of your country."

The king smiled at the request, and said: "I cannot imagine what pleasure you Europeans find in our yellow clay; but take away as much of it as you will, and much good may it do you."

He immediately gave orders to his engineers to make a machine to hoist these two extraordinary men out of the kingdom. Three thousand good machinists went to work and finished it in about fifteen days, and it did not cost more than twenty millions sterling of that country's money. Candide and Cacambo were placed on this machine, and they took with them two large red sheep, bridled and saddled, to ride upon, when they got on the other side of the mountains; twenty others to serve as sumpters for carrying provisions; thirty laden with presents of whatever was most curious in the country, and fifty with gold, diamonds, and other precious stones. The king, at parting with our two adventurers, embraced them with the greatest cordiality.

It was a curious sight to behold the manner of their setting off, and the ingenious method by which they and their sheep were hoisted to the top of the mountains. The machinists and engineers took leave of them as soon as they had conveyed them to a place of safety, and Candide was wholly occupied with the thoughts of presenting his sheep to Cunégonde.

"Now," cried he, "thanks to heaven, we have more than sufficient to pay the governor of Buenos Aires for Cunégonde, if she is redeemable. Let us make the best of our way to Cayenne, where we will take shipping and then we may at leisure think of what kingdom we shall purchase with our riches."

Chapter XIX.

WHAT HAPPENED TO THEM AT SURINAM, AND HOW CANDIDE BECAME ACQUAINTED WITH MARTIN.

Our travellers' first day's journey was very pleasant; they were elated with the prospect of possessing more riches than were to be found in Europe, Asia, and Africa together. Candide, in an ecstasy, cut the name of Cunégonde on almost every tree he came to. The second day two of their sheep sunk in a morass, and were swallowed up with their loads; two more died of fatigue; some few days afterwards seven or eight perished with hunger in a desert, and others, at different times, tumbled down precipices, or were otherwise lost, so that, after travelling about a hundred days they had only two sheep left of the hundred and two they brought with them from El Dorado. Said Candide to Cacambo:

"You see, my dear friend, how perishable the riches of this world are; there is nothing solid but virtue."

"Very true," said Cacambo, "but we have still two sheep remaining, with more treasure than ever the king of Spain will be possessed of; and I see a town at a distance, which I take to be Surinam, a town belonging to the Dutch. We are now at the end of our troubles, and at the beginning of happiness."

As they drew near the town they saw a Negro stretched on the ground with only one half of his habit, which was a kind of linen frock; for the poor man had lost his left leg and his right hand.

"Good God," said Candide in Dutch, "what dost thou here, friend, in this deplorable condition?"

"I am waiting for my master, Mynheer Vanderdendur, the famous trader," answered the Negro.

"Was it Mynheer Vanderdendur that used you in this cruel manner?"

"Yes, sir," said the Negro; "it is the custom here. They give us a linen garment twice a year, and that is all our covering. When we labor in the sugar works, and the mill happens to snatch hold of a finger, they instantly chop off our hand; and when we attempt to run away, they cut off a leg. Both these cases have happened to me, and it is at this expense that you eat sugar in Europe; and yet when my mother sold me for ten patacoons on the coast of Guinea, she said to me, 'My dear child, bless our witch doctors; adore them forever; they will make you live happy; you have the honor to be a slave to our lords the whites, by which you will make the fortune of us your parents.' Alas! I don't know whether I have made their fortunes; but they have not made mine: dogs, monkeys, and parrots are a thousand times less wretched than I. The Dutch witch doctors who converted me tell me every Sunday that the blacks and whites are all children of one father, whom they call Adam. As for me, I do not understand anything of genealogies; but if what these preachers say is true, we are all second cousins; and you must allow that it is impossible to be worse treated by our relations than we are."

"O Pangloss!" cried Candide, "such horrid doings never entered your imagination. Here is an end of the matter; I find myself, after all, obliged to renounce your Optimism."

"Optimism," said Cacambo, "what is that?"

"Alas!" replied Candide, "it is the obstinacy of maintaining that everything is best when it is worst." And so saying he turned his eyes towards the poor Negro, and shed a flood of tears; and in this weeping mood he entered the town of Surinam.

Immediately upon their arrival our travellers inquired if there was any vessel in the harbor which they might send to Buenos Aires. The person they addressed themselves to happened to be the master of a Spanish ship, who offered to agree with them on moderate terms, and appointed them a meeting at an inn. Candide and his faithful Cacambo went there to wait for him, taking with them their two sheep.

Candide, who was all frankness and sincerity, made an ingenuous recital of his adventures to the Spaniard, declaring to him at the same time his resolution of carrying off Cunégonde from the governor of Buenos Aires.

"O ho!" said the shipmaster, "if that is the case, get whom you please to carry you to Buenos Aires; for my part, I wash my hands of the affair. It would prove a hanging matter to us all. The fair Cunégonde is the governor's favorite mistress." These words were like a clap of thunder to Candide; he wept bitterly for a long time, and, taking Cacambo aside, he said to him, "I'll tell you, my dear friend, what you must do. We have each of us in our pockets to the value of five or six millions in diamonds; you are cleverer at these matters than I; you must go to Buenos Aires and bring off Miss Cunégonde. If the governor makes any difficulty give him a million; if he holds out, give him two; as you have not killed an inquisitor, they will have no suspicion of you. I'll fit out another ship and go to Venice, where I will wait for you. Venice is a free country, where we shall have nothing to fear from Bulgarians, Abarians, Jews, or Inquisitors."

Cacambo greatly applauded this wise resolution. He was inconsolable at the thoughts of parting with so good a master, who treated him more like an intimate friend than a servant; but the pleasure of being able to do him a service soon got the better of his sorrow. They embraced each other with a flood of tears. Candide charged him not to forget the old woman. Cacambo set out the same day. This Cacambo was a very honest fellow.

Candide continued some days longer at Surinam, waiting for any captain to carry him and his two remaining sheep to Italy. He hired domestics, and purchased many things necessary for a long voyage; at length Mynheer Vanderdendur, skipper of a large Dutch vessel, came and offered his service.

"What will you charge," said Candide, "to carry me, my servants, my baggage, and these two sheep you see here, directly to Venice?"

The skipper asked ten thousand piastres, and Candide agreed to his demand without hesitation.

"Oho!" said the cunning Vanderdendur to himself, "this stranger must be very rich; he agrees to give me ten thousand piastres without hesitation." Returning a little while after he tells Candide that upon second consideration he could not undertake the voyage for less than twenty thousand. "Very well; you shall have them," said Candide.

"Heavens!" said the skipper to himself, "this man agrees to pay twenty thousand piastres with as much ease as ten." Accordingly he goes back again, and tells him roundly that he will not carry him to Venice for less than thirty thousand piastres.

"Then you shall have thirty thousand," said Candide.

"Oh!" said the Dutchman once more to himself, "thirty thousand piastres seem a trifle to this man. Those sheep must certainly be laden with an immense treasure. I'll even stop here and ask no more; but make him pay down the thirty thousand piastres, and then we may see what is to be done farther." Candide sold two small diamonds, the least of which was worth more than all the skipper asked. He paid him beforehand, the two sheep were put on board, and Candide followed in a small boat to join the vessel in the road. The skipper took advantage of his opportunity, hoisted sail, and put out to sea with a favorable wind. Candide, confounded and amazed, soon lost sight of the ship. "Alas!" said he, "this is a trick like those in our old world!"

He returned back to the shore overwhelmed with grief; and, indeed, he had lost what would have made the fortune of twenty monarchs.

Straightway upon his landing he applied to the Dutch magistrate; being somewhat nervous, he thundered at the door. He went in, told his case, and talked a little louder than was necessary. The magistrate began with fining him ten thousand piastres for his petulance, and then listened very patiently to what he had to say, promised to examine into the affair on the skipper's return, and ordered him to pay ten thousand piastres more for the fees of the court.

This treatment put Candide out of all patience; it is true, he had suffered misfortunes a thousand times more grievous, but the cool insolence
of the judge, and the villainy of the skipper raised his ill humor and threw
him into a deep melancholy. The villainy of mankind presented itself to his
mind in all its deformity, and he was a prey to the most gloomy ideas.
After some time, hearing that a French ship was ready to set sail for Bordeaux, since there were no more sheep loaded with diamonds to put on
board, he hired the cabin at the usual price; and made it known in the
town that he would pay the passage and board of any honest man who
would give him his company during the voyage; besides making him a
present of ten thousand piastres, on condition that such person was the most
dissatisfied with his condition, and the most unfortunate in the whole
province.

At this there appeared such a crowd of candidates that a large fleet could
not have contained them. Candide, willing to choose from among those
who appeared most likely to answer his intention, selected twenty, who
seemed to him the most sociable, and who all pretended to merit the pref-
erence. He invited them to his inn, and promised to treat them with a supper, on condition that every man should bind himself by an oath to relate
his own history; declaring at the same time, that he would choose that
person who should appear to him the most deserving of compassion, and
the most justly dissatisfied with his condition in life; and that he would
make a present to the rest.

This extraordinary assembly continued sitting till four in the morning.
Candide, while he was listening to their adventures, called to mind what
the old woman had said to him in their voyage to Buenos Aires, and the
wager she had laid that there was scarcely a person on board the ship who
had not met with great misfortunes. Every story he heard put him in mind
of Pangloss.

"My old master," said he, "would be confoundedly put to it to demonstrate his favorite system. Would he were here! Certainly if everything is
for the best, it is in El Dorado; and not in the other parts of the world."

At length he determined in favor of a poor scholar, who had labored ten
years for the booksellers at Amsterdam.[1] He thought that no employment
could be more detestable.

This scholar, who was in fact a very honest man, had been robbed by his
wife, beaten by his son, and forsaken by his daughter, who had run away
with a Portuguese. He had been likewise deprived of a small employment
on which he subsisted, and he was persecuted by the clergy of Surinam, who

---

[1] Voltaire suffered from the pirating of his works in Holland where there was freedom of the press and no international copyright laws.

took him for a Socinian.[2] It must be acknowledged that the other competitors were, at least, as wretched as he; but Candide was in hopes that the company of a man of letters would relieve the tediousness of the voyage. All the other candidates complained that Candide had done them a great injustice, but he silenced them by a present of a hundred piastres to each.

Chapter XX.

WHAT BEFELL CANDIDE AND MARTIN ON THEIR PASSAGE.

The old philosopher, whose name was Martin, embarked with Candide for Bordeaux. Both had seen and suffered a great deal, and had the ship been going from Surinam to Japan round the Cape of Good Hope, they could have found sufficient entertainment for each other during the whole voyage, in discoursing upon moral and natural evil.

Candide, however, had one advantage over Martin: he lived in the pleasing hopes of seeing Cunégonde once more; whereas, the poor philosopher had nothing to hope for; besides, Candide had money and jewels, and, notwithstanding he had lost a hundred red sheep laden with the greatest treasure outside of El Dorado, and though he still smarted from the reflection of the Dutch skipper's knavery, yet when he considered what he had still left, and repeated the name of Cunégonde, especially after meal times, he inclined to Pangloss' doctrine.

"And pray," said he to Martin, "what is your opinion of the whole of this system? what notion have you of moral and natural evil?"

"Sir," replied Martin, "our priest accused me of being a Socinian; but the real truth is, I am a Manichaean."[1]

"Nay, now you are jesting," said Candide; "there are no Manichaeans existing at present in the world."

"And yet I am one," said Martin; "but I cannot help it. I cannot for the soul of me think otherwise."

"Surely the devil must be in you," said Candide.

"He concerns himself so much," replied Martin, "in the affairs of this world that it is very probable he may be in me as well as everywhere else; but I must confess, when I cast my eye on this globe, or rather globule, I cannot help thinking that God has abandoned it to some malignant being.

[2] The Socinians denied among other things the Trinity, original sin, and the divinity of Christ. They were "rational" Christians and great optimists.

[1] A follower of the doctrine of the Persian Manichaeus who believed that good and evil are of approximately equal strength, one not able to overcome the other.

I always except El Dorado. I scarce ever knew a city that did not wish the destruction of its neighboring city; nor a family that did not desire to exterminate some other family. The poor in all parts of the world bear an inveterate hatred to the rich, even while they creep and cringe to them; and the rich treat the poor like sheep, whose wool and flesh they barter for money; a million of regimented assassins cross Europe from one end to the other, to get their bread by regular robbery and murder, because it is the most gentlemanlike profession. Even in those cities which seem to enjoy the blessings of peace, and where the arts flourish, the inhabitants are devoured with envy, care, and inquietudes, which are greater plagues than any experienced in a town besieged. Private chagrins are still more dreadful than public calamities. In a word," concluded the philosopher, "I have seen and suffered so much that I am a Manichaean."

"And yet there is some good in the world," replied Candide.

"May be so," said Martin, "but it has escaped my knowledge."

While they were deeply engaged in this dispute they heard the report of cannon, which redoubled every moment. Each took out his glass, and they spied two ships warmly engaged at the distance of about three miles. The wind brought them both so near the French ship that those on board her had the pleasure of seeing the fight with great ease. After several smart broadsides the one gave the other a shot between wind and water which sunk her outright. Then could Candide and Martin plainly perceive a hundred men on the deck of the vessel which was sinking, who, with hands uplifted to heaven, sent forth piercing cries, and were in a moment swallowed up by the waves.

"Well," said Martin, "you now see in what manner men treat one another."

"It is certain," said Candide, "that there is something diabolical in this affair." As he was speaking thus he spied something of a shining red hue, which swam close to the vessel. The boat was hoisted out to see what it might be, when it proved to be one of his sheep. Candide felt more joy at the recovery of this one animal than he did grief when he lost the other hundred, though laden with the large diamonds of El Dorado.

The French captain quickly perceived that the victorious ship belonged to the crown of Spain; that the other was a Dutch pirate, and the very same captain who had robbed Candide. The immense riches which this villain had amassed were buried with him in the deep, and this one sheep saved out of the whole.

"You see," said Candide to Martin, "that vice is sometimes punished; this villain, the Dutch skipper, has met with the fate he deserved."

"Very true," said Martin, "but why should the passengers be doomed also to destruction? God has punished the knave, and the devil has drowned the rest."

The French and Spanish ships continued their cruise, and Candide and Martin their conversation. They disputed fourteen days successively, at the end of which they were just as far advanced as the first moment they began. However, they had the satisfaction of disputing, of communicating their ideas, and of mutually comforting each other. Candide embraced his sheep with ecstasy.

"Since I have found thee again," said he, "I may possibly find my Cunégonde once more."

Chapter XXI.

CANDIDE AND MARTIN, WHILE THUS REASONING
WITH EACH OTHER, DRAW NEAR TO THE
COAST OF FRANCE.

At length they sighted the coast of France, when Candide said to Martin, "Were you ever in France?"

"Yes sir," said Martin, "I have been in several provinces of that kingdom. In some, one-half of the people are fools and madmen; in some, they are too artful; in others, again, they are, in general, either very good-natured or very brutal; while in others, they affect to be witty, and in all, their ruling passion is love, the next is slander, and the last is to talk nonsense."

"But were you ever in Paris?"

"Yes sir, I have been in that city, and it is a place that contains the several species just described; it is a chaos, a confused multitude, where everyone seeks for pleasure without being able to find it; at least, as far as I have observed during my short stay in that city. At my arrival I was robbed of all I had in the world by pickpockets and sharpers at the fair of St. Germain. I was taken up myself for a robber, and confined in prison a whole week; after which I hired myself as proofreader to a press, in order to get a little money towards defraying my expenses back to Holland on foot. I knew the whole tribe of scribblers, malcontents, and fanatics. It is said the people of that city are very polite; I believe they may be."

"For my part, I have no curiosity to see France," said Candide; "you may easily conceive, my friend, that after spending a month in El Dorado, I can desire to behold nothing upon earth but Cunégonde; I am going to wait for her at Venice. I intend to pass through France, on my way to Italy. Will you not bear me company?" "With all my heart," said Martin; "they say Venice is agreeable to none but noble Venetians; but that, nevertheless, strangers are well received there when they have plenty of money; now I have none, but you have, therefore I will attend you wherever you please."

"Now we are upon this subject," said Candide, "do you think that the earth was originally sea, as we read in that great book[1] which belongs to the captain of the ship?" "I believe nothing of it," replied Martin, "any more than I do of the many other chimeras which have been related to us for some time past." "But then, to what end," said Candide, "was the world formed?" "To make us mad," said Martin. "Are you not surprised," continued Candide "at the love which the two girls in the country of the Oreillons had for those two monkeys?—You know I have told you the story." "Surprised?" replied Martin, "not in the least; I see nothing strange in this passion. I have seen so many extraordinary things that there is nothing extraordinary to me now." "Do you think," said Candide, "that men always massacred one another as they do now? were they always guilty of lies, fraud, treachery, ingratitude, inconstancy, envy, ambition, and cruelty? were they always thieves, fools, cowards, gluttons, drunkards, misers, calumniators, debauchees, fanatics, and hypocrites?" "Do you believe," said Martin, "that hawks have always been accustomed to eat pigeons when they came in their way?" "Doubtless," said Candide. "Well then," replied Martin, "if hawks have always had the same nature, why should you pretend that mankind change theirs?" "Oh," said Candide, "there is a great deal of difference; for free will—" and reasoning thus they arrived at Bordeaux.

[In Chapter 22, Candide and Martin go to Paris. Candide grows sick and eventually is cured. He loses a large sum of money at gambling and even has two of his diamond rings stolen. A priest, who hears about Cunégonde, hires a woman to impersonate her and Candide unwittingly gives her most of his diamonds. The police arrest Candide and Martin as suspicious foreigners, but they are bribed. Candide and Martin sail for England.]

Chapter XXIII.

CANDIDE AND MARTIN TOUCH UPON THE ENGLISH COAST—WHAT THEY SEE THERE.

"Ah Pangloss! Pangloss! ah Martin! Martin! ah my dear Cunégonde! what sort of a world is this?" Thus exclaimed Candide as soon as he got on board the Dutch ship. "Why something very foolish, and very abominable," said Martin. "You are acquainted with England," said Candide; "are

---

[1] The Bible or possibly Buffon's *Theorie de la terre* (1749).

they as great fools in that country as in France?" "Yes, but in a different manner," answered Martin. "You know that these two nations are at war about a few acres of barren land in the neighborhood of Canada,[1] and that they have expended much greater sums in the contest than all Canada is worth. To say exactly whether there are a greater number fit to be inhabitants of a madhouse in the one country than the other, exceeds the limits of my imperfect capacity; I know in general that the people we are going to visit are of a very dark and gloomy disposition."

As they were chatting thus together they arrived at Portsmouth. The shore on each side the harbor was lined with a multitude of people, whose eyes were steadfastly fixed on a large man who was kneeling down on the deck of one of the men-of-war, with something tied before his eyes. Opposite to this personage stood four soldiers, each of whom shot three bullets into his skull, with all the composure imaginable; and when it was done, the whole company went away perfectly well satisfied. "What the devil is all this for?" said Candide, "and what demon, or foe of mankind, lords it thus tyranically over the world?" He then asked who was that large man who had been sent out of the world with so much ceremony. When he received for answer, that it was an admiral. "And why do you put your admiral to death?"[2] "Because he did not put a sufficient number of his fellow-creatures to death. You must know, he had an engagement with a French admiral, and it has been proved against him that he was not near enough to his antagonist." "But," replied Candide, "the French admiral must have been as far from him." "There is no doubt of that; but in this country it is found requisite, now and then, to put an admiral to death, in order to encourage the others to fight."

Candide was so shocked at what he saw and heard that he would not set foot on shore, but made a bargain with the Dutch skipper (were he even to rob him like the captain of Surinam) to carry him directly to Venice.

The skipper was ready in two days. They sailed along the coast of France, and passed within sight of Lisbon, at which Candide trembled. From thence they proceeded to the Straits, entered the Mediterranean, and at length arrived at Venice. "God be praised," said Candide, embracing Martin, "this is the place where I am to behold my beloved Cunégonde once again. I can confide in Cacambo, like another self. All is well, all very well, all as well as possible."

---

[1] French and Indian War (1754–1763).

[2] Admiral Byng was executed on March 14, 1757, for failing to win a naval engagement against the French the previous year. Voltaire had attempted to save his life.

[In Chapter 24, Candide and Martin travel to Venice. They do not find Cacambo, but they see Paquette, Pangloss' former mistres, who helps them. Candide goes to visit the nobleman Pococuranté, who has never known grief.]

Chapter XXV.

CANDIDE AND MARTIN PAY A VISIT TO LORD POCOCURANTÉ, A NOBLE VENETIAN.

Candide and his friend Martin went in a gondola on the Brenta, and arrived at the palace of the noble Pococuranté.[1] The gardens were laid out in elegant taste, and adorned with fine marble statues; his palace was built after the most approved rules of architecture. The master of the house, who was a man of affairs, and very rich, received our two travellers with great politeness, but without much ceremony, which somewhat disconcerted Candide, but was not at all displeasing to Martin.

As soon as they were seated, two very pretty girls, neatly dressed, brought in chocolate, which was extremely well prepared. Candide could not help praising their beauty and graceful carriage. "The creatures are well enough," said the senator; "I amuse myself with them sometimes, for I am heartily tired of the women of the town, their coquetry, their jealousy, their quarrels, their humors, their meannesses, their pride, and their folly; I am weary of making sonnets, or of paying for sonnets to be made on them; but after all, these two girls begin to grow very indifferent to me."

After having refreshed himself, Candide walked into a large gallery, where he was struck with the sight of a fine collection of paintings. Candide asked what master painted the two first of these." "They are by Raphael," answered the senator. "I gave a great deal of money for them seven years ago, purely out of curiosity, as they were said to be the finest pieces in Italy; but I cannot say they please me: the coloring is dark and heavy; the figures do not swell nor come out enough; and the drapery is bad. In short, notwithstanding the praise lavished upon them, they are not, in my opinion, a true representation of nature. I approve of no paintings save those wherein I think I behold nature herself; and there are few, if any, of that kind to be met with. I have what is called a fine collection, but I take no manner of delight in it."

---

[1] His name means "small care."

While dinner was being prepared Pococuranté ordered a concert. Candide praised the music to the skies. "This noise," said the noble Venetian, "may amuse one for a little time, but if it were to last above half an hour, it would grow tiresome to everybody, though perhaps no one would care to own it. Music has become the art of executing what is difficult; now, whatever is difficult cannot be long pleasing.

"I believe I might take more pleasure in an opera, if they had not made such a monster of that species of dramatic entertainment as perfectly shocks me; and I am amazed how people can bear to see wretched tragedies set to music; where the scenes are contrived for no other purpose than to lug in, as it were by the ears, three or four ridiculous songs, to give a favorite actress an opportunity of exhibiting her pipe. Let who will die away in raptures at the trills of a eunuch quavering the majestic part of Caesar or Cato, and strutting in a foolish manner upon the stage, but for my part I have long ago renounced these paltry entertainments, which constitute the glory of modern Italy, and are so dearly purchased by crowned heads." Candide opposed these sentiments; but he did it in a discreet manner; as for Martin, he was entirely of the old senator's opinion.

Dinner being served, they sat down to table, and, after a hearty meal, returned to the library. Candide, observing Homer richly bound, commended the noble Venetian's taste. "This," said he, "is a book that was once the delight of the great Pangloss, the best philosopher in Germany." "Homer is no favorite of mine," answered Pococuranté, cooly; "I was made to believe once that I took a pleasure in reading him; but his continual repetition of battles have all such a resemblance with each other; his gods that are forever in haste and bustle, without ever doing anything; his Helen, who is the cause of the war, and yet hardly acts in the whole performance; his Troy, that holds out so long, without being taken: in short, all these things together make the poem very insipid to me. I have asked some learned men, whether they are not in reality as much tired as myself with reading this poet: those who spoke ingenuously, assured me that he had made them fall asleep, and yet that they could not well avoid giving him a place in their libraries; but that it was merely as they would do an antique, or those rusty medals which are kept only for curiosity, and are of no manner of use in commerce."

"But your excellency does not surely form the same opinion of Virgil?" said Candide. "Why, I grant," replied Pococuranté, "that the second, third, fourth, and sixth books of his "Æneid" are excellent; but as for his pious Æneas, his strong Cloanthes, his friendly Achates, his boy Ascanius, his silly King Latinus, his ill-bred Amata, his insipid Lavinia, and some other characters much in the same strain, I think there cannot in nature by anything more flat and disagreeable. I must confess I prefer Tasso far beyond him; nay, even that sleepy tale-teller Ariosto."[2]

"May I take the liberty to ask if you do not experience great pleasure from reading Horace?" said Candide. "There are maxims in this writer," replied Pococuranté, "whence a man of the world may reap some benefit; and the short measure of the verse makes them more easily to be retained in the memory. But I see nothing extraordinary in his journey to Brundusium, and his account of his bad dinner; nor in his dirty, low quarrel between one Pupilus,[3] whose words, as he expresses it, were full of poisonous filth; and another, whose language was dipped in vinegar. His indelicate verses against old women and witches have frequently given me great offence: nor can I discover the great merit of his telling his friend Mæcenas, that if he will but rank him in the class of lyric poets, his lofty head shall touch the stars. Ignorant readers are apt to judge a writer by his reputation. For my part, I read only to please myself. I like nothing but what makes for my purpose." Candide, who had been brought up with a notion of never making use of his own judgment, was astonished at what he heard; but Martin found there was a good deal of reason in the senator's remarks.

"O! here is a Cicero," said Candide; "this great man I fancy you are never tired of reading?" "Indeed I never read him at all," replied Pococuranté. "What is it to me whether he pleads for Rabirius or Cluentius? I try causes enough myself. I had once some liking for his philosophical works; but when I found he doubted everything, I thought I knew as much as himself, and had no need of a guide to learn ignorance."

"Ha!" cried Martin, "here are eighty volumes of the proceedings of the Academy of Sciences; perhaps there may be something curious and valuable in this collection." "Yes," answered Pococuranté; "so there might if any one of these compilers of this rubbish had only invented the art of pin-making: but all these volumes are filled with empty systems, without one single article conducive to real utility."

"I see a prodigious number of plays," said Candide, "in Italian, Spanish, and French." "Yes," replied the Venetian; "there are I think three thousand, and not three dozen of them good for anything. As to those huge volumes of divinity, and those enormous collections of sermons, they are not all together worth one single page in Seneca; and I fancy you will readily believe that neither myself, nor anyone else, ever looks into them."

[2] Tasso (1544–1595) and Ariosto (1474–1533), Italian poets, were two of Voltaire's favorite authors.

[3] "Rupilius" in Horace's *Satires*, I, vii.

Martin, perceiving some shelves filled with English books, said to the senator: "I fancy that a republican must be highly delighted with those books, which are most of them written with a noble spirit of freedom." "It is noble to write as we think," said Pococuranté; "it is the privilege of humanity. Throughout Italy we write only what we do not think; and the present inhabitants of the country of the Cæsars and Antonines dare not acquire a single idea without the permission of a Dominican father.[4] I should be enamored of the spirit of the English nation, did it not utterly frustrate the good effects it would produce by passion and the spirit of party."

Candide, seeing a Milton, asked the senator if he did not think that author a great man. "Who?" said Pococuranté sharply; "that barbarian who writes a tedious commentary in ten books of rumbling verse, on the first chapter of Genesis?[5] That slovenly imitator of the Greeks, who disfigures the creation, by making the Messiah take a pair of compasses from heaven's armory to plan the world; whereas Moses represented the Deity as producing the whole universe by his *fiat?* Can I think you have any esteem for a writer who has spoiled Tasso's hell and the devil; who transforms Lucifer sometimes into a toad, and at others into a pygmy; who makes him say the same thing over again a hundred times; who metamorphoses him into a school-divine; and who, by an absurdly serious imitation of Ariosto's comic invention of firearms, represents the devils and angels cannonading each other in heaven? Neither I nor any other Italian can possibly take pleasure in such melancholy reveries; but the marriage of Sin and Death, and snakes issuing from the womb of the former, are enough to make any person sick that is not lost to all sense of delicacy. This obscene, eccentric, and disagreeable poem met with the neglect it deserved at its first publication; and I only treat the author now as he was treated in his own country by his contemporaries."

Candide was sensibly grieved at this speech, as he had a great respect for Homer, and was fond of Milton. "Alas!" said he softly to Martin, "I am afraid this man holds our German poets in great contempt." "There would be no such great harm in that," said Martin. "O what a surprising man!" said Candide, still to himself; "what a prodigious genius is this Pococuranté! nothing can please him."

After finishing their survey of the library, they went down into the garden, when Candide commended the several beauties that offered themselves to his view. "I know nothing upon earth laid out in such bad taste,"

---

[4] The Dominicans ran the Inquisition.

[5] Milton first published *Paradise Lost* in ten books in 1667; he divided it into twelve books in the second edition in 1674. Although an admirer of Milton, Voltaire became more and more critical of him in his later years.

said Pococuranté; "everything about it is childish and tiring; but I shall have another laid out to-morrow upon a nobler plan."

As soon as our two travellers had taken leave of his excellency, "Well," said Candide to Martin, "I hope you will own that this man is the happiest of all mortals, for he is above everything he possesses." "But do not you see," answered Martin, "that he likewise dislikes everything he possesses? It was an observation of Plato, long since, that those are not the best stomachs that reject, without distinction, all sorts of aliments." "True," said Candide, "but still there must certainly be a pleasure in criticising everything, and in perceiving faults where others think they see beauties." "That is," replied Martin, "there is a pleasure in having no pleasure." "Well, well," said Candide, "I find that I shall be the only happy man at last, when I am blessed with the sight of my dear Cunégonde." "It is good to hope," said Martin.

In the meanwhile, days and weeks passed away, and no news of Cacambo. Candide was so overwhelmed with grief, that he did not reflect on the behavior of Pacquette and Friar Giroflée, who never stayed to return him thanks for the presents he had so generously made them.

Chapter XXVI.

CANDIDE AND MARTIN DINE WITH SIX FOREIGNERS—WHO THEY WERE.

One evening as Candide, with his attendant Martin, was going to sit down to supper with some foreigners who lodged in the same inn where they had taken up their quarters, a man with a face the color of soot came behind him, and taking him by the arm, said, "Hold yourself in readiness to go along with us; be sure you do not fail." Upon this, turning about to see from whom these words came, he beheld Cacambo. Nothing but the sight of Cunégonde could have given him greater joy and surprise. He was almost beside himself. After embracing this dear friend, "Cunégonde!" said he, "is come with you no doubt! Where, where is she? Carry me to her this instant, that I may die with joy in her presence." "Cunégonde is not here," answered Cacambo; "she is in Constantinople." "Good heavens! in Constantinople! but no matter if she were in China, I would fly there. Quick, quick, dear Cacambo, let us be gone." "Soft and fair," said Cacambo, "stay till you have supped. I cannot at present stay to say anything more to you; I am a slave, and my master waits for me; I must go and attend him at table: but say not a word, only get your supper, and hold yourself in readiness."

Candide, divided between joy and grief, charmed to meet with his faithful agent again, and surprised to hear he was a slave, his heart palpitating, his senses confused, but full of the hopes of recovering his dear Cunégonde, sat down to table with Martin, who beheld all these scenes with great unconcern, and with six strangers, who had come to spend the carnival at Venice.

Cacambo waited at table upon one of those strangers. When supper was nearly over, he drew near to his master, and whispered in his ear, "Sir, your majesty may go when you please; the ship is ready"; and so saying he left the room. The guests, surprised at what they had heard, looked at each other without speaking a word; when another servant drawing near to his master, in like manner said, "Sir, your majesty's post-chaise is at Padua, and the ship is ready." The master made him a sign, and he instantly withdrew. The company all stared at each other again, and the general astonishment was increased. A third servant then approached another of the strangers, and said, "Sir, if your majesty will take my advice, you will not make any longer stay in this place; I will go and get everything ready"; and he instantly disappeared.

Candide and Martin then took it for granted that this was some of the diversions of the carnival, and that these were characters in masquerade. Then a fourth domestic said to the fourth stranger, "Your majesty may set off when you please"; saying which, he went away like the rest. A fifth valet said the same to a fifth master. But the sixth domestic spoke in a different style to the person on whom he waited, and who sat near to Candide. "Faith, sir," said he, "they will trust your majesty no longer, nor myself neither; and we may both of us chance to be sent to jail this very night; and therefore I shall take care of myself, and so adieu." The servants being all gone, the six strangers, with Candide and Martin, remained in a profound silence. At length Candide broke it by saying, "Gentlemen, this is a very singular joke upon my word; how come you all to be kings? For my part I admit that neither my friend Martin here, nor I, have any claim to royalty."

Cacambo's master then began, with great gravity, to speak in Italian. "I am not joking in the least, my name is Achmett III.[1] I was grand seignor for many years; I dethroned my brother, my nephew dethroned me, my viziers lost their heads, and I am condemned to end my days in the old seraglio. My nephew, the Grand Sultan Mahomet, gives me permission to travel sometimes for my health, and I have come to spend the carnival at Venice."

[1] The list of kings mentioned is as follows: Achmet III (1673–1736); Ivan VI (1740–1764); "Bonnie Prince Charles, The Young Pretender" (1720–1788); Augustus III (1696–1763); Stanislas Leczinsky (1677–1766); Baron Neuhov (1690–1765).

A young man who sat by Achmet, spoke next, and said: "My name is Ivan. I was once emperor of all the Russias, but was dethroned in my cradle. My parents were confined, and I was brought up in a prison, yet I am sometimes allowed to travel, though always with persons to keep a guard over me, and I have come to spend the carnival at Venice."

The third said: "I am Charles Edward, king of England; my father has renounced his right to the throne in my favor. I have fought in defence of my rights, and almost a thousand of my friends have had their hearts taken out of their bodies alive and thrown in their faces. I have myself been confined in a prison. I am going to Rome to visit the king my father, who was dethroned like me; and my grandfather and I have come to spend the carnival at Venice."

The fourth spoke thus: "I am the king of Poland; the fortune of war has stripped me of my hereditary dominions. My father experienced the same vicissitudes of fate. I resign myself to the will of Providence, in the same manner as Sultan Achmet, the Emperor Ivan, and King Charles Edward, whom God long preserve; and I have come to spend the carnival at Venice."

The fifth said: "I am king of Poland also. I have twice lost my kingdom; but Providence has given me other dominions, where I have done more good than all the Sarmatian kings put together were ever able to do on the banks of the Vistula; I resign myself likewise to Providence; and have come to spend the carnival at Venice."

It now came to the sixth monarch's turn to speak: "Gentlemen," said he, "I am not so great a prince as the rest of you, it is true, but I am, however, a crowned head. I am Theodore, elected king of Corsica. I have had the title of majesty, and am now hardly treated with common civility. I have coined money, and am not now worth a single ducat. I have had two secretaries, and am now without a valet. I was once seated on a throne, and since that have lain upon straw, in a common jail in London, and I very much fear I shall meet with the same fate here in Venice, where I came, like your majesties, to divert myself at the carnival."

The other five kings listened to this speech with great attention; it excited their compassion; each of them made the unhappy Theodore a present of twenty sequins, and Candide gave him a diamond, worth just a hundred times that sum. "Who can this private person be," said the five princes to one another, "who is able to give, and has actually given, a hundred times as much as any of us?"

Just as they rose from table, in came four serene highnesses, who had also been stripped of their territories by the fortune of war, and had come to spend the remainder of the carnival at Venice. Candide took no manner of notice of them; for his thoughts were wholly employed on his voyage to Constantinople, where he intended to go in search of his lovely Cunégonde.

Chapter XXVII.

CANDIDE'S VOYAGE TO CONSTANTINOPLE.

The trusty Cacambo had already engaged the captain of the Turkish ship that was to carry Sultan Achmet back to Constantinople, to take Candide and Martin on board. Accordingly they both embarked, after paying their obeisance to his miserable highness. As they were going on board, Candide said to Martin, "You see we dined with six dethroned kings, and to one of them I gave charity. Perhaps there may be a great many other princes still more unfortunate. For my part I have lost only a hundred sheep, and am now going to fly to the arms of my charming Cunégonde. My dear Martin, I must insist on it, that Pangloss was in the right. All is for the best." "I wish it may be," said Martin. "But this was an odd adventure we met with at Venice. I do not think there ever was an instance before of six dethroned monarchs supping together at a public inn." "This is not more extraordinary," said Martin, "than most of what happened to us. It is a very common thing for kings to be dethroned; and as for our having the honor to eat with six of them, it is a mere accident, not deserving our attention."

As soon as Candide set his foot on board the vessel, he flew to his old friend and valet Cacambo; and throwing his arms about his neck, embraced him with joy. "Well," said he, "what news of Cunégonde? Does she still continue the paragon of beauty? Does she love me still? How does she do? You have, doubtless, purchased a superb palace for her at Constantinople."

"My dear master," replied Cacambo, "Cunégonde washes dishes on the banks of the Propontis, in the house of a prince who has very few to wash. She is at present a slave in the family of an ancient sovereign named Ragotski,[1] whom the grand Turk allows three crowns a day to maintain him in his exile; but the most melancholy circumstance of all is, that she is turned horribly ugly." "Ugly or handsome," said Candide, "I am a man of honour; and, as such am obliged to love her still. But how could she possibly have been reduced to so abject a condition, when I sent five or six millions to her by you?" "Lord bless me," said Cacambo, "was not I obliged to give two millions to Señor Don Fernando d'Ibaraa y Fagueora y Mascarenes y Lampourdos y Souza, the governor of Buenos Aires, for liberty to take Cunégonde away with me? and then did not a brave fellow of a pirate gallantly strip us of all the rest? And then did not this same pirate carry us with him to Cape Matapan, to Milo, to Nicaria, to Samos, to

---

[1] Francis Leopold Rakoczy, king of Transylvania in 1707. He lost his throne and died in 1735.

Petra, to the Dardanelles, to Marmora, to Scutari? Cunégonde and the old woman are now servants to the prince I have told you of; and I myself am slave to the dethroned sultan." "What a chain of shocking accidents!" exclaimed Candide. "But after all, I have still some diamonds left, with which I can easily procure Cunégonde's liberty. It is a pity though she is grown so ugly."

Then turning to Martin, "What think you friend," said he, "whose condition is most to be pitied, the Emperor Achmet's, the Emperor Ivan's, King Charles Edward's, or mine?" "I cannot resolve your question," said Martin, "unless I were in the hearts of you all." "Ah!" cried Candide, "was Pangloss here now, he would have known, and satisfied me at once." "I know not," said Martin, "in what balance your Pangloss could have weighed the misfortunes of mankind and have set a just estimation on their sufferings. All that I pretend to know of the matter is that there are millions of men on the earth, whose conditions are a hundred times more pitiable than those of King Charles Edward, the Emperor Ivan, or Sultan Achmet." "Why, that may be," answered Candide.

In a few days they reached the Bosphorus; and the first thing Candide did was to pay a high ransom for Cacambo: then, without losing time, he and his companions went on board a galley, in order to search for his Cunégonde on the banks of the Propontis, despite the fact she had grown so ugly.

There were two slaves among the crew of the galley, who rowed very badly, and to whose bare backs the master of the vessel frequently applied a lash. Candide, from natural sympathy, looked at these two slaves more attentively than at any of the rest, and drew near them with an eye of pity. Their features, though greatly disfigured, appeared to him to bear a strong resemblance with those of Pangloss and the unhappy baron Jesuit, Cunégonde's brother. This idea affected him with grief and compassion: he examined them more attentively than before. "In truth," said he, turning to Martin, "if I had not seen my master Pangloss fairly hanged, and had not myself been unlucky enough to run my sword through the baron, I should absolutely think those two rowers were the men."

No sooner had Candide uttered the names of the baron and Pangloss, than the two slaves gave a great cry, ceased rowing, and let fall their oars out of their hands. The master of the vessel, seeing this, ran up to them, and redoubled the discipline of the lash. "Hold, hold," cried Candide, "I will give you what money you shall ask for these two persons." "Good heavens! it is Candide," said one of the men. "Candide!" cried the other. "Do I dream," said Candide, "or am I awake? Am I actually on board this galley? Is this my lord baron, whom I killed? and that my master Pangloss, whom I saw hanged before my face?"

"It is I! it is I!" cried they both together. "What! is this your great philosopher?" said Martin. "My dear sir," said Candide to the master of the galley, "how much do you ask for the ransom of the baron of Thunder-ten tronckh, who is one of the first barons of the empire, and of Pangloss, the most profound metaphysician in Germany?" "Why, then, Christian cur," replied the Turkish captain, "since these two dogs of Christian slaves are barons and metaphysicians, who no doubt are of high rank in their own country, you shall give me fifty thousand sequins." "You shall have them, sir; carry me back as quick as thought to Constantinople, and you shall receive the money immediately—No! carry me first to Cunégonde." The captain, upon Candide's first proposal, had already tacked about, and he made the crew ply their oars so effectually that the vessel flew through the water quicker than a bird cleaves the air.

Candide bestowed a thousand embraces on the baron and Pangloss. "And so then, my dear baron, I did not kill you? and you, my dear Pangloss, are come to life again after your hanging? But how came you slaves on board a Turkish galley?" "And is it true that my dear sister is in this country?" said the baron. "Yes," said Cacambo. "And do I once again behold my dear Candide?" said Pangloss. Candide presented Martin and Cacambo to them; they embraced each other, and all spoke together. The galley flew like lightning, and soon they got back to port. Candide instantly sent for a Jew, to whom he sold for fifty thousand sequins a diamond richly worth one hundred thousand, though the fellow swore to him all the time by Father Abraham that he gave him the most he could possibly afford. He no sooner got the money into his hands, than he paid it down for the ransom of the baron and Pangloss. The latter flung himself at the feet of his deliverer, and bathed him with his tears: the former thanked him with a gracious nod, and promised to return him the money the first opportunity. "But is it possible," said he, "that my sister is in Turkey?" "Nothing is more possible," answered Cacambo, "for she scours the dishes in the house of a Transylvanian prince." Candide sent directly for two Jews, and sold more diamonds to them; and then he set out with his companions in another galley, to deliver Cunégonde from slavery.

Chapter XXVIII.

WHAT BEFELL CANDIDE, CUNÉGONDE, PANGLOSS, MARTIN, ETC.

"Pardon," said Candide to the baron; "once more let me entreat your pardon, Reverend Father, for wounding you in the body." "Say no more about it," replied the baron; "I was a little too hasty I must admit; but as you seem to desire to know by what accident I came to be a slave on board the galley where you saw me, I will inform you. After I had been cured of the wound you gave me, by the college apothecary, I was attacked and carried off by a party of Spanish troops, who clapped me in prison in Buenos Aires, at the very time my sister was setting out from there. I asked leave to return to Rome, to the general of my order, who appointed me chaplain to the French ambassador at Constantinople. I had not been a week in my new office, when I happened to meet one evening with a young, extremely handsome ichoglan.[1] The weather was very hot; the young man had an inclination to bathe. I took the opportunity to bathe likewise. I did not know it was a crime for a Christian to be found naked in company with a young Turk. A cadi ordered me to receive a hundred blows on the soles of my feet, and sent me to the galleys. I do not believe that there was ever an act of more flagrant injustice. But I would like to know how my sister came to be a kitchen maid to a Transylvanian prince, who has taken refuge among the Turks?"

"But how does it happen that I behold you again, my dear Pangloss?" said Candide. "It is true," answered Pangloss, "you saw me hanged, though I ought properly to have been burned; but you may remember, that it rained extremely hard when they were going to roast me. The storm was so violent that they found it impossible to light the fire; so they hanged me because they could do no better. A surgeon purchased my body, carried it home, and prepared to dissect me. He began by making a crucial incision from my navel to the clavicle. It is impossible for anyone to have been more poorly hanged than I had been. The executioner was a subdeacon, and knew how to burn people very well, but as for hanging, he was a novice at it, being quite out of practice; the cord being wet, and not slipping properly, the noose did not join. In short, I still continued to breathe; the crucial incision made me scream to such a degree that my surgeon fell flat upon his back; and imagining it was the devil he was dissecting, ran away, and in his fright tumbled down stairs. His wife hearing the noise, flew from the next room, and seeing me stretched upon the table with my crucial incision, was still more terrified than her husband, and fell upon him. When they had a little recovered themselves, I heard her say to her husband, 'My dear, how could you think of dissecting a heretic? Don't you know that the devil is always in them? I'll run directly to a priest to come and drive the evil spirit out.' I trembled from head to foot at hearing her talk in this manner, and exerted what little strength I had left to cry out, 'Have mercy on me!' At length the Portuguese barber[2] took courage, sewed up my

---

[1] The page of a sultan.

[2] The surgeon.

wound, and his wife nursed me; and I was upon my legs in a fortnight's time. The barber got me a place to be lackey to a knight of Malta, who was going to Venice; but finding my master had no money to pay me my wages, I entered into the service of a Venetian merchant, and went with him to Constantinople.

"One day I happened to enter a mosque, where I saw no one but an old man and a very pretty young female devotee, who was telling her beads; her neck was quite bare, and in her bosom she had a beautiful nosegay of tulips, roses, anemones, buttercups, hyacinths, and auriculas; she let fall her nosegay. I ran immediately to take it up, and presented it to her with a most respectful bow. I was so long in delivering it that the imam began to be angry; and, perceiving I was a Christian, he cried out for help; they carried me before the cadi, who ordered me to receive one hundred strokes, and sent me to the galleys. I was chained in the very galley and to the very same bench with the baron. On board this galley there were four young men belonging to Marseilles, five Neapolitan priests, and two monks of Corfu, who told us that similar adventures happened every day. The baron pretended that he had been worse used than myself; and I insisted that there was far less harm in taking up a nosegay, and putting it into a woman's bosom, than to be found stark naked with a young icho-glan. We were continually whipped, and received twenty lashes a day with a heavy thong, when the concatenation of earthly events brought you on board our galley to ransom us from slavery."

"Well, my dear Pangloss," said Candide to him, "when you were hanged, dissected, whipped, and tugging at the oar, did you continue to think that everything in this world happens for the best?" "I have always abided by my first opinion," answered Pangloss; "for, after all, I am a philosopher, and it would not become me to retract my sentiments, especially as Leibnitz could not be in the wrong: and that pre-established harmony is the finest thing in the world, as well as a *plenum* and the *materia subtilis*."[3]

Chapter XXIX.

IN WHAT MANNER CANDIDE FOUND CUNÉGONDE AND THE OLD WOMAN AGAIN.

While Candide, the baron, Pangloss, Martin, and Cacambo were relating their several adventures, and reasoning on the contingent or non-contingent events of this world, on causes and effects; on moral and physical

---

[3] Leibnitz's optimistic determinism requires that all space in the universe be filled with matter (*plenum*) and that there be a soul ("subtle matter") to influence and control all visible material.

evil, on free will and necessity, and on the consolation that may be felt by
a person when a slave and chained to an oar in a Turkish galley, they arrived at the house of the Transylvanian prince on the coasts of the Propontis. The first objects they beheld there were Cunégonde and the old
woman, who were hanging some tablecloths on a line to dry.

The baron turned pale at the sight. Even the tender Candide, that affec-
tionate lover, upon seeing his fair Cunégonde, all sunburnt, with blear eyes,
a withered neck, wrinkled face and arms, all covered with a red scurf,
started back with horror; but recovering himself, he advanced towards her
out of good manners. She embraced Candide and her brother; they embraced the old woman, and Candide ransomed them both.

There was a small farm in the neighborhood, which the old woman proposed to Candide to use till the company should meet with a more favorable
destiny. Cunégonde, not knowing that she had grown ugly, as no one had
informed her of it, reminded Candide of his promise in so peremptory a
manner that the simple lad did not dare to refuse her; he then told the baron
that he was going to marry his sister. "I will never allow," said the baron,
"my sister to be guilty of an action so derogatory to her birth and family;
nor will I bear this insolence on your part: no, I never will be reproached
that my nephews are not qualified for the first ecclesiastical dignities in
Germany; nor shall a sister of mine ever be the wife of any person below
the rank of a baron of the empire." Cunégonde flung herself at her brother's
feet, and bathed them with tears; but he still continued inflexible. "You
foolish fellow," said Candide, "have I not delivered you from the galleys,
paid your ransom, and your sister's, too, who was a dish washer, and is very
ugly, and yet condescended to marry her? And shall you pretend to oppose
the match? If I were to listen only to the dictates of my anger, I would kill
you again." "You may kill me again," said the baron; "but you shall not
marry my sister while I am living."

Chapter XXX.

CONCLUSION.

Candide had, in truth, no great inclination to marry Cunégonde; but the
extreme impertinence of the baron determined him to conclude the match;
and Cunégonde pressed him so warmly that he could not recant. He consulted
Pangloss, Martin, and the faithful Cacambo. Pangloss composed a fine
memoir, by which he proved that the baron had no right over his sister;
and that she might, according to all the laws of the empire, marry Candide
with the left hand.[1] Martin concluded to throw the baron into the sea;

---

[1] A morganatic marriage in which the party with the lower rank would have no
equality with the party of the higher rank.

Cacambo decided that he must be delivered to the Turkish captain and sent to the galleys, after which he should be conveyed by the first ship to the father-general at Rome. This advice was found to be good; the old woman approved of it, and not a syllable was said to his sister; the business was executed for a little money; and they had the pleasure of tricking a Jesuit and punishing the pride of a German baron.

It was altogether natural to imagine that after undergoing so many disasters, Candide, married to his mistress and living with the philosopher Pangloss, the philosopher Martin, the prudent Cacambo, and the old woman, having besides brought home so many diamonds from the country of the ancient Incas, would lead the most agreeable life in the world. But he had been so robbed by the Jews, that he had nothing left but his little farm; his wife, every day growing more and more ugly, became headstrong and insupportable; the old woman was infirm, and more ill-natured yet than Cunégonde. Cacambo, who worked in the garden, and carried the vegetables from it to sell at Constantinople, was above his labor, and cursed his fate. Pangloss despaired of making an impression in any of the German universities. And as for Martin, he was firmly persuaded that a person is equally ill-situated anywhere. He took things with patience. Candide, Martin, and Pangloss disputed sometimes about metaphysics and morality. Boats were often seen passing under the windows of the farm laden with effendis, bashaws, and cadis[2] that were going into banishment to Lemnos, Mitylene and Erzerum. And other cadis, bashaws, and effendis were seen coming back to succeed the place of the exiles, and were driven out in their turn. They saw several heads curiously stuck upon poles, and carried as presents to the Sublime Porte.[3] Such sights gave occasion to frequent dissertations; and when no disputes were in progress, the irksomeness was so excessive that the old woman ventured one day to tell them, "I would be glad to know which is worst, to be ravished a hundred times by Negro pirates, to have one buttock cut off, to run the gauntlet among the Bulgarians, to be whipped and hanged at an *auto-da-fé*, to be dissected, to be chained to an oar in a galley; and, in short, to experience all the miseries through which every one of us has passed or to remain here doing nothing?" "This," said Candide, "is a grand question."

This discourse gave birth to new reflections, and Martin especially concluded that man was born to live in the convulsions of anxiety or in the lethargy of idleness. Though Candide did not absolutely agree on this, yet he did not state an opinion. Pangloss avowed that he had undergone dreadful sufferings; but having once maintained that everything went on as well as possible, he still maintained it, and at the same time believed nothing of it.

---

[2] Turkish civil and military officials.
[3] The gate of the Sultan's palace where once justice was administered.

There was one thing which more than ever confirmed Martin in his detestable principles, made Candide hesitate, and embarrassed Pangloss: the arrival of Pacquette and Brother Giroflée one day at their farm. This couple had been in the utmost distress; they had very speedily made away with their three thousand piastres; they had parted, been reconciled; quarrelled again, been thrown into prison; had made their escape, and at last Brother Giroflée had turned Turk. Pacquette still continued to follow her trade; but she got little or nothing by it. "I foresaw very well," said Martin to Candide, "that your presents would soon be squandered, and only make them more miserable. You and Cacambo have spent millions of piastres, and yet you are not more happy than Brother Giroflée and Pacquette." "Ah!" said Pangloss to Pacquette, "it is heaven that has brought you here among us, my poor child! Do you know that you have cost me the tip of my nose, one eye, and one ear? What a handsome shape is here! And what is this world!" This new adventure engaged them more deeply than ever in philosophical disputations.

In the neighborhood lived a famous dervish who passed for the best philosopher in Turkey; they went to consult him: Pangloss, who was their spokesman, addressed him thus: "Master, we come to ask you to tell us why so strange an animal as man has been formed."

"Why do you trouble your head about it?" said the dervish; "is it any business of yours?" "But, my reverend father," said Candide, "there is a great deal of evil on earth." "What signifies it," said the dervish, "whether there is evil or good? When his highness sends a ship to Egypt does he trouble his head whether the rats in the vessel are at their ease or not?" "What must then be done?" said Pangloss. "Be silent," answered the dervish. "I flattered myself," replied Pangloss, "to have reasoned a little with you on the causes and effects, on the best of possible worlds, the origin of evil, the nature of the soul, and a pre-established harmony." At these words the dervish shut the door in their faces.

During this conversation, news was spread abroad that two viziers[4] of the bench and the mufti[5] had just been strangled at Constantinople, and several of their friends empaled. This catastrophe made a great stir for some hours. Pangloss, Candide, and Martin, as they were returning to the little farm, met with a good-looking old man, who was taking the air at his door, under an alcove formed of the boughs of orange-trees. Pangloss, who was as inquisitive as he was disputative, asked him what was the name of the mufti who was lately strangled. "I cannot tell," answered the good old man; "I never knew the name of any mufti, or vizier breathing. I am entirely ignorant of the event you speak of; I presume that in general such as are

[4] Prime ministers.
[5] An official expounder of Mohammedan law.

concerned in public affairs sometimes come to a miserable end; and that they deserve it: but I never inquire what is doing at Constantinople; I am contented with sending there the produce of my garden, which I cultivate with my own hands." After saying these words, he invited the strangers to come into his house. His two daughters and two sons presented them with various sorts of sherbet of their own making; besides caymac, heightened with the peels of candied citrons, oranges, lemons, pineapples, pistachio nuts, and Mocha coffee unadulterated with the bad coffee of Batavia or the West Indies. After which the two daughters of this good Mussulman perfumed the beards of Candide, Pangloss, and Martin.

"You must certainly have a vast estate," said Candide to the Turk, who replied, "I have no more than twenty acres of ground, the whole of which I cultivate myself with the help of my children; and our labor keeps off from us three great evils—idleness, vice, and want."

Candide, as he was returning home, made profound reflections on the Turk's discourse. "This good old man," he said to Pangloss and Martin, "appears to me to have chosen for himself a lot much preferable to that of the six kings with whom we had the honor to dine." "Human grandeur," said Pangloss, "is very dangerous, if we believe the testimonies of almost all philosophers; for we find Eglon, king of Moab, was assassinated by Aod; Absalom was hanged by the hair of his head, and run through with three darts; King Nadab, son of Jeroboam, was slain by Baaza; King Ela by Zimri; Okosias by Jehu; Athaliah by Jehoiada; the kings of Jehooiakim, Jeconiah, and Zedekiah, were led into captivity: I need not tell you what was the fate of Croesus, Astyages, Darius, Dionysius of Syracuse, Pyrrhus, Perseus, Hannibal, Jugurtha, Ariovistus, Caesar, Pompey, Nero, Otho, Vitellius, Domitian, Richard II of England, Edward II, Henry VI, Richard III, Mary Stuart, Charles I, the three Henrys of France, and the emperor Henry IV." "Neither need you tell me," said Candide, "that we must take care of our garden." "You are in the right," said Pangloss; "for when man was put into the garden of Eden, it was with an intent to toil there: and this proves that man was not born to be idle." "Work then without disputing," said Martin; "it is the only way to render life supportable."

The little society, one and all, entered into this laudable plan and began to exert their different talents. The little piece of ground yielded them a plentiful crop. Cunégonde indeed was very ugly, but she became an excellent hand at pastrywork; Pacquette embroidered; the old woman had the care of the linen. There was none, down to Brother Giroflé, who failed to perform some service; he was a very good carpenter, and became an honest man. Pangloss used now and then to say to Candide, "There is a concatenation of all events in the best of possible worlds; for, in short, had

you not been put into the Inquisition; had you not travelled over America
on foot; had you not run the sword through the baron; and had you not
lost all your sheep, which you brought from the good country of El Dorado, you would not have been here to eat preserved citrons and pistachio
nuts." "Excellently observed." answered Candide; "but let us cultivate our
garden."

Robert Burns

Holy Willie's Prayer

Robert Burns (1759–1796) was born in Alloway, Ayrshire, Scotland, the son of a tenant farmer. He was largely self-educated in poetry, theology, and philosophy. Although he was raised in a strict Calvinist ethos, his opinions in politics and theology were liberal, and he certainly offended many pious Presbyterians of the country. His first volume, *Poems Chiefly in the Scottish Dialect* (1786), had a great success in intellectual Edinburgh and even in London. It should be noted that Burns as satirist was heir to a rich native tradition which had been established in Scotland in the fifteenth century by Henryson, Dunbar, and others. He owes very little to Pope and the other English neoclassical poets. *Tam O'Shanter* (1790) is his most ambitious satire.

O Thou that in the Heavens does dwell,
Wha, as it pleases best Thysel,
Sends ane to Heaven an' ten to Hell
        A' for Thy glory,
And no for onie guid or ill
           They've done before Thee!

I bless and praise Thy matchless might,
When thousands Thou hast left in night,
That I am here before Thy sight,
        For gifts an' grace   10
A burning and a shining light
           To a' this place.

What was I, or my generation,
That I should get sic exaltation?
I, wha deserv'd most just damnation
        For broken laws
Sax thousand years ere my creation,
           Thro' Adam's cause!

---

1 Holy Willie was in real life William Fisher, a Presbyterian Elder, who upheld the Calvinist doctrine of predestination and election. Before the Presbytery of Ayr he charged Gavin Hamilton, a man of good character, with immoral conduct. Robert Aiken successfully defended the accused man.

When from my mither's womb I fell,
Thou might hae plung'd me deep in hell   20
To gnash my gooms, and weep, and wail
      In burning lakes,
Whare damnéd devils roar and yell,
        Chain'd to their stakes.

Yet I am here, a chosen sample,
To show Thy grace is great and ample:
I'm here a pillar o' Thy temple,
        Strong as a rock,
A guide, a buckler,[2] and example
        To a' Thy flock!   30

O Lord, Thou kens[3] what zeal I bear,
When drinkers drink, and swearers swear,
And singin there and dancin here,
        Wi' great an' sma':
For I am keepit by Thy fear,
        Free frae them a'.

But yet, O Lord! confess I must:
At times I'm fash'd[4] wi' fleshly lust;
An' sometimes, too, in warldly trust,
        Vile self gets in;   40
But Thou remembers we are dust,
        Defiled wi' sin.

O Lord! yestreen,[5] Thou kens, wi' Meg—
Thy pardon I sincerely beg—
O, may't ne'er be a living plague
        To my dishonour!
An' I'll ne'er lift a lawless leg
        Again upon her.

Besides, I farther maun[6] avow—

---

[2] Defender.
[3] Knowest.
[4] Troubled.
[5] Last night.
[6] Must.

Wi' Leezie's lass, three times, I trow—   50
But, Lord, that Friday I was fou,[7]
                    When I cam near her,
Or else, Thou kens, Thy servant true
                    Wad never steer[8] her.

Maybe Thou lets this fleshly thorn
Buffet Thy servant e'en and morn,
Lest he owre proud and high should turn
                    That he's sae gifted:
If sae, Thy han' maun e'en be borne
                    Until Thou lift it.   60

Lord, bless Thy chosen in this place,
For here Thou has a chosen race!
But God confound their stubborn face
                    An' blast their name,
Wha bring Thy elders to disgrace
                    An' open shame!

Lord, mind Gau'n Hamilton's deserts:
He drinks, an' swears, an' plays at cartes,
Yet has sae monie takin arts
                    Wi' great and sma',   70
Frae God's ain Priest the people's hearts
                    He steals awa.

And when we chasten'd him therefore
Thou kens how he bred sic a splore,[9]
And set the warld in a roar
                    O' laughin at us:
Curse Thou his basket and his store,
                    Kail[10] an' potatoes!

Lord, hear my earnest cry and pray'r

---

[7] Drunk.
[8] Meddle with.
[9] Such a row.
[10] Broth.

Against that Presbyt'ry of Ayr!   80
Thy strong right hand, Lord, mak it bare
        Upo' their heads!
Lord, visit them, an' dinna spare,
        For their misdeeds!

O Lord, my God! that glib-tongu'd Aiken,
My vera heart and flesh are quakin
To think how we stood sweatin, shakin,
        An' pish'd wi' dread,
While he, wi' hingin[11] lip an' snakin,[12]
        Held up his head.   90

Lord, in Thy day o' vengeance try him!
Lord, visit him wha did employ him!
And pass not in Thy mercy by them,
        Nor hear their pray'r,
But for Thy people's sake destroy them,
        An' dinna spare!

But, Lord, remember me and mine
Wi' mercies temporal and divine,
That I for grace an' gear[13] may shine
        Excell'd by nane;   100
And a' the glory shall be Thine—
        Amen, Amen.

---

[11] Hanging.
[12] Sneering.
[13] Wealth.

George Gordon, Lord Byron

Dedication from *Don Juan*

Although *Don Juan* is essentially a comic epic with a youthful, buoyant adventurer for its hero, satire plays a significant part in the poem. The narrator sets out to show, as Byron insists, "the *abuses* of the present state of society," attacking war, marriage, romantic love, and education as well as all forms of sham and complacency. In his mock encomium of the Lake poets in the "Dedication" he is satirizing, as one critic has pointed out, those who would seek "to restrain life, to bind and force it into some narrow, permanent form." Castlereagh is also seen as a re-straining power intent on thwarting man's natural freedom. Byron (1788–1824) led a turbulent life marked by scandal, exile, and heroism. His marriage ended in a separation when his wife discovered his incestuous relationship with his half-sister. Forced to leave England in 1816, he wandered throughout the Continent, fathering an illegitimate child by the stepsister of Shelley's wife and carrying on numerous affairs until he settled into a permanent liaison with a married Italian countess. He died from fever just after his thirty-sixth birthday as a result of his participation in the Greek war for independence from the Turks and has always been revered by the Greek people as a national hero.

I

Bob Southey! You're a poet—Poet-laureate,
   And representative of all the race;
Although 't is true that you turned out a Tory at
   Last,—yours has lately been a common case;
And now, my Epic Renegade! what are ye at?
   With all the Lakers, in and out of place?[1]
A nest of tuneful persons, to my eye
Like "four and twenty Blackbirds in a pye;"[2]

II

"Which pye being opened they began to sing,"
   (This old song and new simile holds good),
"A dainty dish to set before the King,"
   Or Regent, who admires such kind of food;—
And Coleridge, too, has lately taken wing,
   But like a hawk encumbered with his hood,—
Explaining Metaphysics to the nation—
I wish he would explain his Explanation.[3]

10

---

[1] Derogatory name for Wordsworth, Coleridge, and Southey, residents of the Lake District.

[2] Henry James Pye (1745–1813), ridiculous poet laureate before Southey.

[3] A reference to Coleridge's discussion of German idealism in his *Biographia Literaria*. Although once an admirer of the poet, Byron was disturbed when he heard that Coleridge had told stories about his conduct on the Continent.

III

You, Bob! are rather insolent, you know,
   At being disappointed in your wish
To supersede all warblers here below,
   And be the only Blackbird in the dish;   20
And then you overstrain yourself, or so,
   And tumble downward like the flying fish
Gasping on deck, because you soar too high, Bob,
And fall, for lack of moisture, quite a-dry, Bob![4]

IV

And Wordsworth, in a rather long "Excursion,"
   (I think the quarto holds five hundred pages),
Has given a sample from the vasty version
   Of this new system to perplex the sages;
'T is poetry—at least by his assertion,
   And may appear so when the dog-star rages—   30
And he who understands it would be able
To add a story to the Tower of Babel.

V

You—Gentlemen! by dint of long seclusion
   From better company, have kept your own
At Keswick, and, through still continued fusion
   Of one another's minds, at last have grown
To deem as a most logical conclusion,
   That Poesy has wreaths for you alone:
There is a narrowness in such a notion,
Which makes me wish you'd change your lakes for Ocean.   40

VI

I would not imitate the petty thought,
   Nor coin my self-love to so base a vice,
For all the glory your conversion brought,
   Since gold alone should not have been its price.

---

[4] Unfulfilled coition.

You have your salary; was't for that you wrought?
   And Wordsworth has his place in the Excise.[5]
You're shabby fellows—true—but poets still,
And duly seated on the Immortal Hill.

VII

Your bays may hide the baldness of your brows—
   Perhaps some virtuous blushes;—let them go—   50
To you I envy neither fruit nor boughs—
   And for the fame you would engross below,
The field is universal, and allows
   Scope to all such as feel the inherent glow:
Scott, Rogers, Campbell, Moore and Crabbe,[6] will try
'Gainst you the question with posterity.

VIII

For me, who, wandering with pedestrian Muses,
   Contend not with you on the wingéd steed,
I wish your fate may yield ye, when she chooses,
   The fame you envy, and the skill you need;   60
And, recollect, a poet nothing loses
   In giving to his brethren their full meed
Of merit—and complaint of present days
Is not the certain path to future praise.

IX

He that reserves his laurels for posterity
   (Who does not often claim the bright reversion)
Has generally no great crop to spare it, he
   Being only injured by his own assertion;

---

5 Byron's note: "Wordsworth's place may be in the Customs—it is, I think, in that or the Excise—besides another at Lord Lonsdale's table, where this poetical charlatan and political parasite licks up the crumbs with a hardened alacrity; the converted Jacobin having long subsided into the clownish sycophant of the worst prejudices of the aristocracy." In 1813 Wordsworth received his position as distributor of stamps for the county of Westmoreland through Lord Lonsdale's "patronage."

6 Poets of the Romantic period.

And although here and there some glorious rarity
   Arise like Titan from the sea's immersion,   70
The major part of such appellants go
To—God knows where—for no one else can know.

X

If, fallen in evil days on evil tongues,[7]
   Milton appealed to the Avenger, Time
If Time, the Avenger, execrates his wrongs,
   And makes the word "Miltonic" mean "*Sublime*,"
He deigned not to belie his soul in songs,
   Nor turn his very talent to a crime;
He did not loathe the Sire to laud the Son,[8]
But closed the tyrant-hater he begun.   80

XI

Think'st thou, could he—the blind Old Man—arise
   Like Samuel from the grave, to freeze once more
The blood of monarchs with his prophecies,
   Or be alive again—again all hoar
With time and trials, and those helpless eyes,
   And heartless daughters—worn—and pale—and poor;
Would *he* adore a sultan? *he* obey
The intellectual eunuch Castlereagh?[9]

XII

Cold-blooded, smooth-faced, placid miscreant!
   Dabbling its sleek young hands in Erin's gore,[10]   90
And thus for wider carnage taught to pant,
   Transferred to gorge upon a sister shore,

---

[7] *Paradise Lost*, VII, 25–26.

[8] The Puritan Milton despised Charles I and did not change his attitude toward the monarchy when Charles II came to the throne in the Restoration.

[9] Vicount Castlereagh (1769–1822) was foreign secretary in the conservative government from 1812 to 1822 and was considered by Byron to be a defender of tyranny.

[10] Castlereagh was responsible for putting down the Irish rebellion.

The vulgarest tool that Tyranny could want,
  With just enough of talent, and no more,
To lengthen fetters by another fixed,
And offer poison long already mixed.

XIII

An orator of such set trash of phrase
  Ineffably—legitimately vile,
That even its grossest flatterers dare not praise,
  Nor foes—all nations—condescend to smile,—   100
Nor even a sprightly blunder's spark can blaze
  From that Ixion grindstone's ceaseless toil,[11]
That turns and turns to give the world a notion
Of endless torments and perpetual motion.

XIV

A bungler even in its disgusting trade,
  And botching, patching, leaving still behind
Something of which its masters are afraid—
  States to be curbed, and thoughts to be confined,
Conspiracy or Congress to be made—
  Cobbling at manacles for all mankind—   110
A tinkering slave-maker, who mends old chains,
With God and Man's abhorrence for its gains.

XV

If we may judge of matter by the mind,
  Emasculated to the marrow *It*
Hath but two objects, how to serve, and bind,
  Deeming the chain it wears even men may fit,
Eutropius of its many masters,—blind[12]
  To worth as freedom, wisdom as to wit,

---

[11] Ixion was chained to a wheel for lack of gratitude to Zeus.
[12] Eutropius, a eunuch who seized power at the court of Arcadius in Constantinople.

Fearless—because *no* feeling dwells in ice,
Its very courage stagnates to a vice.[13]   120

XVI

Where shall I turn me not to *view* its bonds,
   For I will never *feel* them?—Italy!
Thy late reviving Roman soul desponds
   Beneath the lie this State-thing breathed o'er thee—
Thy clanking chain, and Erin's yet green wounds,
   Have voices—tongues to cry aloud for me.
Europe has slaves—allies—kings—armies still—
And Southey lives to sing them very ill.

XVII

Meantime, Sir Laureate, I proceed to dedicate.
   In honest simple verse, this song to you,   130
And, if in flattering strains I do not predicate,
   'T is that I still retain my "buff and blue;"[14]
My politics as yet are all to educate:
   Apostasy's so fashionable, too,
To keep *one* creed's a task grown quite Herculean;
Is it not so, my Tory, ultra-Julian?[15]

---

[13] Byron's note: "Mr. John Murray,—As publisher to the Admiralty and of various Government works, if the five stanzas concerning Castlereagh should risk your ears or the Navy List, you may omit them in the publication . . . ." Murray eventually published them.

[14] Colors of the Whig party during the time of Charles James Fox. Byron wore them.

[15] An apostate in the manner of the Roman Emperor Julian.

Thomas Love Peacock

Nightmare Abbey

Thomas Love Peacock (1785–1866) was the son of a London merchant. As a young man he wrote poetry and formed friendships with other writers, especially Shelley, who was temperamentally quite different. But after publishing several books of verse he found his true métier in the satiric novel. *Headlong Hall* (1816), *Melincourt* (1817), *Nightmare Abbey* (1818), *Crotchet Castle* (1831), and *Gryll Grange* (1860) are his chief works in this genre. In most of these books the situation involves a house party in the country, and the characters talk more than act. Peacock is more interested in ideas than in characterization; the people of his books are (to use his words) "abstractions of embodied classifications." His satiric touch is light, however; he is a kind of Horace in prose, and he shares Horace's disciplined hedonism. Unlike so many of his contemporaries, Peacock was not "alienated" from society; in 1819 he entered the service of the East India Company in London and held a bureaucratic post there for many years. *Nightmare Abbey* in a sense grew out of his friendship with Shelley, who is called Scythrop Glowry in the novel. Scythrop means "sullen countenance" in Greek, and certainly this character is only a partial version of the actual Shelley, who did not always take himself so seriously. Some of the other characters are Mr. Flosky, who represents Coleridge, and Mr. Cypress, who represents the early Byron of the *Childe Harold* period. Mr. Hilary, who represents common sense, is largely Peacock's mouthpiece.

Chapter I

Nightmare Abbey, a venerable family mansion, in a highly picturesque state of semi-dilapidation, pleasantly situated on a strip of dry land between the sea and the fens, at the verge of the county of Lincoln, had the honour to be the seat of Christopher Glowry, Esquire. This gentleman was naturally of an atrabilarious temperament, and much troubled with those phantoms of indigestion which are commonly called *blue devils*. He had been deceived in an early friendship: he had been crossed in love; and had offered his hand, from pique, to a lady, who accepted it from interest, and who, in so doing, violently tore asunder the bonds of a tried and youthful attachment. Her vanity was gratified by being the mistress of a very extensive, if not very lively, establishment; but all the springs of her sympathies were frozen. Riches she possessed, but that which enriches them, the participation of affection, was wanting. All that they could purchase for her became indifferent to her, because that which they could not purchase, and which was more valuable than themselves, she had, for their sake, thrown away. She discovered, when it was too late, that she had mistaken the means for the end—that riches, rightly used, are instruments of happiness, but are not in themselves happiness. In this wilful blight of her affections, she found them valueless as means: they had been the end to which she had immolated all her affections, and were now the only end that remained to her. She did not confess this to herself as a principle of action, but it operated through the medium of unconscious self-deception, and terminated in inveterate avarice. She laid on external things the blame of her mind's internal disorder, and thus became by degrees an accomplished scold. She often went her daily rounds through a series of deserted apartments, every creature in the house vanishing at the creak of her shoe, much more at the sound of her voice, to which the nature of things affords no simile; for, as far as the voice of woman, when attuned by gentleness and love, transcends all other sounds in harmony, so far does it surpass all others in discord, when stretched into unnatural shrillness by anger and impatience.

Mr. Glowry used to say that his house was no better than a spacious kennel, for everyone in it led the life of a dog. Disappointed both in love and in friendship, and looking upon human learning as vanity, he had come to a conclusion that there was but one good thing in the world, *videlicet*, a good dinner; and this his parsimonious lady seldom suffered him to enjoy: but, one morning, like Sir Leoline in *Christabel*,[1] 'he woke and found his lady dead', and remained a very consolate widower, with one small child.

This only son and heir Mr. Glowry had christened Scythrop, from the name of a maternal ancestor, who had hanged himself one rainy day in a fit of *taedium vitae*, and had been eulogized by a coroner's jury in the comprehensive phrase of *felo de se*; on which account, Mr. Glowry held his memory in high honour, and made a punchbowl of his skull.

When Scythrop grew up, he was sent, as usual, to a public school, where a little learning was painfully beaten into him, and from thence to the university, where it was carefully taken out of him; and he was sent home like a well-threshed ear of corn, with nothing in his head: having finished his education to the high satisfaction of the master and fellows of his college, who had, in testimony of their approbation, presented him with a silver fish-slice, on which his name figured at the head of a laudatory inscription in some semi-barbarous dialect of Anglo-Saxonized Latin.

His fellow-students, however, who drove tandem and random in great perfection, and were connoisseurs in good inns, had taught him to drink deep ere he departed. He had passed much of his time with these choice spirits, and had seen the rays of the midnight lamp tremble on many a lengthening file of empty bottles. He passed his vacations sometimes at Nightmare Abbey, sometimes in London, at the house of his uncle, Mr. Hilary, a very cheerful and elastic gentleman, who had married the sister of the melancholy Mr. Glowry. The company that frequented his house was the gayest of the gay. Scythrop danced with the ladies and drank with the gentlemen, and was pronounced by both a very accomplished charming fellow, and an honour to the university.

At the house of Mr. Hilary, Scythrop first saw the beautiful Miss Emily

---

[1] An unfinished poem by Samuel Taylor Coleridge that caught the essence of a medieval romance. Sir Leoline is a rich baron in the fragment.

Girouette. He fell in love; which is nothing new. He was favourably received; which is nothing strange. Mr. Glowry and Mr. Girouette had
a meeting on the occasion, and quarrelled about the terms of the bargain;
which is neither new nor strange. The lovers were torn asunder, weeping
and vowing everlasting constancy; and, in three weeks after this tragical
event, the lady was led a smiling bride to the altar, by the Honourable Mr.
Lackwit; which is neither strange nor new.

Scythrop received this intelligence at Nightmare Abbey, and was half
distracted on the occasion. It was his first disappointment, and preyed
deeply on his sensitive spirit. His father, to comfort him, read him a
Commentary on Ecclesiastes, which he had himself composed, and which
demonstrated incontrovertibly that all is vanity. He insisted particularly
on the text, 'One man among a thousand have I found, but a woman
amongst all those have I not found'.

'How could he expect it,' said Scythrop, 'when the whole thousand were
locked up in his seraglio? His experience is no precedent for a free society
like that in which we live.'

'Locked up or at large,' said Mr. Glowry, 'the result is the same: their
minds are always locked up, and vanity and interest keep the key. I speak
feelingly, Scythrop.'

'I am sorry for it, sir,' said Scythrop. 'But how is it that their minds
are locked up? The fault is in their artificial education, which studiously
models them into mere musical dolls, to be set out for sale in the great toyshop of society.'

'To be sure,' said Mr. Glowry, 'their education is not so well finished
as yours has been; and your idea of a musical doll is good. I bought one
myself, but it was confoundedly out of tune; but, whatever be the cause,
Scythrop, the effect is certainly this, that one is pretty nearly as good as
another, as far as any judgment can be formed of them before marriage.
It is only after marriage that they show their true qualities, as I know by
bitter experience. Marriage is, therefore, a lottery, and the less choice and
selection a man bestows on his ticket the better; for, if he has incurred
considerable pains and expense to obtain a lucky number, and his lucky
number proves a blank, he experiences not a simple, but a complicated
disappointment; the loss of labour and money being superadded to the
disappointment of drawing a blank, which, constituting simply and entirely
the grievance of him who has chosen his ticket at random, is, from its
simplicity, the more endurable.' This very excellent reasoning was thrown
away upon Scythrop, who retired to his tower as dismal and disconsolate
as before.

The tower which Scythrop inhabited stood at the south-eastern angle of
the Abbey; and, on the southern side, the foot of the tower opened on a
terrace, which was called the garden, though nothing grew on it but ivy,

and a few amphibious weeds. The south-western tower, which was ruinous
and full of owls, might, with equal propriety, have been called the aviary
This terrace or garden, or terrace-garden, or garden-terrace (the reader
may name it *ad libitum*), took in an oblique view of the open sea, and
fronted a long track of level sea-coast, and a fine monotony of fens and
windmills.

The reader will judge, from what we have said, that this building was
a sort of castellated abbey; and it will, probably, occur to him to inquire
if it had been one of the strongholds of the ancient church militant.
Whether this was the case, or how far it had been indebted to the taste of
Mr. Glowry's ancestors for any transmutations from its original state, are,
unfortunately, circumstances not within the pale of our knowledge.

The north-western tower contained the apartments of Mr. Glowry. The
moat at its base, and the fens beyond, comprised the whole of his prospect.
This moat surrounded the Abbey, and was in immediate contact with the
walls on every side but the south.

The north-eastern tower was appropriate to the domestics, whom Mr.
Glowry always chose by one of two criterions—a long face, or a dismal
name. His butler was Raven; his steward was Crow; his valet was Skellet.
Mr. Glowry maintained that the valet was of French extraction, and that
his name was Squelette. His grooms were Mattocks and Graves. On one
occasion, being in want of a footman, he received a letter from a person
signing himself Diggory Deathshead, and lost no time in securing this
acquisition; but on Diggory's arrival, Mr. Glowry was horror-struck by
the sight of a round, ruddy face, and a pair of laughing eyes. Deathshead
was always grinning—not a ghastly smile, but the grin of a comic mask;
and disturbed the echoes of the hall with so much unhallowed laughter,
that Mr. Glowry gave him his discharge. Diggory, however, had stayed
long enough to make conquests of all the old gentleman's maids, and left
him a flourishing colony of young Deathsheads to join chorus with the
owls, that had before been the exclusive choristers of Nightmare Abbey.

The main body of the building was divided into rooms of state, spacious
apartments for feasting, and numerous bedrooms for visitors, who, however, were few and far between.

Family interests compelled Mr. Glowry to receive occasional visits from
Mr. and Mrs. Hilary, who paid them from the same motive; and, as the
lively gentleman on these occasions found few conductors for his exuberant
gaiety, he became like a double-charged electric jar, which often exploded
in some burst of outrageous merriment, to the signal discomposure of Mr.
Glowry's nerves.

Another occasional visitor, much more to Mr. Glowry's taste, was Mr.

Flosky,[2] a very lachrymose and morbid gentleman, of some note in the literary world, but in his own estimation of much more merit than name. The part of his character which recommended him to Mr. Glowry, was his very fine sense of the grim and the tearful. No one could relate a dismal story with so many minutiae of supererogatory wretchedness. No one could call up a *raw head and bloody bones* with so many adjuncts and circumstances of ghastliness. Mystery was his mental element. He lived in the midst of that visionary world in which nothing is but what is not. He dreamed with his eyes open, and saw ghosts dancing round him at noontide. He had been in his youth an enthusiast for liberty, and had hailed the dawn of the French Revolution as the promise of a day that was to banish war and slavery, and every form of vice and misery, from the face of the earth. Because all this was not done, he deduced that nothing was done; and from this deduction, according to his system of logic, he drew a conclusion that worse than nothing was done: that the overthrow of the feudal fortress of tyranny and superstition was the greatest calamity that had ever befallen mankind; and that their only hope now was to rake the rubbish together, and rebuild it without any of those loopholes by which the light had originally crept in. To qualify himself for a coadjutor in this laudable task, he plunged into the central opacity of Kantian metaphysics, and lay *perdu* several years in transcendental darkness, till the common daylight of common sense became intolerable to his eyes. He called the sun an *ignis fatuus*; and exhorted all who would listen to his friendly voice, which were about as many called 'God save King Richard', to shelter themselves from its delusive radiance in the obscure haunt of Old Philosophy. This word Old had great charms for him. The good old times were always on his lips; meaning the days when polemic theology was in its prime, and rival prelates beat the drum ecclesiastic with Herculean vigour, till the one wound up his series of syllogisms with the very orthodox conclusion of roasting the other.

But the dearest friend of Mr. Glowry, and his most welcome guest, was Mr. Toobad, the Manichaean Millenarian. The twelfth verse of the twelfth chapter of Revelations was always in his mouth: 'Woe to the inhabiters of the earth and of the sea! for the devil is come among you, having great wrath, because he knoweth that he hath but a short time'. He maintained that the supreme dominion of the world was, for wise purposes, given over for a while to the Evil Principle; and that this precise period of time, commonly called the enlightened age, was the point of his plenitude of power. He used to add that by-and-by he would be cast down, and a high

---

[2] A *corruption* of Filosky, quasi Φιλόσκιος, a lover, or sectator, of shadows.

and happy order of things succeed; but he never omitted the saving clause, 'Not in our time': which last words were always echoed in doleful response by the sympathetic Mr. Glowry.

Another and very frequent visitor was the Reverend Mr. Larynx, the vicar of Claydyke, a village about ten miles distant; a good-natured, accommodating divine, who was always most obligingly ready to take a dinner and a bed at the house of any country gentleman in distress for a companion. Nothing came amiss to him, a game at billiards, at chess, at draughts, at backgammon, at piquet, or at all-fours in a *tête-à-tête*, or any game on the cards, round, square, or triangular, in a party of any number exceeding two. He would even dance among friends, rather than that a lady, even if she were on the wrong side of thirty, should sit still for want of a partner. For a ride, a walk, or a sail in the morning, a song after dinner, a ghost story after supper, a bottle of port with the squire, or a cup of green tea with his lady, for all or any of these, or for anything else that was agreeable to anyone else, consistently with the dye of his coat, the Reverend Mr. Larynx was at all times equally ready. When at Nightmare Abbey, he would condole with Mr. Glowry, drink Madeira with Scythrop, crack jokes with Mr. Hilary, hand Mrs. Hilary to the piano, take charge of her fan and gloves, and turn over her music with surprising dexterity, quote Revelations with Mr. Toobad, and lament the good old times of feudal darkness with the transcendental Mr. Flosky.

Chapter XI

Scythrop, attending one day the summons to dinner, found in the drawing-room his friend Mr. Cypress the poet, whom he had known at college, and who was a great favourite of Mr. Glowry. Mr. Cypress said he was on the point of leaving England, but could not think of doing so without a farewell look at Nightmare Abbey and his respected friends, the moody Mr. Glowry and the mysterious Mr. Scythrop, the sublime Mr. Flosky and the pathetic Mr. Listless; to all of whom, and the morbid hospitality of the melancholy dwelling in which they were then assembled he assured them he should always look back with as much affection as his lacerated spirit could feel for anything. The sympathetic condolence of their respective replies was cut short by Raven's announcement of 'dinner on table'.

The conversation that took place when the wine was in circulation, and the ladies were withdrawn, we shall report with our usual scrupulous fidelity.

MR. GLOWRY. You are leaving England, Mr. Cypress. There is a delightful melancholy in saying farewell to an old acquaintance, when the chances are twenty to one against ever meeting again. A smiling bumper to a sad parting, and let us all be unhappy together.

MR. CYPRESS (*filling a bumper*). This is the only social habit that the disappointed spirit never unlearns.

THE REVEREND MR. LARYNX (*filling*). It is the only piece of academical learning that the finished educatee retains.

MR. FLOSKY (*filling*). It is the only objective fact which the sceptic can realize.

SCYTHROP (*filling*). It is the only styptic for a bleeding heart.

THE HONOURABLE MR. LISTLESS (*filling*). It is the only trouble that is very well worth taking.

MR. ASTERIAS (*filling*). It is the only key of conversational truth.

MR. TOOBAD (*filling*). It is the only antidote to the great wrath of the devil.

MR. HILARY (*filling*). It is the only symbol of perfect life. The inscription 'HIC NON BIBITUR' will suit nothing but a tombstone.

MR. GLOWRY. You will see many fine old ruins, Mr. Cypress; crumbling pillars, and mossy walls—many a one-legged Venus and headless Minerva—many a Neptune buried in sand—many a Jupiter turned topsy-turvy—many a perforated Bacchus doing duty as water-pipe— many reminiscences of the ancient world, which I hope was better worth living in than the modern; though, for myself, I care not a straw more for one than the other, and would not go twenty miles to see anything that either could show.

MR. CYPRESS. It is something to seek, Mr. Glowry. The mind is restless, and must persist in seeking, though to find is to be disappointed. Do you feel no aspirations towards the countries of Socrates and Cicero? No wish to wander among the venerable remains of the greatness that has passed for ever?

MR. GLOWRY. Not a grain.

SCYTHROP. It is, indeed, much the same as if a lover should dig up the buried form of his mistress, and gaze upon relics which are anything but herself, to wander among a few mouldy ruins, that are only imperfect indexes to lost volumes of glory, and meet at every step the more melancholy ruins of human nature—a degenerate race of stupid and shriveled slaves, grovelling in the lowest depths of servility and superstition.

THE HONOURABLE MR. LISTLESS. It is the fashion to go abroad. I have thought of it myself, but am hardly equal to the exertion. To be sure, a little eccentricity and originality are allowable in some cases; and the most eccentric and original of all characters is an Englishman who stays at home.

SCYTHROP. I should have no pleasure in visiting countries that are past all hope of regeneration. There is great hope of our own; and it seems to me that an Englishman, who, either by his station in society, or by his genius, or (as in your instance, Mr. Cypress) by both, has the power of essentially serving his country in its arduous struggle with its domestic enemies, yet forsakes his country, which is still so rich in hope, to dwell in others which are only fertile in the ruins of memory, does what none of those ancients, whose fragmentary memorials you venerate, would have done in similar circumstances.

MR. CYPRESS. Sir, I have quarrelled with my wife; and a man who has quarrelled with his wife is absolved from all duty to his country. I have written an ode to tell the people as much, and they may take it as they list.

SCYTHROP. Do you suppose, if Brutus had quarrelled with his wife, he would have given it as a reason to Cassius for having nothing to do with his enterprise? Or would Cassius have been satisfied with such an excuse?

MR. FLOSKY. Brutus was a senator; so is our dear friend: but the cases are different. Brutus had some hope of political good: Mr. Cypress has none. How should he, after what we have seen in France?

SCYTHROP. A Frenchman is born in harness, ready saddled, bitted, and bridled, for any tyrant to ride. He will fawn under his rider one moment, and throw him and kick him to death the next; but another adventurer springs on his back and by dint of whip and spur on he goes as before. We may, without much vanity, hope better of ourselves.

MR. CYPRESS. I have no hope for myself or for others. Our life is a false nature; it is not in the harmony of things; it is an all-blasting upas, whose root is earth, and whose leaves are the skies which rain their poison-dews upon mankind. We wither from our youth; we gasp with unslaked thirst for unattainable good; lured from the first to the last by phantoms—love, fame, ambition, avarice—all idle, and all ill— one meteor of many names, that vanishes in the smoke of death.[1]

MR. FLOSKY. A most delightful speech, Mr. Cypress. A most amiable and instructive philosophy. You have only to impress its truth on the minds of all living men, and life will then, indeed, be the desert and the solitude; and I must do you, myself, and our mutual friends, the justice to observe, that let society only give fair play at one and the same time, as I flatter myself it is inclined to do, to your system of morals, and my system of metaphysics, and Scythrop's system of politics, and Mr. Listless's system of manners, and Mr. Toobad's

---

[1] See Byron's *Childe Harold*, canto 4, cxxiv, cxxvi.

system of religion, and the result will be as fine a mental chaos as even the immortal Kant himself could ever have hoped to see; in the prospect of which I rejoice.

MR. HILARY. 'Certainly, ancient, it is not a thing to rejoice at.' I am one of those who cannot see the good that is to result from all this mystifying and blue-devilling of society. The contrast it presents to the cheerful and solid wisdom of antiquity is too forcible not to strike anyone who has the least knowledge of classical literature. To represent vice and misery as the necessary accompaniments of genius is as mischievous as it is false, and the feeling is as unclassical as the language in which it is usually expressed.

MR. TOOBAD. It is our calamity. The devil has come among us, and has begun by taking possession of all the cleverest fellows. Yet, forsooth, this is the enlightened age. Marry, how? Did our ancestors go peeping about with dark lanterns, and do we walk at our ease in broad sunshine? Where is the manifestation of our light? By what symptoms do you recognize it? What are its signs, its tokens, its symptoms, its categories, its conditions? What is it, and why? How, where, when is it to be seen, felt, and understood? What do we see by it which our ancestors saw not, and which at the same time is worth seeing? We see a hundred men hanged where they saw one. We see five hundred transported, where they saw one. We see five thousand in the workhouse, where they saw one. We see scores of Bible Societies, where they saw none. We see paper, where they saw gold. We see men in stays, where they saw men in armour. We see painted faces, where they saw healthy ones. We see children perishing in manufactories, where they saw them flourishing in the fields. We see prisons, where they saw castles. We see masters, where they saw representatives. In short, they saw true men, where we see false knaves. They saw Milton, and we see Mr. Sackbut.

MR. FLOSKY. The false knave, sir, is my honest friend; therefore, I beseech you, let him be countenanced. God forbid but a knave should have some countenance at his friend's request.

MR. TOOBAD. 'Good men and true' was their common term, like the καλὸς κάγαθός of the Athenians. It is so long since men have been either good or true, that it is to be questioned which is most obsolete, the fact or the phraseology.

MR. CYPRESS. There is no worth nor beauty but in the mind's idea. Love sows the wind and reaps the whirlwind.[2] Confusion, thrice confounded, is the portion of him who rests even for an instant on that

---

[2] *Childe Harold*, canto 4, cxxiii.

most brittle of reeds—the affection of a human being. The sum of our social destiny is to inflict or to endure.[3]

MR. HILARY. Rather to bear and forbear, Mr. Cypress—a maxim which you perhaps despise. Ideal beauty is not the mind's creation: it is real beauty, refined and purified in the mind's alembic, from the alloy which always more or less accompanies it in our mixed and imperfect nature. But still the gold exists in a very ample degree. To expect too much is a disease in the expectant, for which human nature is not responsible; and, in the common name of humanity, I protest against these false and mischievous ravings. To rail against humanity for not being abstract perfection, and against human love for not realizing all the splendid visions of the poets of chivalry, is to rail at the summer for not being all sunshine, and at the rose for not being always in bloom.

MR. CYPRESS. Human love! Love is not an inhabitant of the earth. We worship him as the Athenians did their unknown God: but broken hearts are the martyrs of his faith, and the eye shall never see the form which phantasy paints, and which passion pursues through paths of delusive beauty, among flowers whose odours are agonies, and trees whose gums are poison.[4]

MR. HILARY. You talk like a Rosicrucian, who will love nothing but a sylph, who does not believe in the existence of a sylph, and who yet quarrels with the whole universe for not containing a sylph.

MR. CYPRESS. The mind is diseased of its own beauty, and fevers into false creation. The forms which the sculptor's soul has seized exist only in himself.[5]

MR. FLOSKY. Permit me to discept. They are the mediums of common forms combined and arranged into a common standard. The ideal beauty of the Helen of Zeuxis was the combined medium of the real beauty of the virgins of Crotona.

MR. HILARY. But to make ideal beauty the shadow in the water, and, like the dog in the fable, to throw away the substance in catching at the shadow, is scarcely the characteristic of wisdom, whatever it may be of genius. To reconcile man as he is to the world as it is, to preserve and destroy or alleviate all that is evil, in physical and moral nature— have been the hope and aim of the greatest teachers and ornaments of our species. I will say, too, that the highest wisdom and the highest genius have been invariably accompanied with cheerfulness. We have

---

[3] Ibid., canto 3, lxxi.
[4] *Childe Harold*, canto 4, cxxi, cxxxvi.
[5] Ibid., canto 4, cxxii.

sufficient proofs on record that Shakespeare and Socrates were the most festive of companions. But now the little wisdom and genius we have seem to be entering into a conspiracy against cheerfulness.

MR. TOOBAD. How can we be cheerful with the devil among us?

THE HONOURABLE MR. LISTLESS. How can we be cheerful when our nerves are shattered?

MR. FLOSKY. How can we be cheerful when we are surrounded by a *reading public*, that is growing too wise for its betters?

SCYTHROP. How can we be cheerful when our general designs are crossed every moment by our little particular passions?

MR. CYPRESS. How can we be cheerful in the midst of disappointment and despair?

MR. GLOWRY. Let us all be unhappy together.

MR. HILARY. Let us sing a catch.

MR. GLOWRY. No: a nice tragical ballad. The Norfolk Tragedy to the tune of the Hundredth Psalm.

MR. HILARY. I say a catch.

MR. GLOWRY. I say no. A song from Mr. Cypress.

ALL. A song from Mr. Cypress.

MR. CYPRESS *sang*—

> There is a fever of the spirit,
>   The brand of Cain's unresting doom,
> Which in the lone dark souls that bear it
>   Glows like the lamp in Tullia's tomb:
>
> Unlike that lamp, its subtle fire
>   Burns, blasts, consumes its cell, the heart,
> Till, one by one, hope, joy, desire,
>   Like dreams of shadowy smoke depart.
>
> When hope, love, life itself, are only
>   Dust—spectral memories—dead and cold—
> The unfed fire burns bright and lonely,
>   Like that undying lamp of old:
> And by that dear illumination,
>   Till time its clay-built home has rent,
> Thought broods on feeling's desolation—
>   The soul is its own monument.

MR. GLOWRY. Admirable. Let us all be unhappy together.

MR. HILARY. Now, I say again, a catch.

THE REVEREND MR. LARYNX. I am for you.

MR. HILARY. *Seamen Three.*

THE REVEREND MR. LARYNX. Agreed. I'll be Harry Gill, with the voice of
   three. Begin.

MR. HILARY *and the* REVEREND MR. LARYNX.

> Seamen three! What men by ye?
> Gotham's three wise men we be.
> Whither in your bowl so free?
> To rake the moon from out the sea.
> The bowl goes trim. The moon doth shine.
> And our ballast is old wine;
> And your ballast is old wine.
>
> Who art thou, so fast adrift?
> I am he they call Old Care.
> Here on board we will thee lift.
> No: I may not enter there.
> Wherefore so? 'Tis Jove's decree,
> In a bowl Care may not be;
> In a bowl Care may not be.
>
> Fear ye not the waves that roll?
> No: in charmed bowl we swim.
> What the charm that floats the bowl?
> Water may not pass the brim.
> The bowl goes trim. The moon doth shine.
> And our ballast is old wine;
> And your ballast is old wine.

This catch was so well executed by the spirit and science of Mr. Hilary,
and the deep triune voice of the reverend gentleman, that the whole party,
in spite of themselves, caught the contagion, and joined in chorus at the
conclusion each raising a bumper to his lips:

> The bowl goes trim. The moon doth shine.
> And our ballast is old wine.

Mr. Cypress, having his ballast on board, stepped, the same evening,
into his bowl, or travelling chariot, and departed to rake seas and rivers,
lakes and canals, for the moon of ideal beauty.

Samuel L. Clemens

Advice to Youth

Samuel L. Clemens (1835–1910) was a satirist most of his writing life. He poked fun at American tourists in *Innocents Abroad* (1869), attacked the greed and hypocrisy of American society in *The Gilded Age* (1873), burlesqued King Arthur and his knights in *A Connecticut Yankee* (1889). Even in *The Adventures of Tom Sawyer* (1876) and *Huckleberry Finn* (1885) he mixed jibes at human foibles with comedy and adventure. Nor did age mellow him. His ridicule of racism in *Pudd'nhead Wilson* (1894), his exposure of man's base nature in "The Man That Corrupted Hadleyburg" (1898), and his stark pessimism in the posthumous *The Mysterious Stranger* reveal an increasingly bitter writer. Rarely was he in that "calm judicial good humor" that he considered essential for genuine satire. The fact is he had seen too much of the dark side of life. A printer, riverboat pilot, prospector, reporter, world correspondent and lecturer, and failed businessman, his tendency when confronted with sham or rapacity was to "curse" or "foam at the mouth," lash out with abuse and invective. Yet there were moments when he practiced the art of satire in "a good enough humor." "Advice to Youth" was one of them. His parody of the time-worn topic instead of inciting him to savage indignation inspired him to try his hand at "fine raillery." Wit triumphs over scorn, tolerant good humor over misanthropy.

Being told I would be expected to talk here, I inquired what sort of a talk I ought to make. They said it should be something suitable to youth—something didactic, instructive, or something in the nature of good advice. Very well. I have a few things in my mind which I have often longed to say for the instruction of the young; for it is in one's tender early years that such things will best take root and be most enduring and most valuable. First, then, I will say to you, my young friends—and I say it beseechingly, urgingly——

Always obey your parents, when they are present. This is the best policy in the long run, because if you don't they will make you. Most parents think they know better than you do, and you can generally make more by humoring that superstition than you can by acting on your own better judgment.

Be respectful to your superiors, if you have any, also to strangers, and sometimes to others. If a person offends you, and you are in doubt as to whether it was intentional or not, do not resort to extreme measures; simply watch your chance and hit him with a brick. That will be sufficient. If you shall find that he had not intended any offense, come out frankly and confess yourself in the wrong when you struck him; acknowledge it like a man and say you didn't mean to. Yes, always avoid violence; in this age of charity and kindliness, the time has gone by for such things. Leave dynamite to the low and unrefined.

Go to bed early, get up early—this is wise. Some authorities say get up with the sun; some others say get up with one thing, some with another. But a lark is really the best thing to get up with. It gives you a splendid reputation with everybody to know that you get up with the lark; and if you get the right kind of a lark, and work at him right, you can easily train him to get up at half past nine, every time—it is no trick at all.

Now as to the matter of lying. You want to be very careful about lying; otherwise you are nearly sure to get caught. Once caught, you can never again be, in the eyes of the good and the pure, what you were before. Many a young person has injured himself permanently through a single clumsy and ill-finished lie, the result of carelessness born of incomplete training. Some authorities hold that the young ought not to lie at all. That, of course, is putting it rather stronger than necessary; still, while I cannot go quite so far as that, I do maintain, and I believe I am right, that the young ought to be temperate in the use of this great art until practice and experience shall give them that confidence, elegance, and precision which alone can make the accomplishment graceful and profitable. Patience, diligence, painstaking attention to detail—these are the requirements; these, in time, will make the student perfect; upon these, and upon these only, may he rely as the sure foundation for future eminence. Think what tedious years of study, thought, practice, experience, went to the equipment of that peerless old master who was able to impose upon the whole world the lofty and sounding maxim that "truth is mighty and will prevail" —the most majestic compound fracture of fact which any of woman born has yet achieved. For the history of our race, and each individual's experience, are sown thick with evidence that a truth is not hard to kill and that a lie told well is immortal. There in Boston is a monument of the man who discovered anesthesia; many people are aware, in these latter days, that that man didn't discover it at all, but stole the discovery from another man. Is this truth mighty, and will it prevail? Ah no, my hearers, the monument is made of hardy material, but the lie it tells will outlast it a million years. An awkward, feeble, leaky lie is a thing which you ought to make it your unceasing study to avoid; such a lie as that has no more real permanence than an average truth. Why, you might as well tell the truth at once and be done with it. A feeble, stupid, preposterous lie will not live two years—except it be a slander upon somebody. It is indestructible, then, of course, but that is no merit of yours. A final word: begin your practice of this gracious and beautiful art early—begin now. If I had begun earlier, I could have learned how.

Never handle firearms carelessly. The sorrow and suffering that have been caused through the innocent but heedless handling of firearms by the young! Only four days ago, right in the next farmhouse to the one where I am spending the summer, a grandmother, old and gray and sweet, one of the loveliest spirits in the land, was sitting at her work, when her young grandson crept in and got down an old, battered, rusty gun which had not been touched for many years and was supposed not to be loaded, and pointed it at her, laughing and threatening to shoot. In her fright she ran screaming and pleading toward the door on the other side of the room; but as she passed him he placed the gun almost against her very breast and pulled the trigger! He had supposed it was not loaded. And he was right—it wasn't. So there wasn't any harm done. It is the only case of that kind I ever heard of. Therefore, just the same, don't you meddle with old unloaded firearms; they are the most deadly and unerring things that have ever been created by man. You don't have to take any pains at all with them; you don't have to have a rest, you don't have to have any sights on the gun, you don't have to take aim, even. No, you just pick out a relative and bang away, and you are sure to get him. A youth who can't hit a cathedral at thirty yards with a Gatling gun in three-quarters of an hour, can take up an old empty musket and bag his grandmother every time, at a hundred. Think what Waterloo would have been if one of the armies had been boys armed with old muskets supposed not to be loaded, and the other army had been composed of their female relations. The very thought of it makes one shudder.

There are many sorts of books; but good ones are the sort for the young to read. Remember that. They are a great, an inestimable, an unspeakable means of improvement. Therefore be careful in your selection, my young friends; be very careful; confine yourselves exclusively to Robertson's Sermons, Baxter's *Saint's Rest, The Innocents Abroad,* and works of that kind.

But I have said enough. I hope you will treasure up the instructions which I have given you, and make them a guide to your feet and a light to your understanding. Build your character thoughtfully and painstaking upon these precepts, and by and by, when you have got it built, you will be surprised and gratified to see how nicely and sharply it resembles everybody else's.

H. L. Mencken

Hell and Its Outskirts

H. L. Mencken (1880–1956) was one of America's great prose satirists. Born and educated in Baltimore, he spent most of his life there, writing first for the *Baltimore Morning Herald* and then for the *Baltimore Sun* until 1941. He was also editor of two important periodicals, *The Smart Set* and *The American Mercury*. As journalist, essayist, linguist, and critic he commented on all aspects of American life with remarkable vigor, clarity, and intelligence. Few of our writers have been so wide-ranging and so provocative. His most famous and important work is *The American Language*. The bulk of his satires are contained in *Prejudices*, six volumes of essays he published from 1919 to 1927. Of these pieces the best known are his attack on the South, "The Sahara of the Bozart," and his ridicule of "evangelical Christianity as a going concern" in "The Hills of Zion," an account of the Scopes trial. He demonstrates that he is a "skeptic in religion" in his discussion of the term "hell," a discussion that combines his skepticism with his lifelong interest in language. There is no better description of his role as a satirist than his remarks in 1946: "People are in a state of imbecility. The country is a wreck. Don't ask me for the remedy. It's always been my function to name the disease."

It doesn't matter what they preach,
Of high or low degree:
The old Hell of the Bible
Is Hell enough for me.

'Twas preached by Paul and Peter;
They spread it wide and free;
'Twas Hell for Old John Bunyan
And it's Hell enough for me.

The author of these elegiac strophes, Frank Lebby Stanton, has been moldering in the red clay of Georgia for a long, long while, but what he wrote went straight to the hearts of the American people, and there it still glows warmly. Hell remains the very essence not only of their dogmatic theology but also of their everyday invective. They employ it casually more than any other *Kulturvolk*, and perhaps more than all others put together. They have enriched it with a vast store of combinations, variations, licks, breaks, and riffs. They have made it roar and howl, and they have made it coo and twitter. It helps to lift them when supersonic waves of ecstasy rush through their lymphatic systems, and it soothes them when they roll in the barbed wire of despair. To find its match, you must go to the Buddhist *Om mani padma Hum*, meaning anything you please, or the Moslem *al-hamdu lil'lah*, meaning the same, or the ancient Mesopotamian Word from the Abyss, *Muazaga-gu-abzu*. Even so, *hell* is far ahead, for, compared to it, all these ejaculations have a pale and pansy cast, as does *hell* itself in nearly every other language; e.g., *enfer* in French, *infierno* in Spanish, *helvede* in Danish, *jigoku* in Japanese, and *Hölle* in

German. So long ago as 1880, in the appendix on "The Awful German Language" to "A Tramp Abroad," Mark Twain derided *Hölle* as "chipper, frivolous and unimpressive" and marveled that anyone invited to go there could "rise to the dignity of feeling insulted." He had never heard, apparently, of the even more flaccid Finnish *manala*, which in These States would be the name of an infant food or perhaps of a female infant among the Bible-searchers of the Dust Bowl.

Hell is one of the most ancient and honorable terms in English, and etymologists in their dusty cells have traced it to the first half of the ninth century. It is thus appreciably older than either *home* or *mother* and nearly five centuries older than its great rival, *damn*. But it was not until Shakespeare's time that it began to appear in the numerous blistering phrases that now glorify it—e.g., *go to hell, to hell with, hell to pay, hell is loose, hellcat,* and so on—and even then it rose only to be knocked down, for Shakespeare's time also saw the beginnings of the Puritan murrain, and once the bluenoses were in power they put down all strong language with a brutal hand. At the Restoration, of course, it was reliberated, but only in a spavined state. The Cavaliers, male and female, were great swearers, but their oaths were nearly all cautious and cushioned. Such examples as *gadzooks, zounds, 'sdeath, 'sblood, by'r Lady, a plague on't, rat me, split my windpipe, marry,* and *burn me* are heard in America today, when they are heard at all, only among candidates in theology and Boy Scouts. The English, indeed have never recovered from the blight of Puritanism, and their swearing strikes all other civilized peoples as puny. They are constantly working up a pother over such forms as *bloody*, which to the rest of the world are quite innocuous. *Good gracious*, which appeared in Oliver Goldsmith's "Good Natur'd Man" in 1768, seems to have been regarded in that day as pretty pungent, and *mercy*, which preceded it by some years, was frowned upon as blasphemous. "Our armies," says Uncle Toby in "Tristram Shandy," "swore terribly in Flanders," but at home such virtuosity was rare, even among the military. In the wars of our own time, the swearing of the English has provoked the contempt of both their allies and their enemies. In both World War I and World War II, they depended mainly upon a couple of four-letter words that are obscene but not profane, and what they made of them showed little ingenuity or imagination. The American military borrowed these terms in a spirit probably more derisory than admiring, and dropped them the instant they were restored to Mom.

But as the brethren of the Motherland lost their Elizabethan talent for wicked words it was transferred to these shores. Even the Puritans of New England, once they settled down, took to cussing out one another in a violent manner, and thousands of them were sent to the stocks or whipping post for it by their baffled magistrates. The heroes of the Revolution not only swore in all the orthodox forms but also invented a new expletive, *tarnation*, which survived until the Mexican War. As Dr. Louise Pound has demonstrated with great learning, both *tarnation* and *darn* were derived from *eternal* and the former preceded the latter in refined use. George Washington himself cut loose with *hell* and *damn* whenever the imbecilities of his brass went too far. But it was the great movement into the West following the War of 1812 that really laid the foundations of American profanity and got *hell* firmly on its legs. Such striking forms as *to raise hell, to hell around, hell-bent for election, to be hell on, to play hell with, what the hell, heller, merry hell, hellish, hellcat, hell on wheels, hell and high water, from hell to breakfast, a hoot in hell, the hell of it, hell's a-poppin,' the hell you say, hell with the lid off,* and *the hinges of hell* were then invented by the gallant fellows, many of them fugitives from Eastern sheriffs, who legged it across the great plains to die for humanity at the hands of Indians, buffalo, catamounts, rattlesnakes, bucking broncos, and vigilance committees. For nearly two generations ninetenths of the new terms in America, whether profane or not, came from the region beyond Wheeling, West Virginia, and were commonly called Westernisms. It was not until after the Civil War that the newspaper wits of the East began to contribute to the store, and not until after World War I that concocting such things became the monopoly of Hollywood press agents, radio mountebanks, and Broadway columnists.

The great upsurge of *hell* that rose to a climax in the Mexican War era naturally upset the contemporary wowsers, and they busied themselves launching euphemistic surrogates. Some of these seem to have been imported from the British Isles, along with Dundreary whiskers, soda water, and bathing; for example, *by heck*, which originated there as a substitute for *by Hector*, itself a substitute for *by God*, but was already obsolete at home by the time it appeared in America. Here it not only flourished among the prissy in its prototypical form but also moved over into the domain of *hell* and gave birth to *a heck of a, to raise heck, to run like heck, colder than heck, to play heck with, to beat heck, what the heck,* and *go to heck*. Other deputies for *hell* were invented on American soil, notably *thunder* and *blazes*. *Go to thunder* in the sense of *go to hell* is traced by the "Dictionary of American English" to 1848 and marked an Americanism, and at about the same time *thunderation* began to be used for *damnation*. But soon *thunderation* was used in place of *hell*, as in *what the thunderation*. It is possible that German immigration helped to spread it in its various forms, for a favorite German expletive in those days was *Donnerwetter*; i.e., thundery weather. But this is only a guess, and, like all other learned men, I am suspicious of guessing.

After the Civil War there was another great upsurge of wowserism, culminating in the organization of the Comstock Society in 1873[1] and of the Woman's Christian Temperance Union the year following. Neither organization devoted itself specifically to profanity, but the moral indignation that radiated from both of them soon began to afflict it, and by 1880 it was being denounced violently in thousands of far-flung evangelical pulpits. In this work, the leader was the Reverend Sam Jones, who had been converted and ordained a Methodist clergyman in 1872. Sam roared against cussing as he roared against boozing, but the Devil fetched him by seducing him into using stronger and stronger language himself, and toward the end of his life I more than once heard him let go with objurgations that would have cheered a bouncer clearing out a Sailor's Bethel. Even the Catholics, who ordinarily never mistake the word for the deed, joined the crusade, and in 1882 they were reviving the Holy Name Society, which had been organized back in 1274 and then forgotten. This combined assault had some effect; indeed, it probably had much more effect than it has been given credit for. At all events, the lush profanity of the Civil War era began to shrink and pale, and such unearthly oaths as *Jesus Christ and John Jacob Astor, by the high heels of St. Patrick,* and *by the double-barreled jumping Jiminetty* began to vanish from the American repertory. *God damn* kept going downhill throughout my youth in the eighties and nineties, and by the time I came of age I seldom used it. Many new euphemisms took the places of the forthright oaths of an earlier day. and one of them, *hully gee,* quickly became so innocuous that when Edward W. Townsend introduced it into "Chimmie Fadden," in 1895, it fell almost as flat as the four-letter words with which the lady novelists now pepper their pages.

But *hell* and *damn* somehow survived this massacre—maybe because the new euphemisms left a man choking and gasping when the steam really rose in his gauges, or maybe because some amateur canon lawyer discovered that in their naked state, uncoupled to sacred names, they are not officially blasphemous. Whatever the reason, American profanity was saved, and to this day it revolves around them and recruits itself from their substance. *Damn* is plainly the feebler of the two, despite its crashing effect when used by a master. *Hell* is enormously more effective, if only because it is more protean. For one phrase embodying the former there are at least forty embodying the latter, and many of them are susceptible to elegant and ingenious permutations. It is impossible for *damn*

---

[1] Its legal name was The New York Society for the Suppression of Vice. In 1947 that name was changed to the Society to Maintain Public Decency. Old Anthony Comstock was snatched up to Heaven in 1915 and succeeded by John S. Summer.

to bust loose, or to freeze over; it is impossible to knock it out of anyone, or to give it to anyone, or to beat it, or to raise it, or to think of a snowball or a bat in it, or to link it to high water, or to be *damn*-bent for election, or to plunge from *damn*-to-breakfast, or to *damn* around, or to get the *damn* out of any place, or to pull its lid off, or to think of it as having bulbs or hinges. There is no such thing as a *damn*-hound, a *damn*-cat, a *damn*hole, or a *damn*ion. Nothing is as black as *damn*, as busy as *damn*, as hot (or cold) as *damn*, or as deep, crazy, dumb, clever, cockeyed, crooked, touchy, dead, drunk, nervous, dull, expensive, scared, funny, hungry, lonely, mad, mean, poor, real, rotten, rough, serious, sick, smart, or sore as *damn*. *Damn* is a simple verb and its only child is a simple adjective, but *hell* ranges over all the keys of the grammatical scale and enters into combinations as avidly as oxygen.

There was a time when men learned in the tongues turned trembling backs upon such terms, but in recent years they have shown a libido for studying them, and the result is a rising literature. One of the earliest of the new monographs upon the subject—and still one of the best—was published in *American Speech* in August, 1931, by Dr. L. W. Merryweather. Probing scientifically, he discovered a great deal about *hell* that no one had ever noticed before. It can be slung about, he found, through nearly all the parts of speech. It can be used to represent almost every shade of meaning from yes to no, so that *hell of a time* may mean both the seraphic felicity of a police sergeant in a brewery and the extreme discomfort of a felon in the electric chair. A thing may be either *hotter than hell* or *colder than hell*. A *hellcat* may be either a woman so violent that her husband jumps overboard or nothing worse than a college cheerleader. *What in hell* is a mere expression of friendly interest, but *who the hell says so* is a challenge to fight. Merryweather threw out the suggestion that the upsurge and proliferation of *hell* in the Old West may have been due to Mormon influence. The Saints, he said, were very pious fellows and avoided the vain use of sacred names, but they were also logicians and hence concluded that the use of terms of precisely opposite connotation might be allowable, and even praiseworthy. At all events, they began to swear *by hell* and to call ordinary Christians *hellions* and *sons of hell*, and these terms were quickly borrowed by the miners, trappers, highwaymen, and others who invaded their Zion and out of them flowed some of the most esteemed terms in *hell* of today. Whether Merryweather was right here I do not presume to say, but in another of his conclusions he undoubtedly slipped, as even savants sometimes do. "Today," he said, "*hell* fills so large a place in the American vulgate that it will probably be worn out in a few years more, and will become obsolescent." We all know now that nothing of the sort has happened. *Hell*, in fact, is flourishing as never before. I have many hundreds of examples of its use in my archives, and new ones are being added almost every day.

A large number of swell ones were assembled into a monograph by another scholar, Dr. Bartlett Jere Whiting, published in *Harvard Studies and Notes in Philology and Literature*, Vol. XX, 1938. Whiting, a sequestered philologian interested chiefly in Old and Middle England, sought his material not in the market place but in books—mostly novels of the 1920– 37 period. But even within this narrow and somewhat dephlogisticated field he found enough phrases based on *hell* to fill twenty-four pages of the austere journal in which he wrote. I have space for only a few examples: *holy hell, fifteen kinds of hell, to batter hell into, assorted hell, the seven hinges of hell, thicker than fiddlers in hell, four naked bats out of hell, like a shot out of hell, the chance of a celluloid collar in hell, three hurrahs in hell, hell's own luck, hell up Sixth Street, hell on toast, from hell to Harvard, hell gone from nowhere, like a hangman from hell, hell's half acre, hell-for-leather,* and *what the red* (or *bloody) hell.* Whiting duly noted *hell of a business, hurry, jam, job, life, mess, place, row, time,* and *way* but overlooked George Ade's *hell of a Baptist.* He added some euphemisms for *hell*—for example, *billy-be-damned, billy-ho,* and *blazes*—but he had to admit that these "makeshifts and conscience-easers," as he called them, were all pretty feeble.

Robert Southey, more than a century ago, investigated the names of the principal devils of Hell, and not only printed a list of them in one of his books but also suggested that some might be useful as cuss words; e.g., *Lacahabarrutu, Buzache, Knockadawe, Baa,* and *Ju.* There were, however, no takers for his suggestion and he got no further with the subject. In Harlem, according to Zora Neale Hurston, the dark geographers have discovered that there is a hotter Hell lying somewhat south of the familiar Christian resort, and have given it the name of *Beluthahatchie.* So far, not much has been learned about its amperage, sociology, or public improvements, but its temperature has been fixed tentatively somewhere between that of a blast furnace and that of the sun. These Afro-American explorers also believe that their spectroscopes have found three suburbs of Hell proper, by name *Diddy-wah-diddy, Ginny Gall,* and *West Hell.* Unhappily, not much is known about them, though several ghosts returned to earth report that *Diddy-wah-diddy* is a sort of Long Island, given over mainly to eating houses and night clubs, and that *West Hell* lies beyond the railroad tracks and is somewhat tacky.

T. S. Eliot

Mr. Apollinax

T. S. Eliot (1888–1965), one of the great poets of this century, was born in St. Louis of a distinguished Massachusetts family who had gone west. He studied philosophy at Harvard, where he almost finished his doctorate, at the University of Paris, and at Oxford. He remained in England and eventually became a British subject. Although he was not primarily a satirist, some of his early poems are certainly in this mode, especially the Bostonian portraits such as "Cousin Nancy" and "Mr. Apollinax." In a sense they are a preparation for "Gerontion" and *The Waste Land*. "Mr. Apollinax" is a witty presentation of Bertrand Russell, the famous philosopher-mathematician, who visited Harvard during Eliot's student days. The fictional name suggests that he is a son of Apollo, the god of light, and the epigraph from Lucian's dialogue "Zeuxis and Antiochus" is mock eulogy: "Oh the freshness! By Heracles, the marvel! What an ingenious man!" Mr. Apollinax is both refined and coarse in his social behavior (like Bertrand Russell, as we· now know); and like Proteus, the old man of the sea, he assumes many forms. Mrs. Phlaccus is Mrs. Jack Gardner, the art patron and hostess whose palace still exists in Boston. Professor Channing-Cheetah is probably Charles Eliot Norton, the Harvard art historian. Although "Mr. Apollinax" is the work of a postsymbolist poet, it is Horatian in tone and technique—especially in its use of dialogue.

Ω τῆς καινότητος.   Ἡράκλεις, τῆς, παραδοξολογίας.
εὐμήχανος ἄνθρωπος.

LUCIAN.

When Mr. Apollinax visited the United States
His laughter tinkled among the teacups.
I thought of Fragilion, that shy figure among the birch-trees,
And of Priapus in the shrubbery
Gaping at the lady in the swing.
In the palace of Mrs. Phlaccus, at Professor Channing-Cheetah's
He laughed like an irresponsible fœtus.
His laughter was submarine and profound
Like the old man of the sea's
Hidden under coral islands   10
Where worried bodies of drowned men drift down in the green silence,
Dropping from fingers of surf.
I looked for the head of Mr. Apollinax rolling under a chair

   Or grinning over a screen
With seaweed in its hair.
I heard the beat of centaur's hoofs over the hard turf
As his dry and passionate talk devoured the afternoon.
"He is a charming man"—"But after all what did he mean?"—
"His pointed ears. . . . He must be unbalanced,"—
"There was something he said that I might have challenged."   20
Of dowager Mrs. Phlaccus, and Professor and Mrs. Cheetah
I remember a slice of lemon, and a bitten macaroon.

303

Wallace Stevens

A High-Toned
Old Christian Woman

Wallace Stevens (1879–1955) was born in Reading, Pennsylvania. After attending Harvard and the New York University Law School, he practiced law for some years in New York City. In 1916 he became associated with the Hartford Accident and Indemnity Company, and eventually he was made vice-president of the firm. His first book of poems, *Harmonium*, was not published until 1923 and the second, *Ideas of Order*, until 1935, but the last 20 years of his life were very productive. The *Collected Poems* of 1954 is his most important volume. "A High-Toned Old Christian Woman" (1922) is a satirical treatment of the same theme that is taken up in another way in "Sunday Morning" (1915). Here the poet from his aesthetic point of view (symbolized by the peristyle) taunts the woman, who represents a moralistic point of view (symbolized by the nave).

Poetry is the supreme fiction, madame.
Take the moral law and make a nave[1] of it
And from the nave build haunted heavens. Thus,
The conscience is converted into palms,
Like windy citherns[2] hankering for hymns.
We agree in principle. That's clear. But take
The opposing law and make a peristyle,
And from the peristyle project a masque[3]
Beyond the planets. Thus, our bawdiness,
Unpurged by epitaph, indulged at last,   10
Is equally converted into palms,[4]
Squiggling like saxophones. And palm for palm,
Madame, we are where we began. Allow,
Therefore, that in the planetary scene
Your disaffected flagellants, well-stuffed,
Smacking their muzzy bellies in parade,
Proud of such novelties of the sublime,
Such tink and tank and tunk-a-tunk-tunk,
May, merely may, madame, whip from themselves

---

[1] The area of the Christian church, where the congregation sits. In contrast to it is the peristyle, a colonnade around a building. It is associated with Greek architecture and pagan temples.
[2] Aeolian harps, stringed instruments upon which the wind plays.
[3] A play given at court combining songs, dances, and elaborate scenery and costumes.
[4] Palm leaves belong to pagan as well as Christian ritual.

A jovial hullabaloo among the spheres.[5]   20
This will make widows wince. But fictive things
Wink as they will. Wink most when widows wince.

---

[5] The "music of the spheres" was thought to derive from the motion of the planets revolving around the earth.

W. H. Auden

The Unknown Citizen

W. H. Auden (1907–1973) was born in York, England, and grew up in Birmingham, where his father was a medical officer. By the time he went to Oxford in 1925, he was already writing poetry, and his first little book was printed in 1928. His *Poems* of 1930 was published under the auspices of T. S. Eliot, and it initiated a decade that is sometimes called the "Auden era." His work in poetry and drama was extensive and influential during this period in England. In 1939 he emigrated to the United States, where he lived for most of the rest of his life; in 1946 he became an American citizen. "The Unknown Citizen" was first published in 1939. It easily falls in the ancient genre of antiutopian satire, but its terms and style are modern. The "utopia" in this case is a bureaucratic society in which the individual is gradually subsumed into statistics and reports. The title is a parody of the Unknown Soldier, who, though anonymous, is supposed to have died for a noble cause.

(To JS/07/M/378
This Marble Monument
Is Erected by the State)

He was found by the Bureau of Statistics to be
One against whom there was no official complaint,
And all the reports on his conduct agree
That, in the modern sense of an old-fashioned word, he was a saint,
For in everything he did he served the Greater Community.
Except for the War till the day he retired
He worked in a factory and never got fired,
But satisfied his employers, Fudge Motors Inc.
Yet he wasn't a scab or odd in his views,
For his Union reports that he paid his dues,   10
(Our report on his Union shows it was sound)
And our Social Psychology workers found
That he was popular with his mates and liked a drink.
The Press are convinced that he bought a paper every day
And that his reactions to advertisements were normal in every way.
Policies taken out in his name prove that he was fully insured,
And his Health-card shows he was once in hospital but left it cured.
Both Producers Research and High-Grade Living declare
He was fully sensible to the advantages of the Installment Plan
And had everything necessary to the Modern Man,   20
A phonograph, a radio, a car and a frigidaire.

Our researchers into Public Opinion are content
That he held the proper opinions for the time of year;
When there was peace, he was for peace; when there was war, he went.
He was married and added five children to the population,
Which our Eugenist says was the right number for a parent of his
       generation,
And our teachers report that he never interfered with their education.
Was he free? Was he happy? The question is absurd:
Had anything been wrong, we should certainly have heard.

Criticism

Robert C. Elliott

Satire and Magic: History

You'll accidentally find
    in barrows of books,
wrought-iron lines of long-buried poems;
handle them
    with the care that respects
ancient
    but terrible weapons.
—VLADIMIR MAYAKOVSKY, "AT THE TOP OF MY VOICE"

1. Greece

At the end of his play *Poetaster*, Ben Jonson justifies his satire and threatens his enemies. The climax of the threat comes in these lines:

> I could doe worse,
> Arm'd with ARCHILOCHVS fury, write *Iambicks*,
> Should make the desperate lashers hang themselues.
> Rime 'hem to death, as they doe *Irish* rats
> In drumming tunes.

Behind Jonson's boast lie themes and traditions and beliefs which point both ways in time: backward into the dimmest recesses of history, forward to the latest poetic flyting to come from the press. . . .

Archilochus, whose power Jonson claims, was a Greek satirist of the seventh century B.C. According to tradition, he was the first who "dipt a

313

bitter Muse in snake-venom and stained gentle Helicon with blood"; travelers are warned to pass softly by his tomb, lest the wasps that settle there be aroused.[1] Even today, of course, we speak of satire as "venomous," "cutting," and "stinging," although as we use these terms we may be a little self-conscious about the extravagance of what are, for us, mere metaphors. It was not always so. Our language preserves the memory of a once-powerful belief: Archilochus' verses had demonic power; his satire killed. Indeed, all satire "kills," symbolically at any rate, and Archilochus is the archetypal figure in the tradition.

The curious legend which attributed deadly power to Archilochus' verse was widespread in antiquity, carried great authority. We shall examine it closely, but the best approach is indirect: like so many others, by way of Aristotle. In the *Poetics* Aristotle says that poetry broke into two kinds, the graver sort of poets producing hymns and panegyrics, the meaner sort "invectives" (variously translated: satires, lampoons), which were written in the iambic meter: "hence our present term 'iambic,' because it was the metre of their 'iambs' or invectives against one another." Homer's *Margites* is the first poem of this kind we know, says Aristotle; by presenting "a dramatic picture of the Ridiculous," it outlines the general forms comedy will take. In fact, the *Margites* "stands in the same relation to our comedies as the *Iliad* and *Odyssey* to our tragedies." As soon as comedy appeared in the field, says Aristotle, "those naturally drawn to the one line of poetry became writers of comedies instead of iambs," because the new mode was grander and more highly esteemed than the old.

Comedy originated, according to Aristotle, in improvisations—the improvisations of the authors or leaders of the Phallic Songs, "which still survive as institutions in many of our cities."[2] Thus far we have Aristotle's authority that comedy developed out of invective or satire, and we want now to follow the lead provided by the reference to the Phallic Songs. These songs, we know, were a feature of the fertility rituals common to many peoples over Europe and Asia Minor. The exact form of the songs has not been preserved, although a brief scene in Aristophanes' *Acharnians* (ll. 237 ff.) seems to incorporate the principal elements of the rite. Working with this scene and much analogous material, F. M. Cornford has been able to reconstruct hypothetically the form required by the ceremonial

---

[1] Gaetulicus in *The Greek Anthology*, Bk. vii, No. 71; cited in *Elegy and Iambus*, ed. and trans. J. M. Edmonds (London, 1931), II, 97.

[2] *Aristotle on the Art of Poetry*, 4.1448ᵇ-1449ᵃ, trans. Ingram Bywater (Oxford, 1909), pp. 11-13. The Greeks (for that matter, the Romans) had no single word equivalent to our *satire*. In dealing with early satire I shall not attempt to distinguish among *lampoon, invective, abuse, ridicule*, etc.; and so long as some element of formalization has gone into the utterance, I shall use these terms, together with the Greek *iambi* (iambics), as generally equivalent to *satire*.

purpose. The Phallic Song, in his view, was divided antiphonally between a chorus and a leader or succession of leaders; it consisted of invocation of the god: "Hymen, O Hymenaee" or "O Phales, Phales!" (the image of the god would have been in evidence, erect on a pole) and an iambic element, improvised by the leaders and directed at individuals—presumably stingy persons who had refused to contribute food or money—who were attacked by name.[3] The great purpose of these rituals was to spread the benign influence of fruitfulness throughout the land, among crops, herds, and among the people. Traditionally we associate feelings of gaiety and abandon—even orgiastic abandon—with such ceremonies, as in the Maypole dance, whose kinship with the ancient phallic rites we know. But the iambic component of the Phallic Songs breaks sharply into the mood of solemn joy. How are we to account for it?

The entire rite is magical. Its purpose was to stimulate fertility, the sacred energy of life. Its method was to coerce by magical means the responsible spirits or powers. The ceremonial had two aspects, as it were: the invocation of good influences through the magic potency of the phallus, the expulsion of evil influences through the magical potency of abuse. "The phallus itself is no less a negative charm against evil spirits than a positive agent of fertilisation," writes Cornford. "But the simplest of all methods of expelling . . . malign influences of any kind is to abuse them with the most violent language."[4] Similarly, D. S. Margoliouth in his commentary on the *Poetics* notes that violent abuse forms the most effective spell against demons; he cites Apollonius of Tyana, who got rid of a vampire by insulting her.[5] The scurrilous Fescennine verses sung at Roman wedding processions, and by soldiers at triumphs, had somewhat the same apotropaic function. So, when the joyful invocation of the god Phalles was interrupted by invectives, the purpose was magical, and the iambic verses themselves were thought to have magic properties. Cornford is explicit in

[3] Francis M. Cornford, *The Origin of Attic Comedy* (London, 1914), pp. 35–52.

[4] Cornford, p. 49. Regular choral matches in abuse were apparently connected with certain of the ceremonies; see pp. 110–111. An analogue to these practices may be found in ancient India. Professor A. Berriedale Keith, discussing the elements out of which the Sanskrit drama might have developed, describes a primitive dramatic ritual marked by the following ceremony: "A Brahman student and a hetaera are introduced as engaged in coarse abuse of each other, and in the older form of the ritual we actually find that sexual union as a fertility rite is permitted. . . . The ritual purpose of this abuse is undeniable; it is aimed at producing fertility. . . ." The *Sanskrit Drama* (Oxford, 1924), pp. 24–25. Cf. the rites cited by Mircea Eliade, "Agriculture and Fertility Cults," *Patterns in Comparative Religion*, trans. Rosemary Sheed (London, 1958), pp. 331–66, esp. p. 358.

[5] *The Poetics of Aristotle*, trans. with commentary by D. S. Margoliouth (London, 1911), p. 143.

his summary: "There can be no doubt that the element of invective and personal satire which distinguishes the Old Comedy is directly descended from the magical abuse of the phallic procession, just as its obscenity is due to the sexual magic; and it is likely that this ritual justification was well known to an audience familiar with the phallic ceremony itself."[6] Aristotle's remarks have thus led us to our first evidence that in their early manifestations satire, invective, and ridicule may be closely associated with magic.

A discussion of Archilochus arises naturally out of this background. Despite the anticipations just discussed, ancient tradition is fairly strong that Archilochus was the first individual satirist of record. He was generally credited with having "invented" iambic verse, the measure in which "ruthless warfare ought to be waged," Ovid was to say.[7] More important, however, was the story of Archilochus himself, with its mystery and melodrama, its widely-flung influence. Briefly, it is this: Archilochus was born on the island of Paros; he came, on his father's side, from a family of hereditary priests of Demeter. His father was Telesicles, founder of Thasos, his mother a slave. Archilochus was betrothed to Neobule, daughter of the Parian noble Lycambes. For some reason (perhaps because Archilochus made public the matter of his irregular birth), Lycambes "broke the great oath made by salt and table," as Archilochus put it, and refused to sanction the marriage.[8] In the terrible violence of his rage Archilochus composed iambics against the father and his household and recited (or sang) them at the festival of Demeter. Lycambes and his daughter (according to

---

[6] Cornford, p. 50. Perhaps there is a recollection of the kind of ritual in the Elizabethan Lord of Misrule ceremony. The Puritan Phillip Stubbes has a characteristically brilliant description of the wild goings-on, then adds: "They haue also certain papers, wherein is painted some babblerie or other of Imagery woork, & those they call 'my Lord of mis-rules badges:' these they giue to eury one that wil giue money for them to maintaine them in their hethenrie, diuelrie, whordome, drunkennes, pride, and what not. And who will not be buxom to them, are mocked & flouted at not a little." *Anatomy of Abuses* (1583), Part I, ed. F. J. Furnivall (London, The New Shakespeare Society, 1877–79), p. 148. This may be compared also with Cornford's account (p. 39) of the ancient Greek children's songs in various festal processions: a choral verse was sung by the whole company before every house door; when householders refused to give liberally to the group, iambic verses of ridicule and abuses were improvised against them.

[7] See, for example, Clement of Alexandria, *Miscellanies;* Horace, *Ars Poetica,* l. 79; Plutarch, *Music,* 28—all cited in *Elegy and Iambus,* II, 85–89; and Ovid, *Ibis,* ll. 53–54, 307. The derivation of the word *iambi* is obscure. Archilochus used it of his own poetry, and, writes J. M. Edmonds, "it is certain that when the word came to be used to describe a form of literature, it came to connote ridicule and invective, and the idea of ridicule seems to have joined in it with that of improvisation." "An Account of Greek Lyric Poetry," *Lyra Graeca,* ed. and trans. J. M. Edmonds (London, 1927), III, 604.

[8] Fragment 96, *Elegy and Iambus,* II, 149.

some versions, daughters) hanged themselves.[9] Archilochus went on to further triumphs, and further miseries, in the islands of the Aegean. He established a towering reputation as a poet. Hundreds of years after his death writers compared him to Sophocles, to Pindar, even to Homer, some indeed placing him next to Homer over all other poets. There is evidence that when he was killed in battle, Archilochus became the center of a heroic cult on his native island of Paros; and, according to Dio Chrysostom and others, the man who killed him was banished from the temple by Apollo for having slain a servitor of the Muses.[10] By piecing together scraps of commentary with the Fragments of Archilochus that have survived, we can embellish the story further; but central to it, and crucial, is the account of the poet's terrible triumph over Lycambes and Neobule.

Until recently, modern scholars have been inclined to treat the tale as a late invention (antedating Horace, it is true, who knew it and presumably expected his audience to know it well)—an invention based upon a false interpretation of a Fragment of Archilochus. The improbability of such a theory, however, has been made clear by Professor G. L. Hendrickson: that a story of such wide currency as that of Archilochus and Lycambes could have been spun out of a grammatical interpretation perhaps hundreds of years after Archilochus' death is simply not credible. Instead, Hendrickson shows, the legend, if it be such, grew inevitably out of belief: "the wide-spread popular belief in the destructive, supernatural power of words of ill-omened invective or imprecation, uttered by one who believes himself wronged."[11]

The invectives of Archilochus have much in common with the curses of tragic mythology: that of Thyestes, for example, which doomed the house of Atreus; or that of Oedipus on his sons. For a Greek audience these curses were not a matter of dramatic convention or of supernatural machinery; they were part of reality. When in the *Electra* the chorus, hearing the death agony of Clytemnestra, cries out, "The curses are fulfilled!" the moment must have been charged with a meaning but dimly available to us today. Similarly, there can be no question about the wide-spread belief in the efficacy of the personal curse: witness the curse tablets, *defixiones* (metal tablets engraved with a more or less elaborate imprecation against a personal enemy and then buried), which have been recovered in great numbers over the past fifty years. So common was belief in curse and incantation that Plato proposed extremely harsh penalties for these and

---

[9] For an attempt to account for the varying forms of the story, see François Lasserre, *Les Epodes d'Archiloque* (Paris, 1950), pp. 47 ff.

[10] *Elegy and Iambus*, II, 93.

[11] "Archilochus and the Victims of His Iambics," *AJP*, XLVI (1925), p. 103.

other magical practices.[12] (Plato also forbade iambic poets to hold any citizen up to laughter; but the motivation here seems to have nothing directly to do with fear of magic.) These matters will be discussed more fully later, but the point is this: Archilochus had sources of power similar to those drawn on by the curser. Just as the curse was believed to be fatal, so, as Hendrickson says, "the popular fancy demanded and assumed, as a matter of course, destruction for the objects of the imprecations of the more famous iambists. That their ill-omened vows and invectives should be effective was a part of their preeminence, and that their victims should escape with less than death would have been a derogation of their fame." Whether the iambics of Archilochus were believed to have magic potency because of his own personal command over the Word, which was magical in and of itself, or whether his power derived from his ability to bring about divine intervention, it is difficult to say. But Hendrickson's thesis is convincing: Lycambes and his daughter were driven—or were believed to have been driven—to suicide by the preternatural power of Archilochus' poetry.[13]

The whole tradition is adequately summed up in a sepulchral epigram on Archilochus: "Cerberus, whose bark strikes terror into the dead, there comes a terrible shade before whom even thou must tremble. Archilochus is dead. Beware the acrid iambic wrath engendered by his bitter mouth. Thou knowest the might of his words ever since one boat brought thee the two daughters of Lycambes."[14]

The attribution of magic power need not surprise us. In the early stages of cultural development, poetry is almost always associated with magic, whether white or black, or both. The poet's function has not yet been differentiated; in addition to being celebrant and perhaps mocker or maker of

---

[12] See the discussion by E. R. Dodds, *The Greeks and the Irrational* (Berkeley, Cal., 1951), pp. 194–95, who says that few of the *defixiones* seem to date from earlier than the fourth century B.C. Hendrickson, p. 106, believes, however, that "they merely carry on in written form (perhaps under oriental influence) the same habit of oral imprecation which is implied in the multitudinous curses of early mythology." For Plato, see *The Laws*, Bk. XI, 933, trans. A. E. Taylor (London, 1934), pp. 327–38.

[13] J. Vendryes observes that we treat the Archilochus story as legend, "flattering on the whole for the talent of Archilochus, if not for his character. But it is not correct to interpret it as a legend; it is probably necessary to take the story in a literal sense. Archilochus really condemned Lycambes and Neobule to death; he hurled a magical incantation against them, from which they could not escape. He had the secret of avenging himself on his enemies." *Revue Celtique* (referred to hereafter as *RC*), XXXIV (1913), pp. 94–96.

[14] *The Greek Anthology*, Bk. VII, 69, trans. W. R. Paton (London, 1917), II, 43.

invectives, he is likely to be prophet, historian, genealogist, even healer.[15] All "antique poetry," according to Johan Huizinga, "is at one and the same time ritual, entertainment, artistry, riddle-making, doctrine, persuasion, sorcery, soothsaying, prophecy, and competition."[16] In this cultural situation the poet can hardly be said to *compose* verses; rather, as the more or less passive instrument of divinity, he transmits them. He is inspired, "breathed into," by the god. I do not mean to claim that Archilochus was a shaman or a primitive medicine-man. But it is well to remember that he was a priest of Demeter. Given his status in a relatively "primitive" culture, and given his extraordinary power of utterance, it is not difficult to understand why magical power was attributed to his verse.

The poetry of Archilochus survives in dishearteningly inadequate bits and pieces; at least one Fragment, however, is long enough to give us a sense of the power his satires must have developed. This, the Strassburg Fragment (97A), is a fierce imprecation against a former friend who is embarking on a journey by sea. The poet prays—demands—that the vessel be wrecked, that the traveler be "tossed by the waves and naked [where] the savage Thracians may receive him with their *kindly* hospitality; and there may have his fill of suffering and eat the bread of slavery. Shivering with cold, covered with filth washed up by the sea, with chattering teeth like a dog, may he lie helplessly on his face at the edge of the strand amidst the breakers—this 'tis my wish to see him suffer, who has trodden his oaths under foot, him who was once my friend."[17] The total conviction of hate carries down undiminished through twenty-five centuries: we sense the force of the implacable will behind the words. Even these few lines make a famous characterization of Archilochus more meaningful: "And he

---

[15] Aelian writes (*Various History*, 1250): "If ever the Spartans required the aid of the Muses on occasion of general sickness of body or mind or any like public affliction, their custom was to send for foreigners at the bidding of the Delphic oracle, to act as healers and purifiers. For instance they summoned Terpander . . . Tyrtaeus . . . and Alcman." J. M. Edmonds comments: "Here in 7th Century Greece is the poet as medicine-man . . . doubtless his original role." Both quotations are from Edmonds, "An Account of Greek Lyric Poetry," *Lyra Graeca*, III, 610.

[16] *Homo Ludens*, trans. R. F. C. Hull (London, 1949), p. 120. Cf. N. Kershaw Chadwick, *Poetry and Prophecy* (Cambridge, 1942), p. 14; Dodds, *The Greeks and the Irrational*, pp. 80–82; F. M. Cornford, "Was the Ionian Philosophy Scientific?" *JHS*, LXII (1942), pp. 5–7.

[17] Trans. Hendrickson, "Archilochus and the Victims of His Iambics," p. 115. For an excellent poetic translation of this and other poems of Archilochus, see Richard Lattimore, trans., *Greek Lyrics* (Chicago, 1955). A sizable Fragment of Archilochus probably bearing on the Lycambes story (but not an imprecation) has recently been recovered; see François Lasserre, "Un nouveau poème d'Archiloque," *Museum Helveticum*, XIII (1956), pp. 226–35.

drank the bitter wrath of the dog and the sharp sting of the wasp; from both of these comes the poison of his mouth."[18]

Ancient writers most often characterize Archilochus' satire in terms like these; the emphasis is on the bitterness, the hatred, the abuse. One other element, however, should be noticed. In the Fragment just quoted Archilochus speaks from a sense of outraged justice; the former friend has trampled on his oaths, as had Lycambes. A tone of righteous indignation informs a number of the Fragments: "he shall not escape for this despite done to me" (92); "Lord Apollo, reveal Thou the guilty and destroy them . . ." (27). It is this quality which prompts Bruno Snell to view the Strassburg poem as something more than a curse, something more even than the invectives of the Homeric heroes, who used abuse as a weapon of battle. Here invective is attached to a feeling of moral mission; the satirist (if we may call him so) is at this early date concerned with punishing vice.[19]

One wonders, of course, whether the punishment of Lycambes and Neobule, through the agency of iambic verse, *actually* brought about their deaths; whether we ought to take the story *au pied de la lettre*, as Vendryes thinks we should take it. It is impossible to say. The tradition is strong and it is the tradition, which is founded in and grows out of belief, that is significant. Lycambes and Neobule may in fact have hanged themselves as a result of the satirical onslaught, just as a man of the Murngin tribe in Australia lies down and dies when he feels that his soul has been stolen from him by black magic.[20] On the other hand, they may have survived the imprecations, as Pliny established that, despite the tradition, the sculptor Bupalus survived the iambics of Hipponax a century after Archilochus' death. Historical fact or legend, it hardly matters. For a very long time the story of Archilochus' word-slaying of Lycambes commanded belief. The satirist had access to uncanny powers because the story said he did. In light of the belief, we may read with new insight the simple vaunt

---

[18] The characterization is by Callimachus; see Frag. 37a in *Callimachus and Lycophron*, trans. A. W. Mair (London, 1921), p. 239. Cf. Pindar: "But I must refrain from the violent bite of slanderous calumny; for, though far removed in time, I have seen the bitter-tongued Archilochus full often in distress, because he battened on bitter abuse of his foes." "Pythian Odes," II, 53-56, in *The Odes of Pindar*, trans. Sir John Sandys (London, 1946), p. 177; and Horace's well-known "Archilochum proprio rabies armavit iambo," *Ars Poetica*, l. 79.

[19] *The Discovery of the Mind*, trans. T. G. Rosenmeyer (Oxford, 1953), pp. 54–55. Werner Jaeger emphasizes that the poem is "dictated by a hatred which is *justified*, or which Archilochus believes to be justified," and comes to similar conclusions about the early sense of moral mission. *Paedeia: The Ideals of Greek Culture*, trans. Gilbert Highet (Oxford, 1946), I, 121–24.

[20] W. Lloyd Warner, "The Social Configuration of Magical Behavior," in *Essays in Anthropology Presented to A. L. Kroeber* (Berkeley, Cal., 1936), pp. 405 ff.

of Archilochus: "One great thing I know, how to recompense with evil reproaches him that doeth me evil."[21]

All satirists, of course, have made this boast, although not all have been specific about the nature of their powers. Ben Jonson is blunt enough, as we have seen: armed with Archilochus' fury, he will write iambics which will "make the desperate lashers hang themselves." In the twentieth century Roy Campbell asserts similar claims: just as a lion breaks the spine of a giraffe, so his verse will drive hated rival poets to their doom.[22] The farther we are removed in time from Archilochus and the beliefs of his age, the more incongruous such threats are likely to appear. Dekker refused to be cowed by Jonson, and retaliated with *Satiromastix*. Auden, Spender, MacNeice, Day Lewis were publicly unaffected by Campbell's blast, however "wounded' they must have been privately. Neither Jonson nor Campbell, we may assume, would really have expected otherwise. But although the satirist no longer wields overt magical power, the old tradition remains vital, still exerting a strenuous attraction on our imaginations.

Greek satirists who followed Archilochus were believed to have powers similar to his. Best known of them was Hipponax, the sixth-century poet who wrote the first choliambics and to whom the ancients attributed (mistakenly) the invention of parody.[23] Hipponax, it is said, was a small, misshapen man, sensitive about his appearance. Two sculptors, the brothers Bupalus and Athenis, made a statue of him, exaggerating his deformity and exposing it to public ridicule. Against the distortion of the image Hipponax opposed the power of the word, but with uncertain results. A Renaissance translation of Pliny's account of the affair is colorful: Hipponax "so coursed them with bitter rimes & biting libels, that as some do thinke and verily beleeve, being weary of their lives, they knit their necks in halters, and so hanged themselves. But sure this cannot be true . . . ," for, says Pliny, the sculptors survived the verses and went on to create images of the gods on Delos and elsewhere.[24] Pliny's rationalistic denial could not of course stem the progress of the legend which had long been fixed in tradition and was carried by epigrams like this: "Avoid, O stranger, this terrible tomb of Hipponax, which hails forth verses, Hipponax whose very ashes cry in iambics his hatred of Bupalus, lest thou

[21] Fragment 65. Cf. the similar boast in the recently recovered Fragment. Lasserre translates: "Je sais aimer qui m'aime, haïr mon ennemi, le poursuivre d'injures: la fourmi mord!" In Lasserre's interpretation, these are lines Archilochus claims to have addressed to Neobule, his betrothed. See "Un nouveau poème d'Archiloque," p. 227.

[22] See the last lines of the title poem in Campbell's *Talking Bronco* (London, 1946).

[23] For translations of the surviving Fragments of Hipponax, see *Herodes, Cercidas, and the Greek Choliambic Poets*, trans. A. D. Knox (London, 1929), pp. 15 ff.

[24] *The Historie of the World: commonly called the Natural Historie* . . . , trans. Philemon Holland (London, 1634), Bk. xxxvi, Chap. v.

wake the sleeping wasp, who not even in Hades has lulled his spite to rest, but in a halting measure launcheth straight shafts of song."[25]

Theocritus introduces the theme of justice which often appears in accounts of magical power: "Here lies the bard Hipponax. If you are a rascal, go not nigh his tomb; but if you are a true man of good stock, sit you down and welcome, and if you choose to drop off to sleep you shall."[26]

The common element in these tales of the satirists is obvious. Out of hate and desire for revenge the poet writes iambics against his enemy. We may conjecture that the verses expressed the hatred and the will that the enemy die, directly, and that, perhaps concomitantly, they employed mockery and ridicule, which, under certain circumstances . . . can themselves be fatal. In the Strassburg Fragment of Archilochus the hatred and the willed death are strikingly clear. As to the ridicule, an ingenious reconstruction by Hendrickson enables us to get some sense of the tone of Archilochus' opening attack on Lycambes. The reconstruction is hypothetical, but seems most reasonable: "What is this that you say, father Lycambes? Who has robbed you of the reason on which before you leaned so securely? But now in truth are you become a laughing-stock to your fellow-townsmen. What god pray, or in anger at what, has kindled you to stir up a creature garrulous like me, looking for nothing better than themes for his iambics? You have seized in fact a cicada by the wing, which shrills by nature and without occasion, and when touched shrills the louder. What do you mean? Do you desire to become notorious at any cost? You shall pay for your rashness with a penalty that shall endure for long."[27]

It would be a mistake to build too much on this, but one cannot help being struck by the mocking, supremely self-confident tone and by the explicit reference to ridicule as one of the means of attack. . . . [F]or the moment this much should be clear: the iambic verses of a major poet, expressive of his hate, his will to destroy, his mockery, were believed to exert some kind of malefic power. The power seems to have resided, not in secret, esoteric spells or in the mechanics of sympathetic magic, but in the character of the poet himself—in his command over the word. The word could kill; and in popular belief it *did* kill. This is the essence of Archilochus' story. It is crucial for an understanding of the image of the satirist as it develops over the centuries, as it exists in our own day.

---

[25] *Greek Anthology*, Bk. vii, 405, Paton ed., II, 219. The "halting measure" refers to the fact that Hipponax wrote iambics ending in a spondee.
[26] Number xix of the Inscriptions in *The Greek Bucolic Poets*, trans. J. M. Edmonds (London, 1923), p. 377. Other Greek satirists to whom are ascribed comparable powers are Semonides of Amorgos and Callimachus. See Hendrickson, "Archilochus and the Victims of His Iambics," pp. 103, 111.
[27] The reconstruction is based upon three Fragments of Archilochus (94, 95, 143), a paraphrase of Archilochus by Lucian in "The Mistaken Critic," and an epigram of Catullus (40). See "Archilochus and Catullus," *CP*, xx (1925), pp. 155–57.

Northrop Frye

The Nature of Satire

The word "satire" belongs to that fairly large class of words which have two meanings, one specific and technical, the other more general. In Roman literature, for instance, the study of satire is essentially the study of a specific literary form, or rather two literary forms, of that name: the poetic satire developed by Horace and Juvenal and the prose or "Menippean" satire developed by Petronius and (in Greek) Lucian. In English literature, with which we are at present concerned, the satire may also be and has been the name of a form. Juvenal and Horace are the models of Donne and Pope, and Lucian is the model of Swift. But this idea of a satire form is in English literature a Renaissance and neo-Classical idea: it hardly existed in the Middle Ages, and it hardly exists now, though we still have our Hilaire Bellocs and Roy Campbells trying to blow up its dying fire with antique bellows. The word now means a tone or quality of art which we may find in any form: in a play by Shaw, a novel by Sinclair Lewis or a cartoon by Low. Hence in dealing with English satire we must include not only Swift and Pope, who worked with the traditional models, but all the writers who have ignored the models but have preserved the tone and attitude of satire. A distinction essential to the treatment of Roman, and perhaps also of French, satire is quite unnecessary in English literature, which has never taken kindly to strict forms.

But this, like all our cherished freedoms, was won for us by our ancestors. In the year 1597 Joseph Hall, who later became a bishop, published three books of what he called "Toothless Satires," following them with three books of "Biting Satires." Hall begins by saying that he is in-introducing something radically new into English literature:

> I first adventure, follow me who list,
> And be the second English satirist.

He does not mean that he has never heard of the *Canterbury Tales* or *Piers Plowman:* he means that from the point of view of an imitator of Juvenal and Horace they are not satires. From this point of view his claim to be first is more or less correct: that it, he was about fourth. Later in his life Bishop Hall became involved in a controversy with Milton, who did not care for bishops. Milton carefully goes over Hall's literary output to show, as the custom then was, that his adversary had been a fool from birth. When he comes to the "Toothless Satires" he says that this so-called first English satirist might have learned better from *Piers Plowman,* besides other works, and adds: "But that such a Poem should be toothless I still affirm it to be a bull, taking away the essence of that which it calls itself. For if it bite neither the persons nor the vices, how is it a Satyr, and if it bite either, how is it toothless, so that toothless Satyrs are as much as if he had said toothless teeth." If there can be no toothless satires, it is the tone that makes a work of art a satire: if Langland is a great satirist because of his satiric attitude, Swift and Pope are so for the same reason, not because of their form. On this point posterity has decided for Milton against the bishop.

As a tone or attitude, then, two things are essential to satire. One is wit or humour, the other an object of attack. Attack without humour, or pure denunciation, thus forms one of the boundaries of satire; humour without attack, the humour of pure gaiety or exuberance, is the other. Now these two qualities, it is obvious, are not simply different, but opposed. For satire one needs both pleasure in conflict and determination to win; both the heat of battle and the coolness of calculation. To have too much hatred and too little gaiety will upset the balance of tone. Man is a precocious monkey, and he wins his battles by the sort of cunning that is never far from a sense of mockery. All over the world people have delighted in stories of how some strong but stupid monster was irritated by a tiny human hero into a blind, stampeding fury, and how the hero, by biding his time and keeping cool, polished off his Blunderbore or Polyphemus at leisure. In literature, too, the slugging haymaker has no more chance against an expert pen-fencer than a bull in a bullfight. Milton, a deeply serious prophet haunted by the sense that he was responsible both to God and man for making the best use of his genius, had no gift for satire, and when we see this blind giant flailing at his buzzing assailants, we can only be thankful that he never encountered a first-rate satirist. The same is true of many romantics. Lord Castlereagh, who did not kill himself before he had achieved an all-time high in unpopularity with poets, is described by Shelley, along with his confederate Sidmouth, as:

> two vultures sick for battle,
> Two scorpions under one wet stone,

> Two bloodless wolves whose dry throats rattle,
> Two crows perched on the murrained cattle,
>> Two vipers tangled into one.

This is very fine, but it is not fine satire. The poet is too angry and his victims too abstract. Let us try Byron:

> Cold-blooded, smooth-faced, placid miscreant!
> Dabbling its sleek young hands in Erin's gore,
> And thus for wider carnage taught to pant,
> Transferr'd to gorge upon a sister shore,
> The vulgarest tool that Tyranny could want,
> With just enough of talent, and no more,
> To lengthen fetters of another fix'd,
> And offer poison long already mix'd.

Byron wrote some great satire, but this is evidently not it. Let us turn to Tom Moore:

> Why is a Pump like Viscount Castlereagh?
> Because it is a slender thing of wood,
> That up and down its awkward arm doth sway,
> And coolly spout and spout and spout away,
> In one weak, washy, everlasting flood!

That does it exactly. It is rather flattering to one's ego to be called a wolf or a scorpion; there is a certain thrill in being thought a dark and terrible emissary of the demonic powers. But nobody likes to be called a pump, at any rate not with so much enthusiasm.

The satirist in whom the gift of seeing things absurdly appears most clearly as exuberance of mind is Dryden. He takes a physical pleasure in his victims; he transforms them into fantastic dinosaurs of bulging flesh and peanut brains. He is really impressed by the great bulk of his Falstaffian Og:

> Round as a globe, and liquor'd every chink,
> Goodly and great he sails behind his link.

He really admires the furious energy of the poet Doeg, and his heart is warmed by the spectacle of that noble Buzzard, Bishop Burnet:

> A portly prince, and goodly to the sight . . .
> A prophet form'd to make a female proselyte.

The great effectiveness of such satire comes from the victim's realization that no one could laugh at him with such genuine pleasure unless he were genuinely amused. In other words, one cannot merely adopt satire to express a personal or moral feeling; one must be born with the sardonic vision.

Now both humour and attack depend on certain conventions which are assumed to be in existence before the satirist begins to write. The world of humour is a rigidly stylized world in which generous Scotchmen, obedient wives, beloved mothers-in-law and professors with presence of mind are not permitted to exist. All humour demands common agreement that certain things, such as a picture of a wife beating her husband in a comic strip, are funny. To introduce a comic strip in which a husband beats his wife would distress and perplex the average reader: it would mean learning a new convention. Similarly, in order to attack anything, satirist and audience must agree on its undesirability. The misery and cold of German soldiers in a Russian winter is matter for satire in our newspapers; the misery and cold of Russians is not.

Much in these conventions is only fashion, and quantities of scandal, gossip, pasquinades and lampoons have gone the way of all flashes. Even our sense of what constitutes absurdity has changed. "We laugh at deformed creatures," says Sir Philip Sidney, but he does not speak for the twentieth century. That Milton was blind, Dryden poor and Pope a cripple does not seem as amusing to us as to their contemporary enemies. When Nashe tells of the trick Jack Wilton played on a Captain, and how the best of the joke was, that the Captain was arrested as a spy, racked and flogged, we stop laughing long before Nashe does. Ben Jonson was a bricklayer's stepson, and his many enemies expected every reference to bricklaying they made to be followed by knowing winks, leers and guffaws. But the whole social attitude which enabled that to be humorous has disappeared, and the satire with it. National hatreds are no longer-lived. In the Hundred Years' War, Laurence Minot vituperated the French; at the time of Flodden, Skelton poured scorn on the Scotch; when Holland was England's trade rival, Marvell persuaded himself that he disliked the Dutch; in Napoleon's time Canning's poetry of the *Anti-Jacobin* held all revolutionary ideas up to ridicule. Many of these wrote excellent satire, but it has gone stale and mouldy, and at best is something to be rescued. Now no one would claim that Chaucer or Pope or Swift had any Olympian superiority to the passions and prejudices of their times. To what, then, do they owe their amazing vitality and power of survival?

Denunciation, or humourless attack, is, we said, one of the boundaries of satire. It is a very hazy boundary, because invective is one of the most readable forms of literary art, just as panegyric is one of the dullest. It is simply an established datum of literature that we love to hear people cursed and are bored with hearing them praised; and almost any denunciation, if vigorous enough, is followed by a reader with the kind of pleasure that soon breaks into a smile. Now invective is never the expression of merely personal hatred, whatever the motivation for it may be, because the words for it simply do not exist in the language. About the only ones we have are derived from the animal world, but calling a man a swine or a skunk or even a cholera germ is merely an eructation. For effective attack we must reach some kind of impersonal level, and that commits the attacker, if only by implication, to a moral standard. As Shakespeare's Thersites says of Menelaus, "to what form, but that he is, should wit turn him to? To an ass, were nothing; he is both ass and ox; to an ox, were nothing; he is both ox and ass." In the long run, then, the tone of antagonism or attack in satire must imply an assertion and a defence of a moral principle. The satirist, when attacked, takes a very high moral line. He is a prophet sent to lash the vices and follies of the time, and he will not stop until he has cleansed the foul body of the infected world. Pope says:

> Hear this, and tremble! you, who 'scape the Laws,
>   Yes, while I live, no rich or noble knave
>   Shall walk the World, in credit, to his grave,
>   To VIRTUE ONLY and HER FRIENDS A FRIEND,
>   The world beside may murmur, or commend.

That, you see, is what Pope is really doing when he is reflecting on the cleanliness of the underwear worn by the lady who had jilted him. And as far as the survival power of his satire goes, he is quite right. Hence satire based on persisting moral sentiments has a better chance for immortality than satire based on fluctuating ones, satire which strikes roots in the soil of stupidity, treachery, slovenliness, hypocrisy, and all the other things that are as evil today as in Chaucer's time.

Again, we said that the humour of gaiety was the other boundary of satire. But as Juvenal truly said that whatever men do is the subject of satire, and that in consequence it is difficult not to write it, it follows that most humorous situations are at least indirectly satiric. Nonsatiric humor tends to fantasy: one finds it most clearly in the fairy worlds of Lewis Carroll, Edward Lear and Walt Disney, in Celtic romance and American tall tales. Yet even here one can never be sure, for the humor of fantasy is continually being pulled back into satire by means of that powerful undertow which we call allegory. The White Knight in Alice who felt that one should be provided for everything, and therefore put anklets around his horse's feet to guard against the bites of sharks, may pass without challenge. But what are we to make of the mob of hired revolutionaries in the same author's *Sylvie and Bruno*, who got their instructions mixed and yelled under the palace windows: "More taxes! less bread!"? Here we begin to sniff the acrid, pungent smell of satire. Those fantastic romances, *Gulliver's Travels, Utopia, Erewhon,* work on exactly the same principle.

Now just as denunciation contributes morality to satire, so exuberance or gaiety contributes to it absurdity or grotesqueness. It is absurdity of a special kind, which I should tentatively call a poetic imagination in reverse gear. The imagination of Quixote, who saw a windmill as a hundred-armed giant, was a genuinely poetic one, if overliteral in its application; but it is the business of the satirist to see giants as windmills, Castlereaghs as pumps. Poetry may deepen and intensify the imaginative impact of things; satire belittles and minimizes it. Allegory in high gear gives us a Spenser or a Bunyan; allegory in reverse gear gives us a *Tale of a Tub.* Poetry may be as primitive as you please, and may thrive on superstition or false belief: satire means civilization and a confidence in the invincibility of the intelligence. I should define satire, then, as poetry assuming a special function of analysis, that is, of breaking up the lumber of stereotypes, fossilized beliefs, superstitious terrors, crank theories, pedantic dogmatisms, oppressive fashions, and all other things that impede the free movement of society. I say free movement rather than progress: progress, besides implying a theory of history to which one may or may not subscribe, implies also that all satire is revolutionary, or at least progressive, which is nonsense. This does not explain the total effect of satire, as we shall see, but it covers its primary objectives.

For society to exist at all there must be a delegation of prestige and influence to organized groups: the church, the army, the medical and teaching professions, the government, all consist of individuals given more than individual power by the institution to which they belong. Whether they are given this power for good or for evil depends largely on them. If a satirist presents a clergyman, for instance, as a fool or a hypocrite, he is primarily attacking neither the man nor his church. The former is too petty and the latter carries him outside the range of satire. He is attacking an evil man protected by the prestige of an institution. As such, he represents one of the stumbling-blocks in society which it is the satirist's business to clear out.

We have spoken of the resemblance of the giant-killing myth to the technique of satire: there is in both a victory of intelligence over stupid power. In the sort of case we are considering, the satirist's victim is a gigantic monster; monstrous because really a fool or a hypocrite while pretending to be otherwise; gigantic because protected by his position and by the prestige of the good men in it. The cowl might make the monk if it were not for the satirist. Hence, though Milton's etymology may be wrong, his principle is right: "for a Satyr as it was born out of a Tragedy, so ought to resemble his parentage, to strike high, and adventure dangerously at the most eminent vices among the greatest persons." The larger they come, the easier they fall.

When the Philistine giant comes out to battle with the children of light, he naturally expects to find someone his own size ready to meet him, someone who is head and shoulders over every man in Israel. Such a Titan would have to bear down his opponent by sheer weight of words, and hence be a master of that technique of torrential abuse which we call invective. And as invective is very close to moral denunciation, we should expect it to be a form closely allied to preaching. Another reason for this is that the literary qualities necessary for good invective are essentially those of good swearing: a sense of rhythm, an unlimited vocabulary and a technical knowledge of the two subjects which ordinarily form the subject-matter of swearing, one of which is theology. Now if we want satire on military life and martial courage we should expect to find most of it in the army: *Don Quixote* could only have been the work of an old soldier. Similarly, we should not be surprised to find that the two greatest masters of invective, Rabelais and Swift, have been recruited from the clergy. The association between satire and preaching goes back at least to the Hebrew prophets, runs all through medieval sermons on the Seven Deadly Sins and reaches its peak with the Reformation, when controversy poured oil on the fires.

There is another reason why this last period, the sixteenth century, was the golden age of abuse. Controversy supplies the anger, but not the gaiety, of satire: for the source of the latter we must turn to the great influx of new words then coming in. The Elizabethans had a delight in words of a physical kind which we can hardly comprehend today, a kind of reversed drunkenness that comes from outpouring rather than intake. Words spawn and swarm in every corner of their writings: their expenditure of erudite technicalities, fantastically abusive epithets and dizzily inclusive compounds was as reckless as their resources were inexhaustible both in coinage and in the plunder of every language in Europe, living or dead. They could hardly touch a foreign language without gloating over their own superior resources. Thus Cotgrave's French Dictionary defines the French word *lourdans* as: "a sot, dullard, grotnoll, jobernoll, blockhead; a lowt, lob, lusk, boare, clown, churle, clusterfist; a proud, ignorant and unmannerly swaine." Rabelais tells of a man who retired to the country for quiet, and who found that the animals made such a noise that he could not sleep. Rabelais plagues him with nine sorts of animals; Urquhart of Cromarty, his Scotch translator, expands them to seventy. Urquhart, when not engaged in making Gargantua more Rabelaisian than Rabelais, was busy writing books with such titles as *Trissotetras, Pantochrono-chanon, Exkubalauron* and *Logopandecteison*. In an age when even pedan-

try could produce such a Holofernes, invective is not likely to die of malnu-
trition. Marston, Bishop Hall's chief follower, is put into a play by his
enemy Ben Jonson, given a purge and made to vomit up some of his hard
words. They include glibbery, lubrical, magnificate, turgidous, ventosity,
oblatrant, furibund, fatuate, prorumped and obstupefact. Thomas Nashe,
the greatest prose satirist of the period, calls his opponent, Gabriel Harvey,
an important mote-catching carper, an indigested chaos of doctorship and
a scholastic squitter-book. Here is one sentence from Burton's *Anatomy of
Melancholy*, which, if not directly satirical in itself, certainly illustrates
the method and technique of invective:

> Every lover admires his mistress, though she be very deformed of her-
> self, ill-favoured, wrinkled, pimpled, pale, red, yellow, tanned, tallow-
> faced, have a swollen juggler's platter face, or a thin, lean, chitty face,
> have clouds in her face, be crooked, dry, bald, goggle-eyed, blear-eyed,
> or with staring eyes, she looks like a squis'd cat, hold her head still awry,
> heavy, dull, hollow-eyed, black or yellow about the eyes, or squint-eyed,
> sparrow-mouthed, Persian hook-nosed, have a sharp fox-nose, a red nose,
> China flat, great nose, *nare simo patuloque*, a nose like a promontory,
> grubber-tushed, rotten teeth, black, uneven, brown teeth, beetle-browed,
> a witch's beard, her breath stink all over the room, her nose drop winter
> and summer, with a Bavarian poke under her chin, a sharp chin, lave-
> eared, with a long crane's neck, which stands awry too, *pendulis mammis*,
> "her dugs like two double jugs," or else no dugs, in that other extreme,
> bloody-fallen fingers, she have filthy, long unpared nails, scabbed hands
> or wrists, a tanned skin, a rotten carcass, crooked back, she stoops, is
> lame, splay-footed, "as slender in the middle as a cow in the waist," gouty
> legs, her ankles hang over her shoes, her feet stink, she breed lice, a mere
> changeling, a very monster, an oaf imperfect, her whole complexion
> savours, an harsh voice, incondite gesture, vile gait, a vast virago, or an
> ugly tit, a slug, a fat fustilugs, a truss, a long lean rawbone, a skeleton,
> a sneaker (*si qua latent meliora puta*), and to thy judgment looks like a
> mard in a lanthorn, whom thou couldst not fancy for a word, but hatest,
> loathest, and wouldest have spit in her face, or blow thy nose in her
> bosom, *remedium amoris* to another man, a dowdy, a slut, a scold, a nasty,
> rank, rammy, filthy, beastly quean, dishonest peradventure, obscene, base,
> beggarly, rude, foolish, untaught, peevish, Irus' daughter, Thersites' sis-
> ter, Grobian's scholar; if he love her once, he admires her for all this, he
> takes no notice of any such errors or imperfections of body or mind, *Ipsa
> haec delectant, veluti Balbinum polypus Agnae*; he had rather have her
> than any woman in the world.

Since Dryden, there has been little of this naïve and childlike quality in
satire, which has trusted more to the rapier that stabs the heart than to
the single stick that breaks the head. Abuse of this kind is based on a solid
physical laugh, an earthquake in miniature, a laugh which begins far down

in the abdomen, bursts the vest buttons, rolls the stomach, shakes the diaphragm, suffocates the throat, reddens the face and finally reduces the whole body to rolling and kicking in an epilepsy of joy, then, after quieting down, returns for the next few hours in a couple of dozen squalls of splutters, gasps and reminiscent chortles, and finally sinks into the subconscious to be left until called for. As Carlyle says:

> How much lies in Laughter: the cipher-key, wherewith we decipher the whole man! Some men wear an everlasting barren simper; in the smile of others lies a cold glitter as of ice: the fewest are able to laugh, what can be called laughing, but only sniff and titter and snigger from the throat outwards; or at best, produce some whiffing husky cachinnation, as if they were laughing through wool: of none such comes good.

Urquhart of Cromarty, an ardent Royalist, is reputed to have laughed on King Charles' Restoration until he burst himself and died. And anyone who has glanced at an old copy of *Punch* can see that their cartoons, with their enormous captions, elaborately festooned with garrulous explanations and parenthetic postscripts, are aimed at a John Bull or fox-hunting squire for whom a laugh was an exhausting indoor exercise. Such a fox-hunting squire might survive to hear himself described by Oscar Wilde as the unspeakable in pursuit of the uneatable. There is an entirely different kind of laughter; not the *forte* of invective but the *piano* of irony, which, like the poisoned rings of the Renaissance, distils its venom in a friendly handshake, unnoticed by its bulky victim.

For better or worse, it is the tiny David with his sudden and vicious stones who goes out to battle now, and the great Rabelaisian bellow has dropped out of literature. For that kind of satire flourishes in a world of solid assurances and unshakable values; the whole weight of a confident society is flung into the scales against limp affectation. The less sure society is of its assumptions, the more likely the satire is to take the line of irony, of the method laid down once for all in the dialogues of Plato.

It is impossible not to sympathize with the floundering red-faced brawlers in Plato, with the Thrasymachus or Callicles who is inexorably led on from one trap to another while Socrates sits quietly and smiles. Yet we know that they can never win, because they can never lay a finger on Socrates. Socrates pleads his own ignorance, convicts his opponents of equal ignorance, and there, in most of the shorter dialogues, we are. The master of irony has done nothing but sow doubt and confusion. He calls himself a midwife, but all he does is kill the mother and demonstrate that there is no child.

For irony is not simply the small man's way of fighting a bigger one: it is a kind of intellectual tear-gas that breaks the nerves and paralyses the muscles of everyone in its vicinity, an acid that will corrode healthy as well as decayed tissues. We have said that satire is primarily directed at the impediments of society; but irony has an automatically expansive and destroying force; it is a bomb dropped on an objective which, if it misses that, will at any rate hit something in an enemy's territory. Take, for example, the warfare of science against superstition. Here the satirists have done famously. Chaucer and Ben Jonson riddled the alchemists with a cross-fire of their own jargon; Nashe and Swift hounded astrologers into premature graves; Browning's *Sludge the Medium* annihilated the spiritualists; and a rabble of occultists, numerologists, Pythagoreans and Rosicrucians lie dead in the wake of *Hudibras.* But when triumphant science turns to shake hands with the satirists, there is again that little prick of the poisoned ring. For all satirists are not so ready to see the sharp dividing line between alchemists and chemists, a Rosicrucian cell meeting and the Royal Society. Samuel Butler makes his scientists discover an elephant in the moon which turns out to be a mouse in the telescope. It does not matter; their scientific reputation is at stake, and an elephant in the moon it must be. Swift's Grand Academy of Lagado, in *Gulliver's Travels,* is a vast scientific laboratory in which professors are deeply engaged in such experiments as "to sow land with chaff, wherein he affirmed the true seminal virtue to be contained." In fact there seems to be as perennial a warfare between satire and all forms of science and philosophy, as between satire and superstitution. What Rabelais and Erasmus thought of the scholastics, Swift thought of the Cartesians; and what Voltaire thought of the Leibnitzians, Samuel Butler II thought of the Darwinians. In every case it is not the doctrine but its application to society that is attacked; however, the satirist has a latent distrust of the adequacy of human reason that becomes most articulate in *Gulliver's Travels:*

> I was going on to more particulars, when my master commanded me to silence. He asked whoever understood the nature of Yahoos might easily believe it possible for so vile an animal to be capable of every action I had named, if their strength and cunning equalled their malice. But when a creature pretending to reason could be capable of such enormities, he dreaded lest the corruption of that faculty might be worse than brutality itself. He seemed therefore confident, that instead of reason, we were only possessed of some quality fitted to increase our natural vices.

Similarly with religion. There is a great deal of hypocrisy and corruption in any church, and a great deal of superstition in popular worship. Any really devout person would welcome a satirist who cauterized such infections as an ally of true religion. But once a hypocrite who sounds exactly like a good man is sufficiently blackened, the good man himself may begin to seem a little dingier than he was. Thus Burns' Holy Willie is doubtless only a reprobate, but does not his confession make many others, who would say Amen to much of it, look a little like Holy Willies?

> When frae my mither's womb I fell,
> Thou might hae plunged me in hell,
> To gnash my gums, to weep and wail,
>   In burnin' lake,
> Where damned devils roar and yell,
>   Chain'd to a stake.
>
> Yet I am here a chosen sample,
> To show thy grace is great and ample;
> I'm here a pillar in thy temple,
>   Strong as a rock,
> A guide, a buckler, an example
>   To a' thy flock.

Even the God Holy Willie is praying to begins to take on some of his features, just as the God of the Pharisee's prayer was a Pharisee. The same thing happens to the treatment of superstition. In Lilliput, we are told,

> They bury their dead with their heads directly downwards, because they hold an opinion, that in eleven thousand moons they are all to rise again, in which period the earth (which they conceive to be flat) will turn upside down, and by this means they shall, at their resurrection, be found ready standing on their feet. The learned among them confess the absurdity of this doctrine, but the practice still continues, in compliance to the vulgar.

But does not the satire go on quietly eating its way into the very heart of our own views of immortality, no matter how smug or how vague? In the same writer's *Tale of a Tub* we are much more convinced that Jack and Peter are wrong than that Martin is right.

Or again, take that scene, one of the most powerfully ironic in all literature, at the climax of *Huckleberry Finn*, where Huck has to decide whether he will go to heaven to the white slave-owners' God or to hell for stealing Jim out of slavery. We know that the white slave-owners' God is a bogey, an example, as Goya would say, of what a tailor can do. But Huck does not know that. He is no Prometheus Unbound; it never occurs to him to doubt that the white slave-owners' God is the only true God. And in contemplating his predicament we can only say that the half-gods have gone: we have no evidence that the gods have arrived.

And if we fall back from the outworks of faith and reason to the solid and tangible realities of the senses, satire will follow us even there. A slight shift of perspective, a different tinge in the emotional colouring, and the same real, physical world becomes an intolerable horror. *Gulliver's Travels* show, in rapid review, man from a large perspective as a venomous little rodent, man from a small perspective as a noisome and clumsy pachyderm, the mind of man as a bear-pit and the body of man as a compound of filth and ferocity. Swift shows us everything about the human body that can be made to appear disgusting and nauseating; his account of old age is the most hideous on record; and his sense of the nastiness and sordidness of ordinary life, which oozes through his *Directions to Servants* and his more unquotable poems, seems not so much abnormal as merely perverse. But he is simply following where his satiric genius leads him, and without raising any questions about his "purpose," surely anyone who had attentively read Swift could never again find complete satisfaction in gratifying his senses. And that is an important barrier in civilization removed.

The fact that all great satirists have been obscene suggests that obscenity is an essential characteristic of the satirist. Swift is in the direct tradition of the medieval preachers who painted the repulsiveness of gluttony and lechery; and his account of the Struldbrugs is a late version of the medieval dance of death. The preoccupation of medieval satirists with the theme of death, often assigned to morbidity, is part of the same moral criticism. It is all very well to eat, drink and be merry; but one cannot always put off dying until tomorrow.

We are getting close to one of the fundamental facts about satire: that the sardonic vision is the seamy side of the tragic vision. We usually associate satire with comedy, but to the extent that a comedy is satiric it possesses a more than comic seriousness. A comedy is, or purports to be, a study of human behaviour, and in its most concentrated forms, in a play by Congreve or a novel by Jane Austen, we are superficially conscious of only an amiable and civilized prattle. The satire in such a comedy comes as a kind of backfire or recoil after it is read or seen as a whole. Once read, deserts of futile snobbery and simpering insipidity open up on all sides of it, and we begin to feel that Congreve and Jane Austen are more aware than a less able comedian would be of the importance of being earnest. Collins, in *Pride and Prejudice*, being a mere jackass, is treated as a comic relief; but if the novel's main theme had been the married life of Charlotte and Collins, how long would Collins continue to be funny? And when this chattering world of card-parties and dances comes under direct satiric fire, it turns into a racking nightmare of horror:

> As Hags hold Sabbaths, less for joy than spite,
> So these their merry, miserable Night;
> Still round and round the Ghosts of Beauty glide,
> And haunt the places where their Honour died.

See how the World its Veterans rewards!
A Youth of Frolics, an old Age of Cards;
Fair to no purpose, artful to no end,
Young without Lovers, old without a Friend;
A Fop their Passion, but their Prize a Sot;
Alive, ridiculous, and dead, forgot!

It is possible for comedy on a very high plane, the plane of *The Tempest*, the *Franklin's Tale* or *The Magic Flute*, to escape altogether from satire; but tragedy can never separate itself from irony. Flights of angels sing Hamlet to his rest in the climax of a frantically muddled attempt at revenge which has taken eight lives instead of one. Cleopatra fades away with great dignity and solemn music after a careful search for the easiest way to die. And in *King Lear*, when the mad old king scampers off the stage with his flowers stuck in his hair, or Gloucester makes a noble farewell speech, throws himself from a cliff, and falls a couple of feet, tragedy and irony have completely merged in something which is neither, and yet both at once. The sublime and the ridiculous are convex and concave of the same dark lens. One may find this in the middle of one of the most terrible and bloody tragedies in English literature, Webster's *Duchess of Malfi:*

What's this flesh? A little crudded milk, fantastical puff-paste. Our bodies weaker than those paper-prisons boys use to keep flies in; more contemptible, since ours is to preserve earth-worms. Didst thou ever see a lark in a cage? Such is the soul in the body: this world is like her little turf of grass, and the heaven o'er our heads, like her looking-glass, only gives us a miserable knowledge of the small compass of our prison.

Or one may find this in a modern American ballad, of uncertain parentage:

The old grey hearse goes rolling by,
You don't know whether to laugh or cry,
For you know some day it'll get you too,
And the hearse's next load may consist of you.

They'll take you out, and they'll lower you down
While men with shovels stand all around:
They'll throw in dirt, and they'll throw in rocks,
And they won't give a damn if they break the box.

And your eyes drop out and your teeth fall in,
And worms crawl over your mouth and chin:
They invite their friends and their friends' friends too,
And you look like hell when they're through with you.

At what point does the fact of death cease to be tragic and become a grim joke? When Mr. E. J. Pratt, in his poem called "The Drag-Irons," describes the hauling up of a drowned captain, is his mood the tragic one of violent death or the satiric one of the indignity of the body?

> But with his Captain's blood he did resent,
> With livid silence and with glassy look,
> This fishy treatment when his years were spent
> To come up dead upon a grapnel hook.

The same principle is clear in Chaucer. The *Canterbury Tales* is simply a human comedy: it is not a deliberate satire. Chaucer studies his pilgrims carefully, but does not distort or caricature them. If they are fools and weaklings, they will come out as that, and we may call the result a satire if we wish; if they are decent people, like the knight or the ploughman, they will come out as such. To this larger comic aim both tragedy and satire must be subordinated. The *Knight's Tale* is pathetic rather than tragic; it is sad, but it is told to amuse the pilgrims. The *Merchant's Tale* is bitter and cynical; but, again, that is merely a contributing aspect to the human comedy. In the *Troilus* the case is very different. Here we have a full-dress tragedy, complete in itself, with all the unanswerable problems in it that tragedy raises. And when its hero dies his tragic death, he ascends into the stars and looks down upon the world:

> And in hymself he lough right at the wo
> Of hem that wepten for his deth so faste;
> And dampned al oure werk that foloweth so
> The blynde lust, the which that may nat laste.

The laugh of pure satire is the echo to his tragedy.

Satire at its most concentrated, therefore, is tragedy robbed of all its dignity and nobility, a universal negation that cheapens and belittles everything. *Gulliver's Travels* destroys every standard of values except the life according to reason and nature, and then demonstrates that such a life is impossible. More makes a shambles out of Christian Europe, contrasts it with a heathen Utopia, and finally shows us that there is little hope of Utopian principles being applied to Europe and that Christianity has started to destroy the Utopia. Langland's great vision culminates in something very like a triumph of Antichrist. It is against this background that we are able to see why the most deliberate and self-conscious satire in English literature, Pope's *Dunciad*, comes to the conclusion it does. It is not only the triumph of Dullness but the triumph of satire that the great poem records, and in the complete triumph of satire the victor reigns, like Elizabeth in Ireland, only over ashes and dead carcasses:

> Religion blushing veils her sacred fires,
> And unawares Morality expires.
> Nor public Flame, nor private, dares to shine;
> Nor human Spark is left, nor Glimpse divine!
> Lo! thy dread Empire, CHAOS! is restor'd;
> Light dies before thy uncreating word;
> Thy hand, great Anarch! lets the curtain fall,
> And universal Darkness buries All.

Now, one may reasonably ask, what is the use, or, if that is too vague a question, the motive, of this art of nihilism? For the occupational hazards of satire are very considerable. "Certainly, he that hath a satirical vein," says Lord Bacon, "as he maketh others afraid of his wit, so he had need be afraid of others' memory." Satire got Nashe, Jonson, Marston and Wither into gaol; it got Defoe into both gaol and the pillory; it involved Dryden and Pope in squabbles which their worst detractors will hardly affirm they enjoyed; and it perhaps had more to do than is generally thought with the poverty and neglect of Samuel Butler. Skelton, satiric poet and thrice-crowned laureate, tutor to King Henry VIII in his youth, has put the position of the satirist as plaintively as anyone. It was only fair that he should, for the sixteenth century made him a buffoon, the seventeenth ignored him, in the eighteenth Pope called him "beastly" and in the nineteenth a female historian called him an abandoned wretch whose tutorial influence undoubtedly explained King Henry's Bluebearding tendencies:

> What can it avail . . .
> To rhyme or to rail,
> To write or to indite,
> Either for delight
> Or else for despight?
> Or books to compile
> Of divers manner style,
> Vice to revile
> And sin to exile?
> To teach or to preach,
> As reason will reach?
> Say this, and say that,
> His head is so fat,
> He wotteth never what
> Nor whereof he speaketh . . .
> Or if he speak plain,
> Then he lacketh brain,

> He is but a fool;
> Let him go to school . . .
> And if that he hit
> The nail on the head,
> It standeth in no stead.
> The Devil, they say, is dead,
> The Devil is dead!

As for the use, that is the concern of posterity. The true seminal virtue of satire is not in the chaff, and it takes a good deal of winnowing to separate the harvest from the husks of gossip and insult. The use an age makes of satire thus depends on its own problems. In an age such as ours, when the urgency of radical change is a main pre-occupation, the innate nihilism of satire, reactionary and wrong-headed as it often is, can be put to a revolutionary use. Langland was doubtless what we should now call a Tory, but his identification of Christ with the honest workman Piers Plowman cuts through all the fat of compromise with the world down to the bare bones of an eternally subversive and anarchic Christianity, and that is his meaning for us. Dickens's influence also is for us completely radical, whatever he himself may have been. When his Pickwick goes from the law court into the debtor's prison, it never once occurs to him that the accumulated legal wisdom of his country, which has decided against him, is entitled to the smallest respect whatever. That is a useful frame of mind to have in citizens of a free democracy who are determined not to be hagridden by precedent. That curious self-depreciation in respect to physical courage which is so characteristic of the Englishman is also closer to satire than it looks. It is founded on the profoundly satiric belief that physical dignity can only last as far as the first banana peeling. Cockney cheek and impudence have done much to save England from swaggering and posturing tyrants; the Jorrocks of that neglected Victorian genius Surtees, who is one of the best Cockneys in literature, will do for an example:

"You 'air-dresser on the chestnut 'oss," roars Mr. Jorrocks, during a check, to a gentleman with very big, ginger whiskers, "pray, 'old 'ard!"

"Hair-dresser," replies the gentleman, turning round in a fury, "I'm an officer in the ninety-first regiment."

"Then you hossifer in the ninety-fust regiment, wot looks like an 'air-dresser, 'old 'ard!"

Satire, in short, is the completion of the logical process known as the *reductio ad absurdum,* and that is not designed to hold one in perpetual captivity, but to bring one to the point at which one can escape from an incorrect procedure. Just as a mother tells a timid child afraid of the dark that there is nothing there, so the satirist presents ignorance and confusion with a negation. And when the public tells the satirist that the devil is dead, the very smugness of the response proves that his work has had some effect.

I have said that the sardonic vision is the seamy side of the tragic vision, but Skelton's remark provides me with a more exact image for what I mean. At the bottom of Dante's hell, which is also the centre of the spherical earth, Dante sees Satan standing upright in the circle of ice, and as he cautiously follows Virgil over the hip and thigh of the evil giant, letting himself down by the tufts of hair on his skin, he passes the centre and finds himself no longer going down but going up, climbing out on the other side of the world to see the stars again. From this point of view, the devil is no longer upright, but standing on his head, in the same attitude in which he was hurled downward from heaven upon the other side of the earth. Both tragedy and satire take us into a hell of narrowing circles, a blasted world of repulsiveness and idiocy, a world without pity and without hope. Both culminate in some such vision as that of Dante's, of the source of all evil in a personal form. Tragedy can take us no farther; but if we persevere with the satirist, we shall pass a dead centre, and finally see the gentlemanly Prince of Darkness bottom side up.

Alvin Kernan

Juvenal

In all, over a period of thirty years (roughly A.D. 90–120), Juvenal wrote sixteen satires which purport to deal with the events and characters of preceding reigns but are actually attacks on the Rome of his own time. The first satire is a "program" satire in which "Juvenal" first speaks of the inanity of the multitudinous epics he is forced to listen to, and then delivers a long indictment of the Romans by cataloguing their sins. He then tells us that this is the "real" world and that only satire can reveal it, not the lying epic form which makes heroes where there are none. In the course of this catalogue Juvenal manages to construct his satiric personality, a plain, old-fashioned Roman of good family who has fallen on evil days burning with indignation at the abominations he sees around him and not afraid to speak the truth. The remaining satires, with one exception, deal with various forms of Roman degeneracy: male sexual perversion, the condition of the Roman city, the decay of patronage, the indecent behavior of Roman women, the brutality of the professional army, and the debasement of the great families. One satire only, XV, a description of cannibalism in Egypt, does not seem to bear directly on Rome and its people.

The variety of material constitutes a broad panorama of Roman life about 100 A.D., and it is held together by a simple theme: money, wealth, luxury, and success have debased Rome and destroyed the ancient virtues which made her ruler of the world. Juvenal concentrates his attention on the sensitive areas of cultural life—religion, the law, the arts, the army, the family, the chastity of women—and using a multitude of rhetorical devices paints in vivid terms the corruption of each. By way of contrast we have occasional glimpses of a plainer and more dignified way of life, the way of simplicity, hard work, concern for Rome rather than self, natural sex life, and love of family—the myth of Cicero and Cato which the satirist embodies. Roman depravity is given dramatic life in a number of ways. Sometimes it is presented in the form of a short story as in Satire IV, a mock epic in which obsequious counsellors are consulted about how to cook a large turbot; or as a straight sermon, Satire X, "The Vanity of Human Wishes"; or the satirist will play the part of a sympathetic listener to an attack delivered by another figure. His sympathy is ironic in Satire IX where the professional pathic bewails the "immoral" way in which his patron has treated him, but the sympathy is genuine in Satire III where the satirist listens to an old friend tell why he is leaving Rome. This latter satire is very close to the most characteristic Juvenalian form, a dramatic monologue in which the satirist speaking to an adversarius[1] describes in vivid terms the corruption of Rome. In Satire III Juvenal simply reverses the usual parts and allows the adversarius to deliver a magnificent attack while the satirist listens, no doubt in amazement. This satire is typical in all other respects, and a brief résumé of it will make clear certain features of Juvenalian satire which the Elizabethans imitated.

The satirist begins by saying that an old friend of his is leaving Rome and settling at Cumae, and though he laments the loss of a friend, he can understand anyone wanting to leave the city where one lives, "in perpetual dread of fires and falling houses, and the thousand perils of this terrible city, and poets spouting in the month of August." Without transition we are swept into a scene in which the goods of the departing friend, Umbricius, are being loaded for the journey. The setting for this incident is a grove once sacred to the gods, but now the native grass has been replaced by a marble fountain in bad taste and the whole area has been given over to indigent Jews. This gives the satirist a chance to expatiate on the contrast between the beauties of unspoiled nature and the ugly, ostentatious works of men, and allows him to sneer at the Jews who, along with Greeks and other Eastern peoples, are for him symbols of both the adulteration of the Roman stock and the effeminate customs which have debased the citizenry. With the background established and the major themes hinted at, Umbricius delivers his farewell speech, a speech in which he arouses our sympathy for the man who has to leave his native and rightful home and stirs up our indignation at the evils which are driving him thence. He goes, he says, "while my old age is erect and fresh, while Lachesis has something left to spin, and I can support myself on my own feet without slipping a staff beneath my hand." He leaves the city to those "who turn black into white" and to those who were formerly men of the lowest order but have

---

[1] Persius lays this convention bare in his first satire when he addresses his adversarius in this manner, "*Quisquis es, o modo quem ex adverso dicere feci*" (line 44).

now made fortunes from contracting city works or running a slave market. He leaves it to them since he no longer has any purpose at Rome: he cannot lie, knows nothing of astrology, cannot act as a messenger between a bride and her paramour, and does not wish to know those dangerous secrets which rob one of sleep but ensure the favor of the man whom the relevation might harm.

At this point old Umbricius abandons his skillfully maintained attitude of mock humility and launches into direct invective against the sycophantic and parasitical Greeks and Syrians. His anger rises as he recounts how he, a freeborn Roman citizen, must give place to these foreigners. The foreigner, he says, is a natural actor and even if the true Roman wished to compete with him it would be impossible, for the slave can praise anything, no matter how bad: if one smiles the Greek splits his side with laughter, if one says he is hot the Greek "breaks into a sweat." Besides, this parasite is a lustful creature, and if he fails to debauch the mother of the family, the young daughter, son-in-law, or son, he will attack the grandmother.

Umbricius then commences an attack, still in the vituperative manner, on the prevailing condition where wealth has become the measure of a man in Rome, rather than birth or virtue. You cannot get justice, you cannot even compete for the favors of a courtesan, let alone hope to marry well, unless you have money. And to make these ideas more vivid Umbricius quickly sketches in two brief scenes in which he is forced to give way to slaves while hurrying to see a client, and then because poorly dressed he is forced out of his rightful place at the games by the sons of panders, auctioneers, and gladiators.

Next he turns to a description of rural Italy for contrast. It is here, he says, that the old simplicity is still preserved, and clothes make no difference. We are then shown a sentimental picture of a rustic festival where the "babe on its mother's breast shrinks back affrighted at the gaping of the pallid masks," and where all men are dressed alike. After shifting back briefly to a description of the indignities one must undergo at the hands of a rich man in Rome, Umbricius returns again to the countryside of "cool Praeneste, or at Volsinii," and points out that one can live in these towns in perfect safety, whereas in Rome one is in constant danger of fire and falling buildings.

This is approximately the center of the Satire, and old Umbricius, still breathing easily, having first decried the moral contamination of Rome and contrasted it with the rural areas where the old virtues are maintained, now begins to dramatize the physical ugliness and dangers of the city. He begins with a scene in which a friend living on the third floor is calling futilely for water to put out a fire. This scene fades into a companion piece, a description of the poor scholar Codrus who loses all his miserable possessions in a fire and is forced to beg—unsuccessfully, of course, for nothing but villainy prospers in Juvenal's satire. But if the house of a wealthy man is destroyed, everyone deplores the fact and hastens to offer valuable gifts. After this the speaker again weaves a description of country life into his tapestry of Rome and then hurries on to descriptions of the noise of the city and the dangers of trying to walk through the Roman crowd. The denunciation of the huge drays passing through the city is made more poignant by drawing a scene in which a load of marble falls from a wagon and crushes, in a most horrible manner, a man so poor that he has not the money to pay his passage over Styx. This scene dissolves into a picture, à la Dickens, in which the dead man's family in their humble (but happy) home are waiting for his arrival. Next Umbricius presents the dangers of the street at night, again in dramatic terms. He describes himself as passing quickly along a street where he is first struck by tiles falling from a badly repaired roof and then by the contents of slop-pails. Having endured these trials, he is robbed and beaten by a bravo, who does not, of course, dare attack the rich. But he ironically consoles himself by saying that even if he should get home safely, the chances are he will be robbed by a burglar in a city where there are so many criminals that most of the iron, which should have been used for agricultural tools, goes for making chains. Having completed this magnificent tirade, old Umbricius takes his leave and with mild irony says to the satirist, who has no doubt been listening with mouth agape, "I will come over to your cold country in my thick boots to hear your Satires [i.e. satirists], if they think me worthy of that honour."

Paraphrase is ineffective for rendering the quality of Juvenalian satire for several reasons. First, it misses the lightning speed with which the original moves, an effect achieved by the vigor of the verse and by the rapid shifts from scene to scene and subject to subject without concern for formal transitions. Second, it fails to show the superb manner in which Juvenal manages constantly to keep the ideals of rustic simplicity and antique virtue in contrast with the degenerate city life, not only by alternately presenting scenes of each but by weaving the pastoral world into the texture of the entire satire through the use of imagery and diction which make an invidious comparison with the dirty and wicked town. Finally, it is impossible to suggest the profusion of rhetorical devices used to manipulate the emotions of the reader.[2]

---

[2] My discussion of the rhetorical aspects of Juvenal's satires is largely based upon various analyses by W. S. Anderson. His unpublished Yale dissertation, "The Rhetoric of Juvenal" (1954), is a thorough discussion of the skillful manner in which Juvenal used rhetoric. Some of his work has appeared in "Juvenal 6: A Problem in Structure," *Classical Philology*, 2 (1956), 73–94, and "Studies in Book 1 of Juvenal," *Yale Classical Studies, 15.*

What we have then within the satires is a panoramic view of the dirt and sins of Rome, a camera-eye sweep directed by the satirist over Rome, pausing here and there to focus briefly on a scene or a face, and utilizing every technique known to the rhetorician and the poet to make the pictures vivid and bring into relief their more unsavory aspects. This is one of the primary qualities of formal satire; the display of the world's ills not by concentrating on a single incident, or even a limited number of situations, but rather by presenting a wide variety of brief and carefully constructed pictures and comments, all tending to indict the society in which such things exist. This is the familiar, and difficult, artistic technique of attempting to show the whole through the presentation of as great a number of its parts as possible. The dangers of such a method are characteristic of satire: superficiality and a diversity of events and persons which hinder the emergence of any pattern. But the Juvenalian hodgepodge has a remarkable thematic unity. Each of the innumerable vices and disorders described is traced back to a single source, the possession of excessive wealth which saps Roman vitality and morality.

This horde of hypocrites, foreigners, perverts, whores, sycophants, cowards, murderers, thieves, and sybarites in their dirty, noisy, brawling, and dangerous city is the scene of Juvenalian satire. But strictly speaking this scene, vivid as it is, has no separate existence of its own, for it comes into being entirely through the words of the satirist. He selects the parts, arranges them, and describes them in such a way as to control the reactions of the audience. He stands always in the foreground, pointing out detail after detail, directing our attention from one example of vice to the next, and imparting qualities to each with his language. As a result every detail is reflexive: the words leave the satirist's mouth to describe the scene but they also bounce back to define the satirist who chooses these details and uses this language. This process combined with a variety of direct statements about his feelings and attitudes creates the personality of Juvenal's satirist. He admits to the more attractive characteristics of the satirist—frankness, courage, indignation, and a compulsion to expose vice wherever he finds it. He is a conservative in the best sense, embodying all the primitive virtues Rome now lacks, and as he continues speaking we begin to see the stern old Roman of good family who has fallen on evil days. His money is gone, and since money is the only thing that counts any longer in Rome, he is shoved about by all, dishonored in being made to sit below the salt, turned away by patrons, pushed from his proper seat at the games, and, in general, denied the dignities to which his name, his profession, and his citizenship should entitle him. To such a man everything about modern Rome appears debased, and he reacts with violence. He is the perfect figure to attack Roman depravity, for he represents an older, healthier society and thus stands always in contrast to the decadence around him; and he dislikes everything modern and has the courage to censure it. What Juvenal has done is to create a character something like Cato the Censor and place him in the setting of first-century Rome, and it is as if Cotton Mather were allowed to comment on twentieth-century New York.

But the Juvenalian satirist inevitably has qualities utterly foreign to Cato the Censor, and these involve him in the usual paradoxes. For one thing the satirist is a Stoic—at least from time to time he makes Stoic pronouncements about denying diviniy to Fortune by fortitude, advocates control of both wrath and desire, and speaks, in Stoic fashion, of the necessity for wisdom and reason. But the pose of the Stoic conflicts with the furious indignation which is so omnipresent in Juvenal's satire. The invective is so powerful, the scorn so biting, the lash so vigorously applied, the probing so careful and vindictive, the sense of outrage so apparent, that the satirist is constantly in the position of denying the same ethic by which he is condemning his victim. He attacks the wealthy, the hypocritical, the lecherous on the grounds of their being unreasonable, and simultaneously is outrageously unreasonable, in the Stoic sense, in his anger which knows no bounds. Juvenal was not unaware of this predicament and presents the problem in the line, "si natura negat, facit indignatio versum" (I, 79). Throughout the satires he argues that the crimes he sees are so great that no one could resist scourging them, but the fundamental ambivalence in the character of the satirist remains.

Perhaps even more striking is the contrast between the pose of the plain, simple man and the baroque rhetorician who emerges in the satires. By the end of the first century A.D. rhetoric had degenerated from the Aristotelian and Ciceronian ideal of persuasion through reason to a form of public entertainment in which the orator sought to amuse with a display of ornate styles and sensational subject matter. Emphasis was now placed not on *disposito*, the arrangement of the parts in a logical and orderly fashion, but on *ornatus*, the embellishment of language. The classical ideals of smoothness, concealment, clarity, and organization—*ars est celare artem* —gave way to the baroque rhetoric of the Silver Latin period with its ideals of emotional intensity; elaboration of details; display; and concentration on a single, simple theme. Juvenal was trained in this school of rhetoric, and in his satires the hand of the extravagant rhetorician is apparent in his profuse use of such linguistic devices as synecdoche, metonymy, antonomasia, epithets, allegory, irony, periphrasis. But Juvenal went far beyond the boundaries established by the rhetors for such subjects as he treated. On one hand he made use of elements of the high style: epic catalogues, sonorous meters, archaisms, Hellenisms, weird compounds, and on the other hand he included vulgarisms, obscenities, racy colloquialisms, technical terminology. All this dazzling verbal array is skillfully marshalled to hammer home one single theme, *dépravation du siècle, éloge du temps passé,*[3] one of the standard declamatory topics of the rhetorical schools.

The use of this elaborate, showy rhetoric in Juvenal's satires not only endows his stern Roman satirist with contradictory characteristics, a plain man who is at the same time a sophistic rhetorician, but it has led as well to a questioning of Juvenal's motives for writing satire. Once it was shown that his satires conformed to the declamatory exercises of the rhetorical schools, then, given our modern distrust of rhetoric, the truth of Juvenal's charges against the Romans and his indignation became suspect. As H. J. Rose puts it, "Juvenal sometimes leaves a skeptical reader a little in doubt whether he is more angered at the wickedness of the world or obliged to it for giving him such admirable subjects for his great eloquence and extraordinary power of composing vigorous hexameters."[4] There has been no agreement on this point, however, and another scholar can argue that Juvenal's "honesty cannot be questioned. It comes through everything he writes. He is terrifically in earnest, desperately sincere."[5]

The materials of the satires certainly suggest a conscious attempt to capitalize on human delight in the display of depravity. Juvenal's satirist says that he takes for his subject matter "quidquid agunt homines" (I, 85), but since he is always on the attack he seldom, except by way of contrast, introduces any pictures of virtuous Romans, and there must have been many going about their daily business and leading normal lives.[6]

Instead we are whisked from scene to scene of hypocrisy, gluttony, luxury, effeminacy, and ingratitude. The whole of this is liberally spiced with explicit accounts of the sexual perversions of the Romans, and their moral debilitation is paralleled by descriptions of the ulginess and dangers of

---

[3] Juvenal's use of this theme is treated by Josue de Decker, *Juvenalis Declamans: Etude sur la rhetorique declamatoire dans les Satires de Juvenal* (Gand, 1913). This work provides a picture of rhetorical practice at the time of Juvenal and investigates the relationship of his satires to the rules of declamation.

[4] *A Handbook of Latin Literature* (London, Methuen, 1936), p. 407.

[5] Edith Hamilton, *The Roman Way* (New York, W. W. Norton, 1932), p. 253.

[6] The historian's more balanced view of the Rome of the first and second centuries is ably and most interestingly presented by C. N. Cochrane, *Christianity and Classical Culture,* (Oxford, 1949). In ch. 4, *Regnum Caesaris Regnum Diaboli,* Cochrane argues that satiric poets such as Juvenal and satiric historians such as Tacitus were fashionable conservatives who completely failed to understand the nature of the crisis through which Rome was necessarily passing on its way to the achievement of stability and order, a crisis made unavoidable by the uncompromising attitude taken in the first century B.C. by such rubbed individualists as Cato and Brutus, who were regarded by the new conservatives as models of virtue.

their city. There is, of course, always the possibility that Rome was as thoroughly infected as Juvenal paints it, but it seems unlikely. What we are facing here is a problem brought into being by the use of the realistic perspective on satire: i.e. either Rome was completely corrupt or it wasn't, and if it wasn't then Juvenal's indignation wassham and he was no more than a Roman muckraker. The problem is delusive, for we are dealing with art, albeit highly rhetorical, not history. Rome was somewhat corrupt, and Juvenal constructed his satires in such a way as to reveal that corruption in the most striking manner possible. His satirist, a man who finds everything modern not to his taste and looks only for evidence of decay, is simply one of his poetic tools forged to reveal that corruption in a spectacular manner.

. . . The characteristic action of Juvenal's satires, taken singly or as a group, would seem to be, "to expose the truth," though this could be stated in a number of other metaphorical ways such as "to track down the infection." W. S. Anderson has shown that this action usually takes the form of proving a startling paradox, as in Satire III "whose theme we may state as follows: Rome is no longer Rome. . . . Umbricius . . . takes the Rome of traditional associations—its majesty, justice, wealth, beauty, and honesty—and exposes its self-contradiction. Thus he comments on various conditions, the lack of opportunity, the aliens, the fires, the thieves, etc., all of which signify the loss of traditional Roman qualities and cumulate in a totally negative picture of an uninhabitable city. When he leaves, then, Umbricius symbolizes in his act what he has been saying, that Roman characteristics no longer fit the city, for he is the last Roman."[7] While Juvenal's satirist remains behind to give us thirteen more satires, his conclusions are always as bleak and unproductive as those of Umbricius. In each satire he proves his crushing paradox, which in sum might be stated that men are not men but beasts, but shows us no possibility of change for the better. The few instances of good appear in isolated pockets and seem about to be destroyed. The only "positive" program appears in Satire X where we are advised to cultivate Stoic fortitude to endure a mad world from which the satirist has stripped the last shreds of pretense.

---

[7] "Studies in Book I of Juvenal," p. 88.

John Speirs

The Nun's Priest's Tale

The Host, of course, heartily agrees with the Knight's interruption of the *Monk's Tale*; a melancholy monotony, besides being futile—there is no use in bewailing spilt milk—is unsociable, does not promote the cheerfulness of a company. He turns from the Monk to the Nun's Priest, who has not hitherto figured in the foreground, for a merry tale.

> Be blythe, though thou ryde up-on a jade.
> What though thyn hors be bothe foule and lene,
> If he wol serve thee, rekke nat a bene;
> Look that thyn herte be mery evermo.

Despite his impoverished exterior

> This swete preest, this goodly man, sir John

does indeed tell a blithe, a witty and wise tale, the tale of Chauntecleer and Pertelote; surely Chaucer's masterpiece among the *Canterbury Tales*.

For only a refusal to allow that a tale purporting to be about a cock and a hen could be more than light entertainment with an improving 'moral' added (though its 'skill' as a little masterpiece of comic 'art' might be admired) could have hindered recognition of the moral fable of Chauntecleer and Pertelote as a great and wise poem about human nature, a humane masterpiece. The inclusiveness of the harmony of the poem, the diversity of spheres of human experience and knowledge involved and composed in the harmony, constitutes it perhaps the wisest single poem of all the *Canterbury Tales* and therefore perhaps the supreme expression—and the most urbane expression—of the mediaeval English organic community.

When England, old already, was called merry.[1]

Against the sober realistic background of a peasant widow's poverty, and in contrast to her prudent wisdom, is set the mock-heroic brilliance of the dazzling cock.

> His vois was merier than the mery orgon
> On messe-dayes that in the chirche gon;
> Wel sikerer was his crowing in his logge,
> Than is a clokke, or an abbey orlogge . . .
> His comb was redder than the fyn coral,
> And batailed, as it were a castel-wal.
> His bile was blak, and as the jeet it shoon;
> Lyk asur were his legges, and his toon;
> His nayles whytter than the lilie flour,
> And lyk the burned gold was his colour.

The splendid comparisons (and colours) lavished inordinately upon a cock produce a burlesque in which the gorgeous creature is seen as a proud—perhaps vainglorious—prince of a romance or 'tragedy'; particularly, the glorification of his crowing draws attention at once to that gift of which he is especially vain and which is to be the agency of his fall. Thus is introduced what is to prove the tale's central theme of pride—the pride that goes before a fall. The position of the *Nun's Priest's Tale* immediately after the Monk's solemn succession of tragic instances—

> Of him that stood in greet prosperitee
> And is y-fallen out of heigh degree

—indicates that it is intended (among other things) to parody these; but the comedy of the *Nun's Priest's Tale* is more serious than the solemnity of the Monk's 'tragedies'.

This impression of a court in a farmyard, a castle in a hen-house, Chauntecleer a knight, Pertelote his lady, shifts into a domestic scene between the cock and hen couple—a most natural parody of a human husband and wife. The scene engages the fullest human sympathy for Chauntecleer and Pertelote. When Pertelote says to Chauntecleer (badly shaken by a dream he has had in the night of that beast which we recognize from his description is a fox)

> Now han ye lost myn herte and al my love;
> I can nat love a coward, by my feith . . .
> Have ye no mannes herte, and han a berd?

---

[1] Edward Thomas, *The Manor Farm*.

they are the very words of a wife. The human conjugal relation is rendered the more piquant by the attribution of a man's heart and beard to—when we remember—a cock. But Chauntecleer is more than an aspect of humanity, the cock-like strutting male aspect; Pertelote more than the hen-like female aspect; they are individuals, they are distinct, rounded characters.

The cock and hen *debate* on dreams (like the *debate* on the same theme between Troilus and Pandarus) brings out the contrast between them; it is that old *debate* in a new comic setting. Pertelote is the practical wife. She ascribes a purely physiological cause and significance to dreams and advises a laxative. She has a wealth of knowledge of medicine, of remedies and herbs, at her finger-tips. The diet of worms which she prescribes to be taken before the herbs is (we are told by the scholars) prescribed in Dioscorides as a remedy for the tertian fever which she fears her husband may have contracted; it is, besides, quite the appropriate diet for a cock. The cock thereupon displays himself as a great clerk. He brings to bear his more ponderous erudition, 'ensamples' out of 'olde bokes' of dreams that came true. These vivid and terrifying anecdotes of violent death serve the purpose in the tale of intensifying the suspense, the sense of something dreadful about to happen, an impending catastrophe to Chauntecleer. In the end he rejects the laxatives not after all on any very rational grounds but simply because they are disagreeable.

> I hem defye, I love hem never a del.

He turns instead to earthly pleasures to distract him, and first to female beauty—which to a cock is that of a hen.

> For whan I see the beautee of your face,
> Ye ben so scarlet-reed about your yën,
> It maketh al my drede for to dyen.

But even while his wife's beauty provides him with solace the conceited fellow continues privately to despise her because she does not know Latin, and takes a mean advantage of her ignorance to quote at her expense a Latin allusion to Eve and the Fall; the centuries-old male grimace heightens the bookish cock's own absurdity. The scene exposes the vanity of pedantry, and thus further develops the principal theme of pride.

The coming of day totally dissolves, for Chauntecleer, the disagreeableness of the dream.

> . . . he fley doun fro the beem,
> For it was day, and eek his hennes alle.

In the bright daylight as he struts before his wives and paramours he is no longer afraid. We are made aware again of the 'royal' aspect of Chauntecleer; his looks are the looks of a lion.

> He loketh as it were a grim leoun;
> And on his toes he rometh up and doun,
> Him deyned not to sette his foot to grounde.
> He chukketh, whan he hath a corn y-founde,
> And to him rennen thanne his wyves alle.
> Thus royal, as a prince is in his halle . . .

When at length the fatal day arrives Chauntecleer is once again seen as a prince about to fall through pride.

> . . . Chauntecleer, in al his pryde,
> His seven wyves walking by his syde—

walking through an earthly—and (as it unhappily proves) a fool's—paradise.

> Madame Pertelote, my worldes blis,
> Herkneth thise blisful briddes how they singe,
> And see the fresshe floures how they springe;
> Ful is myn herte of revel and solas.

The Nun's Priest—for the tale is dramatically his—here interposes the warning reminder

> But sodeinly him fil a sorweful cas;
> For ever the latter ende of joye is wo.
> God woot that worldly joye is sone ago.

In Chauntecleer's paradise the serpent is a fox. The fox lurking among the plants is a type of the betrayer; and is identified (in a passage in which the *apostrophe*, *exclamatio* and *exempla* of the mediaeval rhetoric are parodied) with the great historical traitors.

> O false mordrer, lurking in thy den!
> O newe Scariot, newe Genilon!
> False dissimilour, O Greek Sinon,
> That broghtest Troye al outrely to sorwe!

In the ensuing scene with the fox as the tempter, the serpent in paradise, the poem develops as a tragi-comic allegory of the Fall, the major human catastrophe. An allusion to Adam and Eve brings in the relevant associations.

Wommannes counseil broghte us first to wo,
And made Adam fro paradys to go,
Ther-as he was ful mery, and wel at ese.

(From the blame of women the teller of the tale, being a nun's priest, is careful to dissociate himself.) The earthly paradise then vividly recurs with the fox in the role of the serpent among the flowers.

Agayn the sonne; and Chauntecleer so free
Song merier than the mermayde in the see . . .
And so bifel that, as he caste his yë,
Among the wortes, on a boterflye,
He was war of this fox that lay ful lowe.

The temptation is conducted with the smooth, accomplished flattery of the false courtier.

He wolde han fled, but that the fox anon
Seyde, 'Gentil sire, allas! wher wol ye gon?
Be ye affrayed of me that am your freend?
Now certes, I were worse than a feend,
If I to yow wolde harm or vileinye.
I am nat come your counseil for t'espye;
But trewely, the cause of my cominge
Was only for to herkne how that ye singe.
For trewely ye have as mery a stevene
As eny aungel hath, that is in hevene;
Therwith ye han in musik more felinge
Than hadde Boëce, or any that can singe.
My lord your fader (god his soule blesse!)
And eek your moder, of hir gentilesse,
Han in myn hous y-been, to my gret ese;
And certes, sire, ful fayn wolde I yow plese.
But for men speke of singing, I wol saye,
So mote I brouke wel myn eyen tweye,
Save yow, I herde never man so singe,
As dide your fader in the morweninge;
Certes, it was of herte, al that he song.
And for to make his voys the more strong,
He wolde so peyne him, that with bothe his yën
He moste winke, so loude he wolde cryen,
And stonden on his tiptoon ther-with-al,
And strecche forth his nekke long and smal . . .
Now singeth, sire, for seinte Charitee,
Let see, conne ye your fader countrefete?

Chauntecleer, unconscious of the double meanings in the fox's (the fiend's) speech, 'is ravished with his flaterye'. (The Nun's Priest here interposes an admonition against flatterers.

> Allas! ye lordes, many a fals flatour
> Is in your courtes, and many a losengeour.)[2]

In this instance it is Adam (not Eve) who falls, through his personal vanity; vanity of crowing is his downfall.

> This Chauntecleer stood hye up-on his toos,
> Strecching his nekke, and heeld his eyen cloos,
> And gan to crowe loude for the nones.

The fantastic braggadocio creature is caught by the outstretched neck.

The reflections on the event, though necessarily mock-serious when that event is a tragic disaster to a cock, are just as applicable to the affairs of a cock as to human affairs. The age-old *debate* of the Schoolmen concerning free choice and necessity (which the lurking proximity of the fox had earlier in the tale called to mind) now finds its response in the recognition of this fresh instance of the inexorable chain of cause and effect which involves both cocks and men.

> O destinee, that mayst nat been eschewed!
> Allas, that Chauntecleer fleigh fro the bemes!
> Allas, his wyf ne roghte nat of dremes!
> And on a Friday fil al this meschaunce.
> O Venus, that are goddesse of plesaunce,
> Sin that thy servant was this Chauntecleer,
> And in thy service dide al his poweer,
> More for delyt, than world to multiplye.

The drop from high philosophic meditation on destiny to the shocked, but hardly philosophic, consideration that the fatal day was a Friday (Venus's day) and the reference to Chauntecleer as Venus's servant 'more for delyt, than world to multiplye', are rippling comic surface variation over the poem's graver depth. The apostrophes to 'destinee' and Venus are anticlimaxed by an apostrophe to Gaufred (a celebrated mediaeval teacher of rhetoric) whose rhetorical aid is invoked to 'chyde the Friday'.[3]

---

[2] We may compare the court of the God of Love in the *Prolouge* to the *Legend of Good Women*.

For in your court is many a losengeour . . .

[3] 'Every educated man remembered Master Gaufred,' says Professor Manly, 'and some perhaps knew by heart his famous lamentation (on the death of Richard Coeur de Lion who received his fatal wound on a Friday) for the *Nova Poetria* was one of the principal textbooks on rhetoric . . . studied in the schools.'

From this parody of the apostrophes and exclamations of the academic rhetoric which Chaucer was himself sufficiently well grounded in to be able to treat lightly (and deliberately to prefer, in his poetry, 'pleyn' English which all 'may understonde') the poetry rises to a superb mock-heroic climax—a succession of *ensamples* in which the cries of the be-reaved hens sound like the lamentations of famous women on the grand tragic occasions of history.

> Certes, swich cry ne lamentacioun
> Was never of ladies maad, whan Ilioun
> Was wonne, and Pirrus with his streite swerd,
> Whan he hadde hent king Priam by the berd,
> And slayn him (as saith us *Eneydos*),
> As maden alle the hennes in the clos,
> Whan they had seyn of Chauntecleer the sighte.
> But sovereynly dame Pertelote shrighte,
> Ful louder than dide Hasdrubales wyf,
> Whan that hir housbond hadde lost his lyf,
> And that the Romayns hadde brend Cartage;
> She was so ful of torment and of rage,
> That wilfully into the fyr she sterte,
> And brende hir-selven with a steadfast herte.
> O woful hennes, right so cryden ye,
> As, whan that Nero brende the citee
> Of Rome, cryden senatoures wyves,
> For that hir housbondes losten alle hir lyves.

This in its turn leads up to the grand climax in external action—as are the climaxes of other tales and of the Wife of Bath's monologue—moral dis-order, the universal chaos of the Fall as burlesque, a commotion in an English farm-yard.

> Ran Colle our dogge, and Talbot, and Gerland,
> And Malkin, with a distaf in hir hand;
> Ran cow and calf, and eek the verray hogges
> So were they fered for berking of the dogges
> And shouting of the men and wimmen eke,
> They ronne so, hem thoughte hir herte breke.
> They yelleden as feendes doon in helle;
> The dokes cryden as men wolde hem quelle;
> The gees for fere flowen over the trees;
> Out of the hyve cam the swarm of bees;
> So hidous was the noyse, a! *benedicite!* . . .
> Of bras thay broghten bemes, and of box,

> Of horn, of boon, in whiche they blewe and
>   pouped,
> And therwithal thay shryked and they houped;
> It semed as that heven sholde falle.

This comic chaos is given a contemporary reference by an allusion to Jack Straw and to the disorder with which Chaucer's social world had been threatened. The hullabaloo is, by itself, to no purpose. The last-moment reversal of fortune by which the lost cock is saved springs from Chauntecleer's own wit—now that he is wiser—in successfully appealing to the confident vanity of Reynard in *his* turn. When the Nun's Priest remarked 'My tale is of a cok' that was his modesty; this fable of the fall of a cock, this tragi-comic allegory of the Fall of Man, illustrates some central truths about human nature with subtle irony and humane wisdom.

Allen Tate

A Note on Elizabethan Satire

It is ungrateful to impute to Sir Edmund Chambers [Editor of *The Oxford Book of Sixteenth Century Verse*] any trace of wrong insight into the quality of the age. The century as a whole falls into three periods—that of Skelton, lasting until the appearance of Wyat in Tottel's *Songes and Sonets* in 1557; the period of Wyat, the most considerable figure until Sidney and Spenser, whose *Shepherd's Calendar* brought in a new era in 1579. It was by then the English Renaissance full-blown. *The Shepherd's Calendar*, a dull but original exercise in theory, offered to Spenser's successors an example of new possibilities of poetic English, and set up a pastoral convention that was to reach perfection as late as 1637. In singling out the leading impulse of the Elizabethan age one is constantly guided by the genius and magnitude of Spenser. Yet it is Milton in the next age who puts the seal of perfection on the pastoral, mythological school, and who, to no little extent, permits us to rank as highly as we do merely competent poets like Davies and Constable.

Our comparatively low rating of Greville no less than of Raleigh—Saintsbury says that Greville is "sententious and difficult"—is due to the constant introspection, the difficult self-analysis, the cynical melancholy, that break through the courtly pastoral convention to a level of feeling deeper, and historically purer, than the facile despair of the Sidneian sonneteers. Doubtless both Greville and Raleigh, as minor masters, were too much impressed with the glittering style of Sidney, and, later, of Spenser, to understand that their own sensibilities deserved a more perfectly matured style. Their work has the diffuseness of divided purpose.

There has never been enough made of Elizabethan satire. While Raleigh

and Fulke Greville cannot be called pure satirists, they were not comforta-
ble in the courtly, pastoral abstractions. In this negative feature of their
verse they resemble certain of the satirists, Hall, Marston, Tourneur. If we
put Raleigh and Greville together against the background of the wide-
spread influence of Martial,[1] they, too, form a background not only for the
Satires of Donne (1593) but for much of that great poet's most characteristic later writing.

Yet Sir Edmund says: "Only for chronology, indeed, can Donne be an
Elizabethan"—an opinion that obscures the still powerful strain of medieval thought at the end of the sixteenth century. By another kind of
reasoning Donne cannot be a Jacobean. For we find in Donne, significantly
enough, not only the influence of Martial, but a resurgence of scholasticism
—a union of classical satire and medievalism. And it is significant that
"Go, soul, the body's guest" was written by the same Raleigh who wrote
"The Passionate Man's Pilgrimage," a poem that is, I believe, occasionally
described as charming. I cannot believe that, in order to write it, Raleigh
invoked a muse different from the muse of a poem that is sophisticated,
consciously erudite, and subtle. "The Passionate Man's Pilgrimage" is
medieval allegory furbished up with a new awareness of the sensuous
world; "Go, soul, the body's guest" is satire; and the two strains are not
quite the disharmony that we are accustomed to believe them.

Possibly the last use of extended medieval allegory in verse of great
distinction is Sackville's *Induction*. There are the familiar personifications
—Remorse, Dread, Revenge, Misery, Death. Spenser's task was to revive
allegory with a new spirit alien to the medieval mind. Although Spenser's
puritanism is manifest, his allegory has a voluptuous glitter that Sackville's
more medieval spareness lacked; or if you go back to Gower's treatment
of the seven deadly sins it is plain that as a medieval man he was too
serious about them to dress them up.

The medieval minds left over at the end of the sixteenth century tended
to see the world not in terms of a fixed moral system, but with an ingrained
moral prejudice about the nature of man. I allude here to the decline of
Catholic theology in England, and to the rise, conspicuously in the dramatic
poets, of an unmoral and anti-doctrinal point of view. Marlowe is an example. But the moral temper of a less expansive, more melancholy age, a
kind of interregnum between feudalism and Tudorism when the evil of
life was expressed in ideas of all-pervasive mortality—this moral temper,
having lost its theological framework, remained as an almost instinctive

---

[1] See T. K. Whipple, *Martial and the English Epigram from Sir Thomas Wyat to
Ben Jonson.* University of California Press, 1929; and Evelyn M. Simpson, *Paradoxes
and Problems,* in *A Garland for John Donne.* Harvard University Press, 1931.

approach to the nature of man. And the nature of man, far from enjoying the easy conquest of evil that Spenser set forth in six books that might have been twelve, was on the whole unpleasant and depraved. This depravity is the theme of Elizabethan tragedy, I think, as early as *The Jew of Malta*. There is no need to cite Webster and Ford.

It is the prevailing attitude of the satirists and of most of those non-dramatic poets who stand apart from the Spenserian school. In such poets we find a quality that we have shortsightedly ascribed uniquely to modern verse—the analysis of emotion and an eye chiefly to the aesthetic effect. There is here the use of symbols that are too complex to retain, throughout a long work, or from one work to another, a fixed meaning. The allegorical symbol is constant and homogeneous, like the Red Cross Knight; the richer, poetic symbol, like Prospero, does not invite the oversimplification of certain of its qualities, but asks to be taken in all its manifold richness.

It is this stream of Elizabethan poetry that has never been properly evaluated. We tend to forget, in fixing the relation of the Shakespearean drama to its sources, and of its text to the texts of contemporaries, that Shakespeare stands outside the allegorical school. It is thus difficult for us to take a further step and to see that he was closely connected with a much less conspicuous type of poetry that had been only superficially affected by the Renaissance. This was the dormant medieval which, even after the new language of Wyat, survived in Sackville's *Induction*.

In a later poet like Greene the new courtly conventions are too weak to sustain his restless sensibility. Although Greene never mastered a style, his great vitality of image and rhythm is largely due to a naïvely skeptical grasp of the conventions of Sidney and Spenser. He uses them without ever quite believing them: as in the verse of Raleigh the convention offers just enough resistance to expression to lend to the poetry tension and depth. Though Greene is imperfect, he has none of Daniel's complacently perfect dullness.

It is this resistance of the language to full expression, the strain between images and rhythm, opposites "yoked by violence together" in varying degrees of violence, that gives to English lyrical verse its true genius. It is a genius that permitted Milton to bring to the pastoral style richness and subtlety of effect that Spenser never achieved. It is that quality of English style which is superior to age and school. It was perfectly mastered as early as Wyat:

> It was no dream; I lay broad waking:
>   But all is turned, thorough my gentleness
> Into a strange fashion of forsaking;
>   And I have leave to go of her goodness,
>   And she also to use newfangleness.

> But since that I so kindly am served
> I would fain know what she hath deserved.

It is in the lyrics, even in the political satires, of Dryden, but it begins to disappear in Pope, to reappear in the nineteenth century perhaps in Landor and Browning alone. It is a quality, not of system or of doctrine, but of immediate intelligence acting directly; a definite but unpremeditated limitation of moral and metaphysical idea to the problem of the work to be done. It is unmoralistic and anti-allegorical. Out of that long and neglected stream of the English tradition comes a kind of poetry that we have named in our age symbolism—a curious misnomer borrowed from the French; for it has no elaborate symbolism at all in the Spenserian mode.

When Saintsbury thirty-five years ago issued the first edition of his *Short History of English Literature,* he announced that his chief interest throughout would be form—at that time a revolutionary point of view. But he gave to the Elizabethan satirists only a scant paragraph: they were both "coarse" and "insincere." This view will have to be changed before we shall be able to understand the early Donne—not only Donne, but a great deal of the finest work of our own time, poets like Eliot and Yeats. The satirists of the 1590's not only read Martial, they went back through Sackville to Lyndsay and Dunbar. The medieval sense of mortality, of the vanity of the world, survives in the satirists, who use it as a weapon of critical irony upon the vaunting romanticism of the Renaissance. And we, in this age, in so far as we maintain the traditions of English verse, are still criticizing the Renaissance.

Richard Wilbur

Introduction to *The Misanthrope*

The idea that comedy is a ritual in which society's laughter corrects individual extravagance is particularly inapplicable to *The Misanthrope*. In this play, society itself is indicted, and though Alceste's criticisms are indiscriminate, they are not unjustified. It is true that falseness and intrigue are everywhere on view; the conventions enforce a routine dishonesty, justice is subverted by influence, love is overwhelmed by calculation, and these things are accepted, even by the best, as "natural." The cold vanity of Oronte, Acaste, and Clitandre, the malignant hypocrisy of Arsinoé, the insincerity of Célimène, are to be taken as exemplary of the age, and Philinte's philosophic tolerance will not quite do in response to such a condition of things. The honest Éliante is the one we are most to trust, and this is partly because she sees that Alceste's intransigence *A quelque chose en soy de noble & d'héroïque.*

But *The Misanthrope* is not only a critique of society; it is also a study of impurity of motive in a critic of society. If Alceste has rage for the genuine, and he truly has, it is unfortunately compromised and exploited by his vast, unconscious egotism. He is a jealous friend (*Je veux qu'on me distingue*), and it is Philinte's polite effusiveness toward another which prompts his attack on promiscuous civility. He is a jealous lover, and his "frankness" about Oronte's sonnet owes something to the fact that Oronte is his rival, and that the sonnet is addressed to Célimène. Like many humorless and indignant people, he is hard on everybody but himself, and does not perceive it when he fails his own ideal. In one aspect, Alceste seems a moral giant misplaced in a trivial society, having (in George Eliot's phrase) "a certain spiritual grandeur ill-matched with the meanness of opportunity"; in another aspect, he seems an unconscious fraud who magnifies the petty faults of others in order to dramatize himself in his own eyes.

He is, of course, both at once: but the two impressions predominate by turns. A victim, like all around him, of the moral enervation of the times, he cannot consistently be the Man of Honor—simple, magnanimous, passionate, decisive, true. It is his distinction that he is aware of that ideal, and that he can fitfully embody it; his comic flaw consists in a Quixotic confusion of himself with the ideal, a willingness to distort the world for his own self-deceptive and histrionic purposes. Paradoxically, then, the advocate of true feeling and honest intercourse is the one character most artificial, most out-of-touch, most in danger of that nonentity and solitude which all, in the chattery, hollow world of this play, are fleeing. He must play-act continually in order to believe in his own existence, and he welcomes the fact or show of injustice as a dramatic cue. At the close of the play, when Alceste has refused to appeal his lawsuit and has spurned the hand of Célimène, one cannot escape the suspicion that his indignation is in great part instrumental, a desperate means of counterfeiting an identity.

Martin Turnell (whose book *The Classical Moment* contains a fine analysis of *The Misanthrope*) observes that those speeches of Alceste which ring most false are, as it were, parodies of "Cornelian *tirade*." To duplicate this parody-tragic effect in English it was clearly necessary to keep the play in verse, where it would be possible to control the tone more sharply, and to recall our own tragic tradition. There were other reasons, too, for approximating Molière's form. The constant of rhythm and rhyme was needed, in the translation as in the original, for bridging great gaps between high comedy and farce, lofty diction and ordinary talk, deep character and shallow. Again, while prose might preserve the thematic structure of the play, other "musical" elements would be lost, in particular the frequently intricate arrangements of balancing half-lines, liner couplets, quatrains, and sestets. There is no question that words, when dancing within such patterns, are not their prosaic selves, but have a wholly different mood and meaning.

Consider, finally, two peculiarities of the dialogue of the play: redundancy and logic. When Molière has a character repeat essentially the same thing in three successive couplets, it will sometimes have a very clear dramatic point; but it will always have the intention of stabilizing the idea against the movement of the verse, and of giving a specifically rhetorical pleasure. In a prose rendering, these latter effects are lost, and the passage tends to seem merely prolix. As for logic, it is a convention of *The Misanthrope* that its main characters can express themselves logically, and in the most complex grammar; Molière's dramatic verse, which is almost wholly free of metaphor, derives much of its richness from argumentative virtuosity. Here is a bit of logic from Arsinoé:

> *Madame, l'Amitié doit sur tout éclater*
> *Aux choses qui le plus nous peuvent importer:*
> *Et comme il n'en est point de plus grande importance*
> *Que celles de l'Honneur et de la Bienséance,*
> *Je viens par un avis qui touche vostre honneur*
> *Témoigner l'amitié que pour vous a mon Coeur.*

In prose it might come out like this: "Madam, friendship should most display itself when truly vital matters are in question: and since there are no things more vital than decency and honor, I have come to prove heartfelt friendship by giving you some advice which concerns your reputation." Even if that were better rendered, it would still be plain that Molière's logic loses all its baroque exuberance in prose; it sounds lawyerish; without rhyme and verse to phrase and emphasize the steps of its progression, the logic becomes obscure like Congreve's, not crystalline and followable as it was meant to be.

For all these reasons, rhymed verse seemed to me obligatory. The choice did not preclude accuracy, and what follows is, I believe, a line-for-line verse translation quite as faithful as any which have been done in prose. I hasten to say that I am boasting only of patience; a translation may, alas, be faithful on all counts, and still lack quality.

One word about diction. This is a play in which French aristocrats of 1666 converse about their special concerns, and employ the moral and philosophical terms peculiar to their thought. Not all my words, therefore, are strictly modern; I had for example to use "spleen" and "phlegm"; but I think that I have avoided the zounds sort of thing, and that at best the diction mediates between then and now, suggesting no one period. There are occasional vulgarities, but for these there is precedent in the original, Molière's people being aristocrats and therefore not genteel.

Stanley Edgar Hyman

The Rape of the Lock

The occasion for Pope's "The Rape of the Lock," published in 1712 and republished in a considerably revised version in 1714, was a tiny scandal. Lord Petre had cut off a lock of Miss Arabella Fermor's hair and refused to return it, and the incident had caused bad feeling between the two families. Pope's friend Caryll who was friendly with both families, Pope told Spence, "desired me to write a poem to make a jest of it, and laugh them together again." Pope produced a poem of two cantos in iambic pentameter couplets within a fortnight, and it appears to have had the desired effect. Despite Addison's advice that the poem was "a delicious little thing" as it stood and not to tamper with it, Pope felt that it could be made more ambitious, and in 1714 he expanded it to five cantos, with additional scenes and an elaborate mock-epic machinery of Rosicrucian supernaturals that he got from a book called the *Comte de Gabalis.* In its final version, "The Rape of the Lock" first describes the elaborate toilet of Belinda, tended by her guardian sylph, Ariel, and other supernaturals. She and another maiden, Clarissa, then have an epic combat at ombre with the baron and another gentleman, at which the baron cuts off one of Belinda's tresses. The gnome Umbriel journeys to the underworld Cave of Spleen to return with a load of wild female emotions, and there is a furious Homeric battle between men and women, in the course of which the lock disappears, to reappear in the sky as a comet with a hairy tail, writing Belinda's name immortal.

The principal effect the poem gives at every point is of order and control. Its action, described in resounding epic imagery, is always tiny. The baron's madness comes from the mildest of intoxicants:

> Coffee (which makes the politician wise,
> And see through all things with his half-shut eyes)
> Sent up in vapours to the baron's brain
> New stratagems, the radiant lock to gain.

Belinda's reaction when the lock is cut off, which we can assume to be wounded vanity, is put in heroic terms, then ironically undercut:

> Then flash'd the living lightning from her eyes,
> And screams of horror rend th'affrighted skies.
> Not louder shrieks to pitying Heaven are cast,
> When husbands, or when lapdogs breathe their last.

Passions, as Dryden advised, are carefully kept under control. Instead of Cleopatra's soul-consuming love, we are told of such virgins as Belinda:

> With varying vanities, from every part,
> They shift the moving toyshop of their heart.

In the last canto, Clarissa appeals to two of the highest virtues of the Augustan age. She says:

> How vain are all these glories, all our pains,
> Unless good sense preserve what beauty gains . . . .

and adds:

> What then remains, but well our power to use,
> And keep good humour still, whate'er we lose?

The "good sense" and "good humour" Clarissa summons up are the poet's virtues too. Pope told Spence of the critic William Walsh:

> He used to encourage me much, and used to tell me, that there was one way left of excelling; for though we had several great poets, we never had any one great poet that was correct; and desired me to make that my study and aim.

Like its subject, the poem too is a game within clearly defined rules. We can imagine Pope writing his hundreds of couplets, with hardly a two-syllable rhyme in the entire poem, as a *tour de force* not unlike the baron's, and encompassing a whole range of feeling within the confines of the stylized like Belinda playing at ombre.

If we are tempted to read more in'o the poem than its trivialities, we had our warning early. In 1715, a year after the complete "Rape of the Lock" was published, one Esdras Barnivelt published a pamphlet: *A Key to the Lock, or a Treatise proving beyond all contradiction the dangerous tendency of a late Poem, intitled the Rape of the Lock, to Religion and*

Government. In it Barnivelt showed that Belinda represents Great Britain, that the lock is the barrier treaty and the baron who cuts it off the Earl of Oxford, that Clarissa is Lady Masham, Sir Plume Prince Eugene, and so on. "Esdras Barnivelt" was of course Alexander Pope, having some fun with the tendency of his time to find hidden political meanings, and not averse to stirring up a little controversy about his poem. The tendency of our time has been to find other kinds of hidden meanings. It would be equally ludicrous to produce a Freudian interpretation in which the poem is a projection of Pope's castration complex, or Belinda is ego, the baron id, and Clarissa superego; or a Marxian interpretation with Belinda the English yeomanry expropriated by baronial enclosures and forcibly proletarianized; or a Frazerian interpretation in which Belinda is the corn maiden reaped by the annual baron in a fertility ritual. The solar mythologists of the nineteenth century would have shown, with plenty of apt quotations from the poem, that Belinda is the sun, descending at night into the Cave of Spleen and rising in splendor in the heavens the next morning. Esdras Barnivelt might have written any of these.

Nevertheless, the poem is clearly much more meaningful than its surface. We cannot accept it, as the nineteenth century did, as the "bit of filigree-work" William Hazlitt calls it, or as Leslie Stephen's "brilliant, sparkling, vivacious trifle." There is a sense in which Pope is a very knowing Freudian. The poem is one vast comic symbolic defloration, proper to a cruelly deformed poet for whom such ventures were symbolic or nothing. The hair is a fertility or sex symbol, described in the poem as catching men as it traps birds and hooks fish. "Lock" is a pun on Freud's lock that all keys fit, and it is a pun that Pope makes explicit in the title of his Barnivelt pamphlet. Its rape by the baron is a sex act, and the baron cries triumphantly to Belinda at the end of Canto Four:

> What wonder then, fair nymph! thy hairs should feel
> The conquering force of unresisted steel?

Its loss is the unalterable loss of virginity, comically contrasted with "a wretched sylph" who gets in the way of the shears and is cut in half, then is given Pope's parenthetical reassurance "(But airy substance soon unites again)" that he is unlike flesh-and-blood substance. We get the same comedy in the free-for-all, with Belinda's impossible demand:

> "Restore the lock!" she cries; and all around
> "Restore the lock!" the vaulted roofs rebound.

If the card game is a stylized seduction (when the Queen of Hearts is taken, "the blood the virgin's cheek forsook"), Belinda's punishment of the baron, the pinch of snuff that makes him sneeze and sneeze, is parody orgasm. In this world that Freud and Pope share,

> Men prove with child, as powerful fancy works,
> And maids, turn'd bottles, call aloud for corks.

Belinda's remark to the baron,

> O hadst thou, cruel! been content to seize
> Hairs less in sight, or any hairs but these!

may be her conscious pubic-hair joke (Cleanth Brooks, in *The Well Wrought Urn*, thinks it is not) but it is certainly Pope's. The battle in the last canto is a torrent of double entendre. Pope writes:

> Now Jove suspends his golden scales in air,
> Weighs the men's wits against the lady's hair;
> The doubtful beam long nods from side to side;
> At length the wits mount up, the hairs subside.

The baron, "Who sought no more than on his foe to die," warns Belinda when she has him helplessly sneezing, "Thou by some other shalt be laid as low." Brooks has noted the frail china jars that symbolize virginity in the poem: broken as an alternative to breaking "Diana's law" in Canto Two, fallen into fragments when the lock is cut off in Canto Three, recollected as having been tottering that morning in Canto Four.

Without reading Marx, Pope is just as clear about social context in the poem. He carefully shows us the glittering falsity of leisure class life, with much of the gold really gilt: "gilded chariots," "gilded mast," novels "neatly gilt." While Belinda dresses in the third canto, the real world of social institutions, production and exchange goes on:

> The hungry judges soon the sentence sign,
> And wretches hang that jurymen may dine;
> The merchant from th' Exchange returns in peace,
> And the long labours of the toilet cease.

It is this dichotomy of two worlds or classes that underlies the poem's principal stylistic device, the comic yoking of two objects of very different degrees of importance with one verb, a rhetorical device called "zeugma." Thus:

> Or stain her honour, or her new brocade;

> Here Britain's statesmen oft the fall foredoom
> Of foreign tyrants, and of nymphs at home;

Here thou, great Anna! whom three realms obey,
Dost sometimes counsel take—and sometimes tea.

While the lesser world of events—brocades, nymphs, and tea or tay—go on in the poem, the significant events of the social, political, and economic world are clearly visible through its gossamer texture.

Pope certainly knew as much as Frazer and the Cambridge scholars about ritual. Superficially, "The Rape of the Lock" is a parody of religion, and it is interesting to know that both the families involved were Roman Catholic, as was Pope. Belinda's toilet is called a "holy ritual" and is actually, as G. Wilson Knight has pointed out in *The Burning Oracle*, a ritual in the Eros cult, in which Belinda is both priestess and goddess, a priestess in her own worship. The divine tress is naturally "sacred." We see the baron at his worship:

For this, ere Phoebus rose, he had implor'd
Propitious Heaven, and every power ador'd,
But Chiefly Love—to Love an altar built,
Of twelve vast French romances, neatly gilt.
There lay three garters, half a pair of gloves,
And all the trophies of his former loves;
With tender billet-doux he lights the pyre,
And breathes three amorous sighs to raise the fire.

The coffee-making and drinking are described as a sacred ceremonial in Canto Three, and like many such, quickly turn orgiastic.

Deeper than these parodies of religious ritual are the poem's two epic battles, the mock-warfare of the card game and the free-for-all between the beaux and belles at the end, both rigidly stylized and ceremonial. Cards, love, and war are equated as games with identical rules, and sex and mock-death are ambivalent consummations that turn into each other. In the second canto, Belinda arms herself for the fray like a Homeric warrior, putting on a seven-fold petticoat like the shield of Achilles: "stiff with hoops, and arm'd with ribs of whale." She is a mock-combatant in a ritual battle, who must lose and be symbolically slain to win and be reborn. Deeper still, the poem is the great myth or the great journey of ritual, the descent into the belly of the whale or the Cave of Spleen:

Now glaring fiends, and snakes on rolling spires,
Pale spectres, gaping tombs, and purple fires . . . .

followed by emergence transformed. Belinda starts in *hubris* and is chastened, starts in Edenic innocence and has a Fall, becomes another "maid" "to numerous ills betray'd." Then Clarissa as initiator can reveal the mystery to her. Like the Orphic "A kid, I have fallen into milk," this is that in time "locks will turn to gray," but that this one lock, like her immortal soul, can be taken out of time. It will be eternal, perpetually fair, in a comet or a constellation, in heaven, in a poem by Alexander Pope. Initiate maidens in primitive cultures are ritually deflowered, sacrificed, circumcized, have their teeth filed or knocked out; Belinda loses a lock of hair and becomes a woman.

I have thus done precisely what I said I would not and should not do, found vast significances in Pope's poem, written in high spirits in his early twenties, "intended only to divert a few young ladies." The Rosicrucian machinery of air sylphs, earth gnomes, fire salamanders and water nymphs points at Pope's division of women into four comparable types; coquettes, prudes, termagants and acquiescents. But Belinda, a nymph, or docile, aspires to be a sylph or coquette and soon transcends everything by becoming a goddess; Clarissa, identified as a prude, emerges as a true wisdom figure. Here as elsewhere the poem demolishes its own machinery, as though it too aspired to break through the polished surface into significance. When Walsh advised Pope to become the first "correct" poet, he meant, in Austin Warren's paraphrase in *Rage for Order*, "The age of myth-making is over." However, just as a mock-epic is not a mockery of the epic but a kind of epic in symbolic and ironic terms, so it requires a mock-myth equally valid although symbolic and ironic.

A poem that deliberately invites comparison, by specific reference, to Homer and the Bible, Dante and Shakespeare, Spenser and Milton, is less apt to be setting out to parody the whole of our literary culture than attempting to build on it ironically. A good part of the nineteenth century saw Pope's poetry as "spoonfulls of boiling oil, ladled out by a fiendish monkey at an upstairs window." The twentieth century, represented by John Middleton Murry, F. R. Leavis, and Brooks, has tended to see him as a serious metaphysical poet like Donne. He need not be either, really. Brooks reminds us that a few years after Pope published "The Rape of the Lock," his good friend Jonathan Swift wrote "The Lady's Dressing Room," in which the toilet of a society belle like Belinda is seen as infinitely foul and evil. Pope sees everything that Swift sees, but he nevertheless regards the event as comic, absurd, rather touching, somewhat beautiful. Belinda making up, like Pope, is an artist reordering nature. Pope must affirm the incident of the rape of the lock as important to show its ultimate triviality, must mock it in terms of epic and myth to show its considerable significance. He must see whole heavens and earths in a lock of hair to tell us something serious and important about the small spot we live in. Pope's vision of girls like Belinda shifting "the moving toyshop of their heart" is uniquely his own, but it is not so terribly far from Yeats' ultimate vision, the place where all the ladders start, "the foul rag-and-bone shop of the heart."

William H. Barber

Voltaire's Use of Irony

The whole conception of Voltaire's *Candide* as a compact adventure story in which, after the manner of the picaresque novel but in much smaller compass, the central figures are hurried along through a rapid series of encounters, necessarily commits the author to a pungent brevity of manner. The many minor characters must be hit off in a phrase, situations must be presented in a sentence or two, journeys accomplished, intervals of time passed over, without the reader's losing that sense of furious pace which is essential, yet without his feeling that the sketch is too hasty to have life. Such demands were not uncongenial to Voltaire, whose natural manner was the epigrammatic rather than the rhetorical, and whose creative powers were not richly imaginative. And his success in meeting them is considerable. A typical passage is that in which he describes the adventures of Candide and Cacambo when, after leaving the Oreillons, they try to make for Cayenne:

> *Il n'était pas facile d'aller à la Cayenne; ils savaient bien à-peu-près de quel côté il fallait marcher; mais des montagnes, des fleuves, des précipices, des brigands, des sauvages, étaient partout de terribles obstacles. Leurs chevaux moururent de fatigue; leurs provisions furent consumées: ils se nourrirent un mois entier de fruits sauvages, et se trouvèrent enfin auprès d'une petite rivière bordée de cocotiers, qui soutinrent leur vie et leurs espérances.*[1]

Weeks of hardship and manifold dangers are here brought to life for the reader in a paragraph, by a continual emphasis upon detail which is all the

---

[1] See Chap. XVII, paragraph 4, of *Candide*, in Part 2 of this book. All footnotes refer to this selection.

more evocative for being conveyed in a word—'*des précipices, des brigands, des sauvages*'—and by a discreet, but repeated insistence upon the travellers' reactions—'*il n'était pas facile . . .*' , '*de terribles obstacles*', '*soutinrent leur vie et leurs espérances*'. And all this is a necessary preparation for the climax of the hazardous river voyage to Eldorado and the contrasting scenes of comfort and safety which follow it.

Again, the element of parody which, we have seen, is of the essence of the tale, finds reflection in the style. It occasions, for one thing, such caricatures of the conventional rhetorical outbursts of lovers as the one already quoted: '*à quoi me servira de prolonger mes misérables jours, puisque je dois les traîner loin d'elle dans les remords et dans le désespoir?*'[2] But it also permits a degree of caricature which reaches the level of fantasy. The disease-ridden Pangloss whom Candide finds in Holland makes his appearance at first anonymously, as '*un gueux*', and he is a figure of, deliberately, nightmarish repulsiveness—'*tout couvert de pustules, les yeux morts, le bout du nez rongé, la bouche de travers, les dents noires, et parlant de la gorge, tourmenté d'une toux violente, et crachant une dent à chaque effort*'.[3] Voltaire, indeed, insists upon the unreality of this vision by calling him '*le fantôme*' in the next paragraph, immediately before shocking Candide, and the reader, with the revelation of the beggar's identity. This is fantasy of description which is parallel to the narrative fantasy of the resurrection of Pangloss and the Baron at the end of the tale.

The aspect of style in *Candide* which is most characteristic, however, and worth more attention than critics have commonly given it, is Voltaire's use of irony. Here, too, the manner of writing is organically related to the matter, for the central theme of *Candide*, the doctrine of optimism and its critique through the disillusionment of Candide, is one which, so to speak, spontaneously generates the ironical. Optimism, or at least the optimism of Pangloss, is essentially here a dogma, an article of faith which insists upon interpreting in a good sense, as ultimately beneficial, every event in human experience, however negative, degrading, or painful. Its natural tendency in expression is consequently towards euphemism. But neither author nor reader, nor ultimately Candide himself, shares this optimistic faith. Hence what is presented to us in the voice of optimism inevitably acquires the tone of irony: we interpret it as meaning the opposite of what it says, and the events of the story confirm for us, and convince Candide, that this is the correct interpretation. In this way, Voltaire effectively satirizes the optimists by transforming their affirmations of dogmatic faith

---

[2] See Chap. XVI, paragraph 2.
[3] See Chap. III, paragraph 6.

into ironic comments on a grim reality. The reader finds himself continually echoing the words of Candide himself in a moment of disillusionment:
'*Si c'est ici le meilleur des mondes possibles, que sont donc les autres?*'[4]

It is not only optimistic dogma, however, which creates such effects in
Candide. Other satirical themes are also presented as generating irony.
The barbaric primitiveness of life in Westphalia is revealed to the reader,
not by any direct judgment, but through the confident pride of the inhabitants, who in their ignorance believe they live in '*le paradis terrestre*'.
And in the brilliant opening chapter of the book this is combined with our
introduction to Pangloss and his optimism; Voltaire ironically adopts the
tone of both, so that naïveté and dogmatism together give us a picture
full of superlatives and at the same time wholly deflatory in its effect.
'*Monsieur le baron était un des plus puissants seigneurs de la Westphalie,
car son château avait une porte et des fenêtres.*' Pangloss '*prouvait admira-
blement qu'il n'y a pas d'effet sans cause, et que dans ce meilleur des
mondes possibles, le château de monseigneur le baron était le plus beau
des châteaux, et madame la meilleure des baronnes possibles*'.[5] And by
the same means the mock tragedy of Candide's expulsion from Thunder-
ten-tronckh is enhanced: '*tout fut consterné dans le plus beau et le plus
agréable des châteaux possibles*'.[6]

\ War, too, is a satirical theme which can be presented ironically. Here
also a gap exists between euphemism and reality, between the picture of
war which rulers find it useful to sponsor—gay uniforms, cheerful music,
and the splendour of heroism—and the grim and cruel facts. The recruiting officers who enlist Candide into the Bulgarian army themselves use the
flattering convention of military heroism ironically, as a bait, when they
talk of fortune and glory; but the irony is at first lost upon the still innocent Candide—it is only a little later that, shocked by his first taste of the
harsh life of the recruit, he begins to suspect the fraud: '*Candide tout
stupéfait ne démêlait pas encore trop bien comment il était un héros*'.[7] It
is in the battlescene which opens the following chapter, however, that
Voltaire most fully exploits the ironical possibilities of the subject. His
description begins in conventional tones of martial splendour, which are
carefully thrown into discord by the last word of the second sentence:
'*Rien n'était si beau, si leste, si brillant, si bien ordonné que les deux
armées. Les trompettes, les fifres, les haut-bois, les tambours, les canons*

---

[4] See Chap. VI, paragraph 3.
[5] See Chap. I, paragraphs 2 and 4.
[6] See Chap. I, paragraph 8.
[7] See Chap. II, paragraph 2.

formaient une harmonie telle qu'il n'y en eut jamais en enfer.'[8] Then, the jargon of optimism is employed to lend ironical support to the conventionally euphemistic phrasing of the casualty report:

> *Les canons renversèrent d'abord à-peu-près six mille hommes de chaque côté; ensuite la mousquetterie ôta du meilleur des mondes environ neuf à dix mille coquins qui en infectaient la surface. La baïonnette fut aussi la raison suffisante de la mort de quelques milliers d'hommes. Le tout pouvait bien se monter à une trentaine de mille âmes.*[9]

It is only after this, when Candide is fleeing from '*cette boucherie heroïque*'[10] while the *Te Deum* is being sung in both camps, that the realities of the situation, the dead and the dying in the villages sacked '*selon les lois du droit public*',[11] are described in savage detail; and the full force of the irony is brought home to the reader.

Similar opportunities for irony are also offered by the Portuguese Inquisition, in the contrast between the supposedly beneficent purposes of the Holy Office, the redemption of heretics and the protection of divine truth, and the cruelty of its actual practices. The agents of the Inquisition treat Pangloss with extreme courtesy as they extract evidence of his heretical views:

> '*Apparemment que monsieur ne croit pas au péché originel; car si tout est au mieux, il n'y a donc eu ni chute ni punition.*'—'*Je demande très humblement pardon à votre excellence,*' répondit Pangloss encore plus poliment, '*car la chute de l'homme et la malédiction entraient nécessairement dans le meilleur des mondes possibles.*'—'*Monsieur ne croit donc pas à la liberté?*' dit le familier.—'*Votre excellence m'excusera,*' dit Pangloss . . . .*[12]

And this courtly tone is retained by Voltaire when he comes to describe the dungeons in which Pangloss and Candide are imprisoned: '*tous deux furent menés séparément dans des appartements d'une extrême fraîcheur, dans lesquels on n'était jamais incommodé du soleil*' (chap. 6).[13] Similarly, the aesthetic qualities and entertainment value of the auto-da-fé are ironically emphasized: the victims '*entendirent une sermon très pathétique, suivi d'une belle musique en faux-bourdon. Candide fut fessé en cadence*

[8] See Chap. III, paragraph 1.

[9] See Chap. III, paragraph 1.

[10] See Chap. III, paragraph 1.

[11] See Chap. III, paragraph 2.

[12] See Chap. V, paragraphs 6–7.

[13] See Chap. VI, paragraph 2.

pendant qu'on chantait'.[14] Cunégonde was invited as a spectator: *'Je fus très bien placée; on servit aux dames des rafraîchissements entre la messe et l'exécution'.*[15] And by the end of the ceremony Candide is in a position to compare, from experience, the value of the different benefits it has conferred upon him: *'Il s'en retournait se soutenant à peine, prêché, fessé, absous et béni.'*[16]

Irony, then, is here much more than one among many possible satirical devices. It forms an essential part of the whole conception of *Candide*, because the book is above all an attack on systems of thought and attitudes of mind which divorce men from reality and reason, which substitute words for facts and prefer habit to reflection. Such systems and attitudes conceal truth behind a mask; they can be most effectively discredited by setting the truth beside the mask and allowing the spectator to judge for himself. The rosy dogma of the optimists, the euphemistic clichés of Church and State, are thus emptied of their positive content and transformed into ironic statements, and the reader is encouraged by this spectacle to reject all such pronouncements whenever they are not supported by his own experience and his own reasoning. *'Il faut cultiver notre jardin'* is a motto for self-reliance in thought as well as action.

Candide thus emerges as a work of art of considerable complexity. Parody, satire, intellectual debate, all contribute their share of the material; each has its own complexity, and each amuses and interests in its own way. The range is vast, within such a small compass; not merely in subject-matter, but also in tone—from bawdy jokes at the expense of La Vieille to compassionate horror at human suffering in war and earthquake, from ironic bitterness to the almost rhapsodical utopianism of Eldorado. Yet for the most part these diverse elements are organically related to each other: the literary framework of parody encourages in the reader a critical alertness which is also essential for his appreciation of the central intellectual theme; the central theme itself, the disillusionment of Candide, is such that the secondary satirical themes can all take their place as agents in the process; while the distinguishing features of the style, the pungent rapidity of manner, the contrasts of scene and incident, the pervading irony, all arise naturally and inevitably from the nature of the material itself. Such organic unity is not solely the result of literary craftsmanship, however, important as that is: it has its roots much deeper in Voltaire's personality. Not merely is *Candide* a vehicle, among many others, for Voltaire's compassion for human suffering and anger at human cruelty,

---

[14] See Chap. VI, paragraph 2.
[15] See Chap. VIII, paragraph 4.
[16] See Chap. VI, paragraph 4.

intolerance and stupidity; it is above all an expression of perhaps the profoundest force in his nature, the need for activity, for coming to grips with reality and leaving his own mark upon it. It was precisely this need which the static philosophy of 'optimism', unwilling to face facts and destructive of all hope, seemed most to deny; and it is understandable that in reacting against it Voltaire should marshal all the creative and critical powers at his command, and produce a masterpiece.

Ashley Brown

A Note on American Satire

In taking up the general subject of satire in the American literary tradition, one is not surprised to find that it has operated in a somewhat fitful manner. There is in fact no great American writer who is preeminently a satirist; we have no Swift or Pope. At the same time the impulse to denounce (which Aristole says is one of the two salient ways of looking on man and his activities) is certainly widespread in our literature, and one can frequently find it in writers whose main interests are otherwise. Most of our best satire has been in prose fiction. I shall mention, just as small examples, Hawthorne's "The Celestial Railroad" and that very funny story by Poe, "The Man That Was Used Up." But these are not typical of their authors. In the case of Melville the satirical impulse is closer to the center of his work—certain parts of *Moby Dick* show this. And then there is his curious *Confidence Man,* which seems to be a satire by intention— Melville's version of the Ship of Fools. It may be that our writers have created their best satire when they have worked it into a larger context. Mark Twain, for instance, is better with the King and the Duke in *Huckleberry Finn* than he is with the Connecticut Yankee; in the latter case his ambiguous attitude toward Europe often trails off into mere buffoonery. With Henry James the social satire, often very acute, is almost wholly absorbed into the novel of manners, whether it be tragic or comic.

Our classic writers, then, do not offer us a continuous tradition of satire. (In England one can see a line of descent from *Gulliver's Travels* to Samuel Butler's *Erewhon* to Aldous Huxley's *Brave New World,* or from Peacock's novels to the early Huxley of *Crome Yellow.*) Our writers' relations with their various audiences suggest that there has seldom been any agreement about moral and aesthetic standards. The ferocity of some

American satire (I am thinking of Ambrose Bierce and many contemporary writers) seems to prove this point. At any rate, my colleague John Russell and I have noticed a strange national preoccupation with bodily dismemberment—for instance, in Poe's "The Man That Was Used Up," Cummings' "I Sing of Olaf," Nathanael West's *A Cool Million*, and Albee's *The American Dream*. Perhaps a great innocence has given way to a greater disillusionment in some cases. My opinion is that satire has never been more rampant than it is in the United States today. We have already moved into a period like Juvenal's: his famous maxim, *difficile est saturam non scribere*,[1] describes the present mood rather well. But the finished and sustained satire—the *Gulliver's Travels* or the *Dunciad*—is almost unknown in our society.

Turning to the more specific subject of American verse satire, one finds that it has been sporadic indeed. Few readers today would linger on the works of the Connecticut Wits, who were writing a kind of neoclassic satire which had already declined very far in England by 1790. More interesting and still readable is James Russell Lowell's *A Fable for Critics*, but this genial work does not cut deep. His criticism of Emerson, for instance, is far less penetrating than Hawthorne's or Melville's. As for Whitman and Dickinson, our two supreme poets of the period, they are simply incapable of the malice that a satirist must have. In dismissing the Connecticut Wits, one should realize that they were trying to perpetuate an outworn literary mode. The fact is that most of the best nineteenth-century verse satire was written in the forms that poets found congenial in other ways: the dramatic monologue, the romantic ballad, the symbolist lyric, and the portrait poem. These were put to satiric use by poets as different as Heine and Corbière. The moderns have in almost every case continued to use these forms. One could mention, as successful examples from American poetry alone, Stevens' "A High-Toned Old Christian Woman," Ransom's "Captain Carpenter," and Eliot's Bostonian portraits. Eliot, in a late interview in which he is asked about Pound's famous editorial work on the manuscript of *The Waste Land*, reports that "there was another section which was an imitation *Rape of the Lock*. Pound said, 'It's no use trying to do something that somebody else has done as well as it can be done. Do something different.' " Pound, incidentally, has surely written the most brilliantly sustained work of verse satire in our century: *Hugh Selwyn Mauberley*. This is the closest thing we have to a *Dunciad*, but it is done largely in the form of the satiric portrait that Pound evolved from Corbière and Gautier. I am not certain if this miniature panorama of literary London is an American poem, but perhaps only an American could have felt so strongly about the subject.

---

[1] It's hard not to write satire.

Partly because we have lacked a tradition of satire, our writers have sometimes tried to create the sense of one by reference to literary works of the past. Allen Tate and Robert Lowell, who are probably our most "Roman" poets, have written satires along these lines. In 1943 Tate brought out his "Ode to Our Young Pro-Consuls of the Air," an attack on the modern religion of the state; his very title proposes an analogy between America and the Rome of the Empire. (An American poet or statesman in 1790, after the Revolution, would have thought of the Roman Republic, as best represented by Cicero.) Tate complicates his satire by imitating the stanzaic form of an exuberant patriotic ode, "To the Virginian Voyage," by the Elizabethan Michael Drayton. This reference is of course ironic. Three periods of history, including our own, are thus juxtaposed. More recently, also during time of war, Lowell published his version of Juvenal's Satire X, "The Vanity of Human Wishes" (1967). Like Tate, he suggests that the America of the 1960s has gone into an imperial phase, and Juvenal in effect is the commentator on our generation. The prose satirist Gore Vidal has insisted for some time on this historical analogy, and it seems to be the basis for a number of his novels and essays. In a period of literary and social fragmentation, then, writers can still look to the past, not for guidance but for inspiration of a sort.

Selected Bibliography

The list of satires below represents only well-known novels, plays, and poems and is not meant to be exhaustive. The criticism is restricted to important works of the twentieth century. For further commentaries on the genre as well as extensive bibliographies see *Satire Newsletter*, 1963–1973. A selective critical bibliography covering the period 1940–1974 appears in the special satire issue of *Seventeenth-Century News*, Spring–Summer 1975. The student should also consult *PMLA (Publications of the Modern Languages Association)* bibliographical supplements.

The Contemporary Scene

DRAMA

George Bernard Shaw	*Arms and the Man; Man and Superman*
Vladimir Mayakovsky	*The Bedbug*
Bertolt Brecht	*The Three-Penny Opera*
Jean Giraudoux	*The Madwoman of Chaillot*
Friedrich Dürrenmatt	*The Visit*
Jean Genet	*The Balcony*
Eugène Ionesco	*Rhinoceros*
Edward Albee	*The American Dream*
Jean-Claude van Itallie	*America Hurrah*

POETRY

T. S. Eliot	"Sweeney Among the Nightingales"
Ezra Pound	*Hugh Selwyn Mauberley*
John Crowe Ransom	"Captain Carpenter"
Robinson Jeffers	"Shine, Perishing Republic"
Roy Campbell	*The Georgiad*
W. H. Auden	"Miss Gee"
Robert Frost	"Departmental"
John Betjeman	"In Westminster Abbey"
Karl Shapiro	"University"
Allen Tate	"Ode to Our Young Pro-Consuls of the Air"
Allen Ginsberg	*Howl*
Robert Lowell	"The Vanity of Human Wishes"

The Tradition of Satire

FICTION

Petronius	*The Satyricon*
Lucius Apuleius	*The Golden Ass*
Erasmus	*The Praise of Folly*
Rabelais	*Gargantua and Pantagruel*
Anon.	*The Life of Lazarillo de Tormes*
Thomas Nashe	*The Unfortunate Traveller*
Miguel de Cervantes	*Don Quixote*
Jonathan Swift	*Gulliver's Travels*
Henry Fielding	*Jonathan Wild*
Laurence Sterne	*Tristram Shandy*
Jane Austen	*Northanger Abbey*

Nikolai Gogol	*Dead Souls*
Charles Dickens	*Martin Chuzzlewit*
Herman Melville	*The Confidence Man*
Lewis Carroll	*Alice's Adventures in Wonderland*
Samuel Butler	*Erewhon*
Mark Twain	*The Gilded Age;* "The Man that Corrupted Hadleyburg"
Henry Adams	*Democracy*
Machado de Assis	"The Psychiatrist"
Gustave Flaubert	*Bouvard and Pécuchet*
Henry James	*The Bostonians*
Anatole France	*Penguin Island*

DRAMA

Aristophanes	*Lysistrata; Clouds*
William Shakespeare	*Troilus and Cressida; Timon of Athens*
John Marston	*The Malcontent*
Ben Jonson	*Volpone; The Alchemist*
Molière	*Tartuffe*
William Congreve	*The Way of the World*
John Gay	*The Beggar's Opera*
Henry Fielding	*Tom Thumb*
Richard Brinsley Sheridan	*The School for Scandal*
Nikolai Gogol	*The Inspector General*
W. S. Gilbert and Arthur Sullivan	*Patience; Iolanthe*

POETRY

Horace	*Satires*
Juvenal	*Satires*
Martial	*Epigrams*
John Skelton	*Colin Clout*
John Donne	*Satires*
John Marston	*The Scourge of Villany*
Ben Jonson	*Epigrams*
John Cleveland	"The Rebel Scot"
Samuel Butler	*Hudibras*
La Fontaine	*Fables*
Nicolas Boileau	*The Lectern*
John Wilmot, Earl of Rochester	"A Satire Against Mankind"
John Dryden	*MacFlecknoe; Absalom and Achitophel*
Jonathan Swift	"A Description of a City Shower"; "Verses on the Death of Dr. Swift"

Alexander Pope	*The Dunciad; Epistle to Dr. Arbuthnot*
Samuel Johnson	*The Vanity of Human Wishes*
Charles Churchill	"The Dedication"
Lord Byron	*The Vision of Judgment*
James Russell Lowell	*A Fable for Critics*
Thomas Hardy	*Satires of Circumstance*

Criticism

Alter, Robert. *Rogue's Progress: Studies in the Picaresque Novel.* Cambridge, Mass.: Harvard University Press, 1964.

Elliott, Robert C. *The Power of Satire.* Princeton, N.J.: Princeton University Press, 1960.

Frye, Northrop, *The Anatomy of Criticism.* Princeton, N.J.: Princeton University Press, 1957.

Guicharnaud, Jacques, ed. *Molière: A Collection of Critical Essays.* Englewood Cliffs, N.J.: Prentice-Hall, 1964.

Highet, Gilbert. *The Anatomy of Satire.* Princeton, N.J.: Princeton University Press, 1962.

——. *Juvenal the Satirist.* Oxford: Clarendon Press, 1954.

Jack, Ian. *Augustan Satire.* Oxford: Clarendon Press, 1952.

Kaiser, Walter. *Praisers of Folly: Erasmus, Rabelais, Shakespeare.* Cambridge, Mass.: Harvard University Press, 1963.

Kernan, Alvin. *The Cankered Muse: Satire of the English Renaissance.* New Haven, Conn.: Yale University Press, 1959.

——. *The Plot of Satire.* New Haven, Conn.: Yale University Press, 1965.

Lewis, Wyndham. *Men Without Art.* New York: Russell & Russell, 1964.

Leyburn, Ellen D. *Satiric Allegory: Mirror of Man.* New Haven, Conn.: Yale University Press, 1956.

Mack, Maynard. "The Muse of Satire," *Yale Review,* XLI (1951), 80–92.

Paulson, Ronald. *The Fictions of Satire.* Baltimore: Johns Hopkins Press, 1967.

——, ed. *Satire: Modern Essays in Criticism.* Englewood Cliffs, N.J.: Prentice-Hall, 1971.

Rosenheim, Edward W. *Swift and the Satirist's Art.* Chicago: University of Chicago Press, 1963.

Sutherland, W. O. S. *The Art of the Satirist.* Austin: University of Texas Press, 1965.

Worcester, David. *The Art of Satire.* Cambridge, Mass.: Harvard University Press, 1940.

Wright, Austin, ed. *Six Satirists.* Pittsburgh: Carnegie Institute of Technology Press, 1965.

Author and Title Index

77 78 79 80 9 8 7 6 5 4 3 2 1